GW00402197

Contemporary Occupational Health Psychology

Contemporary Occupational Health Psychology

Global Perspectives on Research and Practice, Volume 3

Edited by Stavroula Leka and Robert R. Sinclair

WILEY Blackwell

Contents

About the Editors

Stavroula Leka is an Associate Professor of Occupational Health Psychology at the University of Nottingham, UK, and the Director of the Centre for Organizational Health & Development, a World Health Organization collaborating centre in occupational health. She is a Chartered Psychologist, Chair of the International Commission on Occupational Health Scientific Committee on Work Organization and Psychosocial Factors, and a member of the Executive Committee of the European Academy of Occupational Health Psychology. She is the coeditor of *Occupational Health Psychology* (Wiley Blackwell, 2010) and of the two previous volumes of *Contemporary Occupational Health Psychology*.

Robert R. Sinclair is a Professor of Industrial-Organizational Psychology at Clemson University. Prior to coming to Clemson in 2008, he served as a faculty member at Portland State University from 2000 to 2008 and at the University of Tulsa from 1995 to 1999. He is a founding member and past president of the Society for Occupational Health Psychology. His research focuses on individual and organizational factors that contribute to workers occupational safety, health, and well-being with a particular focus on health care, military, retail, and educational settings.

Contributors

Jessica Allen	*UCL Institute of Health Equity, UK*
Matilda Allen	*UCL Institute of Health Equity, UK*
Lindsey Alley	*Portland State University, USA*
Adalgisa Battistelli	*Université Bordeaux Segalen, France*
Ruth Bell	*UCL Institute of Health Equity, UK*
Linn Iren Vestly Bergh	*University of Nottingham, UK* *Statoil ASA, Norway*
Tristan Casey	*Sentis, USA*
Peter Y. Chen	*University of South Australia, Australia*
Konstantin P. Cigularov	*Old Dominion University, USA*
Hans De Witte	*University of Leuven, Belgium* *North-West University, South Africa*
Evangelia Demerouti	*Eindhoven University of Technology, The Netherlands*
Angela Donkin	*UCL Institute of Health Equity, UK*
Donald E. Eggerth	*National Institute for Occupational Safety* *and Health, USA*
Michael A. Flynn	*National Institute for Occupational Safety* *and Health, USA*

Michael T. Ford   *University at Albany, SUNY, USA*

Omar Ganai   *University of Waterloo, Canada*

Sharon Glazer   *University of Maryland, Center for Advanced Study of Language, USA*

Juan Herrero   *University of Oviedo, Spain*

Siri Hinna   *Statoil ASA, Norway*

Jingyi Huang   *University at Albany, SUNY, USA*

Laurie Jacobs   *Portland State University, USA*

Aditya Jain   *Nottingham University Business School, UK*

Evelyn Kortum   *World Health Organization, Switzerland*

Malgorzata W. Kozusznik *University of Valencia, Spain*

Autumn Krauss   *Sentis, USA*

Stavroula Leka   *University of Nottingham, UK*

Frederick T.L. Leong   *Michigan State University, USA*

Yiqiong Li   *University of South Australia, Australia*

Michael Marmot   *UCL Institute of Health Equity, UK*

Pauliina Mattila-Holappa *Finnish Institute of Occupational Health, Finland*

Cameron McCabe   *Portland State University, USA*

Jacob H. Meyers   *American Psychological Association, USA*

Cynthia Mohr   *Portland State University, USA*

Karina Nielsen   *Norwich Business School, University of East Anglia, UK*

Wendy Niesen   *University of Leuven, Belgium*
                         Università degli Studi di Verona, Italy

Krista Pahkin	*Finnish Institute of Occupational Health, Finland*
Daniel Ripa	*University of Oviedo, Spain*
Ana Isabel Sanz-Vergel	*Norwich Business School, University of East Anglia, UK*
Kyoko Shimada	*The University of Tokyo Graduate School of Medicine, Japan*
Akihito Shimazu	*The University of Tokyo Graduate School of Medicine, Japan*
Michelle Tuckey	*University of South Australia, Australia*
Izumi Watai	*Graduate School of Medicine, Nagoya University, Japan*
Maria Widerszal-Bazyl	*Central Institute of Labour Protection – National Research Institute, Poland*
Noortje Wiezer	*Netherlands Organization for Applied Scientific Research TNO, The Netherlands*
Despoina Xanthopoulou	*Aristotle University of Thessaloniki, Greece*

Preface

Welcome to the third volume of *Contemporary Occupational Health Psychology: Global Perspectives on Research and Practice*. The first two volumes of the series have been well received by researchers, practitioners, and students of the discipline, and we hope that readers will be similarly engaged by the variety of contemporary topics addressed in this volume.

Published by Wiley Blackwell on behalf of the European Academy of Occupational Health Psychology and the Society for Occupational Health Psychology, the series sets out to:

1. Publish authoritative, "stand-alone" reviews in the field of occupational health psychology.
2. Publish new empirical research, where it is appropriate to do so, to enable contributors to advance the field in ways that are not typically possible within the confines of the traditional journal article. This applies particularly to developments in professional practice, education, and training.
3. Attract contributions from an international constituency of experts which, in time, become citation classics.
4. Include topics of contemporary relevance to the interests and activities of occupational health psychology researchers, practitioners, educators, and students.

The series covers a wide range of issues related to the science and practice of occupational health psychology as well as to the development of social policies aimed at fostering safer and healthier workplaces that enable workers to lead more fulfilling lives. For this volume, we have assembled a diverse array of highly qualified scholars who examine issues related to the causes and consequences of occupational health threats, organizational level interventions aimed at improving working conditions, and current developments in social policy around the world. The specific chapters explore many issues including safety training programs, meaningful work, immigrant/migrant workers' occupational health, organizational injustice, social determinants of health, job insecurity, the daily process of recovering from work stressors, work–family issues, organizational restructuring, and sustainable business practices for the healthy workplace.

Discussions are in progress about the fourth volume in the series with an anticipated publication date of Spring 2016. We envision the series continuing with its current balanced focus on science and practice concerns as well as representation from authors around the world. The editors welcome informal inquiries from prospective contributors. Please note that contributions are evaluated on the following criteria:

1. Contemporary relevance of the topic to the activities of researchers, educators, practitioners, and students
2. Appropriateness and strength of the literature review
3. Conceptual strength
4. Strength of methodology and data analysis (where a contribution contains new empirical data)
5. Quality of writing
6. Implications for professional practice

We hope that you enjoy this volume and it becomes a useful resource in your work.

Stavroula Leka
Robert R. Sinclair

1

Social Determinants of Health and the Working-Age Population: Global Challenges and Priorities for Action

Angela Donkin, Matilda Allen, Jessica Allen, Ruth Bell, and Michael Marmot

UCL Institute of Health Equity, UK

Introduction

Health inequalities and the importance of the social determinants of health

In 2008, the Commission on Social Determinants of Health (Commission on the Social Determinants of Health, 2008) reported on global health inequalities and priorities for action. Since then, two reviews have been written on health inequalities: one within the UK (The Marmot Review Team, 2010) and one for the WHO European region (The Institute of Health Equity, 2013).

These reports describe the avoidable inequalities in health and length of life both within and between countries. For example, there is a difference of 17 years in life expectancy within the London Borough of Westminster (The Marmot Review Team, 2010) and also a difference of 17 years in male life expectancy between the richest and poorest countries in Europe (The Institute of Health Equity, 2013). Globally, there is a difference of 36 years between the life expectancy of Sierra Leone (47 years) and Japan (83 years) (World Health Organization, 2013). In many countries, there are even larger differences in "disability-free" or "healthy" life expectancy – the number of years a person can expect to live in full health.

These differences occur because people with a higher socioeconomic position live longer and spend more of their life in good health. The key underlying theme to all the reports is that inequalities in health and mortality are not simply a result of genetic variation, or access to health care, important as these are, but that health inequities arise from the conditions in which people are born, grow, live, work,

Contemporary Occupational Health Psychology: Global Perspectives on Research and Practice, Volume 3,
First Edition. Edited by Stavroula Leka and Robert R. Sinclair.
© 2014 John Wiley & Sons, Ltd. Published 2014 by John Wiley & Sons, Ltd.

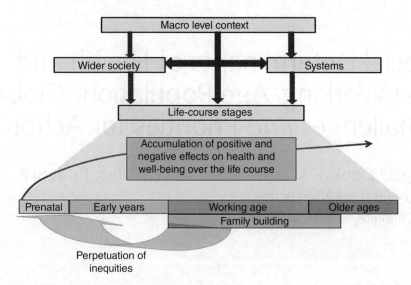

Figure 1.1   A Life Course Approach to Tackling Inequalities in Health.
Source: © The Institute of Health Equity, 2013.

and age and inequities in power, money, and resources that give rise to these conditions of daily life. In order to reduce health inequalities, the evidence-based reports make a number of specific evidence-based recommendations, conceptualized around the life course (see Figure 1.1), which group around the following themes:

- Giving every child the best start in life
- Ensuring good education and enabling all to take control over their lives
- Access to employment and "good jobs"
- Ensuring a sufficient income for healthy living
- Ensuring access to green and sustainable environments
- Placing more focus on ill health prevention
- The need to act across the whole gradient (proportionate universalism)
- A focus on human rights and equality issues

Working age in context

Given the emphasis of this book, we are going to focus on inequalities in the working-age population and the role that work can play, both as a positive and negative social determinant of health. However, it is important to note that social determinants start to influence outcomes from the prenatal period, through childhood, and into education. By the time people are of working age, they may already be unable to make the most of the opportunities available given the cumulative disadvantage that may have built up over their lifetime. Action to give children the best start in life and to ensure good education for all will improve the economic prospects of the working-age population and help build a stronger foundation for mental and physical health. These aspects are covered in more depth in the full reviews (Commission on the Social Determinants of Health, 2008; The Institute of Health Equity, 2013; The Marmot Review Team, 2010) and in a specific piece of work on children's outcomes (Pordes-Bowers, Strelitz, Allen & Donkin, 2012).

Actions and policies focused on the working-age population will also have an effect later on in the life course. As workers retire, the health impacts of their working life, and the level of economic security which they have been able to achieve, will influence their lives in older age. Additionally, increases in longevity and rising pension ages mean there are more people of older age within the workforce and, therefore, more people in the workforce with limiting illnesses and disabilities. It must be ensured that these workers have access to the infrastructure they need to remain in, or be able to return to, work (The Institute of Health Equity, 2013).

The social gradient

In every country, health-adverse material and psychosocial conditions of work and employment are unequally distributed. Those with a higher level of education, income, and a better labor market or occupational position are more likely to be employed and more likely to have better work and employment conditions, which will, in turn, result in better physical and mental health outcomes (Siegrist, Rosskam & Leka, 2012). The following evidence on the effects of employment on health often shows a graded distribution of harm across society. Similarly, there are differences between countries. In general, higher levels of employment and good quality work are more common in higher income countries.

The Nature of Employment Across the Globe and Associated Health Effects

Employment and high-quality work are critically important for population health and health inequalities in several interrelated ways, and the following list summarizes the importance of work to health:

1. Participation in or exclusion from the labor market determines a wide range of life chances, mainly through regular wages and salaries and social status. Deleterious economic conditions can negatively impact on employment rates.
2. Material deprivation, resulting from unemployment or low-paid work and feelings of unfair pay – such as high levels of wage disparities within organizations – contributes to physical and mental ill health.
3. Occupational position is important for people's social status and social identity, and threats to social status from job instability or job loss affect health and well-being.
4. An adverse psychosocial work environment defined by high demand and low control, or an imbalance between efforts spent and rewards received, is associated with an increase in stress-related conditions.

5. Experiences of discrimination, harassment, and injustice aggravate stress and conflict at work, especially in times of high competition and increasing job insecurity.
6. Exposure to physical, ergonomic, and chemical hazards at the workplace, physically demanding or dangerous work, long or irregular work hours, temporary contract and shift work, and prolonged sedentary work can all adversely affect the health of working people.
7. Lack of work, inflexible, or stressful work can not only damage workers health but also have an impact on children, exacerbating the intergenerational transfer of disadvantage.

The following sections look into each of these in more detail. Some of these areas will also be the focus of other chapters in this book, and so we simply provide some examples of why we believe these to be important global challenges.

Participation in or exclusion from the labor market

There is significant variation in working patterns across the globe. In developed nations, the majority (around 85%) of those employed are working for wages, whereas in sub-Saharan Africa and South Asia, this accounts for less than 25% of workers. In the poorer regions, there is a higher percentage of own account (self-employed) and contributing family workers. The graph in the succeeding text illustrates these differences by showing the proportion of work of different statuses in 10 different countries. The percentage of workers employed in the formal compared to the informal economy varies significantly (Figure 1.2).

In 2012, there was a 55.7% employment rate (the proportion of people of working age who have a job) (International Labour Organization, 2013a). However, if we consider own account workers and contributing family workers, global unemployment has reached 5.9%. It has been rising since 2007 and is forecast to continue to increase by 8 million (up to 208 million) by 2015 (International Labour Organization & International Institute for Labour Studies, 2013). Rising unemployment is particularly an issue in high-income countries, 60% of which have experienced an increase in long-term unemployment over the last year (International Labour Organization & International Institute for Labour Studies, 2013).

Unemployment also occurs unequally across society, as those in lower socio-economic positions tend to be at higher risk of losing their jobs and/or failing to find new work. In most countries, those with a lower level of education also tend to be more vulnerable to unemployment. For example, in the 27 countries of the European Union, the unemployment rate was only 3.4% among those who went to university or had other tertiary education, but almost three times this rate, at 9.8%, for those who only had secondary education (Eurostat, 2012).

Unemployment tends to be bad for health. The graph in the succeeding text, based on data from the UK, shows that the male standardized mortality rate is significantly

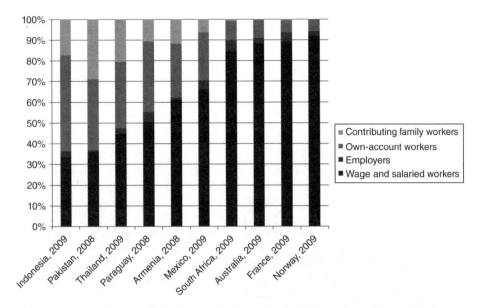

Figure 1.2   Distribution of Employment by Type, Selected Countries, and Latest Years.
Source: Key Indicators of the Labour Market (International Labour Organization, 2011). Reprinted with permission of the International Labour Organization.

higher for those who have been unemployed and that this applies across the social class gradient (Figure 1.3).

The increased mortality rate is likely to be caused by a range of factors, including the fact that unemployed people have increased rates of limiting long-term illness (Bartley, 2004), cardiovascular disease (Gallo *et al.*, 2004, 2006), and mental illness. For example, in America, unemployed workers are twice as likely as their employed counterparts to experience depression, anxiety, psychosomatic symptoms, and other psychological problems (Paul & Moser, 2009). There is also evidence that unemployment impacts on health behaviors, resulting in increased smoking and alcohol consumption and decreased physical exercise (Maier *et al.*, 2006). This, in turn, is likely to have negative effects on health.

The economic impact of a loss of earnings can also have a negative impact on health through a decrease in living standards, as well as a negative effect on self-esteem and general levels of well-being (The Institute of Health Equity, 2013). This can also affect the families of unemployed people.

There are both immediate and long-term health impacts of unemployment. The immediate impacts include the shock and stress of being made redundant (Stuckler *et al.*, 2009), but negative impacts also increase with the duration of unemployment, meaning that those who experience long-term unemployment are likely to be the worst affected (Bethune, 1997).

Younger people tend to be disproportionately affected by rising unemployment. A recent ILO report showed that young people (aged 16–24) are almost three times

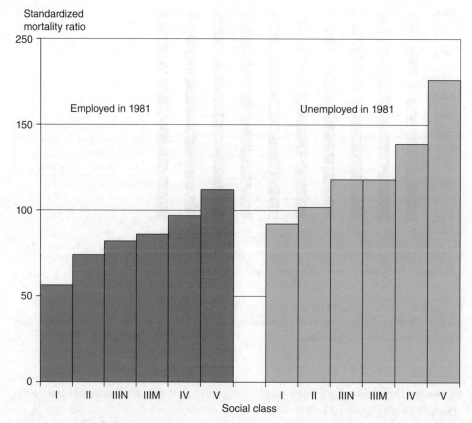

Figure 1.3   Mortality of Men in England and Wales in 1981–1992, by Social Class and Employment Status at the 1981 Census.
Source: The Marmot Review (The Marmot Review Team, 2010).

more likely to be unemployed than adults, with young women being particularly negatively affected (International Labour Organization, 2013b). In OECD countries, the number of young people not in employment, education, or training has been rising recently and has now reached 15.8% (International Labour Organization, 2013b). Unemployment among young people can have negative health impacts that stretch across the rest of their life course.

Economic change can affect large proportions of the workforce resulting in loss of work and poorer health. For example, the economic and social upheaval in Russia and other post-communist countries following the collapse of the Soviet Union in 1989 had demonstrable negative effects on population health (Stuckler *et al.*, 2009). Male life expectancy in Russia in 2009 was still lower than it was in 1965; this is partly due to deaths from cardiovascular disease and injury as a result of increased alcohol consumption (The Institute of Health Equity, 2013).

The current economic crisis is also predicted to have wide-ranging adverse health effects (Marmot & Bell, 2009). Stuckler and Basu's recent book *The Body Economic* outlines the health effects of the recession, particularly in countries that have pursued austerity policies. Greece, for example, has experienced a 52% rise in HIV, a doubling in suicide, rising homicides, and a return of malaria (Stuckler & Basu, 2013). Similarly, our work on the likely effects of the economic downturn on health in London finds that it is likely that there will be more suicides, more homicides and domestic violence, an increase in mental health problems, and worse infectious disease outcomes (Bloomer *et al.*, 2012). These effects are partly as a result of increasing unemployment, decreasing security of employment, and insufficient income in employment.

It is the responsibility of governments, businesses, and other organizations to protect workers against these impacts wherever possible. One way to protect health is to ensure strong social protection policies. There is evidence that in countries with weak social protection systems, there is a greater fluctuation in mortality rates across economic cycles (Gerdtham & Ruhm, 2006; Stuckler *et al.*, 2009).

Material deprivation and pay

Another global issue is that work does not ensure economic security. In 32 developing countries, 23 million of the 209 million wage earners were earning less than US$1.25 a day, and 64 million were earning less than US$2.50 a day (International Labour Organization, 2013c). The regional variation in the working poor is significant, and people in this form of severe poverty are not found in the developed world. Those working in subsistence activities are also more likely to be earning these very low amounts – four out of five workers in extreme poverty (below US$1.25 a day) live in rural areas, and 68% are employed in the agricultural sector (Kapsos & Horne, 2011). Insufficient income from work will often prevent workers from achieving a healthy life and leave them vulnerable to increased morbidity and mortality.

However, this is not to say that all those living in developed nations earn enough to live a healthy life. For example, in the UK, over half of those who are in poverty are in work. The proportion of children in poverty belonging to working families has risen from 30% in the mid-1980s to 60% in 2012 (Aldridge, Kenway, MacInnes & Parekh, 2012). Insufficient income will not only impact on the health of the workers but will also have a knock on effect on their local economies and families.

Unfair pay is also an issue. Since 2003, there has been a decrease in real wages for one-third of European workers, and two-thirds have seen their wages grow at a lower rate than their labor productivity (Franzini & Pianta, 2009). This is particularly the case for low-income workers. The figures demonstrate an increasing discrepancy between workers' effort and their pay (or reward). This is discussed further in Section 4 – Adverse Psychosocial Work Environment.

Social protection policies have an important role to play in ensuring that the working-age population has sufficient resources to survive in times of unemployment. However, they are increasingly being utilized to subsidize low pay and are not just for those who do not work. This stretches the budgets, minimizing the amounts available to those who need it most. Where companies are doing well and senior executive pay is particularly high, it seems rather perverse that tax payers should subsidize their workers on low pay. Data from the ILO shows that workers' share of national income has decreased in most countries. More money is going to profits, to be distributed to shareholders, and less to workers (International Labour Organization, 2013c). New structures to prevent this need to be explored. Further consideration of the benefits of good social protection policies to prevent poverty is given in our full reports (Commission on the Social Determinants of Health, 2008; The Institute of Health Equity, 2013; The Marmot Review Team, 2010).

Occupational position

Most of the world's workforce, particularly in low- and middle-income countries, operate within the informal economy. Informal employment tends to be temporary (e.g., seasonal work), and those in temporary work tend to be exposed to a lack of statutory regulation to protect working conditions, low wages, and poor-quality occupational health and safety. Workers also tend to be excluded from benefits schemes (such as pensions) and receive very little social protection.

Being part of the formal economy is generally more advantageous in terms of socio-economic position and rights; however, the increasing power of large transnational corporations and international institutions to determine the labor policy agenda within countries has led to disempowerment of workers, unions, and those seeking work; and a growth in health-damaging working arrangements and conditions (Benach, Muntaner & Santana, 2007). Indeed in higher income countries, there has been a growth in job insecurity and precarious employment arrangements, as well as an increase in intensity of work and long working hours and a weakening of regulatory protection. In Italy, for example, atypical employment grew from 6% (of all employed people) in 1970 to 18% in 2000 (The Institute of Health Equity, 2013).

There is comprehensive scientific evidence on increased risk of poor mental health resulting from precarious employment (e.g., informal work, non-fixed term temporary contracts, and part-time work) (Artazcoz, Benach, Borrell & Cortes, 2005; Kim et al., 2006). The security of work has also been shown to have an impact on mental and physical health. A 2012 study found that perceived job insecurity predicted much higher odds of fair or poor self-reported health, depression, and anxiety attacks. These effects still occurred even controlling for sociodemographic characteristics, previous health problems, temporary work, or recent job loss (Burgard, Kalousova & Seefeldt, 2012). Other studies (Ferrie, Shipley, Stansfeld & Marmot, 2002) have also found adverse effects on physical and mental health as a result of work insecurity. Insecure jobs can also make it harder for workers to ensure economic stability for their families.

Our work on the effect of the recession in London also shows that the numbers who are in part-time work as a ratio to those who are in full-time work have increased, and there has been a decline in real wages (Bloomer *et al.*, 2012). A recent increase in involuntary temporary and part-time employment has also been noted across most advanced economies, particularly in those countries that have managed to prevent a further increase in unemployment (International Labour Organization & International Institute for Labour Studies, 2013).

Finally, social status is partly determined by occupational status and position and can affect health. Good quality paid work can provide individuals with experiences of learning, achievement, and performance, which, in turn, improve their social status and increase feelings of self-efficacy and self-esteem. On the other hand, insecurity, demotion, or other negative experiences at work can create feelings of anxiety, anger, and helplessness associated with a perceived low social status. These divergent experiences often contribute to positive health outcomes (for good work) and negative health outcomes (for insecure or negative experiences at work) (Siegrist, Rosskam & Leka, 2012). Status inconsistency is a discrepancy between skills and demand – for example, those with a high level of skills and qualifications experiencing limited demand and control at work. This results in increased chances of stress-related disorders (Siegrist, Rosskam & Leka, 2012).

Adverse psychosocial work environment

Not only are there negative health effects from unemployment, but there are also deleterious effects on health for those in employment. Firstly, as detailed earlier, the pay received and the type of work (formal/informal; secure/insecure) affect health, but there are also a range of psychosocial conditions of employment – including the level of control an employee has and the balance of effort and reward that are important for health.

An imbalance between a high amount of effort put into work and low reward is associated with an increase in stress-related disorders (European Commission, 2010). Data from Australia found that unemployed people and those in jobs that had low autonomy, high strain, and insecurity had equally bad health outcomes (Broom *et al.*, 2006).

Psychosocial stress also follows a social gradient – the graph in the succeeding text shows the varying levels of psychosocial stress (measured by effort reward imbalance and low control) across different occupational classes, using data from 11 European countries (Figure 1.4).

Mental health problems (sometimes as a result of physical ill health) account for a large degree of work-related health problems in high-income countries. However, the WHO has also highlighted the growing issue of work-related stress and other psychosocial risks in developing countries (World Health Organization, 2007).

Discrimination, harassment, and injustice

Gender-related risk

In low-income countries, work-related health risks often differ between men and women. Despite a comparative lack of evidence, the WHO concludes that women in low-income countries are often involved in work that is physically demanding, which can have negative health effects. Regular exposure to dirty water and cooking on open

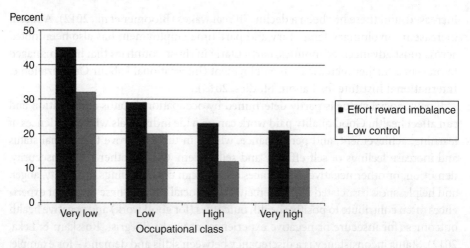

Figure 1.4 The Social Gradient of Adverse Psychosocial Work Environments (Effort–Reward Imbalance and Low Control) by Occupational Class.
Source: Wahrendorf, Dragano and Siegrist (2012), with permission of Oxford University Press.

stoves can also cause sickness. Men experience more occupational accidents and violence at work than women and are often more exposed to extreme temperatures, chemicals, and other harmful conditions (World Health Organization, 2006).

Differences in male and female employment can also be seen in generally more developed areas – for example, in the EU, women are less likely to be employed than men but more likely to work part time (30% of women work part time in the region, compared to only 8% of men) (Eurostat, 2012). Often, women are forced to work part time due to reduced access to the labor market compared to men (Eurofound, 2012).

Socially excluded workers
As shown earlier, the health effects of work apply in varying degrees across all social classes. However, there are some in society that are further away from the workforce, for example, employment rates may be lower for migrants or for those who are disabled. In some countries, up to 80% of disabled people are unemployed, often as employers assume they will be unable to perform the necessary tasks that constitute the job (United Nations Enable, 2013). In India, 70 million people (5% of the population) are disabled. However, only 100,000 have found employment in industry (United Nations Enable, 2013).

Migrants in the labor force are often more vulnerable to exploitation, limited protection, and lower wages than citizens (International Labour Organization, 2004). Data has also shown that some vulnerable migrants, such as asylum seekers, find it particularly difficult to find employment. In 2005, the unemployment rate among refugees in the UK was six times the national average (Archer *et al.*, 2005). On the other hand, those migrants who do find work often support families in their home countries. Global remittances totalled approximately $534 billion in 2012 (Migration and Remittances Unit Development Prospects Group, 2012).

In addition, in some countries, non-standard work includes children working illegally, and migrants can be trafficked for the purposes of sexual exploitation. The health effects of these extreme forms of exploitation are particularly severe.

From the perspective of the social determinants of health, it is important to understand exclusion, vulnerability, and resilience as dynamic multidimensional processes operating through relationships of power. Previously, exclusion has too often been approached by focusing on the attributes of specific excluded groups. We would therefore advocate for efforts to focus on ensuring that people do not become excluded from the workforce, rather than a set of policies that are initiated once they are. This approach should also increase understanding of the processes at work and how these might be reversed and shift the focus from passive victims towards the potential for disadvantaged groups to be resilient in the face of vulnerability (The Institute of Health Equity, 2013).

Exposure to physical, ergonomic, and chemical hazards

There are also material work-related health risks, including injuries, carcinogens, airborne particulates, ergonomic stressors, and noise (World Health Organization, 2009). Damaging physical conditions at work include experiencing noise, vibrations, heavy lifting, chemical hazards, or tiring positions. Levels of exposure to these risks have not significantly diminished in the last 20 years and tend to be experienced by men, with few qualifications, working in manufacturing and other construction jobs (Eurofound, 2012). These conditions often result in increased sickness absence (Chandola, 2011) and disability pensions (Blekesaune & Solem, 2005), reflecting the overall increased morbidity and mortality associated with hazardous work (Aldabe et al., 2011).

These have varying levels of incidence globally. In higher income countries, musculo-skeletal disorders (MSDs) make up a greater proportion of work-related illnesses – for example, in the European Union, MSDs account for nearly half of all absences from work and 60% of permanent work incapacity (Bevan et al., 2009). People of lower socio-economic position, those who have less educational qualifications, or those in jobs with a low level of skills tend to be more highly exposed to dangerous working conditions (World Health Organization, 2007).

Impact on children

Although we have not discussed the early years of life in depth in this chapter, we do need to acknowledge the role of employers and societal systems in ensuring that future generations grow up to be as fulfilled and productive as they can. After all, employers need workers and workers become parents. At the very least, in order to enable everyone to have the opportunity to work, we need to ensure universal access to high-quality, affordable early years education and childcare systems. Access to high-quality early years provision and education is an essential bedrock in leveling social inequalities in educational attainment, reducing poverty, and promoting gender equity, for childhood and beyond. Workplaces and governments should do all they can to encourage such provision and to support employees in their important role as parents of the next generation of workers.

However, the importance of supporting workers as parents goes deeper than merely ensuring that children are looked after well by others so that people are free to work. Flexible working practices and supportive working environments that protect workers' mental health are important so that parents can spend sufficient quality time, free from work stresses, with their children. Work stress and low income significantly impact on workers' mental health, and poor parental mental health has a serious negative impact on children's health and well-being and their future outcomes. Impacts of maternal depression on children include delayed language development, greater levels of misconduct, reduced social and emotional competence, sleeping problems, physical ill health, and lower levels of attachment with its associated detrimental effects (Smith, 2004).

This is not an argument for one parent staying at home. While such an arrangement is common, given the traditions and the cost of childcare, it is not proven to be better for children, and can be disempowering for women. In addition, given average wage levels, it is often not possible. Instead, we need to wake up to the notion that both parents might need or want to work and build better systems and support to recognize this reality.

Priorities for Action

Every country should aspire to reduce exposure to unhealthy, unsafe work and strengthen measures to secure healthy workplaces, as well as taking action to minimize both unemployment and the negative health effects that are caused by being out of work.

The following priorities for action are adapted from the Commission on the Social Determinants of Health Report (Commission on the Social Determinants of Health, 2008) and the European Review on the Social Determinants of Health (The Institute of Health Equity, 2013).

Strengthening employment opportunities

1. Full and fair employment and decent work should be made a shared objective of international institutions and a central part of national policy agendas and development strategies, with strengthened representation of workers in the creation of policy, legislation, and programs relating to employment and work.
2. Countries with rising levels of unemployment among the young should seek to counteract this by creating employment opportunities and ensuring they take up good quality work through education, training, and active labor market policies.

Ensuring sufficient income for healthy living

3. Social protection policies should be in place to protect the most vulnerable, but care should be taken to utilize these budgets to best effect. Social protection should not incentivize employers to pay low wages. National governments should develop and implement economic and social policies that provide secure work and a living wage that takes into account the real and current cost of living for health.

Decent work

4. Governments should reduce insecurity among people in precarious work arrangements including informal work, temporary work, and part-time work through policy and legislation to ensure that wages are based on real cost of living, social security, and support for parents.
5. Public capacity should be strengthened to implement regulatory mechanisms to promote and enforce fair employment and decent work standards for all workers.
6. There should be a reduction in the burden of occupational injuries, diseases, and other health risks by enforcing national legislation and regulations to remove health hazards at work.
7. At the international level, we should intensify and extend the transfer of knowledge and skills in the area of work-related health and safety from European/international organizations, institutions, and networks to national organizations.
8. Employers should be required to improve psychosocial conditions in workplaces characterized by unhealthy stress levels.
9. Occupational health and safety policies and programs should be applied to all workers – formal and informal – and the range be expanded to include work-related stressors and behavior as well as exposure to material hazards.
10. Society should maintain or develop occupational health services that are financed publicly and are independent of employers.

Economic conditions and policy responses

11. In low- and medium-income countries, measures of economic growth, in accordance with an "Environmental and Sustainability Strategy", that are considered most effective in reducing poverty, lack of education, and high levels of unemployment should be prioritized. To achieve this, there needs to be an investment in training, improved infrastructure and technology, and extension of access to employment and good quality work throughout major sectors of the workforce.
12. In high-income countries, a high level of employment, in accordance with principles of a sustainable economy, needs to be ensured, without compromising standards of decent work and policies of basic social protection.

Vulnerable and excluded workers

13. Protection of the employment rights of, and strengthening of preventive efforts among, the most vulnerable (in particular, those with insecure contracts, low-paid part-time workers, the unemployed, and migrant workers) is important.

Proportionate universalism

14. A "proportionate universalism" approach should be adopted. Action on the social determinants of health, including employment and unemployment, should occur for all members of society but targeted progressively more towards those with higher levels of need – those lower down the "social gradient". If approaches are successful in this approach, the "gradient" in health outcomes should be levelled up, meaning that everyone's health outcomes improve, moving towards those of the most advantaged.

Changing values and ethics

15. A key stepping stone to improving working conditions is to promote a more "worker-friendly" culture within business. Efforts to change the articles of association for businesses to enshrine fairness and responsibility into business ethics, for example, could be effective in driving forward such a culture particularly in the current context where the current inequities of the system are being written about on a daily basis (newspaper articles relating to squeezes on income, bankers' bonuses, chief executive payouts, and unsatisfactory working conditions in low- and middle-income countries proliferate).

Conclusion

Avoidable and unjust inequalities in health exist in every society, and reducing these inequalities is a matter of fairness and social justice. The conditions in which people are born, grow, live, work, and age influence morbidity and mortality along a social gradient – those with more resources, opportunities, control, and support are more likely to live longer, healthier lives.

Generally, unemployment tends to have a negative effect on physical and mental health. Being in work can protect and enhance health, but in order for this to occur, it must be "good" work. This is characterized by sufficient economic compensation, security and flexibility, and healthy physical and psychosocial working conditions. Good work should also offer opportunities for development and include vulnerable or excluded groups.

Globally, there is a variety in the types of work people are engaged in, and responses should, therefore, be modified depending on context. However, we have set out a list of priorities for action which provides guidance and direction to improve the effect that work has on the lives of everyone in society.

References

Aldabe, B., Anderson, R., Lyly-Yrjanainen, M., Parent-Thirion, A., Vermeylen, G., Kelleher, C. C., *et al.* (2011). Contribution of material, occupational, and psychosocial factors in the explanation of social inequalities in health in 28 countries in Europe. *Journal of Epidemiology and Community Health, 65,* 1123–1131.

Aldridge, H., Kenway, P., MacInnes, T., & Parekh, A. (2012). *Monitoring poverty and social exclusion 2012.* York, UK: Joseph Rowntree Foundation.

Archer, L., Hollingworth, S., Maylor, U., Sheibani, A., & Kowarzik, U. (2005). *Challenging barriers to employment for refugees and asylum seekers in London.* Surrey, UK: University of Surrey.

Artazcoz, L., Benach, J., Borrell, C., & Cortes, I. (2005). Social inequalities in the impact of flexible employment on different domains of psychosocial health. *Journal of Epidemiology & Community Health, 59,* 761–767.

Bartley, M. (2004). *Health Inequality: An introduction to theories, concepts and methods.* Cambridge, UK: Polity.

Benach, J., Muntaner, C., & Santana, V. (2007). *Employment conditions and health inequalities.* Geneva, Switzerland: WHO.

Bethune, A. (1997). Unemployment and mortality. In F. Drever & M. Whitehead (Eds.), *Health inequalities.* London: TSO.

Bevan, S., Quadrello, T., McGee, R., Mahdon, M., Vavrovsky, A., & Barham, L. (2009). *Fit for Work? Musculoskeletal disorders in the European workforce.* London: The Work Foundation.

Blekesaune, M., & Solem, P. E. (2005). Working conditions and early retirement: A prospective study of retirement behavior. *Research on Aging, 27*(1), 3–30.

Bloomer, E., Allen, J., Donkin, A., Findlay, G., & Gamsu, M. (2012). *The impact of the economic downturn and policy changes on health inequalities in London.* London: UCL Institute of Health Equity.

Broom, D. H., D'Souza, R. M., Strazdins, L., Butterworth, P., Parslow, R., & Rodgers, B. (2006). The lesser evil: Bad jobs or unemployment? A survey of mid-aged Australians. *Social Science & Medicine, 63*(3), 575–586.

Burgard, S. A., Kalousova, L. B. A., & Seefeldt, K. S. (2012). Perceived job insecurity and health: The Michigan recession and recovery study. *Journal of Occupational and Environmental Medicine, 54*(9), 1101–1106.

Chandola, T. (2011). The recession and stress at work. *British Academy Review, 17,* 4–5.

Commission on the Social Determinants of Health. (2008). *Closing the gap in a generation: Health equity through action on the social determinants of health.* Final report of the Commission on Social Determinants of Health. Geneva, Switzerland: WHO.

Eurofound. (2012). *Fifth European working conditions survey.* Luxembourg City, Luxembourg: Publications Office of the European Union.

European Commission. (2010). *Why socio-economic inequalities increase? Facts and policy responses in Europe.* Luxembourg City, Luxembourg: Publications office of the European Union.

Eurostat. (2012). *Unemployment statistics.* Retrieved August 2, 2013, from http://epp.eurostat. ec.europa.eu/statistics_explained/index.php/Unemployment_statistics. Accessed on November 13, 2013.

Ferrie, J. E., Shipley, M., Stansfeld, S., & Marmot, M. (2002). Effects of chronic job insecurity and change of job security on self-reported health, minor psychiatry morbidity, psychological measures, and health related behaviour in British civil servants: The Whitehall II study. *Journal of Epidemiology & Community Health, 56,* 450–454.

Franzini, M., & Pianta, M. (2009). Mechanisms of inequality. *International Review of Applied Economics*, *23*(3), 233–237.

Gallo, W. T., Bradley, E. H., Falba, T. A., Dubin, J. A., Cramer, L. D., Bogardus, S. T., *et al.* (2004). Involuntary job loss as a risk factor for subsequent myocardial infarction and stroke: Findings from the Health and Retirement Survey. *American Journal of Industrial Medicine*, *45*(5), 408–416.

Gallo, W. T., Teng, H., Kasj, S., Krumholz, H., & Bradley, E. (2006). The impact of late career job loss on myocardial infarction and stroke: A 10 year follow up using the health and retirement survey. *Occupational and Environmental Medicine*, *63*, 683–687.

Gerdtham, U. G., & Ruhm, C. J. (2006). Deaths rise in good economic times: Evidence from the OECD. *Economics and Human Biology*, *4*, 298–316.

International Labour Organization. (2004). *Towards a fair deal for migrant workers in the global economy*. Paper presented at the International Labour Conference. Retrieved November 9, 2013, from http://www.ilo.org/public/libdoc/ilo/2004/104B09_110_engl. pdf. Accessed on November 13, 2013.

International Labour Organization. (2011). Status in employment. In *Key indicators of the labour market* (7th ed.). Retrieved August 2, 2013, from http://kilm.ilo.org/manuscript/ kilm03.asp. Accessed on November 13, 2013.

International Labour Organization. (2013a). *Global Employment Trends 2013. Recovering from a second jobs dip*. Geneva, Switzerland: ILO.

International Labour Organization. (2013b). *Global Employment Trends for Youth 2013: A generation at risk*. Geneva, Switzerland: ILO.

International Labour Organization. (2013c). *Global Wage Report 2012/13. Wages and equitable growth*. Geneva, Switzerland: ILO.

International Labour Organization, & International Institute for Labour Studies. (2013). *World of work report 2013: Repairing the economic and social fabric*. Geneva, Switzerland: ILO.

Kapsos, S. , & Horne, R. (2011). Working poverty in the world: Introducing new estimates using household survey data. In *Key Indicators of the Labour Market* (7th ed.). Geneva, Switzerland: ILO.

Kim, I. H., Muntaner, C., Khang, Y. H., Paek, D., & Cho, S. I. (2006). The relationship between nonstandard working and mental health in a representative sample of the South Korean population. *Social Science & Medicine*, *63*(3), 566–574.

Maier, R., Egger, A., Barth, A., Winker, R., Osterode, W., Kundi, M., et al. (2006). Effects of short- and long-term unemployment on physical work capacity and on serum cortisol. *International Archives of Occupational and Environmental Health*, *79*(3), 193–198.

Marmot, M., Allen, J., Bell, R., Bloomer, E., & Goldblatt, P. (2012). WHO European review of social determinants of health and the health divide. *Lancet*, *380*(9846), 1011–1029.

Marmot, M., & Bell, R. (2009). How will the financial crisis affect health? *British Medical Journal*, *338*, b1314.

Migration and Remittances Unit Development Prospects Group. (2012). *Migration and Development Brief 19*. Retrieved August 2, 2012, from http://siteresources.worldbank.org/ INTPROSPECTS/Resources/334934-1288990760745/MigrationDevelopmentBrief19.pdf. Accessed on November 13, 2013.

Paul, K., & Moser, K. (2009). Unemployment impairs mental health: Meta-analyses. *Journal of Vocational Behavior*, *74*(3), 264–282.

Pordes-Bowers, A., Strelitz, J., Allen, J., & Donkin, A. (2012). *An equal start: Improving outcomes in Children's Centres*. London: UCL Institute of Health Equity.

Siegrist, J., Rosskam, E., & Leka, S. (2012, August 13). *Report of task group 2: Employment and working conditions including occupation, unemployment and migrant workers.* Retrieved November 9, 2013, from Publication forthcoming.

Smith, M. (2004). Parental mental health: Disruptions to parenting and outcomes for children. *Child & Family Social Work, 9*(1), 3–11.

Stuckler, D., & Basu, S. (2013). *The body economic: Why austerity kills.* New York: Basic Books.

Stuckler, D., Basu, S., Suhrcke, M., Coutts, A., & McKee, M. (2009). The public health effect of economic crises and alternative policy responses in Europe: An empirical analysis. *Lancet, 374*(9686), 315–323.

The Institute of Health Equity. (2013). Review of the social determinants of health and the health divide in the WHO European Region: Final Report. WHO Europe: Geneva. Available from - https://www.instituteofhealthequity.org/projects/who-european-review

The Marmot Review Team. (2010). *Fair society, healthy lives: Strategic review of health inequalities in England post-2010.* London: Marmot Review Team.

United Nations Enable. (2013). *Factsheet on persons with disabilities.* Retrieved November 9, 2013, from http://www.un.org/disabilities/default.asp?id=18. Accessed on November 13, 2013.

Wahrendorf, M., Dragano, N., & Siegrist, J. (2012). *Social position, work stress, and retirement intentions: A study with older employees from 11 European Countries.* Retrieved November 9, 2013, from http://esr.oxfordjournals.org/content/early/2012/06/21/esr.jcs058.short?rss=1. Accessed on November 13, 2013.

World Health Organization. (2006). *Gender equality, work and health: A review of the evidence.* Geneva, Switzerland: WHO.

World Health Organization. (2007). *Raising awareness of stress at work in developing countries: A modern hazard in a traditional working environment. Advice to employers and worker representatives.* Geneva, Switzerland: WHO.

World Health Organization. (2009). *Global health risks. Mortality and burden of disease attributable to selected major risks.* Geneva, Switzerland: WHO.

World Health Organization. (2013). *Life expectancy: Life expectancy by country.* Retrieved August 2, 2013, from http://apps.who.int/gho/data/node.main.688?lang=en. Accessed on November 13, 2013.

2

An Explanatory Model of Job Insecurity and Innovative Work Behavior: Insights from Social Exchange and Threat Rigidity Theory

Wendy Niesen
University of Leuven, Belgium
Università degli Studi di Verona, Italy

Hans De Witte
University of Leuven, Belgium
North-West University, South Africa

Adalgisa Battistelli
Université Bordeaux Segalen, France

Introduction

Since the late 1970s, economic recessions, industrial restructuring, technological change, and intensified global competition have dramatically changed the nature of work (Burke & Ng, 2006; Howard, 1995). To survive and remain competitive, organizations mainly made use of two strategies.

Downsizing and layoffs may be considered a first type of such organizational strategy. By decreasing employee numbers, organizations hope to improve efficiency and productivity (Sadri, 1996), thereby aiming for long-term gains. In reality, however, this strategy is accompanied by an anticipation phase in which employees experience a higher level of insecurity concerning their occupational future in the company, a phenomenon known as job insecurity. In general, job insecurity refers to "the subjective perceived likelihood of involuntary job loss" (Sverke, Hellgren & Näswall, 2002, p. 243).

Contemporary Occupational Health Psychology: Global Perspectives on Research and Practice, Volume 3,
First Edition. Edited by Stavroula Leka and Robert R. Sinclair.
© 2014 John Wiley & Sons, Ltd. Published 2014 by John Wiley & Sons, Ltd.

Job insecurity is considered as a subjective work stressor (Sinclair, Sears, Zajack & Probst, 2010), causing strain and influencing work-related behaviors (Cheng & Chan, 2008; Sverke, Hellgren & Näswall, 2002). Accordingly, job insecurity has been found to reduce organizational effectiveness, implying the ineffectiveness of the first organizational strategy (Greenhalgh & Rosenblatt, 1984).

The second type of organizational strategy for survival and competitiveness perceives organizational survival as dependent on innovation (Dess & Pickens, 2000; Tushman & O'Reilly, 1997). One way for organizations to become more innovative is to no longer rely only on their research and development (R&D) department, but to capitalize on the innovative abilities of all employees (Axtell et al., 2000; De Jong & Den Hartog, 2007). This has resulted in an increased need for employees who take initiative, are not afraid of risks and uncertainty, and stimulate innovation (Block, 1987; Kizilos, 1990; Spreitzer, 1995). Hence, any employee may help his organization to innovate and improve business performance by generating ideas and by using these ideas as building blocks for new and better products, services, and work processes. Such behavior may be coined as innovative work behavior (IWB) and is formally defined as "the intentional introduction and application, within a role, group or organization of ideas, processes, products or procedures, new to the relevant unit of adoption designed to significantly benefit the individual, the group, organization or wider society" (West & Farr, 1990, p. 9). Using this definition, IWB is considered a "construct that captures all behaviours through which employees can contribute to the innovation process" (De Jong & Den Hartog, 2007, p. 43). IWB includes behaviors related to the different stages in the innovation process: generating ideas, promoting these ideas, and introducing or realizing them, all with the intention to improve organizational functioning (Ramamoorthy, Flood, Slattery & Sardessai, 2005; Scott & Bruce, 1994). Some authors investigate these behaviors separately, assuming that they are influenced by different antecedents. In this chapter, we treat IWB as one dimensional (De Jong & Den Hartog, 2010).

Little is known about how both strategies relate to one another on the individual level. In this respect, the crucial issue is whether employees undergoing the threat of job loss are still likely to help their organization to innovate. Put differently, little is known about the relationship between job insecurity and IWB: research on IWB is often limited to the elements that motivate employees to be more innovative (Picci & Battistelli, 2010), while most studies on job insecurity focus on the negative effects of this phenomenon (Sverke, Hellgren & Näswall, 2002). This chapter addresses this issue by constructing a theory-driven model. This way we attempt to improve our understanding of the processes that explain the effects of job insecurity and the nature and antecedents of IWB. Consequently, the first aim of the current study is to explore whether there is a relationship between job insecurity and IWB. Despite the low number of relevant studies, based on research focusing on innovation as a response to stressors (Janssen, 2000, 2004) and research on job insecurity and creativity (Probst, Steward, Gruys & Tierney, 2007), we may hypothesize that job insecurity and IWB are negatively related. The second aim of this study is to gain insight into the processes that may account for this relationship. Several processes have been proposed to explain the negative associations of job insecurity with a variety of outcomes, such as psychological contract (PC) theory

(Robinson & Rousseau, 1994), the latent deprivation model (Jahoda, 1982), and the lack of predictability and controllability that employees experience when they are no longer secure about their position in the organization (De Witte, 2005). The present study examines both social exchange theory and threat rigidity theory as mediating mechanisms underlying the relationship between job insecurity and IWB. By studying both frameworks simultaneously, we hope to deepen our understanding of how fear about losing one's job might affect IWB. The third aim of this chapter is to direct future research in order to find empirical evidence for the theoretical model presented in this chapter.

The Model

Building on and extending previous research on job insecurity (Bultena, 1998; De Witte, 2005; Greenhalgh & Rosenblatt, 1984), social exchange theory (Cropanzano & Mitchell, 2005; Emerson, 1976), stress theory (Staw, Sandelands & Dutton, 1981), and IWB (Janssen, 2000, 2004; West, 2002), we constructed a comprehensive model of job insecurity and IWB (see Figure 2.1). The concepts used in this model will be explained later on.

Relationship between job insecurity and IWB

Job insecurity, and especially quantitative job insecurity (e.g., the perceived probability of job loss and the worries associated with this perception), is a phenomenon situated between employment and unemployment, since it refers to employed people who fear of becoming unemployed (De Witte, 2005). In general, job insecurity is perceived as a hindrance stressor, that is, an undesirable work demand that

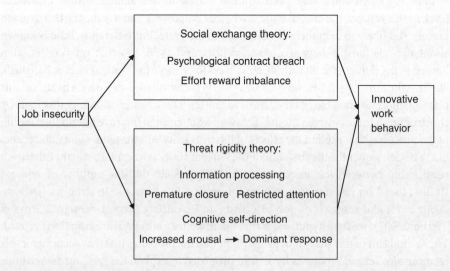

Figure 2.1   A Model of Job Insecurity and IWB.

interferes with the work achievement of an employee (Cavanaugh, Boswell, Roehling & Boudreau, 2000). Furthermore, its demanding nature may thwart personal growth and goal attainment (LePine, Podsakoff & LePine, 2005). Not surprisingly, job insecurity has been found to be associated with multiple behavioral stress reactions, such as resistance against organizational change (Greenhalgh & Rosenblatt, 1984), more exit behavior of the best employees (Rosenblatt & Scheaffer, 2001), and a decrease of both in-role performance (Cheng & Chan, 2008; De Witte, 2000) and organizational citizenship behavior (Bultena, 1998). More specifically related to IWB as an outcome variable, empirical studies suggest that the detrimental effects of job insecurity extend to employees' IWB. To start, a threatened job has been found to make employees play it safe and to take fewer risks, influencing innovation in a negative way (Ford & Gioa, 1995). Moreover, downsizing causes employees to shift priorities to a more output-centered focus (Sadri, 1996). Such focus has a negative impact on innovation, as no output can be assured with certainty, when innovating. As a result, when employees feel insecure at work, individual innovation is inhibited (West & Farr, 1990), and well-known routines will be performed more frequently (West & Altink, 1996).

Based on the presented theoretical motives and research results, a negative relationship between job insecurity and IWB can be expected.

Social exchange theory

Social exchange theory may (partly) explain the association between job insecurity and IWB, as it is an influential paradigm concerning organizational behavior (Cropanzano & Mitchell, 2005). Accordingly, social exchange theory can offer insights into the negative spiral that job insecurity causes (Bultena, 1998). As with all other exchanges, exchanges at work require a bidirectional transaction: after something is given, something is expected in return (Cropanzano & Mitchell, 2005). As such, social exchange involves interactions that generate obligations, resulting in a mutually rewarding exchange or transaction between two mutually contingent parties (Emerson, 1976, p. 336). Such exchanges may include an exchange of activity, tangible or intangible, that is more or less rewarding or costly for at least one party (Homans, 1961, p. 13).

In this regard, the employment relationship can be described in terms of resources, rewards, costs, outcomes, transactions, and payoffs, validating the use of this framework for understanding the employee–employer relationship. Given that a certain level of performance is exchanged for fair rewards and continuous employment, a change in the latter may instigate a change in employees' performance. Given the intensity of the exchange, feelings of imbalance and unfairness are likely in the work environment (Hanson *et al.*, 2000).

As such, job insecurity can be interpreted as a violation by the employer of the long-term obligation of providing stable and continuous employment for employees (Wong, Wong, Ngo & Lui, 2005), impacting the social exchange process and employees' subsequent behavior. Job-secure employees, through the obligation to reciprocate, perform as expected of them (Rousseau & McLean Parks, 1993). Job-insecure employees, on the other hand, may reduce work effort and commitment, as fewer benefits are received.

As argued by Ashford, Lee and Bobko (1989), Bultena (1998) and Wong, Wong, Ngo & Lui (2005), such exchange processes may be responsible for the outcomes of job insecurity. In particular, in reaction to employers' withdrawal from the exchange relationship, job insecurity is expected to impact employees' decision on what to invest in the firm concerning efforts and behaviors. As such, King (2000) and McLean Parks and Kiddler (1994) explain the decrease in organizational citizenship behavior of insecure employees by referring to processes of social exchange.

Concerning the outcome variable, IWB, several authors have related social exchange to employees' innovative behavior. A first social exchange model of creativity was developed by Khazanchi and Masterson (2011), who focused on perceived organizational support and leader–member exchange. Moreover, in her research on the antecedents of IWB, Janssen (2000) explicitly links the quality of the social exchange relationship with the organization as determining employees' innovative behavior. Furthermore, previous research by Scott and Bruce (1994) found a direct relationship between quality of the exchange relationship with the supervisor and creativity. In line with these authors, we believe that an environment characterized by positive relationships, reflected through positive social exchange, may facilitate IWB.

Such positive social exchanges may refer to many concepts, as social exchange theory can be considered as a frame of reference for all theories whose scope is limited to "actions that are contingent on rewarding reactions from others" (Blau, 1964, p. 6). Therefore, and in line with the second aim of this chapter, two more tangible measures of an unjust social exchange framework, PC breach and effort–reward imbalance (ERI), are presented as possible explaining mechanisms in connecting job insecurity with IWB. A PC can be defined as "an individual's belief in mutual obligations between that person and another party, such as an employer" (Rousseau & Tijoriwala, 1998, p. 679). While employees promise to make specific contributions to the organization, the employer offers some benefits in return, and these reciprocal obligations form the essence of the PC (Rousseau & McLean Parks, 1993). ERI fairness is considered another possible mechanism underlying the relationship between job insecurity and IWB. The ERI model states that the effort one exerts at work forms part of a socially organized exchange process to which society at large contributes in terms of rewards (Tsutsumi & Kawakami, 2004). In line with social exchange theory, Adams (1965) stated that employees are preoccupied with being treated fairly: when they perceive an imbalance between work inputs and work outcomes, behaviors and beliefs will be changed in order to restore fairness.

Both models are alike with respect to stressing the idea of reciprocity of costs and gains, shaped through some kind of contract, which makes them fit the social exchange framework (Siegrist *et al.*, 2004). Hence, both PC breach and ERI may cause the employee to experience a "reciprocity deficit". What essentially distinguishes PC breach from ERI is what the employee puts to the scale when evaluating his situation in terms of reciprocity. Concerning the PC, an inter-individual comparison is dominant in which the employee considers whether each party (e.g., employer–employee) fulfills their promises. Concerning ERI, an intra-individual comparison is made in which the employee weights efforts and rewards made and received. Moreover, the ERI model is considered as a more economic approach concerning gains and costs, while PC theory also includes a relational aspect: the decreased quality of the employer–employee relationship is partly responsible for the negative consequences. This different perspective may lead us to expect complementary effects concerning the relationship between job insecurity and IWB. We, therefore, believe that both concepts represent two distinct pathways that influence IWB.

Breach of the psychological contract
Scholars distinguish between two types of PC, namely, transactional and relational PC (Robinson & Rousseau, 1994). The first type is characterized by a short-term agreement in which the limited involvement of each party in the lives and activities of the other is specified and the employee promises to exert some tasks in return for a specific monetary reward. In contrast, the second type is open ended and concerns a long-term agreement with the exchange of socio-emotional elements (Rousseau & McLean Parks, 1993), more specifically an exchange between loyalty (to the organization) and security (for the employee). Given that the relational PC is dominant in most Western societies, most employees will expect a long-term employment relationship, including job security (Van den Brande, Janssens, Sels & Overlaet, 2003). As a result, job insecurity is a possible antecedent of PC breach (Lo & Ayree, 2003). More specifically, an employee expects that when his or her work efforts benefit an organization, this organization will reciprocate by offering him or her rewards in terms of job security (De Cuyper & De Witte, 2006). Furthermore, De Witte and Näswall (2003) found that when confronted with job insecurity, employees experience their PC as violated.

Based on PC theory, breach may be associated with decreased levels of IWB. Following PC theory, the extent to which the PC is fulfilled predicts employees' behavior. When the employees' PC is violated, the promise of future exchange that was made is no longer valid. As this implies that future rewards are possibly jeopardized, employees' incentive to contribute to the organization disappears (Robinson & Rousseau, 1994). This leads to less investment of the employee, as a way to no longer feel deprived (Robinson, 1996). Ng, Feldman and Lam (2010) were the first to empirically test the relationship between PC breach and IWB and found that an increased perception of PC breach was associated with lower levels of innovation-related behavior. This negative effect was interpreted as a form of negative reciprocation and considered as a reaction to the breached PC.

Until now, no previous studies have examined if PC breach mediates the relationship between job insecurity and IWB. De Cuyper and De Witte (2006), however, found relational PC breach to explain the associations between job insecurity and several outcome variables, although this relation was only valid for attitudes such as job and life satisfaction and organizational commitment and not for behaviors such as self-rated performance. This chapter builds on the research of De Cuyper and De Witte (2006) by hypothesizing that PC breach can also be considered as a mediator in the relationship between job insecurity and IWB.

Fairness in the balance in efforts and rewards

Job security can be interpreted as a possible reward, in return for employees' investment. Experiencing job insecurity implies the loss of this reward, and when the efforts remain at the same level, an imbalance is created. While the rewards that an employee receives can take different forms, such as money, esteem, and career opportunities, job security is a reward highly valued by many employees in our current society. Therefore, losing job security as a reward for demonstrated efforts results in a lack of reciprocity or fairness between "costs" and "gains" (Tsutsumi & Kawakami, 2004). As a result, an imbalance in efforts and rewards will appear. This leads us to conclude that job insecurity is a possible antecedent of ERI.

Concerning behavior at work, the ERI model predicts that under high-effort–low-reward circumstances, people will cognitively and behaviorally reduce their efforts and/or maximize their rewards, which is in line with the cognitive theory of emotion (Lazarus, 1991) and the expectancy theory of motivation (Schönpflug & Batman, 1989, in Van Vegchel *et al.*, 2005). Empirical evidence confirmed the influence of ERI on employees' IWB. First, De Jong & Den Hartog (2007) found a positive relationship between rewards and employees' innovative behavior. In addition, an imbalance in rewards and effort is perceived as stressful (Tsutsumi & Kawakami, 2004), thereby leading to sustained strain reactions (Van Vegchel *et al.*, 2005), inhibiting IWB, as will be explained further. Another important contribution was made by Janssen (2000), who investigated the role of effort–reward fairness in the relationship between job demands and IWB. According to Janssen, employees are motivated to respond to higher job demands with IWB if they perceive their efforts as being fairly rewarded by the organization. Likewise, employees behave less innovatively if they perceive their efforts as under-rewarded, to prevent further exploitation. In contrast to Janssen (2000), who attributes a moderating role to ERI, all other authors assign an explanatory role to ERI.

Hence, restricting innovative efforts could be seen as a means to prevent or reduce feelings of being under-rewarded (Adams, 1965, in Janssen, 2004). As job insecurity leads to a decrease in the rewards received by the employee, he/she can try to restore the balance by choosing not to perform this behavior in order to avoid further exploitation by the company (Janssen, 2004). Therefore, perceptions or effort–reward fairness seems to influence the extent to which an employee responds innovatively to a demanding work situation.

Threat rigidity theory

While the previous part of this literature review focused on employees' decreased intention to be innovative as a response to job insecurity in order to restore the perceived imbalance in the social exchange caused by job insecurity, this part will concern the impact of job insecurity on employees' cognitive rigidity, impeding IWB. Based on threat rigidity theory, we hypothesize that the strain caused by job insecurity has a harmful impact on the way employees process information and impacts on the control they exert over their own behavior, thereby decreasing innovative behavior.

The threat of job loss

Threat rigidity theory states that a perceived threat leads to rigid forms of behavior. Rigid behavior can be defined as "persistence or perseverance in an induced method of problem solution that is possibly no longer the best way to solve the presented problem or to reduce the threat" (Cowen, 1952, p. 512). Concerning this threat, threat rigidity theory focuses on the subjective perception of a threat, that is, the perception of "an environmental event that has impending negative or harmful consequences for the entity" (Lazarus, 1966, in Staw, Sandelands & Dutton, 1981, p. 502).

Two aspects of this theory require attention. First, while this theory is applicable to different levels of analysis (individual, group, and organizational behavior), in this chapter, our focus is restricted to the individual's response, and theoretical and empirical evidence will be limited to the individual level. Second, it is important to realize that a rigid response is not always negative. Depending on the magnitude of environmental change causing the threat, a rigid response may prove either functional or dysfunctional (Staw, Sandelands & Dutton, 1981).

Concerning the process through which a threat causes rigid behavior, two mechanisms are proposed: both the person's ability to process information and cognitive self-direction are restricted, causing a more rigid response (Staw, Sandelands & Dutton, 1981).

Regarding the first mechanism, threat impacts employee behavior through a reduction in *information processing*. Accordingly, some authors define a threat rigidity response by means of this process, that is, "the tendency when exposed to externally sourced stress to access only a subset of information or engage in what has been called in the psychological literature premature closure" (Muurlink, Wilkinson, Peetz & Townsend, 2012, p. 75). Hence, restricted information processing is expected to manifest itself in two ways: by an increased reliance upon internal hypotheses and prior expectations (premature closure) on the one hand and by restricted attention on the other hand. Concerning premature closure, the increased reliance on internal hypotheses may manifest itself through the interpretation of unfamiliar stimuli in terms of "internal hypotheses" about the identity of such stimuli (Walsh, 1988), implying that an individual reaches a decision before considering all available alternatives (Muurlink, Wilkinson, Peetz & Townsend, 2012, p. 75). Exposure to a stressor was found to cause such premature closure (Keinan, 1987). Concerning restricted attention, the second manifestation of restricted information processing, strain draws attention towards the dominant or central cues and away from peripheral cues (Staw, Sandelands & Dutton, 1981). Strain has been found to consistently channel attention, thereby impacting information processing (Staal, 2004), coined as the tunneling hypothesis. Channeling of attention implies an increased focus on the threat and a reduction of the focus on non-threat-related, peripheral information or tasks. Already in 1954, Kohn stated that perceptual relationships are influenced by strong emotions (Kohn, 1954); "the perceptual field is constricted and narrowed, and the scope or span of behavior tends to be restricted to those elements which contribute most to the direction of behavior, or to those elements which appear to be most threatening" (p. 290). Studies by Easterbrook offered empirical support that stress decreases the perceptive field and affects the scan that an individual makes of his surroundings (Easterbrook, 1959). Easterbrook concluded that as arousal increased, the ability to focus on peripheral cues was eroded (Muurlink, Wilkinson, Peetz & Townsend, 2012). The tunneling hypothesis has received empirical support regarding a large range of stressors (electric shocks, threats to self-esteem, noise, pharmacological, ego threats, time pressure, or fire) and tasks (pursuit-rotor tracking, mathematical calculations, visual judgment, social perception, attention and memory, and vigilance), both in laboratory and real-world settings (Staal, 2004, p. 36). In sum, while attention seems to be the most affected part of information processing caused by a narrowed attention field and a declined sensitivity to peripheral cues, employees also suffer from premature closure, demonstrated by an increased reliance on prior expectations and internal hypotheses, all causing a more rigid response (Gladstein & Reilly, 1985; Staw, Sandelands & Dutton, 1981).

According to Staw, Sandelands & Dutton (1981), a second mechanism is also responsible for causing rigidity in response to a threat. When a treat occurs, employees may experience a "constriction in control," which corresponds to "the tendency of individuals to emit dominant, well-learned or habituated responses in threat situations" (p. 506) and an increased drive. In this chapter, we adapt this second mechanism in two ways. First, given the prevailing confusion over the concept of control in job insecurity research (Vander Elst, De Cuyper & De Witte, 2011) and the availability of a synonym, we opt for another label to describe this mechanism: a *limitation in cognitive self-direction*.[1] Second, while Staw, Sandelands & Dutton (1981) view increased drive and a tendency towards emitting well-learned or dominant responses as two manifestations of this limited cognitive self-direction occurring at the same time, we follow Zajonc (1965), stating that limited cognitive self-direction, manifested by an increased tendency to emit a dominant response, is a direct consequence of the increased arousal. Put differently, increased drive and emitting dominant responses do not happen simultaneously, with the first being the cause of the latter and the latter being merely a manifestation of limited cognitive self-direction.

Thus, the second mechanism can be described as follows: stressors, such as job insecurity, are found to heighten arousal (Johnson & Anderson, 1990; Koob, 1991; Koob *et al.*, 1990), and this high arousal increases the likelihood of a dominant and thus an inflexible response (Easterbrook, 1959).

Information processing as mediating mechanism
Based on the categorization as a threat, job insecurity is expected to exert similar effects on information processing. Job insecurity has been repeatedly associated with changes in information processing such as increased risk-adverse thinking (Cascio, 1993) and decreased cognitive flexibility (Carnevale & Probst, 1998). While both are manifestations of decreased information processing, we believe that a focus on channeled attention adheres most closely to the threat rigidity framework.

Translated to the work setting, restriction in information processing, and attention in particular, implies that an employee will be more attentive to threat-related information and—based on a cognitive resources framework (Kanfer & Ackerman, 1989)—less attentive to job execution. According to this framework, our cognitive resources are limited and need to be distributed between on-tasks, off-tasks, and self-regulatory activities. A threat is likely to direct attention to one of them, dependent on the source of threat. When job insecurity is the threat under consideration, employees are cognitively occupied with self-regulatory activities such as monitoring their level of job insecurity by estimating the probability to suffer from restructuring or keeping up to date with rumors (Probst & Brubaker, 2001, p. 142). In particular, attentional resources are allocated to self-regulatory processes rather than to the task. Furthermore, worries over the future and possible unemployment may require employees' cognitive resources, diverging their attention further away from work-related tasks (Sverke, Hellgren & Näswall, 2002). Consequently, a negative relationship between job insecurity and task-related attention was found (Probst & Brubaker, 2001).

As innovative behaviors at work often result from experiencing work-related problems or incongruities (Drucker, 1985), attention to work-related aspects is crucial. Accordingly, employees who are less attentive concerning work-related tasks may not perceive these incongruities. As a consequence, they will not experience the need to innovate in order to solve these problems, by generating new ways of working. Moreover, evidence was found that even if they perceive a work-related problem, they may experience problems gathering information from multiple sources and recognizing new and unusual connections, aspects that are crucial for idea generation (Probst, Steward, Gruys & Tierney, 2007). Hence, we may infer that the negative relationship between job insecurity and IWB is (at least partly) explained by a restriction in information processing.

Limited cognitive self-direction as mediating mechanism
When applying the second pathway, a limitation in cognitive self-direction, to the relationship between job insecurity and IWB, an increased drive and a tendency towards emitting well-learned or dominant responses are assumed responsible for this negative relationship.

Applied to job insecurity, empirical evidence identified job insecurity as a stressor, as a determinant of biological reactions, causing cognitive arousal, raised blood pressure, and energy mobilization (Brunner, 1997). Following increased arousal, the dominant response is more likely to be emitted. When experiencing job insecurity, the dominant response consists of behaviors related to emotion-focused coping such as withdrawal and intentions to quit (Dekker & Schaufeli, 1995; Probst, Steward, Gruys & Tierney, 2007). This may be explained by the fact that employees perceive insecurity as uncontrollable and unpredictable and thus experience behavior related to problem-focused coping as useless (De Witte, 2005). Performing IWB contrasts with withdrawal as it demands extra effort and engagement from employees (Janssen, 2000). Hence, we may conclude that IWB is unlikely to follow from job insecurity due to increased arousal.

Moreover, the increased tendency towards emitting well-learned or dominant responses may also decrease employees' innovative behavior. Given that IWB is rarely required of employees, it is unlikely to be a dominant response (George & Brief, 1992; Katz, 1964). As job insecurity and the associated arousal increase, IWB is likely to decrease. Hence, we expect that a limitation in the cognitive self-direction of one's behavior (caused by an increased arousal and an increased performance of dominant responses) mediates the relationship between job insecurity and IWB.

Research Directions

The model presented in this chapter incorporates some hypotheses about the nature of the relationship between job insecurity and IWB. In response, we propose three directions for future research that may improve theoretical knowledge. These suggestions include the following: (1a) testing whether there is a relationship between job insecurity and IWB and (1b) testing if this relationship can be explained by threat rigidity theory (cognitive consequences of stress), by an unjust exchange (social exchange theory), or by both and (1c) investigating the causality of the relationship by testing the proposed model; (2) investigating the validity of these relationships when employees suffer from insecurity regarding valued aspects of the job (qualitative job insecurity) as opposed to quantitative job insecurity; and (3) contributing to the debate about whether sub-dimensions of IWB such as idea generation and idea implementation are influenced by different antecedents.

Concerning the first suggestion, regarding the relationship, its direction, and the explaining mechanisms, only limited attention has been paid to these topics. Concerning the existence of the relationship, this chapter assumes a negative relationship. Note that based on the threat rigidity theory and the rationale behind dominant responses, another relationship might be possible in organizations and sectors focusing on innovation. As innovative reactions to work-related problems at work may be required and expected in such contexts, hence performed frequently, searching for new solutions to problems may be a dominant response, hence a response that increases under threat.[2] This rationale—suggesting a positive relationship—may be supported by employees' perception that IWB are positively related to job and image outcomes (Yuan & Woodman, 2010). As such, IWB could be considered instrumental in decreasing employees' feelings of job insecurity. However, empirical evidence regarding this positive link has been scarce (Staufenbiel & König, 2010). Following this rationale, the direction of the relationship is reversed, with feelings of job insecurity being impacted by IWB. Hence, longitudinal studies are needed to clarify both the existence and the direction of the relationship between both variables. In addition, testing the explaining mechanisms presented in this chapter might increase our understanding of this relationship.

Each aspect of this relationship may have implications for practice. If job insecurity is identified as negatively impacting IWB, insecure feelings may be reduced by organizational communication and participation to ensure optimal levels of IWB (Vander Elst, Baillien, De Cuyper & De Witte, 2010). However, if the order is reversed and IWB increases employees' feelings of job security, the HR department may stimulate these behaviors by explicitly expecting them of each employee. Finally, a better understanding of the process explaining job insecurity's negative impact on employees' IWB could help to counter a decrease in IWB. For example, if the validity of ERI as an explaining framework is confirmed, organizations should guarantee a sufficient level of rewards to insecure employees.

The second suggestion concerns expanding the relationship between job insecurity and IWB to the qualitative component of job insecurity. When experiencing qualitative job insecurity, employees perceive certain aspects of their job to be threatened, such as working conditions, career opportunities, or salary (Hellgren, Sverke & Isaksson, 1999). As this qualitative component has received little critical attention, even less evidence is present about its relationship with various outcomes, such as IWB (De Witte *et al.*, 2012). Nonetheless, both frameworks seem applicable to the qualitative component as well. Concerning social exchange theory, qualitative job insecurity may also imply a violation of the employers' promises concerning salary or career opportunities or elicit feelings of being under-rewarded among employees. Concerning threat rigidity theory, also qualitative job insecurity is a stressful experience, demonstrated by its effect on intention to quit, commitment, satisfaction, and well-being (De Witte *et al.*, 2010; Hellgren, Sverke & Isaksson, 1999). As a consequence, a negative relationship with IWB may be inferred. Further research may conclude if qualitative job insecurity is related to IWB and whether the proposed framework proves useful in explaining this relationship.

The third suggestion relates to the multidimensionality of IWB. First, while we considered IWB as a one-dimensional concept in this chapter, several scholars hold different opinions concerning the number of dimensions (one, two, three, or four) of IWB (De Jong & Den Hartog, 2010; Janssen, 2000; Scott & Bruce, 1994). Put differently, both the relationship and the mechanisms responsible for the association may differ concerning the relationship between job insecurity and each dimension of IWB, such as idea generation, idea promotion, and idea implementation. Hence, although not the focus of this chapter, differentiating the dimensions of IWB could be an important precondition for identifying the most relevant antecedents.

Conclusion

By connecting research on job insecurity, IWB, social exchange theory, and threat rigidity theory, this chapter extends previous knowledge and insights on the innovative behavioral outcomes of job insecurity. Based on previous findings, a negative relationship between job insecurity and IWB is expected. Two possible explaining frameworks have been presented, each representing another aspect of job insecurity's consequences. While social exchange theory is concerned with decreased fairness and broken promises, threat rigidity theory provides insight in how the strain caused by job insecurity may impact employees' innovative behavior. While the current literature offers (indirect) support for our hypotheses, empirical evidence is lacking. In response, this chapter has offered some suggestions for future research.

Notes

1. As cognitive self-direction is concerned with freedom/autonomy of an individual to decide whether or not to perform certain behaviors, the same mechanism is covered. In other words, an increased tendency to emit dominant responses and an increased drive are likely to limit one's cognitive self-direction.
2. Note that the assumption that developing "new and creative ideas" can be a "dominant response" (e.g., "emitting well-learned and habitual responses") could be a contradiction, however.

References

Adams, J. S. (1965). Inequity in social exchange. In L. Berkowitz (Ed.), *Advances in experimental social psychology 2* (pp. 267–299). New York: Academic Press.

Ashford, S. J., Lee, C.L., & Bobko, P. (1989). Content, causes, and consequences of job insecurity: A theory-based measure and substantive test. *Academy of Management Journal, 32*, 803–829.

Axtell, C. M., Holman, D. J., Unsworth, K. L., Wall, T. D., & Waterson, P. E. (2000). Shopfloor innovation: Facilitating the suggestion and implementation of ideas. *Journal of Occupational and Organizational Psychology, 73*, 265–285.

Blau, P. M. (1964). *Exchange and power in social life*. New York: Wiley.

Block, P. (1987). *The empowered manager: Positive political skills at work*. San Francisco: Jossey-Bass.

Brunner, E. (1997). Socioeconomic determinants of health: Stress and the biology of inequality. *British Medical Journal, 314*, 1472–1476.

Bultena, C. (1998). Social exchange under fire: Direct and moderated effects of job insecurity on social exchange. *Dissertation Abstracts International, 59*(4-B), 1894.

Burke, R. J., & Ng, E. (2006). The changing nature of work and organizations: Implications for human resource management. *Human Resource Management Review, 16*(2), 86–94.

Carnevale, P. J., & Probst, T. M. (1998). Social values and social conflict in creative problem solving and categorization. *Journal of Personality and Social Psychology, 74*(5), 1300–1309.

Cascio, W. (1993). Downsizing: What do we know? What have we learned? *Academy of Management Executive, 7*, 95–104.

Cavanaugh, M. A., Boswell, W. E., Roehling, M. V., & Boudreau, J. W. (2000). An empirical examination of self-reported work stress among US managers. *Journal of Applied Psychology, 85*, 65–74.

Cheng, C. H.-L., & Chan, D. K.-S. (2008). Who suffers more from job insecurity? A meta-analytic review. *Applied Psychology: An International Review, 57*(2), 272–303.

Cowen, E. L. (1952). The influence of varying degrees of psychological stress on problem-solving rigidity. *Journal of Abnormal Psychology, 47*(2 suppl.), 512–519.

Cropanzano, R., & Mitchell, M. S. (2005). Social exchange theory: An interdisciplinary review. *Journal of Management, 31*, 874–900.

De Cuyper, N., & De Witte, H. (2006). The impact of job insecurity and contract type on attitudes, well-being and behavioural response: A psychological contract perspective. *Journal of Occupational and Organizational Psychology, 79*, 395–409.

De Jong, J. P. J., & Den Hartog, D. N. (2007). Leadership and employees' innovative behaviour. *European Journal of Innovation Management*, *10*(1), 41–64.

De Jong, J. P. J., & Den Hartog, D. (2010). Measuring innovative work behavior. *Creativity and Innovation Management*, *19*(1), 23–36.

De Witte, H. (2000). Arbeidsethos en jobonzekerheid: Meting en gevolgen voor welzijn, tevredenheid en inzet op het werk (Work ethics and job insecurity: Measurement and consequences for well-being, satisfaction and performance at work). In R. Bouwen, K. De Witte, H. De Witte, & T. Tailleu (Eds.), *Van groep naar gemeenschap (From Group to community)* (pp. 325–350). Leuven, Belgium: Garant.

De Witte, H. (2005). Job insecurity: Review of the international literature on definitions, prevalence, antecedents and consequences. *SA Journal of Industrial Psychology*, *31*(4), 1–6.

De Witte, H., De Cuyper, N., Handaja, Y., Sverke M., Näswall, K., & Hellgren, J. (2010). Associations between quantitative and qualitative job insecurity and well-being: A test in Belgian banks. *International Studies of Management*, *40*(1), 40–56.

De Witte, H., De Cuyper, N., Vander Elst, E., Vanbelle, E., & Niesen, W. (2012). Job insecurity: Review of the literature and a summary of recent studies from Belgium. *Romanian Journal of Applied Psychology*, *14*(1), 11–17.

De Witte, H., & Näswall, K. (2003). Objective versus subjective job insecurity: Consequences of temporary work for job satisfaction and organizational commitment in four European Countries. *Economic and Industrial Democracy*, *24*(2), 149–188.

Dekker, S. W., & Schaufeli, W. B. (1995). The effects of job insecurity on psychological health and withdrawal: A longitudinal study. *Australian Psychologist*, *30*(1), 57–63.

Dess, G. G., & Pickens, J. C. (2000). Changing roles: Leadership in the 21st century. *Organizational Dynamics*, *28*, 18–34.

Drucker, P. F. (1985). *Innovation and entrepreneurship: Practice and principles*. London: Heinemann.

Easterbrook, J. A. (1959). The effect of emotion on cue utilization and the organization of behaviour. *Psychological Review*, *66*(3), 183–201.

Emerson, R. M. (1976). Social Exchange Theory. *Annual Review of Sociology*, *2*, 335–362.

Ford, C. M., & Gioia, D. A. (Eds.). (1995). *Creative action in organizations: Ivory tower visions and real world voices*. London: SAGE Publications.

George, J. M., & Brief, A. P. (1992). Feeling good-doing good: A conceptual analysis of the mood at work-organizational spontaneity relationship. *Psychological Bulletin*, *112*(2), 310–329.

Gladstein, D. L., & Reilly, P. R. (1985). Group decision making under threat: The Tycoon Game. *The Academy of Management Journal*, *28*(3), 613–627.

Greenhalgh, L., & Rosenblatt, Z., (1984). Job insecurity: Towards conceptual clarity. *The Academy of Management Review*, *9*(3), 438–448.

Hanson, E. K., Schaufeli, W., Vrijkotte, T., Plomp, N. H., & Godaert, G. L. (2000). The validity and reliability of the Dutch Effort-Reward Imbalance Questionnaire. *Journal of Occupational Health Psychology*, *5*(1), 142–155.

Hellgren, J., Sverke, M., & Isaksson, K. (1999). A two-dimensional approach to job insecurity: Consequences for employee attitudes and well-being. *European Journal of Work and Organizational Psychology*, *8*(2), 179–195.

Homans, G. C. (1961). *Social behavior and its elementary forms*. New York: Harcourt, Brace and World.

Howard, A. (1995). *The changing nature of work*. San Francisco, CA: Jossey-Bass.

Jahoda, M. (1982). *Employment and unemployment: A social-psychological analysis.* Cambridge, UK: University Press.

Janssen, O. (2000). Job demands, perceptions of effort-reward fairness and innovative work behaviour. *Journal of Occupational and Organizational Psychology, 73,* 287–302.

Janssen, O. (2004). How fairness perceptions make innovative behaviour more or less stressful. *Journal of Organizational Behavior, 25*(2), 201–215.

Johnson, A. K., & Anderson, E. A. (1990). Stress and arousal. In J.T. Cacioppo (Ed.), *Principles of psychophysiology: Physical, social and inferential elements* (pp. 216–252). New York: Cambridge University Press.

Kanfer, R., & Ackerman, P. L. (1989). Motivation and cognitive abilities: An integrative/aptitude-treatment interaction approach to skill acquisition [Monograph]. *Journal of Applied Psychology, 74,* 657–690.

Katz, D. (1964). The motivational basis of organizational behavior. *Behavioral Science, 9*(2), 131–146.

Keinan, G. (1987). Decision making under stress: Scanning of alternatives under controllable and uncontrollable threats. *Journal of Personality and Social Psychology, 52*(3), 639–644.

Khazanchi, S., & Masterson, S. S. (2011). Who and what is fair matters: A multi-foci social exchange model of creativity. *Journal of Organizational Behavior, 32*(1), 86–106.

King, J. E. (2000). White-collar reactions to job insecurity and the role of psychological contract: Implications for human resource management. *Human Resource Management, 39*(1), 79–92.

Kizilos, P. (1990). Crazy about empowerment. *Training, 27*(12), 47–56.

Kohn, H. (1954). The effects of variations of intensity of experimentally induced stress situations upon certain aspects of perception and performance. *The Journal of Genetic Psychology, 85*(2), 289–304.

Koob, G. F. (1991). Arousal, stress, and inverted U-shaped curves: Implications for cognitive function. In R. G. Lister & H. J. Weingartner (Eds.), *Perspectives on cognitive neuroscience* (pp. 301–313). New York: Oxford University Press.

Koob, G. F., Cole, B. J., Swerdlow, N. R., Le Moal, M., & Britton, K. T. (1990). Stress, performance, and arousal: Focus on CRF. *NIDA Research Monograph, 97,* 163–176.

Lazarus, R. S. (1966). *Psychological stress and the coping process.* New York: McGraw-Hill.

Lazarus, R. S. (1991). Progress on a cognitive-motivational theory of emotion. *American Psychologist, 46*(8), 819–834.

LePine, J. A., Podsakoff, N. P., & LePine, M. A. (2005). A meta-analytic test of the Challenge Stressor—Hindrance Stressor framework: An explanation for inconsistent relationships among stressors and performance. *The Academy of Management Journal, 48*(5), 764–775.

Lo, S., & Ayree, S. (2003). Psychological contract breach in a Chinese context: An integrative approach. *Journal of Management Studies, 40*(4), 1005–1020.

McLean Parks, J., & Kiddler, D. L. (1994). Till death do us part…: Changing work relationships in the 90's. *Trends in Organizational Behavior, 1,* 111–136.

Muurlink, O., Wilkinson, A., Peetz, D., & Townsend, K. (2012). Managerial autism: Threat-rigidity and rigidity's threat. *British Journal of Management, 23*(1), s74–s87.

Ng, T. H. H., Feldman, D. C., & Lam, S. S. K. (2010). Psychological contract breaches, organisational commitment, and innovation-related behaviors: A latent growth modeling approach. *Journal of Applied Psychology, 95*(4), 744–751.

Picci, P., & Battistelli, A. (2010). The psychosocial research on innovation at work between antecedents and processes. *Giornale Italiano di Psicologia*, *37*(2), 341–368.

Probst, T., Steward, S., Gruys, M., & Tierney, B. (2007). Productivity, counterproductivity and creativity: The ups and downs of job insecurity. *Journal of Occupational and Organizational Psychology*, *80*, 479–497.

Probst, T. M., & Brubaker, T. L. (2001). The effects of job insecurity on employee safety outcomes: Cross-sectional and longitudinal explorations. *Journal of Occupational Health Psychology*, *6*(2), 139–159.

Ramamoorthy, N., Flood, P. C., Slattery, T., & Sardessai, R. (2005). Determinants of innovative work behaviour: Development and test of an integrated model. *Creativity and Innovation Management*, *14*(2), 142–150.

Robinson, S. L. (1996). Trust and breach of psychological contract. *Administrative Science Quarterly*, *41*(4), 574–599.

Robinson, S. L., & Rousseau, D. M. (1994). Violating the psychological contract: Not the exception but the norm. *Journal of Organizational Behavior*, *15*(3), 245–259.

Rousseau, D. M., & McLean Parks, J. (1993). The contracts of individuals and organizations. *Research in Organizational Behavior*, *15*, 1–43.

Rousseau, D. M., & Tijoriwala, S. A. (1998). Assessing psychological contracts: Issues, alternatives and measures. *Journal of Organizational Behavior*, *19*, 679–695.

Rosenblatt, Z., & Schaeffer, Z. (2001). Brain drain in declining organizations: Toward a research agenda. *Journal of Organizational Behavior*, *22*, 409–424.

Sadri, G. (1996). Reflections: The impact of downsizing on survivors—Some findings and recommendations. *Journal of Managerial Psychology*, *11*(4), 56–59.

Schönpflug, W., & Batman, W. (1989). The costs and benefits of coping. In S. Fisher & J. Reason (Eds.), *Handbook of stress, cognition and health* (pp. 699–714). Chichester, UK: Wiley.

Scott, S. G., & Bruce, R. A. (1994). Determinants of innovative behavior: A path model of individual innovation in the workplace. *The Academy of Management Journal*, *37*(3), 580–607.

Siegrist, J., Starke, D., Chandola, T., Godin, I., Marmot, M., Niedhammer, I., *et al*. (2004). The measurement of effort-reward imbalance at work: European comparisons. *Social Science and Medicine*, *58*, 1483–1499.

Sinclair, R. R., Sears, L. E., Zajack, M., & Probst, T. (2010). A multilevel model of economic stress and employee well-being. In J. Houdmont & S. Leka (Eds.), *Contemporary occupational health psychology: Global perspectives on research and practice* (Vol. 1, pp. 1–21). Chichester, UK: Wiley-Blackwell.

Spreitzer, G. M. (1995). Psychological empowerment in the workplace: Dimensions, measurement and validation. *The Academy of Management Journal*, *35*(5), 1442–1465.

Staal, M. A. (2004). *Stress, cognition, and human performance: A literature review and conceptual framework* (NASA Technical Memorandum 212824). Moffett Field, CA: NASA-Ames Research Center.

Staufenbiel, T., & König, C. J. (2010). A model for the effects of job insecurity on performance, turnover intention and absenteeism. *Journal of Occupational and Organizational Psychology*, *83*, 101–117.

Staw, B. M., Sandelands, L. E., & Dutton, J. E. (1981). Threat rigidity effects in organizational behavior: A multilevel analysis. *Administrative Science Quarterly*, *26*(4), 501–524.

Sverke, M., Hellgren, J., & Näswall, K. (2002). No security: A meta analysis and review of job insecurity and its consequences. *Journal of Occupational Health Psychology*, *7*(3), 242–264.

Tushman, M. L., & O'Reilly, C. A. (1997). *Winning through innovation*. Cambridge, MA: Harvard Business School Press.

Tsutsumi, A., & Kawakami, N. (2004). A review of empirical studies on the model of effort-reward imbalance at work: Reducing occupational stress by implementing a new theory. *Social Science and Medicine, 59*, 2335–2359.

Van den Brande, I., Janssens, M., Sels, L., & Overlaet, R. (2003). Multiple types of psychological contracts: A six-cluster solution. *Human Relations, 56*(1), 1349–1378.

Van Vegchtel, N., De Jonge, J., Bosma, H., & Schaufeli, W. (2005).Reviewing the effort-reward imbalance model: drawing up the balance of 45 empirical studies. *Social science & medicine, 60*(5), 1117–1131.

Vander Elst, T., Baillien, E., De Cuyper, N., & De Witte, H. (2010). The role of organizational communication and participation in reducing job insecurity and its negative association with work-related well-being. *Economic and Industrial Democracy, 31*(2), 249–264.

Vander Elst, T., De Cuyper, N., & De Witte, H. (2011). The role of perceived control in the relationship between job insecurity and psychosocial outcomes: Moderator or mediator? *Stress and Health, 27*(3), e215–e227.

Walsh, J. P. (1988). Selectivity and selective perception: An investigation of managers' belief structures and information processing. *Academy of Management Journal, 31*(4), 873–896.

West, M. A. (2002). Sparkling fountains or stagnant ponds: An integrative model of creativity and innovation implementation in work groups. *Applied Psychology, 51*(3), 355–424.

West, M. A., & Altink, W. M. (1996). Innovation at work: Individual, group, organizational and socio-historical perspectives. *European Journal of Work and Organizational Psychology, 5*(1), 3–11.

West, M. A., & Farr, J. L. (1990). Innovation at work. In M. A. West & J. L. Farr (Eds.), *Innovation and creativity at work: Psychological and organizational strategies* (pp. 3–13). Chichester, UK: Wiley.

Wong, Y. T., Wong, C. S., Ngo, H. Y., & Lui, H. K. (2005). Different responses to job insecurity of Chinese workers in joint ventures and state-owned enterprises. *Human Relations, 58*(11), 1391–1418.

Yuan, F., & Woodman, R. W. (2010). Innovative behaviour in the workplace: The role of performance and image outcome expectations. *Academy of Management Journal, 53*(2), 323–342.

Zajonc, R. B. (1965). Social facilitation. *Science, 149*, 269–275.

3

The Health Consequences of Organizational Injustice: Why Do They Exist and What Can Be Done?

Michael T. Ford and Jingyi Huang
University at Albany, SUNY, USA

Research in occupational health psychology (OHP) has shown that workers in demanding jobs, with little control over what they do and with unsupportive coworkers, tend to have poorer health. There is now a smaller but impressive and growing body of research identifying unfair treatment as a risk factor for employee stress and ill health (Cropanzano & Wright, 2010; Greenberg, 2010; Robbins, Ford & Tetrick, 2012). The primary goal of this chapter is to discuss unique theoretical mechanisms that explain *why* unfair treatment is associated with poor employee health. Some of these mechanisms, which have yet to be clarified and integrated with existing theoretical models of work stress, are distinct from those linking demands, control, and support to health. Unfair treatment can be a uniquely potent stressor because it influences the trust a worker has in his/her organization, threatens one's self-worth, and violates moral principles, activating unhealthy stress responses and moral emotions. In discussing mechanisms linking unfairness and health, we also propose new avenues for research and integrate elements of organizational injustice with job stress interventions.

Organizational Justice Theory

Organizational justice theory and research is currently dominated by a 3-dimensional framework (e.g., Cohen-Charash & Spector, 2001; Colquitt *et al.*, 2001; Cropanzano, Byrne, Bobocel & Rupp, 2001). This framework differentiates *distributive*, *procedural*, and *interactional* justice. Distributive justice traditionally refers to the fair allocation of monetary rewards, although it can also refer to the fair distribution of other important working conditions such as workload, schedules, fringe benefits, and opportunities for development. Although some outcome distributions may be universally considered unfair, the allocation rules people use to make distributive fairness judgments can vary substantially across workers. Three of the justice principles that workers use include (1) an equal ratio of inputs to outputs across workers (i.e., equity), (2) the equal distribution of outcomes across workers, and (3) the distribution of outcomes based on need. Employees may compare their outcomes to different reference points such as those of coworkers, peers in other organizations, or from their own past experience (Greenberg, 2001). The same person may also use different justice principles for different outcomes. For example, employees may use the equity principle to assess pay fairness, whereas they may use a need-based distribution principle to assess the fairness of flexible work arrangements for individuals with families. Thus, there can be substantial variability in perceptions of distributive justice across workers in a given work situation. Still, regardless of whom the referent is and what distribution principle is being used, the unfair allocation of outcomes is the focus of distributive injustice.

Going beyond outcome fairness, procedural justice refers to the process through which outcome allocations are determined. Key features of procedural *in*justice include the inconsistent application of policies, procedures, and practices; systematic biases among decision-makers when making outcome decisions; the use of inaccurate information when making decisions; having no mechanism to correct bad decisions; unethical behavior; and a failure to consider those affected by the decisions (Leventhal, 1980). The third form of organizational justice, interactional justice refers to the respect and dignity with which one is treated and the information one receives about organizational decisions (Bies & Moag, 1986; Greenberg, 1990). Procedural and interactional injustice both reflect the unfairness of the process through which outcome decisions are made and implemented, whereas distributive injustice reflects the unfairness of the outcomes themselves. There is evidence that individuals react less adversely to unfair outcomes when the process is deemed to be fair (e.g., Greenberg, 2006), pointing to the importance of fair processes in addition to fair outcomes. So, for example, if a worker did not receive a deserved promotion but the promotion decision was made through carefully conducted and unbiased performance review and the worker was informed of the decision in a respectful manner, distributive injustice might be high but procedural and interactional injustice would likely be low, attenuating the worker's adverse reactions to the unfair promotion decision.

Research has linked each of these types of injustice to psychological and physical health (Cropanzano & Wright, 2010; Robbins, Ford & Tetrick, 2012). Outcomes that have been correlated with injustice include, but are not limited to, burnout (Moliner et al., 2005), anger (Rupp & Spencer, 2006), anxiety and depression (Spell & Arnold, 2007; Tepper, 2000), physical symptoms (De Boer, Bakker, Syroit & Schaufeli, 2002), blood pressure (Wager, Feldman & Hussey, 2003), and coronary heart disease (Kivimaki et al., 2006). Studies reviewed by Siegrist (1996) also suggest that workers in jobs combining high effort with low rewards (e.g., support, compensation), which often violate the equity principle of distributive justice, tend to have a higher risk for cardiovascular disease.

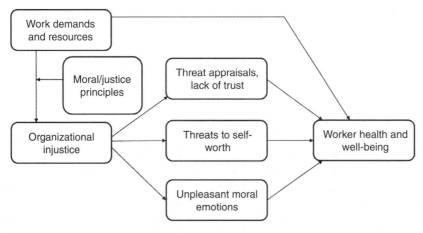

Figure 3.1   Theoretical Framework Linking Organizational Justice to Worker Health and Well-being.

Although researchers have established an empirical link between organizational injustice and employee health, the pathways linking justice to health are not as well understood. These theoretical pathways imply mediators that explain why injustice causes health problems. It is possible that injustice is correlated with health problems merely because they share a common cause such as the unhealthy disposition of the employee. To make the case that injustice is truly the cause of correlated health problems, we must explain why injustice would lead to health problems and, more importantly, why reducing organizational injustice would improve employee health. Here, we propose four key reasons injustice at work and health are associated (see Figure 3.1 for an illustration): (1) injustice decreases a worker's trust in the organization, influencing threat appraisals that are implicated in stress responses; (2) injustice elicits threats to self-worth and unhealthy responses that accompany such threats; (3) injustice threatens basic needs for morality, eliciting moral emotions that have negative health consequences; (4) injustice is associated with structural working conditions that are in and of themselves known risk factors for ill-health. Each of these pathways offers different explanations, points to different core features of injustice that may be targeted by interventions, and suggests new avenues for future research.

Injustice, Trust, and Threat Appraisals

The first reason injustice at work may be associated with employee health is that it decreases the trust workers have that their organizations will not harm them, activating unhealthy stress responses. Applying Lazarus and Folkman's (1984) model of stress to organizations, the work stress process occurs when workers engage in primary appraisals where they appraise their work situations as threatening and/or challenging. Workers then engage in secondary appraisals where they decide how to cope with the threatening or challenging situation (Perrewe & Zellars, 1999). Workers who have been the victims of unfair outcome decisions or are in situations where fair procedures are not in place may appraise their work situations as uncertain and threatening, eliciting unhealthy stress reactions such as arousal, worry, and anxiety.

One reason that organizational injustice may elicit threat appraisals and stress responses is that it causes distrust in the organization and its agents. Mayer, Davis and Schoorman (1995) conceptualized organizational trust as the willingness to make oneself vulnerable to the organization's actions because of a belief that the organization will not act harmfully. Organizational justice, in all of its forms, is a strong predictor of trust in the organization and supervisor (Colquitt *et al.*, 2013). Trust, in turn, has been found to be a strong predictor of psychological strain and burnout (Harvey, Kelloway & Duncan-Leiper, 2003), making trust a potential explanation for some injustice–health relationships. Trust also relates strongly to job security, and workers in insecure work situations tend to have poorer psychological and physical well-being (Sverke, Hellgren & Naswall, 2002), likely because of their threat appraisals and anxiety. Thus, injustice at work may lead to psychological and physical health problems by creating mistrust, uncertainty, and chronic threat appraisals.

Injustice and Social Self-Threat

A second explanation for the relationship between injustice and health is that its unfair treatment is offensive and appraised as a threat to one's self-worth. Semmer and colleagues' (Semmer, Jacobshagen, Meier & Elfering, 2007) "stress-as-offense-to-self" perspective suggests that injustice threatens one's sense of self-worth, while Lind and Tyler's (1988) group-value model of procedural justice proposes that workers care about procedural justice largely because it validates their social standing. From both theoretical perspectives, injustice is interpreted as a signal that the organization does not value its workers. Workers go to great lengths to protect their sense of self-worth (Crocker & Park, 2004) and thus are motivated to act in response to unjust situations. Threats to one's self-worth have indeed been found to explain some of the effects of unfairness on counterproductive behavior and negative work attitudes (Ferris, Spence, Brown & Heller, 2012; Goldman *et al.*, 2008). Dickerson, Gruenwald and Kemeny's (2004) social self-preservation model proposes that threats to self-worth also elicit unhealthy physiological stress responses.

From this perspective, distributive, procedural, and interactional injustice threaten one's self-worth and influence stress independent of the threat appraisals that injustice elicits through mistrust. Injustice-based threats to self-worth can be damaging to one's self-esteem (De Cremer *et al.*, 2005) and may lead to unhealthy levels of physiological arousal. Furthermore, recent empirical work (Ferris, Spence, Brown & Heller, 2012; Meier & Semmer, 2013) has found that high self-esteem and a vulnerable and inflated sense of self (i.e., narcissism) are associated with heightened reactions to unfair treatment, further supporting the role of threats to self-worth in reactions to injustice. Presumably, individuals high in self-esteem and narcissism feel an elevated need to defend their self-worth when treated unfairly. Therefore, injustice likely influences psychological and physical health by threatening self-worth, especially among individuals with high self-esteem.

It is not clear exactly how these effects would vary across the types of justice, although it is possible that the episodic and personal nature of interactional injustice would cause it to be particularly offensive and threatening to self-worth. Ferris, Spence, Brown & Heller (2012) study on threats to self-worth focused specifically on interactional justice. Research on the construct of incivility, which overlaps conceptually with interactional injustice, has shown that rude and disrespectful interpersonal behavior is also associated with poorer psychological and physical health (e.g., Lim, Cortina & Magley, 2008). The offensive nature of this behavior may help explain some of these effects. Distributive and procedural injustice may also be considered offensive, however. Employees experiencing procedural injustice have been found to be more likely to get into angry exchanges with their supervisors, suggesting that individuals do take some personal offense to procedural injustice (Liu, Yang & Nauta, 2013). Semmer and colleagues (Semmer *et al.*, 2010) have developed the concept of illegitimate tasks, which refer to the assignment of tasks that are seen as unreasonable, outside of the range of one's occupation or status, or unnecessary. Such tasks are highly correlated with perceptions of injustice and have been found to predict counterproductive behavior and cortisol release among some individuals (e.g., Kottwitz *et al.*, 2013; Semmer *et al.*, 2010). Thus, interactional injustice, procedural injustice, and the assignment of illegitimate working conditions, which is one form of distributive injustice, all can threaten one's self-worth and in turn elicit unhealthy responses.

Injustice Is Associated with Moral Emotions

Another way injustice might influence health outcomes concerns its relationship with moral judgments and reactions, some of which may be unhealthy or distressing. Using Haidt's (2003) definition, moral emotions are emotions that concern the interests of society whether or not one's own interests are implicated. Of particular interest here are other-condemning emotions, which are directed at others who are perceived to have acted immorally. These moral emotional reactions may have additional power to explain negative health effects of injustice. Moral emotions may also help explain the stressful nature of unjust situations or environments that do not directly affect the worker, such as coworker layoffs or observed discriminatory treatment. Research on deontic justice has shown that individuals become angry and motivated to restore justice when they observe unfair actions toward others (Cropanzano, Goldman & Folger, 2003; Skarlicki & Kulik, 2005), suggesting that unfair situations elicit active physical responses even when the individual is not directly harmed or threatened. There is even evidence that fairness has neuropsychological correlates that are distinct from those of outcome favorability, further suggesting that fairness is a distinct, fundamental psychological need (Tabibnia, Sapute & Lieberman, 2008) that may elicit emotional reactions independent of threats to other needs.

Haidt, Rozin, and colleagues (Haidt, 2003; Rozin, Lowery, Imada & Haidt, 1999) identified three types of other-condemning moral emotions: anger, disgust, and contempt. They describe anger as an emotion that involves motivation to correct injustice and exact revenge on the offender. Disgust, in contrast, is an emotion associated with a motivation to avoid and break off contact with the transgressor. Contempt involves "looking down" at the transgressor and shares elements of anger and disgust (Haidt, 2003). Although all of the other-condemning moral emotions may have negative effects on worker psychological well-being, anger may have the strongest potential of the three to influence psychological and physical health. There is evidence that anger is related to efforts to remove the moral violation, correct the unjust situation, and inflict harm on the offending person, suggesting anger is fundamentally associated with an approach motivational system (Carver & Harmon-Jones, 2009). To the extent that anger results in a desire to engage and correct the unjust situations, it may result in chronic physical overactivation and poor health. Anger in response to injustice at work may also make it more difficult for individuals to disengage from their jobs, inhibiting recovery and sleep (Elovainio *et al.*, 2003; Sonnentag, Binnewies & Mojza, 2008). In addition, anger at work has been shown to predict alcohol consumption and other risky health behavior (O'Neill, Vandenberg, DeJoy & Wilson, 2009), suggesting it may influence health-relevant coping.

While some of the health effects of injustice may be the result of moral outrage, further research is needed on the functional role of discrete moral emotions in responses to injustice, which may have implications for health. In particular, very little is known about disgust or contempt reactions and whether there are distinct workplace situations that lead to these emotions without necessarily resulting in anger. This distinction is worth pursuing because disgust and contempt may have implications for health that are different from anger. Disgust and contempt would logically tend to motivate withdrawal reactions from workers and may be less likely to result in unhealthy chronic arousal. Research suggests anger reactions tend to be more immediate, short term, and event based (Fischer & Roseman, 2007), turning over time into contempt or disgust, which are more lasting, reflect a judgment of the transgressor's disposition, and motivate exclusion of the transgressor rather than correction of the transgressor's actions. Based on this evidence and logic, episodic experiences of injustice, such as negative interpersonal interactions or unfair decisions, may be more likely to elicit anger, whereas structural injustice, such as procedural policies or pay conditions, may tend to elicit disgust reactions once they become chronic elements of the work situation. These distinctions may provide a greater understanding of different reactions to injustice and how they unfold across time.

Injustice and Working Conditions

Finally, injustice may be linked to health because it is the product of working conditions that are unhealthy in and of themselves. At the same time, working conditions may influence worker health *because* they influence perceived injustice, which in turn activates the injustice–health mechanisms described earlier (see Figure 3.1). Two general categories of work role characteristics that have been identified as important for employee health are the demands of the job and the organizational and social resources available to the employee. Demands can include physical and mental workload and time pressure, among other things (Karasek, 1979; Demerouti, Bakker, Nachreiner & Schaufeli, 2001). Resources include pay, benefits, control over one's work, feedback, social support, supervisor support, and other things that help workers overcome work demands (Demerouti, Bakker, Nachreiner & Schaufeli, 2001). Each of these, while associated directly with health, is also associated with distributive and procedural justice. This interrelation needs to be considered when interpreting injustice–health effects.

Distributive justice may be related to ill-health in part through its association with work demands and resources. One of the seminal principles of distributive injustice is Adams' (1963) equity theory, which posits that inequity results from an unequal ratio across workers of *inputs*, or effort expended on the job, to *outcomes*, or pay and benefits. When work demands are high, expected inputs will tend to be high as well. Holding pay, benefits, and other resources offered by the organization constant, individuals with higher demands are also more likely to perceive inequity than individuals with lower demands. For this reason, if all else is held equal, workers in more demanding jobs will tend to also experience higher levels of distributive injustice. Demands may have a direct effect on strain and health by creating excessive task demands that elicit stress appraisals (Blascovich, 2008), increasing effort expenditure, and depleting personal resources (Hobfoll, 1989). From these perspectives, job demands have an indirect effect on health through their effects on inequity and distributive injustice, as well as a direct effect on health that is independent of injustice.

A similar logic can be applied to resources, which reflect the outcome side of Adams' equity principle. When resources are low, the work situation is more likely to be seen as unfair, holding all else equal. Decreases in control, autonomy, and support, which are potential risk factors for ill-health (Demerouti, Bakker, Nachreiner & Schaufeli, 2001; Karasek, 1979), may also be perceived as unfair if this resource distribution violates the principles of distributive justice. In such cases, resources may be related to health in part through effects on distributive injustice and in part through other mechanisms.

As depicted in Figure 3.1, the worker's justice perceptions and moral principles moderate the effect of working conditions on perceived injustice. Workers only perceive demands or resources as unjust if they violate their principles of fairness and morality. As noted earlier, not all workers use the same principles or referents when making these judgments. These moral principles are sources of between-individual variability in whether demand and resource levels are perceived as unjust. When they are perceived as unjust, demands and resources may influence health through the injustice–health mechanisms, adding to their effects through other stress mechanisms.

Procedural justice also has considerable conceptual overlap with perceived control, autonomy, and predictability. Basic social psychological research has pointed to the integral role of procedural justice in fulfilling needs for autonomy and information. Research in this domain has shown that participative voice influences procedural justice perceptions through its effects on perceived control (Lind, Kanfer & Earley, 1990). Individuals have also been found to be more sensitive to procedural injustice when in roles that are less formally autonomous, in situations of uncertainty, and in situations where the leader was not known or trustworthy, suggesting that procedural justice helps fulfill needs for autonomy, control, and predictability when other situational factors fail to do so (van den Bos, 2001; van den Bos, Wilke & Lind, 1998; van Prooijen, 2009). This research also suggests that individuals in low-autonomy jobs are more likely to be sensitive to procedural injustice. Given these findings, it makes sense that in one of the first studies explicitly linking injustice to psychological strain, Elovainio, Kivimaki and Helkama (2001) found that the association between control and psychological strain was largely accounted for by procedural justice. A study of Canadian correctional institution workers also found that procedural injustice predicted psychological distress to a greater degree among workers with low levels of autonomy (Rousseau, Salek, Aube & Morin, 2009). This further supports the notion that procedural justice helps fulfill autonomy needs at work by acting as a substitute for direct control. Autonomy, control, information, and voice are all aspects of procedural justice and yet in and of themselves may be protective factors against ill-health (Demerouti, Bakker, Nachreiner & Schaufeli, 2001; Karasek, 1979). As such, procedural injustice may be associated with health because it is also associated with working conditions that fulfill employee needs for autonomy, control, and predictability that influence health through other mechanisms.

In summary, a final reason that injustice is related to health is that the job demands and resources that have direct effects on health are also major determinants of distributive and procedural injustice, meaning some injustice–health effects may be spurious. However, high-demand, low-resource situations may also be related to health in part *because* of their effects on injustice perceptions, which are in turn related to health through their effects on trust, self-worth, and unpleasant moral emotions as discussed earlier. Future research on the effects of injustice on health should consider the interrelatedness of injustice, demands, resources, and individual differences in moral and justice principles to further clarify and disentangle these main and interactive effects of each on health.

Implications for Interventions

As noted at the beginning of this chapter, the primary goal of this chapter is to highlight theoretical mechanisms that may explain why injustice at work is associated with poor employee health. Although our discussion has largely focused on theoretical issues, understanding the various injustice–ill health pathways also has some practical implications for occupational health interventions. Here, we describe the implications of these theoretical explanations for two types of interventions, those that target work demands and resources and those that target interpersonal treatment.

Work demands and resources

As discussed earlier, work demands and resources such as workload, autonomy, and support likely have effects on health through injustice as well as through other mechanisms independent of injustice. Thus, improving work role conditions by reducing workload, giving workers more control over their work and schedules, and providing more material and social support may improve health in part by increasing the perceived fairness of the situation, especially when these improvements align with the worker's moral principles.

Many intervention studies have been conducted targeting control and workload (LaMontagne *et al.*, 2007), and although these studies usually do not directly measure justice, distributive and procedural justice principles are often implicated in working conditions targeted in these interventions for reasons described earlier. In one intervention study, Bond and Bunce (2001) found that increases in workers' control over assignment distribution, communication, and obtaining performance feedback led to increases in physical and mental health. Kompier, Aust, van den Berg and Siegrist (2000) reported on 13 cases of job redesign among bus drivers, with interventions addressing issues such as job enrichment, shift work, participation and voice, and communication. These interventions were found to influence health-related outcomes such as absenteeism, disability cases, psychophysiological indicators of health, and subjective well-being and distress. In another example, Mikkelsen, Saksvik and Langsbergis (2000) reported on a participatory organizational intervention as part of Norway's "Health in Working Life" research program. As part of this intervention, employee groups identified key work environmental issues and ways to improve on the current work environment. This participative intervention gave employees control over the process and resulted in increases in perceived control and decreases in job demands and work-related stress, at least in the short term. The Results Only Work Environment intervention (Moen, Kelly & Lam, 2013), which gives employees freedom to modify their work schedules and location as long as they achieve agreed-upon results, has also been shown to increase perceived schedule control and the time available to spend on personal life, which in turn may have health benefits.

These and other interventions (e.g., Neilsen, Kristensen & Smith-Hansen, 2002) that are intended to help reduce or manage workload distribution, give workers more control over work processes, and increase worker participation in organizational decision-making have been shown to have benefits for worker health and well-being. These interventions may work in part *because* they also improve distributive and procedural fairness and their effects on health may be more powerful to the extent that the interventions align with the moral principles of the workforce. Future research on interventions targeting these aspects of work roles might consider fairness as a potential explanation for their effects.

Interpersonal treatment

Interventions targeting incivility and supervisor interpersonal skills also have potential to improve health by reducing interactional injustice. One example is the Civility, Respect, and Engagement in the Workplace (CREW) intervention (Leiter, Day, Gilin-Oore & Laschinger, 2012), which was developed to encourage civil and respectful interactions among employees. The CREW intervention was found to result in improvements in civility and job attitudes and decreases in workplace distress and absenteeism (Leiter, Laschinger, Day & Gilin-Oore, 2011), with some of these gains maintained over a 1-year period (Leiter, Day, Gilin-Oore & Laschinger, 2012). Although targeting incivility *per se*, these interventions likely address issues of interactional injustice as well and reduce the threats that interactional injustice poses to workers' self-worth.

Other work by Greenberg (2006) suggests that supervisor training in interactional justice may also reduce negative and insomniac reactions to unfavorable changes in reward distribution. In Greenberg's study, nonunionized nurses in two private hospitals were experiencing a change in pay policy that was going to result in a significant pay reduction. At the same time, two other hospitals were not undergoing such a change. Supervisors from two of the hospitals, one undergoing the change and one not undergoing the change, participated in training sessions that involved descriptions of interactional justice, reviews of case studies, role-playing exercises, and group discussions on the topic. Topics covered as part of the training included treating others with politeness and respect, showing emotional support, avoiding degrading behavior, providing explanations for decisions in a timely manner, and being accessible. Insomnia was measured once before the change and three times after the change. Results showed that nurses reported increases in insomnia after experiencing the pay change, regardless of supervisor training. However, insomniac reactions diminished among nurses whose supervisors were trained in interactional justice, whereas they did not among those whose supervisors were not trained. These results suggest that interactional justice may attenuate some of the negative health effects of undesirable changes in pay that are seen as unfair. It is possible that this attenuation occurred because the interactional justice reduced threats to the workers' self-worth and negated the offensive nature of the pay decisions.

Other interventions to improve supervisor supportive behavior through training have been found to have benefits for the health and well-being of workers (e.g., Hammer *et al.*, 2011). Interactional justice, which is conceptually related to considerate and supportive managerial behavior, may be one explanation for these effects. Future research on interventions to improve supervisor supportiveness and communication might consider interactional and procedural justice and the resulting emotions of workers as explanations for some of the effects these interventions have on worker health and well-being.

In summary, injustice may be reduced through interventions that improve work demands, resources, and interpersonal treatment. To the extent that injustice explains some of the effects of these conditions on health, interventions that improve working conditions and interpersonal treatment may influence health in part because they decrease distributive, procedural, and interactional injustice. More intervention research is needed to further clarify these effects and identify ways to improve these interventions so that they align with the moral principles of the workforce and have the maximum positive impact.

Other Future Research Directions

The aforementioned results point to the promise of interventions to improve distributive, procedural, and interactional justice through changes in work role conditions and training to improve workplace social interactions. There are other theoretical and practical aspects of organizational justice–health relations that also warrant further research. One potential research avenue might be to study the role of workplace injustice in health disparities. Health disparities across socio-economic and ethnic categories continue to be a major public health concern (Braveman, 2006). Individuals in occupations that are lower in socio-economic status likely have a greater exposure to conditions of distributive, procedural, and interactional injustice. Workers in less powerful positions typically have less voice in the decisions that affect them and are more likely to experience inequitable treatment. Workers with less power and status may also be disproportionately targeted by unfair treatment (Cortina, 2008; Cortina, Magley, Williams & Langhout, 2001). To the extent that exposure to these aspects of injustice is a causal factor in mental and physical well-being, organizational injustice may be a contributing factor in health disparities across workers that are systemically exposed to different levels of unfair treatment. Hence, organizational injustice–health research might contribute to further understanding of this important public health problem.

Another potential avenue for future research stems from the role of moral emotions in reactions to injustice. If moral emotions help explain some injustice–health effects, these emotions may also point to other forms of immoral behavior that are not captured by current conceptualizations of organizational justice. For example, Haidt and Graham (2007) identified five foundations for morality. The first is to care for others and to not harm them. The second involves fair distribution and reciprocation. The third is based on loyalty to or betrayal of one's in-group. The fourth involves respect for legitimate authority. The fifth and final principle involves purity and sanctity. Principles of distributive, procedural, and interactional justice overlap with some but not all of these moral foundations, and as such, there may be other events and conditions that also evoke distressing moral emotions. For example, a lack of reciprocity or a failure to keep promises, which results in a psychological contract breach and violation, may lead to distress through the moral emotion of anger (Gakovic & Tetrick, 2003; Robbins, Ford & Tetrick, 2012). Some employees may also believe the organization is morally obligated to be sensitive to family-related issues and thus become angry when the organization fails to do so, whether or not this violates justice principles within the dominant three-dimensional framework. Alternatively, prosocial or moral behavior by the organization and its agents may increase the pleasantness of work through positive moral emotions of gratitude and admiration and in turn have health benefits. Hence, by considering moral emotions as implicated in distress and well-being, we may identify other work situations and experiences that influence worker health in ways similar to the effects of injustice on moral emotions.

Finally, it is also worth considering the difference between episodic or event-based injustice and structural injustice in injustice–health effects. Some justice-relevant experiences, such as disrespectful interpersonal treatment, are discrete and episodic, whereas others, such as inequitable pay or a lack of voice in organizational decisions, tend to be more structural and less tied to a particular event. Relatedly, injustice can reference specific occurrences, such as an unfair decision, or collective entities, such as a person or the organization (Colquitt *et al.*, 2013). It is possible that discrete experiences lead to more intense but less enduring stress reactions, whereas chronic conditions or situations where a person or organization is judged to have an unjust disposition may have more lasting but less intense effects. Research on the distinction between anger and disgust (Fischer & Roseman, 2007) has looked at this issue and suggests that anger tends to occur in response to events, whereas disgust tends to occur in response to more chronic situations and dispositional attributions of immoral behavior. Still, it is not clear when and how discrete events, when repeated, become part of one's chronic, structural situation and how this influences these emotional stress reactions. Such processes need further research and deserve consideration in studying the time course of unhealthy reactions to injustice.

Conclusion

Previous narrative and empirical reviews have demonstrated a correlation between organizational injustice and worker health. The goal of this chapter was to propose theoretical reasons for a causal relationship between organizational injustice and health, consider implications for job stress interventions, and propose some future directions for research on the health implications of unfair treatment at work. We propose four potential explanations for injustice–health effects based on the relations among injustice, trust, self-worth, moral emotional responses, and work demands and resources that have implications for health. Other explanations for injustice–health relationships may also exist, but we believe these factors have significant explanatory value. Further research is also needed examining the ways that worker health can be improved by aligning job stress interventions with workers' fairness and moral principles. Knowledge about why injustice influences employee health has great potential to improve occupational health theory and interventions, while also pointing to new avenues for research that illuminate other working conditions and experiences implicated in these same mechanisms.

References

Adams, J. S. (1963). Toward an understanding of inequity. *Journal of Abnormal and Social Psychology, 67,* 422–436.

Bies, R. J., & Moag, J. F. (1986). Interactional justice: Communication criteria of fairness. In R. J. Lewicki, B. H., Sheppard, & M. H. Bazerman (Eds.), *Research on negotiations in organizations* (Vol. 1, pp. 43–55). Greenwich, CT: JAI Press.

Blascovich, J. (2008). Challenge and threat appraisal. In A. J. Elliot (Ed.), *Handbook of approach and avoidance motivation.* New York: Taylor & Francis Group.

Bond, F. W., & Bunce, D. (2001). Job control mediates change in a work reorganization intervention for stress reduction. *Journal of Occupational Health Psychology, 6,* 290–302.

Braveman, P. (2006). Health disparities and health equity: Concepts and measurement. *Annual Review of Public Health, 27,* 167–194.

Carver, C. S., & Harmon-Jones, E. (2009). Anger is an approach-related affect: Evidence and implications. *Psychological Bulletin, 135,* 183–204.

Cohen-Charash, Y., & Spector, P. E. (2001). The role of justice in organizations: A meta-analysis. *Organizational Behavior and Human Decision Processes, 86,* 278–321.

Colquitt, J. A., Conlon, D. E., Wesson, M. J., Porter, C. O. L. H., & Ng, K. Y. (2001). Justice at the millennium: A meta-analytic review of 25 years of organizational justice research. *Journal of Applied Psychology, 86,* 425–445.

Colquitt, J. A., Scott, B. A., Rodell, J. B., Long, D. M., Zapata, C. P., Conlon, D., *et al.* (2013). Justice at the millennium, a decade later: A meta-analytic test of social exchange and affect-based perspectives. *Journal of Applied Psychology, 98,* 199–236.

Cortina, L. M. (2008). Unseen injustice: Incivility as modern discrimination in organizations. *Academy of Management Review, 33,* 55–75.

Cortina, L. M., Magley, V. J., Williams, J. H., & Langhout, R. D. (2001). Incivility in the workplace: Incidence and impact. *Journal of Occupational Health Psychology, 6,* 64–80.

Crocker, J., & Park, L. E. (2004). The costly pursuit of self-esteem. *Psychological Bulletin, 130,* 392–414.

Cropanzano, R., Byrne, Z. S., Bobocel, D. R., & Rupp. D. E. (2001). Moral virtues, fairness heuristics, social entities, and other denizens of organizational justice. *Journal of Vocational Behavior, 58,* 164–209.

Cropanzano, R., Goldman, B., & Folger, R. (2003). Deontic justice: The role of moral principles in workplace fairness. *Journal of Organizational Behavior, 24,* 1019–1024.

Cropanzano, R., & Wright, T. A. (2010). The impact of organizational justice on occupational health. In J. C. Quick, & L. E. Tetrick (Eds.), *Handbook of occupational health psychology* (2nd ed.). Washington, DC: American Psychological Association.

De Boer, E. M., Bakker, A. B., Syroit, J. E., & Schaufeli, W. B. (2002). Unfairness at work as a predictor of absenteeism. *Journal of Organizational Behavior, 23,* 181–197.

De Cremer, D., van Knippenberg, B., van Knippenberg, D., Mullenders, D., & Stinglhamber, F. (2005). Rewarding leadership and fair procedures as determinants of self-esteem. *Journal of Applied Psychology, 90,* 3–12.

Demerouti, E., Bakker, A. B., Nachreiner, F., & Schaufeli, W. B. (2001). The job demands-resources model of burnout. *Journal of Applied Psychology, 86,* 499–512.

Dickerson, S. S., Gruenewald, T. L., & Kemeny, M. E. (2004). When the social self is threatened: Shame, physiology, and health. *Journal of Personality, 72,* 1191–1216.

Elovainio, M., Kivimaki, M., & Helkama, K. (2001). Organizational justice evaluations, job control, and occupational strain. *Journal of Applied Psychology*, *86*, 418–424.

Elovainio, M., Kivimaki, M., Vahtera, J., Keltikangas-Jjarvinen, L., & Virtanen, M. (2003). Sleeping problems and health behavior as mediators between organizational justice and health. *Health Psychology*, *22*, 287–293.

Ferris, D. L., Spence, J. R., Brown, D. J., & Heller, D. (2012). Interpersonal deviance and workplace deviance: The role of esteem threat. *Journal of Management*, *38*, 1788–1811.

Fischer, A. H., & Roseman, I. J. (2007). Beat them or ban them: The characteristics and social functions of anger and contempt. *Journal of Personality and Social Psychology*, *93*, 103–115.

Gakovic, A., & Tetrick, L. E. (2003). Psychological contract breach as a source of strain for employees. *Journal of Business and Psychology*, *18*, 235–246.

Goldman, B. M., Slaughter, J. E., Schmit, M. J., Wiley, J. W., & Brooks, S. M. (2008). Perceptions of discrimination: A multiple needs model perspective. *Journal of Management*, *34*, 952–977.

Greenberg, J. (1990). Organizational justice: Yesterday, today, and tomorrow. *Journal of Management*, *16*, 399–432.

Greenberg, J. (2001). Setting the justice agenda: Seven unanswered questions about "what, why, and how". *Journal of Vocational Behavior*, *58*, 210–219.

Greenberg, J. (2006). Losing sleep over organizational injustice: Attenuating insomniac reactions to underpayment inequity with supervisor training in interactional justice. *Journal of Applied Psychology*, *91*, 58–69.

Greenberg, J. (2010). Organizational injustice as an occupational health risk. *The Academy of Management Annals*, *4*, 205–243.

Haidt, J. (2003). The moral emotions. In R. J., Davidson, K. R. Scherer, & H. H. Goldsmith (Eds.), *Handbook of affective sciences* (pp. 852–870). Oxford, UK: Oxford University Press.

Haidt, J., & Graham, J. (2007). When morality opposes justice: Conservatives have moral intuitions that liberals may not recognize. *Social Justice Research*, *20*, 98–116.

Hammer, L. B., Kossek, E. E., Anger, W. K., Bodner, T., & Zimmerman, K. L. (2011). Clarifying work-family intervention processes: The roles of work-family conflict and family-supportive supervisor behaviors. *Journal of Applied Psychology*, *96*, 134–150.

Harvey, S., Kelloway, E. K., & Duncan-Leiper, L. (2003). Trust in management as a buffer of the relationships between overload and strain. *Journal of Occupational Health Psychology*, *8*, 306–315.

Hobfoll, S. E. (1989). Conservation of resources: A new attempt at conceptualizing stress. *American Psychologist*, *44*, 513–524.

Karasek, R. A. (1979). Job demands, job decision latitude, and mental strain: Implications for job redesign. *Administrative Science Quarterly*, *24*, 285–308.

Kivimaki, M., Virtanen, M., Elovainio, M., Kouvonen, Vaananen, A., & Vahtera, J. (2006). Work stress in the etiology of coronary heart disease—A meta-analysis. *Scandinavian Journal of Work, Environment, and Health*, *32*, 431–442.

Kompier, M. A. J., Aust, B., van den Berg, A.-M., & Siegrist, J. (2000). Stress prevention in bus drivers: Evaluation of 13 natural experiments. *Journal of Occupational Health Psychology*, *5*, 11–31.

Kottwitz, M. U., Meier, L. L., Jacobshagen, N., Kalin, W., Elfering, A., Hennig, J., & Semmer, N. K. (2013). Illegitimate tasks associated with higher cortisol levels among male employees when subjective health is relatively low: An intra-individual analysis. *Scandinavian Journal of Work, Environment, and Health, 39*, 310–318.

LaMontagne, A. D., Keegel, T., Louie, A. M., Ostry, A., & Landsbergis, P. A. (2007). A systematic review of the job-stress intervention evaluation literature, 1990–2005. *Journal of Occupational and Environmental Health, 13*, 268–280.

Lazarus, R. S., & Folkman, S. (1984). *Stress, appraisal, and coping.* New York: Springer.

Leiter, M. P., Day, A., Gilin-Oore, D., & Laschinger, H. K. S. (2012). Getting better and staying better: Assessing civility, incivility, distress, and job attitudes on year after a civility intervention. *Journal of Occupational Health Psychology, 17*, 425–434.

Leiter, M. P., Laschinger, H. K. S., Day, A., & Gilin-Oore, D. (2011). The impact of civility interventions on employee social behavior, distress, and attitudes. *Journal of Applied Psychology, 96*, 1258–1274.

Leventhal, G. S. (1980). What should be done with equity theory? New approaches to the study of fairness in social relationships. In K. Gergen, M. Greenberg, & R. Willis (Eds.), *Social exchange: Advances in theory and research* (pp. 27–55). New York: Plenum.

Lim, S., Cortina, L. M., & Magley, V. J. (2008). Personal and workgroup incivility: Impact on work and health outcomes. *Journal of Applied Psychology, 93*, 95–107.

Lind, E. A., Kanfer, R., & Earley, P. C. (1990). Voice, control, and procedural justice: Instrumental and noninstrumental concerns in fairness judgments. *Journal of Personality and Social Psychology, 59*, 952–959.

Lind, E. A., & Tyler, T. R. (1988). *The social psychology of procedural justice.* New York: Plenum Press.

Liu, C., Yang, L.-Q., & Nauta, M. M. (2013). Examining the mediating effect of supervisor conflict on procedural injustice-job strain relations: The function of power distance. *Journal of Occupational Health Psychology, 18*, 64–74.

Mayer, R. C., Davis, J. H., & Schoorman, F. D. (1995). An integrative model of organizational trust. *Academy of Management Review, 20*, 709–734.

Meier, L. L., & Semmer, N. K. (2013). Lack of reciprocity, narcissism, anger, and instigated workplace incivility: A moderated mediation model. *European Journal of Work and Organizational Psychology, 22*, 461–475.

Mikkelsen, A., Saksvik, P. O., & Landsbergis, P. (2000). The impact of a participatory organizational intervention on job stress in community health care institutions. *Work & Stress, 14*, 156–170.

Moen, P., Kelly, E. L., & Lam, J. (2013). Healthy work revisited: Do changes in time strain predict well-being? *Journal of Occupational Health Psychology, 18*, 157–172.

Moliner, C., Martinez-Tur, V., Peiro, J. M., Ramos, J., & Cropanzano, R. (2005). Relationship between organizational justice and burnout at the work unit level. *International Journal of Stress Management, 12*, 99–116.

Neilsen, M. L., Kristensen, T. S., & Smith-Hansen, L. (2002). The Intervention Project on Absence and Well-being (IPAW): Design and results from the baseline of a 5-year study. *Work & Stress, 16*, 191–206.

O'Neill, O. A., Vandenberg, R. J., DeJoy, D. M., & Wilson, M. G. (2009). Exploring relationships among anger, perceived organizational support, and workplace outcomes. *Journal of Occupational Health Psychology, 14*, 318–333.

Perrewe, P. L., & Zellars, K. L. (1999). An examination of attributions and emotions in the transactional approach to the organizational stress process. *Journal of Organizational Behavior, 20*, 739–752.

Robbins, J. M., Ford, M. T., & Tetrick, L. E. (2012). Perceived unfairness and employee health: A meta-analytic integration. *Journal of Applied Psychology, 97*, 235–272.

Rousseau, V., Salek, S., Aube, C., & Morin, E. M. (2009). Distributive justice, procedural justice, and psychological distress: The moderating effect of coworker support and work autonomy. *Journal of Occupational Health Psychology, 14*, 305–317.

Rozin, P., Lowery, L., Imada, S., & Haidt, J. (1999). The CAD triad hypothesis: A mapping between three moral emotions (contempt, anger, disgust) and three moral codes (community, autonomy, divinity). *Journal of Personality and Social Psychology, 76*, 574–586.

Rupp, D. E., & Spencer, S. (2006). When customers lash out: The effects of customer interactional injustice on emotional labor and the mediating role of discrete emotions. *Journal of Applied Psychology, 91*, 971–978.

Semmer, N. K., Jacobshaben, N., Meier, L. L., & Elfering, A. (2007). Occupational stress research: The "stress-as-offense-to-self" perspective. In J. Houdmont & S. McIntyre (Eds.), *Occupational health psychology: European perspectives on research, education, and practice* (Vol. 2, pp. 43–60). Maia, Portugal: ISMAI Publishers.

Semmer, N. K., Tschan, F., Meier, L. L., Facchin, S., & Jacobshagen, N. (2010). Illegitimate tasks and counterproductive work behavior. *Applied Psychology: An International Review, 59*, 70–96.

Siegrist, J. (1996). Adverse health effects of high-effort/low-reward conditions. *Journal of Occupational Health Psychology, 1*, 27–41.

Skarlicki, D. P., & Kulik, C. T. (2005). Third-party reactions to employee (mis)treatment: A justice perspective. *Research in Organizational Behavior, 26*, 183–229.

Sonnentag, S., Binnewies, C., & Mojza, E. J. (2008). "Did you have a nice evening?" A day-level study on recovery experiences, sleep, and affect. *Journal of Applied Psychology, 93*, 674–684.

Spell, C. S., & Arnold, T. J. (2007). An appraisal perspective of justice, structure, and job control as antecedents to psychological distress. *Journal of Organizational Behavior, 28*, 729–751.

Sverke, M., Hellgren, J., & Naswall, K. (2002). No security: A meta-analysis and review of job insecurity and its consequences. *Journal of Occupational Health Psychology, 7*, 242–264.

Tabibnia, G., Satpute, A. B., & Lieberman, M. D. (2008). The sunny side of fairness: Preference for fairness activates reward circuitry (and disregarding unfairness activates self-control circuitry). *Psychological Science, 19*, 339–347.

Tepper, B. J. (2000). Consequences of abusive supervision. *Academy of Management Journal, 43*, 178–190.

van den Bos, K. (2001). Uncertainty management: The influence of uncertainty salience on reactions to perceived procedural fairness. *Journal of Personality and Social Psychology, 80*, 931–941.

van den Bos, K., Wilke, H. A. M., & Lind, E. A. (1998). When do we need procedural fairness? The role of trust in authority. *Journal of Personality and Social Psychology, 75*, 1449–1458.

van Prooijen, J.-W. (2009). Procedural justice as autonomy regulation. *Journal of Personality and Social Psychology, 96*, 1166–1180.

Wager, N., Feldman, G., & Hussey, T. (2003). The effect on ambulatory blood pressure of working under favourably and unfavourably perceived supervisors. *Occupational and Environmental Medicine, 60*, 468–474.

4

Reconsidering the Daily Recovery Process: New Insights and Related Methodological Challenges

Despoina Xanthopoulou
Aristotle University of Thessaloniki, Greece

Ana Isabel Sanz-Vergel
Norwich Business School, University of East Anglia, UK

Evangelia Demerouti
Eindhoven University of Technology, The Netherlands

Introduction

During the past decade, empirical research on recovery from work-related demands has flourished (Demerouti, Bakker, Geurts & Taris, 2009; Demerouti & Sanz-Vergel, 2012). Why is recovery important both for occupational health psychologists and managers? The answer to this question is straightforward. Inadequate recovery is detrimental for employee well-being and job performance both in the short and in the long run. Lack of daily recovery is likely to result in fatigue accumulation that consequently leads to chronic – physical and psychological – health impairment (Geurts & Sonnentag, 2006). In contrast, successful recovery enhances both employee well-being and productive behaviors. Sonnentag (2003) showed that on days that employees feel more recovered than usual, they are also more engaged and, consequently, more proactive during work. In a similar vein, Binnewies, Sonnentag and Mojza (2009) found that employees who start a workday recovered are more likely to report higher task performance, personal initiative, and organizational citizenship behaviors. This highlights how essential employee recovery is for flourishing organizations.

In this chapter, we review recent empirical evidence with the aim to enhance our understanding of the daily recovery process. We focus on the mechanisms that may explain the relationship between daily job demands and recovery by discussing potential

Contemporary Occupational Health Psychology: Global Perspectives on Research and Practice, Volume 3,
First Edition. Edited by Stavroula Leka and Robert R. Sinclair.
© 2014 John Wiley & Sons, Ltd. Published 2014 by John Wiley & Sons, Ltd.

mediators (e.g., work-related well-being) and moderators (e.g., resources). Special emphasis is placed on need for recovery as the threshold that determines the degree and the way in which work-related experiences spill over to non-work experiences and influence recovery. Also, we investigate the role of intra-individual (e.g., employee traits) and inter-individual (e.g., the role of significant others) factors in explaining the effect of non-work experiences on recovery. The outmost purpose is to put together an updated theoretical framework for the study of daily recovery that could be used as a guide for future studies.

Understanding the Recovery Process

Geurts and Sonnentag (2006) defined recovery from work as "a process of psychological unwinding after effort expenditure" (p. 485). In the same vein, recovery has been considered as a process through which depleted resources are replenished, as opposing to the process of the building up of stress (Sonnentag & Fritz, 2007; Sonnentag & Zijlstra, 2006). Thus, recovery is operationalized as a dynamic phenomenon that evolves from moment to moment over the course of consecutive workdays, where work and non-work experiences unfold in a reciprocal manner over time. As such, recovery may occur both at work during the work breaks and after work. The former is known as internal and the latter as external recovery (Geurts & Sonnentag, 2006). An important issue is to understand how and when recovery occurs and what makes a complete or incomplete recovery. In what follows, two theoretical models that help understand this process are presented.

The *effort–recovery model* (Meijman & Mulder, 1998) explains how reactions to normal workloads may lead to chronic health problems, when incomplete recovery occurs. The main assumption is that effort expenditure at work leads to acute responses (e.g., physiological activation or fatigue) that can be overcome through adequate recovery. Successful recovery means that the psycho-physiological systems that were activated during work return to baseline once the stressor is no longer present. However, when the same functional systems remain activated, the process of recovery cannot take place, resulting in fatigue accumulation. Take, for instance, a teacher who has graded students' assignments at work and who continues this activity during non-work time. This person is functioning under cognitive load that will deplete his/her energy at the end of the day and probably also the next day. What people do is counteracting this suboptimal state by investing extra effort. However, in this case, the functional systems cannot return to the pre-stressor levels. This fuels a "vicious cycle" where what should be "normal" reactions become chronic problems (Sluiter, Van der Beek & Frings-Dresen, 1999). In this context, Geurts and Sonnentag (2006) suggested that incomplete recovery may be perceived as the link that explains the relationship between acute stress and chronic health impairment.

The *Conservation of Resources* (COR) theory (Hobfoll, 1998, 2001) highlights the concept of "resources" as a key element of the stress process. Resources refer both to external entities, including objects (e.g., house) or conditions (e.g., job security), as well as personal characteristics (e.g., optimism) or energies (e.g., levels of vigor). COR theory assumes that people strive to obtain, retain, and protect those resources that they value. Thus, the threat of losing or the actual loss of resources generates high levels of stress. Applying this theory to the recovery process, it is argued that recovery during work breaks or leisure time may help individuals to restore depleted resources (e.g., by engaging in relaxing activities during the evening) but also to build up new resources (e.g., new skills can be acquired when one is busy with a new hobby). In the latter case, it is implied that in order to gain resources, people need to invest resources. At first sight, it seems difficult to conceive how recovery is achieved when people need to make an extra effort. However, effort to recover can be beneficial when the invested resources are different from those that are activated when facing job demands. For instance, doing some sport after a day with many cognitive demands may help recovery. What we learn from COR theory is that to achieve recovery, people need to restore depleted resources and to invest other types of resources than those used at work in order to acquire additional resources.

The effort–recovery model and the COR theory are complementary in explaining the recovery process since the former emphasizes the need to avoid overwhelming job demands or activities that require the same resources as job tasks, while the latter suggests that the acquisition of resources during recovery helps restoring depleted resources or gaining new resources (Sonnentag & Fritz, 2007). Before reviewing related empirical evidence, it is important to clarify that recovery is either measured by asking participants to report how recovered they feel before going to work or at bedtime (e.g., Bakker, Demerouti, Oerlemans & Sonnentag, 2013; Sonnentag, 2003) or by using daily well-being indicators (e.g., fatigue; Rook & Zijlstra, 2006) as a proxy.

Daily Job Demands, Work-Related Well-Being, and Need for Recovery

Theoretical assumptions clearly suggest that the daily recovery process develops over the course of the day from the moment that employees wake up to the moment they go to rest at night, while the previous day's recovery and sleep quality determines employee functioning the next day. Also, it is evident that the demands that employees face on a daily basis are the main triggers of this process. There is substantial evidence linking job demands to recovery. For instance, Sonnentag (2003) found a negative relationship between situational constraints at work and daily recovery, while Sanz-Vergel, Demerouti, Moreno-Jiménez and Mayo (2010) in their study among Spanish employees found that daily work pressure related negatively to recovery after work breaks. Evidence from different studies underlines the detrimental role of long working hours for daily recovery (Sonnentag & Bayer, 2005; Sonnentag & Jelden, 2009). In this section, we take job demands as the starting point, and we discuss the underlying mechanisms that may explain their impact on daily recovery.

The focus on the demands–recovery link is important because job demands determine the effort that employees invest at work. In turn, the amount of invested effort influences fatigue levels during work and need for recovery at the end of work. When fatigue builds up, people feel a sense of urgency to take a break from job demands (Sonnentag & Zijlstra, 2006). This emotional state, where people are reluctant to continue dealing with their demands or to take over extra demands, has been termed *need for recovery* and has been found to be distinct from fatigue or psychological distress (Jansen, Kant & van den Brandt, 2002). Need for recovery is central in the daily recovery process since it may be perceived as the threshold through which work-related experiences spill over to off-work experiences and determine the degree to which one will finally manage to recover successfully at the end of the day. This is in line with Sonnentag and Zijlstra who showed that need for recovery is more pronounced on days that employees face particularly high demands thus leading to well-being impairments at bedtime.

Despite its importance, the proposition that need for recovery mediates the relationship between daily job demands and well-being at bedtime neglects the main tenet that need for recovery emerges when fatigue builds up at work (Sonnentag & Zijlstra, 2006). Need for recovery at the end of the workday is not only a function of the job demands of that day but also of employee well-being during the preceding hours. In other words, the job demands–need for recovery link may be further explained by the intervening role of employee well-being. Indeed, in a diary study among 111 employees from 30 organizations in Germany, Sonnentag, Mojza, Demerouti and Bakker (2012) found that employees' morning recovery levels related positively to indicators of work-related well-being (i.e., work engagement) during work that in turn were associated with recovery at bedtime, over and above the role of daily job demands and constraints.

Furthermore, the results of a diary study among 50 employees in the Netherlands and Poland showed that well-being during work related to need for recovery at the end of the workday that in turn determined recovery after work (Xanthopoulou, Bakker, Oerlemans & Koszucka, 2012). This study, also highlighted the intervening role of two emotion regulation strategies (i.e., deep acting and surface acting) as the mechanism that explains how emotionally demanding jobs determine work-related well-being and, in turn, daily recovery. Analyses showed that employees' generalized perceptions of organizational display rules (i.e., required emotional displays during interactions at work) related positively to day levels of surface acting (i.e., the expression of required emotions without changing the inner feelings) but not deep acting (i.e., the active attempt to feel the required emotions). Furthermore, surface acting had a positive indirect effect on need for recovery through exhaustion, while deep acting had a negative indirect effect on need for recovery via flow (i.e., enjoyment, intrinsic motivation, and total absorption in the task). In turn, need for recovery related negatively to relaxation after work and vigor at bedtime. These results emphasize the significance of the regulation of emotional demands in explaining well-being during, and recovery from, emotional work.

Moderators in the Job Demands–Recovery Link

Daily job demands seem to trigger the recovery process, since demands determine – through employee well-being during work – the need for recovery at the end of the workday and, consequently, recovery after work (see Figure 4.1). In an attempt to explain under which conditions job demands are particularly problematic for recovery, we present results of diary studies concerning specific moderators in the job demands–recovery link.

Next to the mediating role of emotional regulation in the job demands–recovery relationship, *emotional expression* during work was also found to play a moderating role. Sanz-Vergel, Demerouti, Moreno-Jiménez and Mayo (2010) followed up 49 employees from different domains (i.e., finance, construction, trade, health, media, and education) in Spain for five consecutive workdays, three times a day: in the morning before going to work, in the afternoon after work, and at bedtime. Results highlighted that emotional expression at work plays a significant role in determining the effect of demands on exhaustion. More specifically, it was shown that the positive relation between daily work pressure and exhaustion at bedtime was particularly strong in conditions where employees avoided expressing their positive emotions at work. In contrast, this relationship was non-existent on days that employees were expressing their positive emotions at work. These results suggest that talking to colleagues about one's positive emotions seems to be a strategy that helps distracting

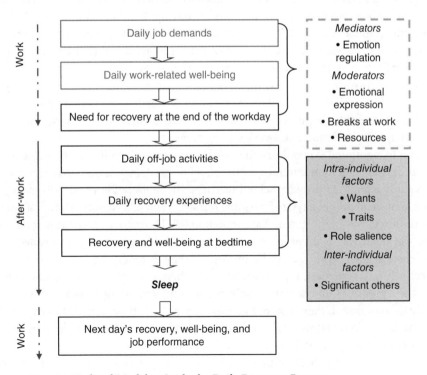

Figure 4.1   An Updated Model to Study the Daily Recovery Process.

from the stressful events at work, thus facilitating recovery. Employees who deal effectively with their daily work pressure by expressing their positive emotions are more likely to avoid a negative spillover from work to home domain and facilitate recovery.

Within-work breaks also play a crucial role in determining the degree and the way in which daily job demands influence recovery. Trougakos and Hideg (2009) proposed that employees must utilize work breaks in order to engage in activities that reduce demands and the associated taxing on resources. Thus, the nature of work breaks determines the degree to which employees replenish their resources during work. Indeed, Trougakos, Hideg and Cheng (2011) found that employees who engaged in relaxing activities during their lunch break experienced lower levels of fatigue, while those who spent their lunch on work-related or social activities that are more effortful were more fatigued at the end of the day. In a similar vein, Sanz-Vergel, Demerouti, Moreno-Jiménez and Mayo (2010) showed that employees who were feeling recovered after within-work breaks were less exhausted at bedtime, particularly when they avoided expressing their negative emotions at work. In this context, it may be proposed that fruitful use of within-work breaks may buffer the positive effect of daily job demands on fatigue and need for recovery and, in turn, facilitate the recovery process. This proposition is in line with COR theory (Hobfoll, 1998) since employees who use their work breaks to refill constantly their resources will be better able to deal with the demanding aspects of their job, thus preventing fatigue accumulation and an increased need for recovery at the end of work. What happens when employees fail to recover during breaks? Demerouti, Bakker, Sonnentag and Fullagar (2012) found that this is not detrimental for employee recovery (i.e., levels of energy) on days that employees enjoy their work tasks. Specifically, it was found that positive experiences at work like enjoyment may enhance energy after work only on days that employees would fail to recover successfully during work breaks. The explanation of this finding is that enjoyment at work may overrule fatigue effects that are caused by daily job demands and may protect against inadequate recovery during breaks.

Next to emotional expression and work breaks, the availability of job and personal resources has been found to mitigate the effect of job demands on need for recovery. In a study among 45 primary school teachers, the moderating role of dispositional time management (i.e., a type of personal resource) and daily autonomy (i.e., a typical job resource) was investigated (Xanthopoulou, 2011). Analyses showed that on days that workload was high, employees were more likely to be happy, motivated, and absorbed in their work (i.e., to be in flow) if they were able to manage their time effectively (i.e., systematically set and prioritize their goals, plan their tasks, and monitor their progress). In contrast, employees dealing with a high workload were less likely to be in flow, if they were not able to manage their time well. Furthermore, the results suggested that flow was lowest on days that high workload was combined with low levels of autonomy and low time management.

All in all, these empirical findings shed light on the psychological mechanisms that explain the job demands–recovery link, as well as on the conditions under which job demands hinder or facilitate recovery. We will now shift the attention to external recovery and the part of the daily process that concerns the hours after work.

Daily Off-Job Activities and Recovery Experiences

Traditionally, research on recovery emphasized that the type of *activities* that are pursued after work are of great significance for successful recovery. Sonnentag (2001) distinguished five basic activity categories: work-related (e.g., being busy with work-related or administration tasks), household (e.g., cleaning or cooking), physical (e.g., sports and exercise), social (e.g., going out with friends), and passive (e.g., watching TV) activities. In line with COR theory (Hobfoll, 1998), the degree to which an activity facilitates or inhibits recovery depends on the type of resources that are invested. Similar to within-work breaks, leisure activities that do not require investing similar resources to those of work tasks are expected to be more beneficial.

Due to its recuperative nature, *sleep* is perhaps the most beneficial activity for recovery (Demerouti, Bakker, Geurts & Taris, 2009). Next to the amount of sleep, researchers have also emphasized the importance of sleep quality. For instance, Sonnentag, Binnewies and Mojza (2008) found that sleep quality associated positively with mood (positive affect, serenity) and negatively with negative affect and fatigue over and above sleep duration. Next to sleep, there is consistent empirical evidence regarding the beneficial role of *physical activities*. A series of studies have shown that on days that employees engage in physical activities during the hours after work, they feel more recovered at bedtime (Rook & Zijlstra, 2006; Sonnentag, 2001; Sonnentag & Bayer, 2005; Sonnentag & Natter, 2004).

Empirical evidence concerning the role of other activity types for recovery is quite inconsistent. Contrary to expectations, Rook and Zijlstra (2006) did not find any effect of spending leisure time on *work-related activities* on fatigue, while Volman, Bakker and Xanthopoulou (2013) did show that work-related activities inhibit recovery. In a similar vein, Sonnentag (2001) found that teachers who engaged in low-effort activities reported higher well-being at bedtime, while this was not the case for flight attendants for whom low-effort activities had no effect on well-being (Sonnentag & Natter, 2004; see also Rook & Zijlstra, 2006). The findings concerning the role of *social activities* are also inconsistent. In some studies, social activities were found to associate positively to recovery (e.g., Sonnentag & Zijlstra, 2006), in others to be unrelated (e.g., Sonnentag & Bayer, 2005), and in others to be detrimental for recovery (Sonnentag & Natter, 2004).

In an attempt to explain these mixed results, scholars suggested that the type of activity is not the most important issue for recovery. Rather, recovery is determined by the degree to which activities facilitate individuals' *recovery experiences*. Sonnentag and Fritz (2007) recognized four recovery experiences. The first is *psychological detachment* that refers to being physically and mentally away from work or switching off from work-related demands. *Relaxation* is a state of low activation and enhanced positive affect that facilitates recovery because it limits the prolonged activation of the functional system and counteracts the effects of negative emotional states. *Mastery experiences* concern activities that offer opportunities to learn new things and to face new challenges. Finally, being in *control* implies that leisure time is spent freely which, consequently, may result in gaining additional resources. Having control on how to spend your time has been found to be significant for recovery during within-work breaks as well (Trougakos, Hideg & Cheng, 2011). According to Sonnentag and Fritz, any activity that provides recovery experiences to employees facilitates recovery. This explains why certain activities that may be taxing and may require investing similar resources to the ones that were used up at work may facilitate recovery. For instance, Mojza, Lorenz, Sonnentag and Binnewies (2010) found that spending leisure time on volunteer work is good for daily recovery because it helps individuals to forget about their job demands and to gain new mastery experiences.

Going beyond the Activity

To our view, recovery is not solely explained by the recovery experiences. In what follows, we discuss certain intra-individual and inter-individual factors that help to better understand when and why leisure-time experiences are beneficial for recovery.

Intra-individual factors

Volman, Bakker and Xanthopoulou (2013) proposed that recovery is most likely to take place when there is a match between the activities people engage in after work and the degree to which people want to spend time in these activities. The notion of individual *wants* relates closely to the notion of control over leisure time since it concerns the degree to which the choice of activities is a preferred and not a forced one. Based on person–environment fit theory (Edwards & Van Harrison, 1993), Volman *et al.* suggested that leisure activities hinder recovery particularly when there is a discrepancy between the person's preferences (i.e., wants) on how to spend leisure time and how time is actually spent. This implies that even activities that require substantial effort or a significant amount of resource investment may facilitate recovery if people have the inner drive to be involved in such activities. For instance, for people who cook a meal because they have to, cooking is most likely to function as a burden. In contrast, people who cook after work because they like to do it (i.e., find value in the activity) have a better chance to recover. The diary study by Volman *et al.* provided preliminary support for this proposition since it was found that people find it hard to detach from work-related demands particularly on days that they engage in household activities that they do not want to do.

Employee traits also contribute in explaining external recovery. Due to their compulsive drive to work excessive long hours and their tendency to think about work all the time, *workaholics* are at high risk because of their reluctance to detach psychologically from work (Bakker, Demerouti, Oerlemans & Sonnentag, 2013). Recent studies tried to explain why workaholics find it difficult to recover, and which recovery activities are particularly beneficial for them. The results of a diary study among 42 Dutch teachers showed that the relationship between need for recovery and relaxation during the hours after work was particularly negative for workaholics (Xanthopoulou & Bakker, 2010). In turn, inability to relax related to lower recovery the next day before going to work. These findings imply that workaholics fail to recognize their need to recover that consequently may initiate a negative spiral of fatigue accumulation. Bakker, Demerouti, Oerlemans and Sonnentag (2013) focused on the moderating role of workaholism in the relationship between various leisure activities (i.e., physical, social, relaxing, routine, cognitive, and work related), on the one hand, and recovery at the end of the day, on the other hand. Eighty-five employees from various occupations filled in a diary for nine working days by using the day reconstruction method. At the end of each day, participants were asked to report what they did during the hours after work and how they felt with regard to the activities pursued. Results suggested that engaging in physical activities (i.e., exercise, sports) on a daily basis facilitates recovery particularly for workaholics (vs. non-workaholics). This finding is of particular importance since it shows that physical activities can be the antidote to workaholics' inability to detach from work-related demands.

Humor has been considered as a facilitator of the recovery process because of its demonstrated benefits on health-related outcomes (Demerouti, Bakker, Geurts & Taris, 2009). Nevertheless, not all types of humor are beneficial, while there are individual differences in the use of humor (Martin *et al.*, 2003). Martin and colleagues distinguished between two types of humor, namely, affiliative and aggressive humor. The former is aimed at enhancing one's relationships with others and it can be considered as benign, whereas the latter enhances the self at the expense of others, and it may be detrimental for the individual since it may impair close relationships. In an exploratory study among couples, Sanz-Vergel, Rodríguez-Muñoz, Demerouti and Bakker (2012) analyzed the impact of these two interpersonal humor styles on partners' daily psychological detachment from work. Results showed that when one partner reported high levels of trait affiliative humor, it was easier for the other partner to disconnect from work on a daily basis. Interestingly, one's own levels of humor did not have an impact on his/her own daily detachment, while the impact of aggressive humor was non-significant. These findings support those by Martin and colleagues who suggested that the use of beneficial humor styles in a dyad may have a positive impact on the partner.

Finally, individual differences in *role salience* or the extent to which a (work-related or family) role is central in an employee's everyday life were found to impact the transition from work to non-work experiences (and *vice versa*) within the recovery process. In a daily diary study among 49 employees, Sanz-Vergel, Demerouti, Bakker and Moreno-Jiménez (2011) examined how the significance of work and family roles affected the impact of employee psychological detachment on family- and health-related outcomes. Next to psychological detachment from work-related demands, these authors also emphasize the need to detach from home in order to function properly at work. Based on Clark's (2000) Border Theory, it was suggested that when the work domain is not central to the individual, it may be easier to cross borders and think of family-related issues at work. In such situations, detaching from home would be particularly necessary to maintain performance. Indeed, results showed that psychological detachment from home related positively to performance among those employees with low work-role salience. Moreover, it was found that detaching from work was especially important for employees with a high home-role salience, increasing evening cognitive liveliness and reducing work–home interference. These results suggest that the importance that employees place to the different roles that they fulfill in their everyday life plays a crucial role in how successful their daily recovery will be.

Inter-individual factors

Although recovery is mainly an individual issue, research starts to recognize that significant others may also play a role in one's recovery. As discussed earlier, one partner's humor style may affect the other partner's recovery. Also, studies on recovery activities showed that spending time on "household and childcare" activities is not always negative for recovery (e.g., Rook & Zijlstra, 2006; Sonnentag, 2001; Sonnentag & Natter, 2004). One explanation may be that this is a very broad activity category comprising of both enjoyable and unpleasant activities (Sonnentag & Braun, 2013). Ten Brummelhuis and Bakker (2012) showed in their diary study that household chores related negatively to relaxation and psychological detachment. In contrast, childcare tasks had no influence on recovery experiences. This implies that household and childcare activities may have two antagonistic effects on recovery. One is detrimental due to energy consumption, and one can be beneficial due to distraction from work-related issues.

   Hahn and Dormann (2013), in a study among 114 dual-earner couples, examined the role of employees' private environment (i.e., partners and children) for their psychological detachment from work during off-job time and well-being. It was found that employees' own and their partners' work–home segmentation preference associated positively with employees' detachment. The presence of children attenuated the relation of partners' work–home segmentation preferences on employees' detachment. Moreover, employees' and partners' detachment were positively associated. Again, the relation was weaker when there were children living in the household. This study indicates that employees are more likely to react to their partners' work-related cues when these resemble their own work-related cues. Moreover, the presence of children is an important boundary condition for the effects of partners' preferences and experiences on employees' detachment. Hahn, Binnewies and Haun (2012) further showed that absorption in joint activities with the partner predicted recovery experiences during the weekend and increased positive affective states at the beginning of the following work week.

Energy levels as a proxy of recovery have also been found to influence work–non-work facilitation among partners. Demerouti (2012), in a study among dual-earner couples, found that the availability of job resources influences one's own individual energy because favorable working conditions facilitate employees to fulfill their personal interests after work (i.e., work–self facilitation). Consequently, one's energy influences positively the partner's perception of home resources, which eventually spills over to the partner's energy through experienced family–self facilitation. Work–self and family–self facilitation occur when resource gains generated at work or in the family domain promote functioning and/or positive affect during time devoted to personal interests. Such facilitation is useful in explaining why job and family resources enhance the levels of energy that individuals invest in different life domains. To conclude, these findings indicate that recovery is not only a personal issue but it is also a social issue since both the mere presence of others and the quality of social interactions may shape off-job experiences and determine one's level of recovery at the end of the day.

An Updated Model to Study Recovery

After reviewing recent empirical studies that explain how the recovery process unfolds from the hours at work to the hours after work and from one day to another, as well as the factors that facilitate or inhibit this process, we synthesized an updated framework that advances our understanding of the daily recovery process. This updated model is depicted in Figure 4.1.

In line with the effort–recovery model (Meijman & Mulder, 1998), we view job demands as the main triggers of the daily recovery process. Job demands determine employee well-being (i.e., fatigue, energy) during work that consequently forms need for recovery levels at the end of work. The need for recovery plays a central role in the model since it is the threshold that determines the degree and the way (facilitating or inhibiting) in which work-related experiences transmit to non-work experiences. For instance, on a day that a waiter faces high levels of work pressure (e.g., many customers to serve in a limited amount of time), he is likely to feel fatigued. Fatigue accumulation over the workday is likely to enhance his need for recovery at the end of the shift. A high need for recovery is likely to inhibit the recovery process further, since the more depleted employees' resources are at the end of their shift, the more effort they will need to spend in finding recovery experiences and, thus, successful recovery will be more difficult to occur at the end of the day (Sonnentag & Zijlstra, 2006). If factors that facilitate employees to deal with daily demands successfully (e.g., personal and job resources or fruitful breaks) are omnipresent, the need for recovery will most likely be less elevated, and thus, recovery experiences after work will be facilitated. Despite the fact that the need for recovery is a crucial mediator that explains the transition from work to non-work experiences in the daily recovery process, the number of studies focusing on the role of need for recovery is rather limited (e.g., Xanthopoulou, Bakker, Oerlemans & Koszucka, 2012). Thus, this should be an interesting way to go in future studies.

As the recovery process evolves within the course of a workday, work experiences are followed by non-work experiences that are also central in determining whether successful recovery will occur. Employees who manage to engage in leisure activities that facilitate psychological detachment from work-related demands, relaxation, and mastery experiences are more likely to restore their energy resources and feel recovered at the end of the day (Sonnentag & Fritz, 2007). We have discussed factors that may shape the recovery experiences during hours after work and facilitate or inhibit recovery. Despite their significance, these factors are by no means the only ones that may determine the recovery process. Furthermore, it should not be assumed that the factors that were discussed with regard to recovery during work may not be significant in the hours after work and vice versa. Based on the findings of Sanz-Vergel, Demerouti, Moreno-Jiménez and Mayo (2010), emotional expression at home may also determine recovery experiences during hours after work. Similarly, affiliative humor may help employees to deal more effectively with the demanding aspects at work, particularly those that have to do with interpersonal conflicts.

As shown in Figure 4.1, sleep is best perceived as a mediator between the previous and next day's recovery. Think of a lawyer at a period that she is busy with a very important and difficult case. Despite the fact that she manages to detach from work during the hours after work, she cannot stop ruminating about next day's job demands when she goes to bed. This may cause sleep disturbances that do not allow conserving the resources that were refilled in the evening, resulting in poor recovery and consequently well-being and performance the next day (Volman, Bakker & Xanthopoulou, 2013).

Finally, our model highlights the role of others as a boundary condition in the recovery process. Our overview suggests that recovery and the work–life interface are closely linked phenomena and their relationship can take three different forms. First, recovery activities and experiences during and after work facilitate participation in family life and personal interests, while the absence of recovery makes participation in different life domains more difficult. In this sense, recovery represents a resource that can benefit the work–life interface when sufficiently present or inhibit inter-role management when absent. Second, recovery and work–life interface represent social processes in several respects. The mere presence of others can facilitate recovery either by being involved in activities with others (e.g., social activities; cf. Demerouti, Bakker, Geurts & Taris, 2009) or by having others facilitating one's own recovery (e.g., through the provision of social support during non-work time; Demerouti, 2012) or by the crossover of energy and the strategies to manage work–life domains (Hahn & Dormann, 2013). Third, on a more abstract level, recovery activities can be viewed as overlapping with the work–life interface. Take, for instance, a father who arranges his working time so that after work he can bring his child to the sport center in order to train. By doing this, this father helps family functioning (i.e., work–family facilitation) but also facilitates his own recovery as he can read his book while waiting for his child (i.e., a relaxation activity). This example illustrates that these constructs are closely related and future research should be devoted to uncover the ways through which they can be distinguished or integrated.

Methodological Challenges

The view of recovery as a dynamic process that evolves within the person over short periods of time explains why it has been mainly investigated by means of daily diary studies (Sonnentag & Geurts, 2009). The use of such designs has many advantages, but also entails a series of challenges for researchers (for a detailed discussion, refer to Oerlemans & Bakker, 2013). The main contribution of these designs is that they allow following up the same employee on a daily basis across a short period of time and for several times during the day. This helps capturing how the experience changes and evolves from one moment to the other.

We would like to underline two methodological challenges that relate closely to the propositions of the updated recovery model. The first has to do with the complexity of the recovery process and the fact that it depends on many different experiences that take place at many different instances throughout a day. Considering that recovery can occur at different moments and in different ways during a day, it is evident that this phenomenon can best be tested with diaries that consist of multiple measurement points throughout a day. Such an example is the study by Sanz-Vergel, Demerouti, Moreno-Jiménez and Mayo (2010) where participants were asked to report on their experiences three times a day: in the morning after waking up and before going to work, in the afternoon right after the end of work, and at bedtime. The main challenge with such designs is that they are extremely demanding and time-consuming for participants. Thus, researchers should place special effort in recruiting participants and keep them engaged in the study. Oerlemans and Bakker (2013) proposed that this can be done either by giving some compensation for participation (i.e., money or gift vouchers) or by providing personalized feedback to employees. A third way is to develop innovative designs (i.e., by using web-based questionnaires or other devices like smartphones), since these seem to attract participants. In addition, such designs entail statistical challenges because in some cases it may be important not only to capture how experiences vary from one day to another within the same person, but also whether they vary within the course of the day (e.g., feelings of recovery). This means that three-level models should be tested where moments are nested within days, and days are nested within individuals.

The second challenge relates to the role of significant others in the recovery process that underlines the need of methods that may take dyadic effects into account. Our model suggests that the degree to which an employee will manage to recover also depends on how his/her partner/friend or children behave, think, and feel. In order to capture such dyadic effects, it is not enough to follow employees over the course of a week, one or more times during a day. Rather, it is necessary to also follow their partners or significant others, who complement the dyad. The use of such dyadic designs may be proven fruitful in the study of the recovery process, since next to actor effects (i.e., whether an employee's recovery activities have an effect on his/her *own* recovery), it is possible to estimate also partner effects (i.e., whether the *partner's* experiences may have an effect on the employee's recovery; Kenny & Cook, 1999). Typically, dyadic data can be analyzed with hierarchical linear modeling, where the dyad is considered to be the highest level of analysis; individuals nested within the dyad consist of the meso-level, while daily recovery experiences are nested within individuals and correspond to the lowest level of analysis. Such designs require the use of elaborate statistical analyses. However, more and more studies on daily recovery have started to make use of these advanced techniques (e.g., Hahn & Dormann, 2013).

Practical Implications

Given that recovery is crucial for employee health and organizational flourishing, researchers and practitioners should uncover ways that facilitate recovery. With regard to job (re)design, our review suggests that special emphasis should be given to the design of within-work breaks. Based on the work of Trougakos, Hideg and Cheng (2011), an important recommendation to organizations would be to protect employees' right to recover by carefully designing work breaks (e.g., a longer lunch break and several micro-breaks during the day). As concerns the hours after work, Hahn, Binnewies, Sonnentag and Mojza (2011) developed and tested the effectiveness of a training aiming at promoting the four recovery experiences (psychological detachment, relaxation, mastery, control). The program consisted of four modules, one for each type of experience. Each module encompassed educational parts where participants were informed of the importance of the recovery experience and the techniques that can be used to enhance these experiences, as well as individual and group exercises. For instance, at the end of the psychological detachment module, participants had to formulate specific goals to promote their recovery till the next training. Importantly, results supported the effectiveness of this training since an increase in recovery experiences before and after the training has been observed.

To conclude, although this chapter offers an updated framework to test the daily recovery process, it is by no means an exhaustive analysis of all the potential processes and factors that may explain what facilitates and what inhibits recovery. Despite this limitation, we do hope that this model will constitute an inspiring context to guide researchers in their study of the interplay between work and non-work experiences in the recovery process.

References

Bakker, A. B., Demerouti, E., Oerlemans, W., & Sonnentag, S. (2013). Workaholism and daily recovery: A day reconstruction study of leisure activities. *Journal of Organizational Behavior, 34,* 87–107.

Binnewies, C., Sonnentag, S., & Mojza, E. J. (2009). Daily performance at work: Feeling recovered in the morning as a predictor of day-level job performance. *Journal of Organizational Behavior, 30,* 67–93.

Clark, S. C. (2000). Work/family border theory: A new theory of work/family balance. *Human Relations, 53,* 747–770.

Demerouti, E. (2012). The spillover and crossover of resources among partners: The role of work-self and family-self facilitation. *Journal of Occupational Health Psychology, 17,* 184–195.

Demerouti, E., Bakker, A. B., Geurts, S. A. E., & Taris, T. W. (2009). Daily recovery from work-related effort during non-work time. In S. Sonnentag, P. L. Parrewé, & D. C. Ganster (Eds.), *Current perspectives on job-stress research in occupational stress and well being* (Vol. 7, pp. 85–123). Bingley, UK: Emerald.

Demerouti, E., Bakker, A. B., Sonnentag, S., & Fullagar, K. (2012). Work-related flow and energy at work and at home: A study on the role of daily recovery. *Journal of Organizational Behavior, 33,* 276–295.

Demerouti, E., & Sanz-Vergel, A. I. (2012). Daily recovery and well-being: An overview. *Psicothema, 24,* 73–78.

Edwards, J. R., & Van Harrison, R. (1993). Job demands and worker health: Three-dimensional re-examination of the relationship between person-environment fit and strain. *Journal of Applied Psychology, 78,* 628–648.

Geurts, S. A. E., & Sonnentag, S. (2006). Recovery as an explanatory mechanism in the relation between acute stress reactions and chronic health impairment. *Scandinavian Journal of Work, Environment and Health, 32,* 482–492.

Hahn, V. C., Binnewies, C., & Haun, S. (2012). The role of partners for employees' recovery during the weekend. *Journal of Vocational Behavior, 80,* 288–298.

Hahn, V. C., Binnewies, C., Sonnentag, S., & Mojza, E. J. (2011). Learning how to recover from job stress: Effects of a recovery training program on recovery, recovery-related self-efficacy, and well-being. *Journal of Occupational Health Psychology, 16,* 202–216.

Hahn, V. C., & Dormann, C. (2013). The role of partners and children for employees' psychological detachment from work and well-being. *Journal of Applied Psychology, 98,* 26–36.

Hobfoll, S. E. (1998). *Stress, culture, and community: The psychology and physiology of stress.* New York: Plenum Press.

Hobfoll, S. E. (2001). The influence of culture, community, and the nested-self in the stress process: Advancing conservation of resources theory. *Applied Psychology: An International Review, 50,* 337–421.

Jansen, N. W. H., Kant, I. J., & Van den Brandt, P. A. (2002). Need for recovery in the working population: Description and associations with fatigue and psychological distress. *International Journal of Behavioral Medicine, 9,* 322–340.

Kenny, D. A., & Cook, W. (1999). Partner effects in relationship research: Conceptual issues, analytic difficulties, and illustrations. *Personal Relationships, 6,* 433–448.

Martin, R. A., Puhlik-Doris, P., Larsen, G., Gray, J., & Weir, K. (2003). Individual differences in uses of humor and their relation to psychological well-being: Development of the Humor Styles Questionnaire. *Journal of Research in Personality, 37,* 48–75.

Meijman, T. F., & Mulder, G. (1998). Psychological aspects of workload. In P. J. D. Drenth & H. Thierry (Eds.), *Handbook of work and organizational psychology: Vol. 2. Work psychology* (pp. 5–33). Hove, England: Psychology Press.

Mojza, E. J., Lorenz, C., Sonnentag, S., & Binnewies, C. (2010). Daily recovery experiences: The role of volunteer work during leisure time. *Journal of Occupational Health Psychology, 15,* 60–74.

Oerlemans, W. G. M., & Bakker, A. B. (2013). Capturing the moment in the workplace: Two methods to study momentary subjective well-being. In A. B. Bakker (Ed.), *Advances in positive organizational psychology* (Vol. 1, pp. 329–346). Bingley, UK: Emerald.

Rook, J. W., & Zijlstra, F. R. H. (2006). The contribution of various types of activities to recovery. *European Journal of Work & Organizational Psychology, 15*, 218–240.

Sanz-Vergel, A. I., Demerouti, E., Bakker, A. B., & Moreno-Jiménez, B. (2011). Daily detachment from work and home: The moderating effect of role salience. *Human Relations, 64*, 775–799.

Sanz-Vergel, A., Demerouti, E., Moreno-Jiménez, B., & Mayo, M. (2010). Work-family balance and energy: A day-levels study on recovery conditions. *Journal of Vocational Behavior, 76*, 118–130.

Sanz-Vergel, A. I., Rodríguez-Muñoz, A., Demerouti, E., & Bakker, A. B. (2012). The daily spillover and crossover of emotional labor: Faking emotions at work and at home. *Journal of Vocational Behavior, 81*, 209–217.

Sluiter, J. K., Van der Beek, A. J., & Frings-Dresen, M. H. (1999). The influence of work characteristics in the need for recovery and experiences health: A study on coach drivers. *Ergonomics, 42*, 573–583.

Sonnentag, S. (2001). Work, recovery activities, and individual well-being: A diary study. *Journal of Occupational Health Psychology, 6*, 196–210.

Sonnentag, S. (2003). Recovery, work engagement, and proactive behavior: A new look at the interface between nonwork and work. *Journal of Applied Psychology, 88*, 518–528.

Sonnentag, S., & Bayer, U.-V. (2005). Switching off mentally: Predictors and consequences of psychological detachment from work during off-job time. *Journal of Occupational Health Psychology, 10*, 393–414.

Sonnentag, S., Binnewies, C., & Mojza, E. J. (2008). "Did you have a nice evening?" A day-level study on recovery experiences, sleep, and affect. *Journal of Applied Psychology, 93*, 674–684.

Sonnentag, S., & Braun, I. (2013). Not always a sweet home: Family and job responsibilities constrain recovery processes. In J. G. Grywacz & E. Demerouti (Eds.), *New frontiers in work and family research* (pp. 71–92). Hove, UK: Psychology Press.

Sonnentag, S., & Fritz, C. (2007). The recovery experience questionnaire: Development and validation of a measure for assessing recuperation and unwinding from work. *Journal of Occupational Health Psychology, 12*, 204–221.

Sonnentag, S., & Geurts, S. A. E. (2009). Methodological issues in recovery research. In S. Sonnentag, P. L. Perrewé, & D. C. Ganster (Eds.), *Research in occupational stress and well-being: Current perspectives on job-stress recovery* (Vol. 7, pp. 1–36). Bingley, UK: Emerald.

Sonnentag, S., & Jelden, S. (2009). Job stressors and the pursuit of sport activities: A day-level perspective. *Journal of Occupational Health Psychology, 14*, 165–181.

Sonnentag, S., Mojza, E. J., Demerouti, E., & Bakker, A. B. (2012). Reciprocal relations between recovery and work engagement: The moderating role of job stressors. *Journal of Applied Psychology, 97*, 842–853.

Sonnentag, S., & Natter, E. (2004). Flight attendants' daily recovery from work: Is there no place like home? *International Journal of Stress Management, 11*, 366–391.

Sonnentag, S., & Zijlstra, F. R. H. (2006). Job characteristics and off-job activities as predictors of need for recovery, well-being, and fatigue. *Journal of Applied Psychology, 91*, 330–350.

Ten Brummelhuis, L. L., & Bakker, A. B. (2012). Staying engaged during the week: The effect of off-job activities on next day work engagement. *Journal of Occupational Health Psychology, 17*, 445–455.

Trougakos, J. P., & Hideg, I. (2009). Momentary work recovery: The role of within-day work breaks. In S. Sonnentag, P. L. Perrewé, & D. C. Ganster (Eds.), *Research in occupational stress and well-being: Current perspectives on job-stress recovery* (Vol. 7, pp. 37–84). Bingley, UK: Emerald.

Trougakos, J. P., Hideg, I., & Cheng, B. H. (2011). *Lunch breaks unpacked: Examining the effect of daily lunch activities and control over lunch breaks.* Academy of Management 2011 Annual Meeting—West Meets East: Enlightening, Balancing, Transcending, AOM 2011, San Antonio, TX.

Volman, F., Bakker, A. B., & Xanthopoulou, D. (2013). Recovery at home and performance at work: A diary study on self-family facilitation. *European Journal of Work & Organizational Psychology, 22,* 218–234.

Xanthopoulou, D. (2011, May). *Is the day enough to be happy? Relationship of time-management to daily flow and recovery.* Paper presented at the 15th Conference of the European Association of Work & Organizational Psychology, Maastricht, the Netherlands.

Xanthopoulou, D. & Bakker, A. B. (2010, March). *Relaxation or psychological detachment? A diary study on recovery among workaholics.* Paper presented at the 9th Conference of the European Academy of Occupational Health Psychology, Rome, Italy.

Xanthopoulou, D., Bakker, A. B., Oerlemans, W., & Koszucka, M. (2012, April). *Recovering from emotional labour: A diary study on the role of deep and surface acting.* Paper presented at the 10th Conference of the European Academy of Occupational Health Psychology, Zurich, Switzerland.

5

Psychological Reactivity: Implications for Occupational Health Psychology

Cynthia Mohr, Laurie Jacobs, Cameron McCabe, and Lindsey Alley

Portland State University, USA

In an effort to reduce the detrimental effects of work stress, occupational health psychologists have focused significant attention on work design features (e.g., job demands, resources). Although these efforts are critically important, the fact remains that individual differences exist in terms of how people respond to stressful aspects of work, even among individuals sharing the same or similar job demands (e.g., Podsakoff, LePine & LePine, 2007). Thus, a better understanding of such individual differences is necessary in order to elucidate the circumstances under which occupational health psychology (OHP) interventions will be beneficial for some workers and not others. One such individual difference that psychologists have begun to examine concerns psychological or emotional reactivity to stressors; that is, when daily experiences such as work stressors occur, individuals have an immediate reaction to them, defined as reactivity. In general, emotional or psychological reactivity represents the extent to which events (both positive and negative) influence individuals psychologically and physiologically (Almeida, 2005; Neupert, Almeida & Charles, 2007). Research has also investigated how stressful events trigger physiological responses, including cardiovascular, endocrine, and immune function (Cohen & Hamrick, 2003). Reactions to proximal stressors vary in terms of strength or intensity of reaction, as well as valence. Such reactivity is often viewed as a stable individual difference (Cohen & Hamrick, 2003). From a resilience perspective, reactivity represents the opposite to resilience, as described by Bonanno (2004), such that those who are more resilient show more modest disruption to daily life even in the face of traumatic events compared to those who are less resilient. Conversely, more reactive individuals demonstrate a stronger reaction to stressors than their counterparts, depending

Contemporary Occupational Health Psychology: Global Perspectives on Research and Practice, Volume 3, First Edition. Edited by Stavroula Leka and Robert R. Sinclair.

© 2014 John Wiley & Sons, Ltd. Published 2014 by John Wiley & Sons, Ltd.

on context. At the same time, reactivity can also vary by situation or context (e.g., on a high work demand day, workers may experience greater reactivity).

Given the numerous negative health consequences of workplace stressors, as well as the likely health benefits of experiencing positive events at work, between stress and health outcomes, it is logical to consider what role psychological reactivity might play in these associations. Specifically, does psychological reactivity influence longer-term health and well-being, physical health, or social functioning? These are questions that researchers are just beginning to examine, with a mere handful of studies investigating reactivity in relation to health outcomes. Following stress induction, physiological reactivity as assessed in a laboratory has been linked with increased cortisol release, elevated systolic and diastolic blood pressure (Smith, Birmingham & Uchino, 2012), and even performance decrements (McGraw et al., 2013). Additionally, chronic stress exposure, particularly among more psychologically reactive individuals, has been linked with slower recovery following acute stressful experiences (Lepore, Miles & Levy, 1997) and, consistent with theories of allostatic load (e.g., McEwen, 1998), has been found to be a vulnerability factor for illness, injury, hypertension, cardiovascular disease, and cognitive decline (Brunner & Marmot, 2011; Lepore, Miles & Levy, 1997; Ming et al., 2004). Studies have also demonstrated longer-term outcomes of reactivity to daily stressors, such that those with greater psychological reactivity reveal higher subsequent levels of depression (e.g., Cohen et al., 2005), higher levels of general affective distress and likelihood of affective disorder after 10 years (Charles et al., 2013), as well as enhanced risk of chronic physical health conditions 10 years later (Piazza et al., 2012). These stress-related patterns may be particularly pronounced and impactful for high-risk–high-stress occupations (e.g., law enforcement, corrections). Importantly, Cohen et al. (2008) also found that those who are more reactive (i.e., show next day negative mood elevation following negative events) demonstrated less early responsiveness to treatment. This suggests that people with stronger reactivity may be relatively more resistant to OHP-related interventions and consequently need additional support.

In another important set of studies, intra-individual variability in single variables such as mood or pain was shown to predict long-term critical health outcomes, including well-being and mortality, contributing over and above an individual's average mood or pain level (Nesselroade, 2004; Nesselroade & Salthouse, 2004). However, few studies have investigated the extent to which psychological reactivity is related to these and other occupational health outcomes. We view this as a fruitful direction for future research. Determining the degree to which short-term psychological reactions to work stressors are determinative of critical job- and personal-level outcomes, over and above mean levels of stress or negative emotions or stressor exposure, would provide invaluable directions for intervention work.

Thus, the goal of this chapter is to introduce the concept of reactivity to OHP. Specifically, we aim to (1) define the construct of reactivity, (2) discuss how it is measured, and (3) describe the implications of reactivity to OHP.

What Is Psychological Reactivity?

Psychologists have delineated two mechanisms by which stressors have an influence on health and well-being: stressor exposure and stressor reactivity (Almeida, 2005). In other words, one reason people experience ill health due to stress is by virtue of the number of stressors they experience (i.e., stressor exposure). Yet, stressors also exert influence through reactivity, or the degree to which one is affected by the intensity and nature of those stressors (regardless of the number). Research on psychological reactivity has examined multiple aspects of this process including emotional, cognitive, behavioral, and physiological, all of which are interrelated, though formal models have yet to be developed that explicate those relationships. Further, there is a lack of consistency in how terminology is used. For purposes of the present chapter, we conceptualize psychological reactivity in the broadest terms, encompassing all forms of reaction. However, we focus our interest mostly on emotional aspects of psychological reactivity.

Early work in psychological reactivity began with a focus on everyday positive and negative experiences, such as receiving praise from one's employer or having an argument with a coworker, and the extent to which such daily occurrences were related to increases in negative and positive moods (Bolger, DeLongis, Kessler & Schilling, 1989; David, Green, Martin & Suls, 1997). The research reflects four common features. First, it is built upon the assumption that the cumulative effects of exposure to multiple daily stressors can have greater ultimate impact on an individual than major life stressors (e.g., divorce, job loss); indeed, the impact of a major event such as job loss may be partially or fully due to the disruption to everyday life (Pillow, Zautra & Sandler, 1996).

Second, the majority of psychological reactivity research has explored emotional reactions to events ideographically, as a within-person process. That is, instead of correlating stress and moods at an aggregate or between-person level, researchers have measured the direct influence of a stressor on a person's mood repeatedly over time to discern patterns of response and the extent to which a given stressor alters mood from that individual's typical baseline mood level. For example, Joe's typical negative mood may be low, but on days with even "minor" work stressors, he may experience large increases in negative mood. Janet, on the other hand, may not react strongly to work stressors, maintaining her typical low negative mood, even on what would appear to others as a highly stressful work day. By examining events and moods ideographically, researchers are able to capture these unique individual differences. Third, and related to the preceding two points, research in this area focuses on more proximal or immediate responses, as opposed to more distal responses. The underlying assumption is that reactivity is experienced and expressed close in time to the stressor exposure.

Finally, this approach differentiates between positive and negative affective processes, based on models specifying the independence of positive and negative affect (Diener & Emmons, 1984). In other words, whereas events perceived negatively (i.e., stressors) may increase negative mood (to varying degrees), positive events should be related to increases in positive mood rather than decreases in negative mood. This allows for two potential reactivity processes: one in which people vary in the extent to which they experience an increase in negative moods associated with stressors and another in which they experience varying levels of positive mood enhancement as a function of positive events. Although the potential for positive reactivity or increases in positive mood associated with positive events is clear, substantially less research has examined this process relative to stress reactivity, creating an opportunity for future research.

Beyond those core features of psychological reactivity, researchers have considered other facets of reactivity when developing a conceptual definition. The first question of interest has been whether reactivity is stable or contextual. Indeed, evidence suggests that psychological reactivity may well be both stable and dynamic. On one hand, it seems likely that reactivity is, to an extent, innate (Belsky & Pluess, 2009), which would suggest a certain degree of stability. Studies of physiological reactivity and comparisons of different types of physiological reactivity or between physiological and psychological reactivity have found that individuals often display a characteristic pattern of response to stressors (Cohen *et al.*, 2000; Cohen & Hamrick, 2003), supporting stability. On the other hand, Lepore, Miles and Levy (1997) found that physiological reactivity seemed to be altered by chronic stress; if physiological reactivity is subject to change, it seems reasonable that other forms of psychological reactivity also would be. Moreover, multiple studies have found age differences in psychological reactivity, with some finding older adults to be more reactive (Mroczek & Almeida, 2004) and others finding them to be less so (Neupert, Almeida & Charles, 2007). Whereas longitudinal research has suggested that reactivity tends to be stable across much of the lifespan, changes in levels over time have also been demonstrated (Sliwinski, Almeida, Smyth & Stawski, 2009).

Additional support for the idea that reactivity can be shaped by context comes from studies that address moderating factors of reactivity. In addition to age differences, Neupert, Almeida and Charles (2007) found that control beliefs played a role in reactivity to different types of events and that individuals exhibited lower reactivity to interpersonal stressors when they had fewer perceived constraints. Overall stress levels and mental health are also known to relate to reactivity. Sliwinski, Almeida and Charles (2009) found that reactivity was higher in times of greater global stress levels, and Steger and Kashdan (2009) found that those who were more depressed were more reactive to both positive and negative social interactions. Thus, a reasonable amount of evidence exists to suggest that reactivity can be both trait-like and state-like.

Research has also considered the potential conceptual distinctiveness (or similarity) of reactivity and neuroticism (Bolger & Zuckerman, 1995; Suls & Martin, 2005), with those higher in neuroticism found to both report more stressors and react more strongly to them, particularly if those stressors are interpersonal (Bolger & Schilling, 1991). However, despite its demonstrated relationship to neuroticism, there is evidence to support the proposition that they are separate but related constructs. In the Bolger and Zuckerman (1995) study, for instance, reactivity was found to be a stronger predictor of psychological distress than mere exposure to stressors for high-neuroticism individuals. Suls and Martin (2005) found no association between neuroticism and positive reactivity. Moreover, Schwebel and Suls (1999) found no association between neuroticism and physiological measures of reactivity. Based on these studies, it might be expected that neuroticism and reactivity would be related in most studies but offer distinct contributions to the results.

The extent to which psychological reactivity relates to other well-known stress constructs such as resources and cognitive appraisals is another important question. In essence, psychological reactivity, as a trait-based construct, could be interpreted through the lens of Hobfoll's (1989, 2001) resource-based model of stress, specifying that stress results from a threat or actual net loss of resources, which then initiates a process of resource replacement. Presumably, how one typically responds to resource loss would correspond to one's long-term pattern of psychological reactivity. Further, individuals would demonstrate stronger reactions to threat to more valued resources. Although offering insight to understanding psychological reactivity, Hobfall's model does not easily relate to the more dynamic aspects of this process, in terms of how people might have a uniquely strong or weak reaction to a stressor on a particular day or week or in response to different types of events/stressors – dynamics which are better captured by transactional models of stress and coping.

Transactional models describe the process of how individuals uniquely respond to a given potential stressor based on their cognitive appraisal of the stressor (Lazarus & Folkman, 1984). Whereas positive/benign or irrelevant appraisals do not result in the experience of stress (and trigger the secondary appraisal or coping process), harm/loss, threat, and challenge appraisals do initiate further analysis of the situation to determine how best to proceed. According to Lazarus (1999), emotional reactions to a stressor and cognitive appraisals are interrelated, in which case cognitive appraisal represents the interpretation of the event and determines the ultimate emotional outcome. Further, studies of physiological reactivity have demonstrated clear patterns of association with cognitive appraisals (e.g., Tomaka, Blascovich, Kelsey & Leitten, 1993). Yet, Houston (1992) argued that cognitive appraisal provides only a distal influence on physiological reactivity, whereas affective and motivational responses serve as more proximal determinants of cardiovascular reactions to stress. Thus, while psychological reactivity is a related but distinct process from cognitive appraisal, it can be easily incorporated into the transactional model of stress and coping, given that the model specifies individual differences in how people typically respond to stressors as well as situational differences in how one responds from day to day.

How Is Psychological Reactivity Measured?

In order to best capture the within-person processes inherent in psychological reactivity, it is necessary to measure stressors (or positive events) and emotional experiences repeatedly over time. Thus, researchers interested in reactivity have often employed daily process (diary) or experience sampling methodologies to assess the extent to which individuals experience different degrees of emotional reaction to events (e.g., Bolger, DeLongis, Kessler & Schilling, 1989; Marco & Suls, 1993). Specifically, daily process methodology involves time-intensive investigations in which individuals record their experiences, thoughts, moods, and behaviors (depending on study purposes) daily or multiple times per day for periods ranging from short periods (e.g., 48 hours) to several months. Such repeated observations allow for the assessment of typical patterns of response to stressors, as well as differences between individuals in their responses. Further, given that mood states are dynamic and changeable (e.g., Larsen & Kasimatis, 1990), it is crucial to capture changes in mood close to the time at which they occur, as opposed to retrospectively (e.g., Tennen, Affleck, Armeli & Carney, 2000). That is, longer-term recall of mood is influenced by recall bias (e.g., Bolger, DeLongis, Kessler & Schilling, 1989), and furthermore, people are unable to recall contingencies in emotional reactions or behaviors, which are the subjects of interest to reactivity researchers. As with other repeated measures studies, each person acts as his/her own control, such that each person's natural baseline (i.e., his/her general level of stress/negative affect) is factored into the study (with person-centered data). Furthermore, depending on the design of the diary study, it is possible to assess delayed (i.e., lagged) emotional reactions to stressors. As an example, Mohr *et al.* (2003) employed a thrice-daily interview to study how stressful experiences at one time point predicted increases in subsequent negative mood.

By examining patterns of responses over time to varying situational and emotional contexts (e.g., differing levels and types of work stressors), an overall pattern of behavioral consistency can be gleaned. Whereas one individual (let's call him Andy) may respond to a higher workload than normal by experiencing greater anxiety (compared to Andy's usual level of anxiety), a different individual (Kurt) may not experience an increase in anxiety (from Kurt's norm) to the same workload. Thus, consistent individual differences are inherent in these psychological reactivity estimates. Further, reactivity can take different forms. In one instance, you might have someone who reacts strongly to relatively mundane events (in a normative sense), that is, "flies off the handle easily," colloquially, whereas another person who may already be experiencing a high level of stress in their daily life, in which case a relatively mundane event might be "the last straw" resulting in an unexpectedly strong reaction compared to others in a less stressed state (Suls & Martin, 2005).

To statistically determine these patterns from daily process data, researchers typically use multilevel modeling programs to analyze associations between events and moods. This is due, in large part, to the unbalanced nature of daily process data (e.g., different numbers of missing data points per person). Studies using these analyses usually report the average within-person association between stressors and negative moods, which reflect the extent to which, on average, participants experienced a significant increase in negative mood as a result of a stressor. Yet, from a psychological reactivity standpoint, the more interesting value is the variance in within-person slopes, which represents the degree to which people vary in their response to stressors. We advocate that it should be standard protocol for researchers reporting on daily diary or experience sampling data to include the variance component estimates (and associated significance levels) to allow for examination of differences in patterns of psychological reactivity. Readers interested in learning more about this statistical and methodological approach are encouraged to consult Mohr *et al.* (2013).

Psychological reactivity has also been explored in experimental studies, in which affective reactions to stressors are induced through emotionally laden stimuli, such as photos or movies (e.g., Crum, Salovey & Achor, 2013), or through stress-induction tasks. For instance, Cohen and colleagues (2000) asked participants to perform a simulated public-speaking task in which they defended themselves against a suggested transgression, and found that both anxiety and task engagement increased in response to the stressor. Similarly, a meta-analysis of 208 laboratory studies investigating physiological and psychological responses to acute stressors (challenge tasks) revealed that personal control and perceptions of social evaluation are most indicative of high cortisol level increases, based on plasma or salivary samples (Dickerson & Kemeny, 2004). Physiological responses to stress are, in fact, most often studied in controlled laboratory settings, using heart monitoring devices and immune-response measuring techniques to gauge participant reactions to such acute stressors. Thus, such lab-based, experimental methodology can allow for the testing of multiple facets of physiological and psychological reactivity that may be more difficult to control and measure in field settings.

Yet, daily process assessments provide some unique advantages over other methods and contribute significantly to our understanding of these and other behavioral processes. In particular, they afford a naturalistic assessment of people's responses to stressors occurring in everyday life. By gathering information over (typically) longer periods of time, researchers are able to gauge deviations from usual patterns of responding and have access to many more observations of mood responses than provided by a much briefer laboratory experiment. Further, mobile monitoring devices, such as heart rate monitors or actigraphs, and easily administered cortisol cheek swabs can be included as part of a daily process protocol to enable the investigation of both physiological and psychological reactivity, while retaining a naturalistic approach. Finally, it is important to note that it is not feasible to glean these critical patterns of response from a one-time self-report assessment, though such measures of emotional or psychological reactivity do exist (e.g., Carlson *et al.*, 1989; Gratz & Roemer, 2004). One's understanding of his/her own reactivity is undoubtedly meaningful but also likely distinct from their daily patterns of response.

Implications of Stress Reactivity for the Workplace

Throughout this chapter, we have attempted to frame psychological reactivity as a quality which fluctuates between as well as within individuals. The type of event experienced in conjunction with one's appraisal of the event and available resources to cope with this event each contribute to the subjective experience of stress. Stress is ubiquitous in workers' everyday lives. As stress accumulates throughout the day, the added strain depletes physical and emotional resources necessary for coping (Almeida, 2005; Ganster & Perrewé, 2011; Hobfoll, 1989). As a result, individuals may become more reactive to future threats leading to negative health outcomes. Poor worker health (e.g., lowered immune functioning, fatigue, depression), in turn, places added burden on the organization, primarily through worker absenteeism, lost production, and higher health-care costs (Cavanaugh, Boswell, Roehling & Boudreau, 2000; Sonnentag & Frese, 2003).

Moreover, the experience of stress and related consequences is not restricted to the workplace. Work–family researchers have repeatedly shown that work-related stressors may spill over into the family domain and produce conflict (Grzywacz, Almeida & McDonald, 2002; Hammer *et al.*, 2005; Story & Repetti, 2006). Similarly, negative mood, stress, and conflict experienced in the home may lead to negative outcomes in the workplace (Byron, 2005). Reactivity may play a crucial role in such spillover, such that individuals who are more reactive to everyday stressors in the workplace may be more apt to experience negative work–family spillover. Conversely, those who experience more positive "bounce" from positive work experiences may have greater positive spillover. Individual reactivity remains particularly relevant for the study of work–family conflict and spillover given that exposure to seemingly innocuous stressors may provoke unique and immediate responses, which have potentially negative consequences for the individual's and family's health and well-being and to their employer.

Importantly, given empirical evidence supporting the dynamic or situational nature of reactivity, it is logical to conclude that intervention efforts to reduce one's reactivity have merit. We see several potential avenues for and targets of work-place intervention to reduce reactivity, as described in the following sections.

Resiliency and support

Resiliency and hardiness have been identified as two of the most prominent factors contributing to observed differences in reactivity–health associations (Almeida, 2005; Kobasa, Maddi & Kahn, 1982). These potential buffers are a function of an individual's capacity and resources to adapt to, overcome, and cope with demands placed on them. More resilient individuals may be more likely to appraise stressful situations as challenging rather than threatening and may be more apt to successfully navigate stressful experiences and avoid potential negative health consequences as a result. From an employer's perspective, an important strategy to retain effective and efficient workers may be to incorporate stress management trainings that emphasize the strengths of resiliency and hardiness to promote positive health and coping behaviors (Bond & Bunce, 2000; Richardson & Rothstein, 2008). Individuals who are more resilient and those with adequate resources to cope with everyday stressors may be more apt at reappraising events previously perceived to be threatening as challenges and can thereby reduce the deleterious impact of stress on individual functioning. Although this process may not come as naturally to individuals who are more reactive to daily stressors, the reappraisal of threats as challenges can produce feelings of mastery and accomplishment and provide a boost to positive affectivity (Folkman & Moskowitz, 2000), furthering individual ability to recover during intense or difficult periods. In their recent study, Limm and colleagues (2011) showed that those receiving stress management training perceived their own reactivity to be significantly lower relative to their counterparts who had not received training. A related point to make is that because of individual differences in reactivity, some employees may need longer or more intensive exposure to resiliency training to achieve comparable benefits.

In concert with the goal of creating more resilient employees, social and organizational supports remain key determinants of health functioning and well-being (Cohen & Wills, 1985). Effective supports have been shown to buffer emotional (Koerner, Shirai & Kenyon, 2010) and physiological reactivity (Heaphy & Dutton, 2008; Uchino *et al.*, 2006). Positive social interactions and supports may buffer aversive experiences through two pathways: (1) through the provision of emotional supports to help navigate and alter perceptions of stressful situations and (2) through the provision of instrumental resources which may facilitate problem-solving (Heaphy & Dutton, 2008). Moreover, while previous research has emphasized the importance of support perceptions, a recent study conducted by Nahum-Shani and Bamberger (2011) demonstrated that the balance between the receipt and provision of support (i.e., reciprocal support) is critical in terms of how individuals cope with work-related stressors (e.g., long work hours). This balance was shown to improve subsequent mental and physical health functioning. Thus, systematic efforts to enhance employee resources in the form of support would be beneficial at reducing reactivity.

Job design

Job design characteristics, such as level of decision latitude (e.g., autonomy and control), have a substantial impact on employee health and well-being. Jobs characterized by high demands but low levels of control place added strain on the individual (Karasek, 1979), and individuals who are more reactive to stress and who have less control and flexibility with their work may be particularly at risk. In line with transactional models of stress (e.g., Lazarus & Folkman, 1984), LePine, Podsakoff and LePine (2005) meta-analysis revealed how challenges (e.g., time pressures, workload, and responsibility) can motivate individuals and benefit job performance while events which hinder performance (e.g., role conflict, daily hassles, job insecurity) may serve to reduce motivation. Individuals who are more reactive to aversive experiences may experience these negative outcomes to a greater extent. Organizations should seek to provide employees with sufficient control over their decision-making while simultaneously providing resources for individuals to develop effective coping skills. Above and beyond the intrinsic benefits, having a sense of control and purpose in one's work not only improves well-being but also physical health (Rodin, 1986). When re-designing a workplace or empowering employees by increasing perceptions of control and reducing extraneous job demands, changes should be made which benefit all employees (Taris, 2006). These efforts will likely differentially benefit some individuals (i.e., those who are highly reactive to stress) more so than others.

Workplace flexibility may be one workplace redesign that could have a powerful impact on both stress exposure and reactivity (Almeida & Davis, 2011). In a sample of hotel employees who completed daily diaries, Almeida and Davis demonstrated a significant relationship between workplace flexibility and stress reactivity. In particular, there was a significant relationship between daily work tension and negative affect, but only for those with low flexibility – the relationship was not significant for those with high flexibility. In a sense, job flexibility buffered the effect of increases in a given day's work stress on negative affect. The less flexible workers also experienced greater stressor exposure and physical health symptoms, and there was some evidence that their increased work stress spilled over onto their children's negative affect. In addition to the stress-buffering effects which benefit the individual, flexible work conditions may also reduce work–family conflict (Hill, Hawkins, Martinson & Ferris, 2003), whereas a lack of flexibility has been linked with higher levels of stress and strain and worse perceived physical health (Butler, Grzywacz, Ettner & Liu, 2009).

High-risk professions

The impact of stress on health may be particularly pronounced among those who are engaged in certain types of work (e.g., nursing), given that some occupations place higher emotional labor demands on employees, or when the likelihood of experiencing significant stressors is higher simply by nature of the tasks and/or environment involved. In addition to negative health consequences reported earlier, particularly within high-stress occupations, burnout or emotional exhaustion, decreased performance (Cavanaugh, Boswell, Roehling & Boudreau, 2000), decreased organizational commitment (Bishop *et al.*, 2008), and turnover intentions as well as actual worker turnover (Chen & Spector, 1992) are commonplace. Highly reactive individuals who show increased sensitivity to daily stressors may experience these negative work outcomes to a greater extent relative to those who are less reactive. For those who lack alternative prospects for employment, the depletion of resources resulting from continued exposure to stress may present challenges in other areas of functioning (e.g., in a dip in job performance). In occupations where the stakes are high, such as in construction, performance decrements on behalf of employees produce significant consequences (e.g., work-related injuries). Highly stressful occupations may indeed engender higher levels of reactivity, given that chronic levels of stress are shown to exacerbate psychological reactivity. At the same time, those in high-stress/low-resource occupations may experience a ceiling effect, wherein the significant numbers of stressors attenuate the influence of any given stressor (because presumably the employees simply do not have the resources to cope with it). Further exploration of this potential phenomenon is needed in order to better understand the impact of occupation type on psychological reactivity.

Implications for behavioral reactivity

Finally, in addition to exploring psychological changes to mood in response to acute stressors, researchers should also be mindful of how reactivity can be expressed behaviorally, resulting in significant health consequences for employees. For example, daily hassles have been found to be correlated to greater snacking in a two-week daily study of women (Newman, O'Connor & Conner, 2007). Motivation to eat has also been found to increase when individuals are experiencing negative emotions, as has experience of hunger (Macht & Simons, 2000). Work-related stress has also been implicated in research related to alcohol consumption. Research has suggested that craving and use of alcohol is higher on days where individuals experience more stress (Liu, Wang, Zhan & Shi, 2009). Drinking as a means of tension reduction (Conger, 1956; Mohr *et al.*, 2001) has received considerable attention in the literature, and continued use of alcohol to cope with stress and negative affect is associated with greater likelihood of developing alcohol problems (Cooper, Russell & George, 1988). Translated to the workplace, daily and problematic alcohol consumption has been linked with increased work–family conflict (Wang, Liu, Zhan & Shi, 2010) and can result in lost productivity, increased absenteeism, and increased risk of workplace accidents.

It is important to consider that not all forms of behavioral reactivity are inherently negative or produce deleterious health outcomes. For example, individuals who exercise in response to high levels of stress are likely to receive both physical and mental health benefits (Thayer, Newman & McClain, 1994; Thayer, 1987). In line with Broaden-and-Build Theory (Fredrickson, 1998, 2001), it is possible that exercise, and the positive moods it generates, could act as a resource that increases health and well-being and improves future coping. Organizational efforts to promote a healthy workforce should educate and encourage employees on these and other healthy behaviors (e.g., adequate sleep, regular exercise, healthy diet) and to avoid negative health behaviors (e.g., poor diet, smoking, stress drinking). Future research and investigation is needed to explore the impacts of different forms of behavioral reactivity on worker health and well-being and their subsequent impact on the broader organizational context.

In conclusion, we believe there is great potential in incorporating the construct of psychological reactivity to existing research on work stress and related outcomes. This approach builds on existing research demonstrating the utility of studying day-to-day fluctuations in work stress on a variety of health and well-being outcomes, as well as the use of daily diary methods to explore individuals' patterns of behavior. However, rather than examining how workers typically respond to a given set of stressors, we advocate looking more closely at individual differences in those reactions. Psychological reactivity represents a distinct individual difference measure that captures both context-specific and more enduring patterns of response to work-related stressors, with resulting impacts on job- and health-related outcomes.

There are myriad future research directions represented in this area of work. A better understanding of how different types of reactivity are interrelated – in terms of emotional, physiological, cognitive, and behavioral – is critically important. It also remains unclear whether individuals who are more reactive tend to be so to many different types of stressors or are mostly reactive to a particular kind of stressor (e.g., reactive to work stress in general vs. reactive to conflicts with one's supervisor). For example, are individuals differentially reactive to workplace demands versus conflicts or conversely supports versus successes? Are identity-relevant stressors particularly powerful at triggering strong reactivity (e.g., Thoits, 1991)? Further, there are likely distinct profiles of reactivity, wherein some individuals react with externalizing emotions/behaviors (e.g., anger), whereas others may internalize their reaction (e.g., depression). Greater information regarding the contextual influences on reactivity is also a key area of interest – for example, how does one's baseline level of stress or the accumulation of stressors influence his or her reactivity to a given work-related stressor? Although much of the present discussion has been focused on more mundane, daily stressors, how might that reactivity differ from reactivity to traumatic events?

References

Almeida, D. M. (2005). Resilience and vulnerability to daily stressors assessed via diary methods. *Current Directions in Psychological Science, 14*, 64–68.

Almeida, D. M., & Davis, K. D. (2011). Workplace flexibility and daily stress processes in hotel employees and their children. *The ANNALS of the American Academy of Political and Social Science, 638*, 123–140.

Belsky, J., & Pluess, M. (2009). Beyond diathesis stress: Differential susceptibility to environmental influences. *Psychological Bulletin, 135*, 885–908.

Bishop, C. E., Weinberg, D. B., Leutz, W., Dossa, A., Pfefferle, S. G., & Zincavage, R. M. (2008). Nursing assistants' job commitment: Effect of nursing home organizational factors and impact on resident well-being. *The Gerontologist, 48*, 36–45.

Bolger, N., DeLongis, A., Kessler, R. C., & Schilling, E. A. (1989). Effects of daily stress on negative mood. *Journal of Personality and Social Psychology, 57*, 808–818.

Bolger, N., & Schilling, E. A. (1991). Personality and the problems of everyday life: The role of neuroticism in exposure and reactivity to daily stressors. *Journal of Personality, 59*, 355–386.

Bolger, N., & Zuckerman, A. (1995). A framework for studying personality in the stress process. *Journal of Personality and Social Psychology, 69*, 890–902.

Bonanno, G. (2004). Loss, trauma, and human resilience: Have we underestimated the human capacity to thrive after extremely aversive events? *American Psychologist, 59*(1), 20–28.

Bond, F. W., & Bunce, D. (2000). Mediators of change in emotion-focused and problem-focused worksite stress management interventions. *Journal of Occupational Health Psychology, 5*(1), 156–163.

Brunner, E., & Marmot, M. (2011). Social organization, stress, and health. In M. Marmot & R. Wilkinson (Eds.), *Social determinants of health* (2nd ed., pp. 97–129). New York: Oxford University Press.

Butler, A. B., Grzywacz, J. G., Ettner, S. L., & Liu, B. (2009). Workplace flexibility, self-reported health, and health care utilization. *Work & Stress, 23*, 45–59.

Byron, K. (2005). A meta-analytic review of work-family conflict and its antecedents. *Journal of Vocational Behavior, 67*, 169–198.

Carlson, C. R., Collins, F. L., Jr., Stewart, J. F., Porzelius, J., Nitz, J. A., & Lind, C. O. (1989). The assessment of emotional reactivity: A scale development and validation study. *Journal of Psychopathology and Behavioral Assessment, 11*(4), 313–325.

Cavanaugh, M. A., Boswell, W. R., Roehling, M. V., & Boudreau, J. W. (2000). An empirical examination of self-reported work stress among U.S. managers. *Journal of Applied Psychology, 85*, 65–74.

Charles, S. T., Piazza, J. R., Mogle, J., Sliwinski, M. J., & Almeida, D. M. (2013). The wear and tear of daily stressors on mental health. *Psychological Science, 24*(5), 733–741.

Chen, P. Y., & Spector, P. E. (1992). Relationships of work stressors with aggression, withdrawal, theft and substance use: An exploratory study. *Journal of Occupational and Organizational Psychology, 65*, 177–184.

Cohen, L. H., Gunthert, K. C., Butler, A. C., O'Neill, S. C., & Tolpin, L. H. (2005). Daily affective reactivity as a prospective predictor of depressive symptoms. *Journal of Personality, 73*, 1687–1714.

Cohen, L. H., Gunthert, K. C., Butler, A. C., Parrish, B. P., Wenze, S. J., & Beck, J. S. (2008). Negative affective spillover from daily events predicts early response to cognitive therapy for depression. *Journal of Consulting and Clinical Psychology, 76*, 955–965.

Cohen, S., & Hamrick, N. (2003). Stable individual differences in physiological response to stressors: Implications for stress-elicited changes in immune related health. *Brain, Behavior, and Immunity, 17*, 407–414.

Cohen, S., Hamrick, N., Rodriguez, M. S., Feldman, P. J., Rabin, B. S., & Manuck, S. B. (2000). The stability of and intercorrelations among cardiovascular, immune, endocrine, and psychological reactivity. *Annals of Behavioral Medicine, 22*(3), 171–179.

Cohen, S., & Wills, T. A. (1985). Stress, social support, and the buffering hypothesis. *Psychological Bulletin, 98*, 310–357.

Conger, J. J. (1956). Reinforcement theory and the dynamics of alcoholism. *Quarterly Journal of Studies on Alcohol, 17*, 296–305.

Cooper, M. L., Russell, M., & George, W. H. (1988). Coping, expectancies, and alcohol abuse: A test of social learning formulations. *Journal of Abnormal Psychology, 97*, 218–230.

Crum, A. J., Salovey, P., & Achor, S. (2013). Rethinking stress: The role of mindsets in determining the stress response. *Journal of Personality and Social Psychology, 104*(4), 716–733.

David, J. P., Green, P. J., Martin, R., & Suls, J. (1997). Differential roles of neuroticism, extraversion, and event desirability for mood in daily life: An integrative model of top-down and bottom-up influences. *Journal of Personality and Social Psychology, 73*, 149–159.

Dickerson, S. S., & Kemeny, M. E. (2004). Acute stressors and cortisol responses: A theoretical integration and synthesis of laboratory research. *Psychological Bulletin, 130*(3), 355–391.

Diener, E., & Emmons, R. A. (1984). The independence of positive and negative affect. *Journal of Personality and Social Psychology, 47*, 1105–1117.

Folkman, S., & Moskowitz, J. T. (2000). Positive affect and the other side of coping. *American Psychologist, 55*, 647–654.

Fredrickson, B. L. (1998). What good are positive emotions? *Review of General Psychology, 2*, 300–319.

Fredrickson, B. L. (2001). The role of positive emotions in positive psychology: The broaden-and-build theory of positive emotions. *American Psychologist, 56*, 218–226.

Ganster, D. C., & Perrewé, P. L. (2011). Theories of occupational stress. In J. C. Quick & L. E. Terrick (Eds.), *Handbook of occupational health psychology* (2nd ed.). Washington, DC: American Psychological Association.

Gratz, K. L., & Roemer, L. (2004). Multidimensional assessment of emotion regulation and dysregulation: Development, factor structure, and initial validation of the difficulties in Emotion Regulation Scale. *Journal of Psychopathology and Behavioral Assessment, 26*(1), 41–54.

Grzywacz, J. G., Almeida, D. M., & McDonald, D. A. (2002). Work-family spillover and daily reports of work and family stress in the adult labor force. *Family Relations, 51*, 28–36.

Hammer, L. B., Cullen, J. C., Neal, M. B., Sinclair, R. R., & Shafiro, M. (2005). The longitudinal effects of work-family conflict and positive spillover on depressive symptoms among dual-earner couples. *Journal of Occupational Health Psychology, 10*, 138–154.

Heaphy, E. D., & Dutton, J. E. (2008). Positive social interactions and the human body at work: Linking organizations and physiology. *Academy of Management Review, 33*(1), 137–162.

Hill, E. J., Hawkins, A. J., Martinson, V., & Ferris, M. (2003). Studying "working fathers": Comparing fathers' and mothers' work-family conflict, fit, and adaptive strategies in a high-tech global company. *Fathering, 1*, 239–261.

Hobfoll, S. E. (1989). Conservation of resources: A new attempt at conceptualizing stress. *American Psychologist, 44*, 513–524.

Hobfoll, S. E. (2001). The influence of culture, community, and the nested-self in the stress process: Advancing conservation of resources theory. *Applied Psychology, 50*, 337–421.

Houston, B. K. (1992). Personality characteristics, reactivity, and cardiovascular disease. In J. R. Turner, A. Sherwood, & K. C. Light (Eds.), *Individual differences in cardiovascular response to stress* (pp. 103–123). New York: Plenum.

Karasek, R. A. (1979). Job demands, job decision latitude, and mental strain: Implications for job redesign. *Administrative Science Quarterly, 24*, 285–308.

Kobasa, S. C., Maddi, S. R., & Kahn, S. (1982). Hardiness and health: A prospective study. *Journal of Personality and Social Psychology, 42*, 168–177.

Koerner, S. S., Shirai, Y., & Kenyon, D. B. (2010). Socio-contextual circumstances in daily stress reactivity among caregivers for elder relatives. *The Journals of Gerontology: Psychology Sciences, 65B*, 561–572.

Larsen, R. J., & Kasimatis, M. (1990). Individual difference in entrainment of mood to the weekly calendar. *Journal of Personality and Social Psychology, 58*(1), 164–171.

Lazarus, R. S. (1999). *Stress and emotion: A new synthesis.* New York: Springer Publishing Company.

Lazarus, R. S., & Folkman, S. (1984). *Stress, appraisal, and coping.* New York: Springer Publishing Company.

LePine, J. A., Podsakoff, N. P., & LePine, M. A. (2005). A meta-analytic test of the challenge stressor-hindrance stressor framework: An explanation for inconsistent relationships among stressors and performance. *Academy of Management Journal, 48*, 764–775.

Lepore, S. J., Miles, H. J., & Levy, J. S. (1997). Relation of chronic and episodic stressors to psychological distress, reactivity, and health problems. *International Journal of Behavioral Medicine, 4*, 39–59.

Limm, H., Gündel, H., Heinmüller, M., Marten-Mittag, B., Nater, U. M., Siegrist, J., et al. (2011). Stress management interventions in the workplace improve stress reactivity: A randomized controlled trial. *Occupational and Environmental Medicine, 68*, 126–133.

Liu, S., Wang, M., Zhan, Y., & Shi, J. (2009). Daily work stress and alcohol use: Testing the cross-level moderation effects of neuroticism and job involvement. *Personnel Psychology, 62*, 575–597.

Macht, M., & Simons, G. (2000). Emotions and eating in everyday life. *Appetite, 35*, 65–71.

Marco, C. A., & Suls, J. (1993). Daily stress and the trajectory of mood: Spillover, response assimilation, contrast, and chronic negative affectivity. *Journal of Personality and Social Psychology, 64*(6), 1053–1063.

McEwen, B. S. (1998). Protective and damaging effects of stress mediators. *New England Journal of Medicine, 338*, 171–179.

McGraw, L. K., Out, D., Hammermeister, J. J., Ohlson, C. J., Pickering, M. A., & Granger, D. A. (2013). Nature, correlates, and consequences of stress-related biological reactivity and regulation in Army nurses during combat casualty simulation. *Psychoneuroendocrinology, 38*(1), 135–144.

Ming, E. E., Adler, G. K., Kessler, R. C., Fogg, L. F., Matthews, K. A., Herd, J. A., *et al.* (2004). Cardiovascular reactivity to work stress predicts subsequent onset of hypertension: The air traffic controller health change study. *Psychosomatic Medicine, 66*, 459–465.

Mohr, C. D., Armeli, S., Ohannessian, C. M., Tennen, H., Carney, M. A., Affleck, G., *et al.* (2003). Daily interpersonal experiences and distress: Are women more vulnerable? *Journal of Social and Clinical Psychology, 22*(4), 393–423.

Mohr, C. D., Armeli, S., Tennen, H., Carney, M. A., Affleck, G., & Hromi, A. (2001). Daily interpersonal experiences, context, and alcohol consumption: Crying in your beer and toasting good times. *Journal of Personality and Social Psychology, 80*, 489–500.

Mohr, C. D., Brannan, D., Wendt, S., Jacobs, L. M., Wright, R. R., & Wang, M. (2013). Daily mood-drinking slopes as predictors: A new take on drinking motives and related outcomes. *Psychology of Addictive Behaviors, 27*(4), 944–955. doi: 10.1037/a0032633.

Mroczek, D. K., & Almeida, D. M. (2004). The effect of daily stress, personality, and age on daily negative affect. *Journal of Personality, 72*, 355–378.

Nahum-Shani, I., & Bamberger, P. A. (2011). Explaining the variable effects of social support on work-based stressor-strain relations: The role of perceived pattern of support exchange. *Organizational Behavior and Human Decision Processes, 114*, 49–63.

Nesselroade, J. R. (2004). Intraindividual variability and short-term change. *Gerontology, 50*, 44–47.

Nesselroade, J. R., & Salthouse, T. A. (2004). Methodological and theoretical implications of intraindividual variability in perceptual-motor performance. *Journal of Gerontology: Psychological Sciences, 59*, 49–55.

Neupert, S. D., Almeida, D. M., & Charles, S. T. (2007). Age differences in reactivity to daily stressors: The role of personal control. *Journal of Gerontology: Psychological Sciences, 62*, 216–225.

Newman, E., O'Connor, D. B., & Conner, M. (2007). Daily hassles and eating behaviour: The role of cortisol reactivity status. *Psychoneuroendocrinology, 32*, 125–132.

Piazza, J. R., Charles, S. T., Sliwinski, M. J., Mogle, J., & Almeida, D. M. (2012). Affective reactivity to daily stressors and long-term risk of reporting a chronic physical health condition. *Annals of Behavioral Medicine, 45*(1), 110–120.

Pillow, D. R., Zautra, A. J., & Sandler, I. (1996). Major life events and minor stressors: Identifying mediational links in the stress process. *Journal of Personality and Social Psychology, 70*, 381–394.

Podsakoff, N. P., LePine, J. A., & LePine, M. A. (2007). Differential challenge stressor-hindrance stressor relationships with job attitudes, turnover intentions, turnover, and withdrawal behavior: A meta-analysis. *Journal of Applied Psychology, 92*(2), 438–454.

Richardson, K. M., & Rothstein, H. R. (2008). Effects of occupational stress management intervention programs: A meta-analysis. *Journal of Occupational Health Psychology, 13*(1), 69–93.

Rodin, J. (1986). Aging and health: Effects of the sense of control. *Science, 233*(4770), 1271–1276.

Schwebel, D. C., & Suls, J. (1999). Cardiovascular reactivity and neuroticism: Results from a laboratory and controlled ambulatory stress protocol. *Journal of Personality, 67,* 67–92.

Sliwinski, M. J., Almeida, D. M., Smyth, J., & Stawski, R. S. (2009). Intraindividual change and variability in daily stress processes: Findings from two measurement-burst diary studies. *Psychology and Aging, 24,* 828–840.

Smith, T. W., Birmingham, W., & Uchino, B. N. (2012). Evaluative threat and ambulatory blood pressure: Cardiovascular effects of social stress in daily experience. *Health Psychology, 31*(6), 763–766.

Sonnentag, S., & Frese, M. (2003). Stress in organizations. In W. C. Borman, D. R. Ilgen & R. J. Klimoski (Eds.), *Comprehensive handbook of psychology: Vol. 12. Industrial and organizational psychology* (pp. 453–491). Hoboken, NJ: Wiley.

Steger, M. F., & Kashdan, T. B. (2009). Depression and everyday social activity, belonging, and well-being. *Journal of Counseling Psychology, 56,* 289–300.

Story, L. B., & Repetti, R. (2006). Daily occupational stressors and marital behavior. *Journal of Family Psychology, 20,* 690–700.

Suls, J., & Martin, R. (2005). The daily life of the garden-variety neurotic: Reactivity, stressor exposure, mood spillover, and maladaptive coping. *Journal of Personality, 73,* 1485–1510.

Taris, T. W. (2006). Bricks without clay: On urban myths in occupational health psychology. *Work and Stress, 20,* 99–104.

Tennen, H., Affleck, G., Armeli, S., & Carney, M. A. (2000). A daily process approach to coping: Linking theory, research, and practice. *American Psychologist, 55*(66), 626–636.

Thayer, R. E. (1987). Energy, tiredness, and tension effects of a sugar snack versus moderate exercise. *Journal of Personality and Social Psychology, 52,* 119–125.

Thayer, R. E., Newman, J. R., & McClain, T. M. (1994). Self-regulation of mood: Strategies for changing a bad mood, raising energy, and reducing tension. *Journal of Personality and Social Psychology, 67,* 910–925.

Thoits, P. A. (1991). On merging identity theory and stress research. *Social Psychology Quarterly, 54*(2), 101–112.

Tomaka, J., Blascovich, J., Kelsey, R. M., & Leitten, C. L. (1993). Subjective, physiological, and behavioral effects of threat and challenge appraisal. *Journal of Personality and Social Psychology, 65*(2), 248–260.

Uchino, B. N., Berg, C. A., Smith, T. W., Pearce, G., & Skinner, M. (2006). Age-related differences in ambulatory blood pressure reactivity during stress: Evidence for greater blood pressure reactivity with age. *Psychology and Aging, 21,* 231–239.

Wang, M., Liu, S., Zhan, Y., & Shi, J. (2010). Daily work-family conflict and alcohol use: Testing the cross-level moderation effects of peer drinking norms and social support. *The Journal of Applied Psychology, 95*(2), 377–386.

6

Work–Family Balance and Well-Being among Japanese Dual-Earner Couples: A Spillover–Crossover Perspective

Akihito Shimazu and Kyoko Shimada
The University of Tokyo Graduate School of Medicine, Japan

Izumi Watai
Graduate School of Medicine, Nagoya University, Japan

Introduction

In Japan, the entry of women into the work force has become increasingly common (Ministry of Health, Labour and Welfare, 2010). The number of dual-earner families has been larger than that of single-earner families (i.e., male worker and female housewife) since 1997. However, wives play a more important role in child care and housework in dual-earner couples with one or more children (Cabinet Office, 2006) because of their husbands' longer working hours (Cabinet Office, 2006) and because they conform to traditional gender roles (Kato & Kanai, 2007). Thus, there is a potential for interference or conflict between the work and non-work lives of dual-earner couples (especially for the wives).

This chapter examines work–family balance and its impact on well-being among Japanese dual-earner couples from a spillover–crossover perspective (Bakker & Demerouti, 2009, 2013; Bakker, Demerouti & Burke, 2009; Bakker, Demerouti & Dollard, 2008).

Working Conditions and Family Structure in Japan

It is well known that in Japan, members of the workforce have significant difficulty in balancing their work and family lives (Rebick & Takenaka, 2006). This characteristic can be explained by recent economic trends and the employment situation.

Contemporary Occupational Health Psychology: Global Perspectives on Research and Practice, Volume 3,
First Edition. Edited by Stavroula Leka and Robert R. Sinclair.

The collapse of the bubble economy in 1991, which was followed by an economic depression, led many companies to increase competition, resulting in a widespread restructuring (e.g., layoffs) and an increase in non-regular employment, such as part-time employment, employment on lease, and temporary employment. Consequently, regular workers are required to work longer hours in order to deal with increased organizational demands (Ohashi, 2000). Indeed, working hours among male regular workers in their late 20s, 30s, and early 40s are particularly longer than those of other groups (Kanai, 2006).

However, the reasons for working long hours in Japan are not only economic but also sociocultural (Snir & Harpaz, 2004). To the Japanese, work is an end in itself: it is the process of carrying out obligations owed to society and to oneself as a social being (Snir & Harpaz, 2004). In the Japanese culture, time logged at one's desk or workstation is often a symbol of submission to managerial power and loyalty to the organization (Japan Institute for Labour Policy and Training, 2010), and hard work and effort are more highly valued than ability in collectivistic cultures (Scholz, Gutierrez-Dona, Sud & Schwarzer, 2002). Consequently, workers in Japan are often asked to volunteer for overtime or to work considerable amounts of unpaid extra time (Snir & Harpaz, 2004).

The difficulty in balancing work and family life among the Japanese can also be explained by family structure. In Japan, though it is increasingly common for women to enter the work force (Ministry of Health, Labour and Welfare, 2010), gender inequality remains in terms of political and economic participation of women, particularly compared to many of the European Organization for Economic Co-operation and Development (OECD) nations. For instance, Japan ranks 57 out of 109 countries on the Gender Empowerment Measure, with female legislators, senior officials, and managers totaling only 9% of its workforce (United Nations Development Programme, 2009). In addition, work hours and hours spent on childcare and housework are polarized by gender. According to the Cabinet Office (2006), Japanese husbands with pre-school children spend 7.7 hours on work at their worksite and 0.8 hours on child care and housework at their homes per day. In contrast, Japanese wives with pre-school children spend 3.7 hours on work at their worksite and 5.7 hours on childcare and housework at their homes per day. This condition suggests that wives play a more important role than husbands in childcare and housework in dual-earner couples with children.

Spillover–Crossover Model

Earlier studies have identified two different ways in which strain is carried over from the work to the family domain (Bolger, DeLongis, Kessler & Wethington, 1989; Westman, 2002). *Work–family conflict (WFC) or spillover* is a within-person, across-domains transmission of strain from one area of life to another. In contrast, *crossover* involves transmission across individuals, whereby strain crosses over between closely related persons (Westman, 2001).

WFC is defined as "a form of inter-role conflict in which the role pressures from the work and family domains are mutually incompatible in some respect, such that participation in one role makes it difficult to participate in the other" (Greenhaus & Beutell, 1985, p. 77). This definition of WFC implies a bidirectional relation between work and family life in such a way that work can interfere with family life (i.e., WFC) and family life can interfere with work (i.e., family-to-work conflict (FWC)) (Frone, 2000). Previous research has focused primarily on how experiences in the work domain are transferred to, and interfere with, the non-work domain for the same individual (Byron, 2005).

It should be noted that although the focus in previous work–family studies has been primarily on negative spillover, research has clearly indicated that positive spillover is also possible. Work–family facilitation is defined as "the extent to which participation at work (or home) is made easier by virtue of the experiences, skills, and opportunities gained or developed at home (or work)" (Frone, 2003, p. 145). That is, participation in the family role may be facilitated by what has happened at work.

In *crossover*, an individual's stress in the workplace may lead to stress for the individual's partner at home. Westman (2006) suggested several possible mechanisms to explain the crossover process. First, direct crossover can take place between the two partners through empathy – that is, because partners spend considerable time together, they become aware of, and affected by, each other's affective states (Bakker & Demerouti, 2009). Second, partners may share some common stressors (e.g., financial pressures, life events) that may lead to increased levels of common strains (e.g., negative affect). Third, crossover may be an indirect process wherein the crossover of strain is mediated by the communication and interaction of the partners (e.g., by coping strategies, social undermining, and lack of social support). So far, social undermining and social support have been particularly examined as behavioral mediators of crossover in the spillover–crossover model.

In sum, the spillover–crossover model proposes an intra-individual transmission of stress or strain from work to home and vice versa (i.e., spillover) and a dyadic, inter-individual transmission of stress or strain from husbands to wives and vice versa (i.e., crossover) as the ways through which work and family influence each other (Bakker & Demerouti, 2013) (Figure 6.1).

Evidence for Spillover Perspective

Previous research on work–family spillover in Japan can be classified into the following three categories according to its focus: (1) predictors of work–family spillover, (2) outcomes of work–family spillover, and (3) the process that connects work and family factors with the outcomes (i.e., mediating role of spillover).

Predictors of work–family spillover

Watai, Nishikido and Murashima (2008) focused on individual characteristics (e.g., age, education, number of children), work environment (i.e., job status, overtime work, job strain characterized by job demands and control), and family environment (e.g., family

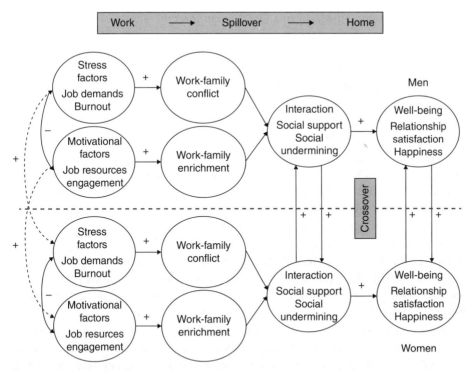

Figure 6.1   The Spillover–Crossover Model (Copyright Bakker & Demerouti (2013) p. 58, Figure 4.1).

stress, time spent on childrearing and housework, partner support) as predictors of work-family conflict and examined their relation to WFC and FWC. A questionnaire survey was conducted among 180 Japanese information technology engineers (78 males and 102 females) with preschool children. Multiple regression analyses of WFC revealed that among males, job strain and family stress were positively related with WFC, and family-friendly culture and age of youngest child were negatively related with WFC. However, among females, family stress was positively related with WFC, and overtime work was negatively related with WFC. In terms of FWC, time spent on childrearing and housework and family stress were positively related with FWC, and the number of children was negatively related with FWC among males, whereas family stress was positively related with FWC among females. These results suggest that family stress may play an important role in predicting both WFC and FWC for both genders.

Outcomes of spillover

Several studies have revealed that work–family negative spillover has adverse effects on psychological health, including depression and psychological distress (Seto, Morimoto & Maruyama, 2004; Shimada *et al.*, 2010, 2013; Watai, Nishikido & Murashima, 2008) and family functioning (Shimazu *et al.*, 2013). However, only a few studies have examined the effects of positive spillover on outcomes.

Seto, Morimoto and Maruyama (2004) examined the effects of WFC as well as work-related factors on depression among 501 women with preschool children. Multiple regression analyses revealed that WFC and such work-related factors as perceived poor relationships at work, job insecurity, and underutilization of skills were significantly related to a greater presence of depressive symptoms. Unfortunately, this study did not differentiate between the directions of spillover – that is, between work to family and family to work.

Watai, Nishikido and Murashima (2008) examined the effects of WFC and FWC on cumulative fatigue and depression among regularly employed information technology engineers with preschool children in Japan. A positive relationship was found between WFC and cumulative fatigue in both genders. WFC was also significantly associated with depression in both genders.

A significant amount of evidence on the effects of work–family spillover on health outcomes also comes from a Tokyo Work–family INterface (TWIN) study. The TWIN study aims at examining intra-individual (i.e., spillover) and inter-individual (i.e., crossover) processes of well-being among dual-earner couples with pre-school children in Tokyo, Japan. Shimada *et al.* (2010) examined the effects of multiple types of work–family spillover on psychological distress. Whereas most previous studies in Japan have focused mainly on the unidirectional relation from work to family and the negative side of spillover (i.e., WFC), Shimada *et al.* included the bidirectional relation between work and family life and the positive side of spillover (work–family positive spillover). A hierarchical multiple regression analysis among 2346 respondents revealed that (1) both FWC and WFC were positively related with psychological distress, although FWC had a stronger relation with psychological distress than WFC, and (2) both work-to-family positive spillover and family-to-work positive spillover were negatively but weakly related to psychological distress. These results suggest that Japanese working parents are more concerned about the adverse impact of family responsibilities on their work than they are about the workplace burden affecting their family life. They also suggest that even if Japanese working parents experience benefits from combining work and family roles, such experiences coincide only to a small extent with psychological distress. Hence, decreasing negative spillover, compared to increasing positive spillover, should have a higher priority in decreasing the psychological distress of Japanese working parents.

Shimazu *et al.* (2013) examined the effects of WFC and FWC on the psychological distress and relationship quality between partners using the baseline data from the TWIN study. Whereas previous research had focused mainly on the bivariate effects of WFC and FWC, this study examined the independent and combined effects of WFC and FWC. The results of logistic regression analyses showed that dual experiences of WFC and FWC have adverse associations with employees' own psychological health and with the relationship quality between partners for both genders.

Mediating role of spillover

Although there have been several studies regarding WFC (Eby *et al.*, 2005; Edward & Rothbard, 2000; Ford, Heinen & Langkamer 2007; Greenhaus & Beutell, 1985), their primary focus has been the direct effects of work-family conflicts on health outcomes (Eby *et al.*, 2005). This means that the process by which job/home demands have an impact on health outcomes through work-family conflict is less often examined. Therefore, Shimazu, Bakker, Demerouti and Peeters (2010) examined the processes (i.e., job demands → FC → psychological distress and home demands → FWC → psychological distress) among 196 Japanese working parents with preschool children. The results of structural equation modeling revealed that home demands were partially related to psychological distress, both directly and indirectly through FWC. However, job demands were only directly related to psychological distress. These results provided empirical support for a partial mediating effect of FWC in the relationship between home demands and psychological distress but not of WFC in the relationship between job demands and psychological distress.

In sum, work–family spillover is generally associated with Japanese workers' well-being, as in other Western countries (Allen, Herst & Bruck, 2000). However, further research is needed in terms of the positive aspect of spillover and the longitudinal effects of spillovers.

Evidence for Crossover Perspective

Westman defined *crossover* as the process that occurs when a stressor or psychological strain experienced by one person affects the level of stress or strain of another person in the same social environment (Westman, 2006). In Western countries, the existence of crossover effects between spouses in the work–family literature has been demonstrated in a number of studies. For example, the effects of job stress on the spouse's family stress and well-being have been supported (Bolger, DeLongis, Kessler & Wethington, 1989; Westman & Etzion, 2005). Likewise, the crossover effect of one's work and family involvement on the spouse's level of work-family conflict has also been established (Greenhaus *et al.*, 1989). Recently, the bidirectional crossover of stress or strain was simultaneously investigated for both spouses, from wives to husbands and vice versa (Hammer, Allen & Grigsby, 1997; Westman, 2006; Westman & Etzion, 2005).

According to Aycan's (2008) review, the cultural context moderates the relationship between demands in the family and work domain and work-family conflict. She indicated that most Asian countries have a different culture in terms of a patterned way of thinking, feeling, and reacting compared to Western countries (e.g., collectivism vs. individualism). The question arises then: are there any differences between Japan and Western countries in the crossover relationship between wife and husband? To date, only a limited amount of research has investigated the relationship of one's work–family balance with the well-being of other family members, such as partner and child, in Japan. Later, we refer to several empirical studies conducted in Japan.

Spillover–crossover in dual-earner couples

Fukumaru (2003) conducted a questionnaire survey ($N = 124$ couples) and telephone interviews ($N = 42$ couples) to examine the impact of one's job and parent roles, positive and negative spillovers, and negative attitude toward the partner's working on partner depression in a sample of dual-earner couples with pre-school children. The results of path analyses showed that WFC had no significant relation with the partner's depression in either gender. However, the husband's WFC was significantly related to his wife's depression only when the husband had a highly negative attitude toward a working wife. This result suggests that the husband's attitude toward the wife plays an important role in determining his wife's psychological health.

Kato and Kanai (2007) examined the relationship between one's and one partner's work-family conflicts and one's and one partner's outcomes (i.e., marital satisfaction and mental health) in 187 dual-earner couples with pre-school children. They conceptualized one's coping behaviors as mediators of the relationship whereby the following three types of coping behaviors were examined: role assignment between partners, family role reduction, and family role fulfillment (Kato & Kanai, 2006). The results of path analyses revealed that only the role assignment between partners played a mediating role among the three types of coping. However, the effects of coping on outcomes were different according to gender. Specifically, the wife's role assignment, increased by the husband's FWC and decreased by his time conflict, had favorable effects on her own and her husband's marital satisfaction. On the other hand, the husband's role assignment, increased by his FWC and his wife's time conflict and decreased by his and his wife's WFC, had a favorable effect on his own marital satisfaction but adverse effects on his wife's mental health. This discrepancy may reflect the gender role difference (at least) among Japanese couples. In Japan, women play a more important role in child care in dual-earner couples with children (Cabinet Office, 2006). Hence, the husband's role assignment may contribute to the reduction of his own family demands, which leads to his own marital satisfaction, whereas it may lead to an increase in his wife's family demands, which results in her poor mental health.

Recently, Shimazu, Bakker and Demerouti (2009) demonstrated the spillover–crossover effect in a sample of 99 Japanese dual-earner couples with pre-school children. They hypothesized that job demands have a negative influence on partner well-being because of WFC and an impaired quality of the relationship (reduced social support and increased social undermining with regard to the partner). The analysis with structural equation modeling revealed that men's job demands (i.e., overload and emotional demands) were positively related to their own reports of WFC and indirectly to women's rating of men's WFC. Consequently, women's rating of men's WFC was negatively related to the quality of the relationship (i.e., decreased social support from, and increased social undermining by, men), which, in turn, led to women's ill health (i.e., depressive symptoms and physical complaints). The findings were similar for the model starting with women's job demands; gender did not affect the strength of the relationships in the model.

In another large-scale study, Shimazu *et al.* (2011) examined the impact of workaholism on employees' and their partners' work-family conflicts and psychological distress using data from the TWIN study: 994 Japanese dual-earner couples with pre-school children in Tokyo. The results of logistic analyses showed that, compared to relaxed workers, workaholics were more likely to report WFC after adjusting for demographic variables. They also found that the association of workaholism with an employee's WFC and psychological distress was stronger in men than in women. Moreover, husbands of workaholic women were more likely to report FWC compared to the husbands of relaxed women, but wives of workaholic men were not more likely to report FWC. Based on this result, they indicated that a solid gender role exists among Japanese couples, even if the wife has a full-time job.

Finally, Watai (2011) examined the crossover of WFC and depression between partners in a sample of 284 Japanese dual-earner couples with elementary-school children. In her study, she hypothesized that crossover effects would be moderated by the employment status of couples (i.e., regular employed husband and wife vs. regular employed husband and non-regular employed wife). The results of structural equation modeling revealed positive relationships between the husband's and wife's depression and between husband's and wife's FWC among couples consisting of a regular employed husband and wife. On the other hand, they did not find any significant relationships among couples consisting of regular employed husband and non-regular employed wife. These results suggest that the employment status of couples (especially of the wife) would play an important role in determining the crossover effects of WFC and depression among dual-earner couples.

Crossover from parents to children

How maternal employment affects children's well-being or development has been a dominant issue in the work–family interface research. However, numerous studies over the past half century have concluded that maternal employment has no consistent positive or negative effects on children's well-being (Harvey, 1999). Hence, researchers have begun to focus more on identifying the processes that may mediate the relationship between employment and family life, such as maternal depression, marital discord, and marital conflict (Davies & Cummings, 1998; Emery & O'Leary, 1982; Kovacs, 1997).

As a corollary to *crossover theory*, the WFC experienced by parents may lead to negative behaviors or emotions in the children at home. Although little of the empirical research has examined the relationship in Japan, some evidence has shown that parents' WFC has adverse effects on family functioning. For instance, Koizumi, Sugawara, Maekawa and Kitamura (2003) examined the impact of one's WFC on one's own depression, marital relationship, and child rearing stress among 246 dual-earner couples with school-aged children using longitudinal data. The results of path analyses showed that parents' WFC was positively related to their marital discord and childrearing stress, which resulted in depressive symptoms in the parents. However, this relationship was found only among mothers.

Sugawara *et al.* (2002) investigated the process, starting with marital relationships (i.e., marital love: mother to father and father to mother) to children's depression, whereby they conceptualized family functioning (i.e., family atmosphere and family cohesion) and parental warm attitudes toward child as mediators. The results of path analyses showed that both mother-to-father love and father-to-mother love were positively related to favorable family atmosphere and family cohesion, which resulted in lowering of children's depression. This suggests that family functioning plays a mediating role in the relationship between marital relationships and children's depression. However, in terms of the role of parental attitudes toward children, both mother-to-father love and father-to-mother love were positively related to their warm attitudes toward children, but only the mother's warm attitudes were negatively related to the children's depression, as the father's warm attitudes were not significant. This suggests that parental warm attitudes toward children may play a mediating role in the relationship between marital relationships and children's depression, but this applies only to the mother.

In another study, Watai, Nishikido and Murashima (2007) examined the relationship between parents' work-family conflict and their attitudes toward childrearing using 401 Japanese working mothers and 292 working fathers with school-aged children in Tokyo. The results of multiple regression analysis showed that WFC was negatively associated with an acceptant parental attitude in fathers and with responsibility for childrearing in mothers. In addition, FWC was positively associated with an excessively controlling attitude in mothers toward the children. These findings suggest that parents experiencing work-family conflict are more likely to show impaired attitudes toward their children.

In sum, our literature review shows that one's work-family conflict and its mental health consequences may cross over to a partner. In addition, we discussed the possibility that the work-family conflict of parents may cross over to their children through parental attitudes toward childrearing and family functioning. Future research needs to examine the crossover from parents to children and vice versa and to clarify the underlying mechanisms in the relationships between them. Given the increasing number of dual-earner couples in Japan, more research is needed from a spillover–crossover perspective.

Future Directions and Conclusion

In this chapter, we have discussed work–family balance and well-being among Japanese dual-earner couples. In doing so, we referred to the spillover–crossover model and introduced empirical studies conducted in Japan. However, several issues remain unexamined.

First, although most of the studies introduced in this chapter examined the crossover between employees and their partners among dual-earner couples, crossover may also be found among employees and other members of the family, such as children and parents. For instance, Breevaart and Bakker (2012) mentioned that employees' psychological distress may lead to the detrimental involvement of their children, fewer modeling opportunities, and less secure attachment, which, in turn, have a negative impact on adaptive child development. In addition, even though, owing to demographic changes, a growing number of employees provide in-home care to an elderly family member (e.g., Major & Germano, 2006; Neal & Hammer, 2007), previous work–family research literature has neglected employees who care informally for aging parents (Neal & Hammer, 2007). Hence, the focus of crossover research should be extended in the family from spouses to children as well as live-in elderly parents.

Second, although this chapter focuses on a particularly negative pathway in terms of the spillover–crossover model, several previous findings have suggested that the spillover and crossover processes can also be positive. Many studies have now provided evidence for positive spillover (see Byron, 2005, for a meta-analysis). Because positive experiences are just as likely to cross over to the partner as negative experiences (Bakker & Demerouti, 2009; Bakker, Demerouti & Burke, 2009), there is promise for future research in testing positive pathways in the spillover–crossover model.

Finally, most studies mentioned in this chapter were conducted among participants living in a big city, such as Tokyo. These characteristics may limit the generalizability of the current findings not only around the globe but also in Japan. Thus, further research is needed to determine whether we can generalize these findings to other areas and other (Western) countries.

References

Allen, T., Herst, D., Bruck, C., & Sutton, M. (2000). Consequences associated with work-to-family conflict: A review and agenda for future research. *Journal of Occupational Health Psychology, 5*, 278–308.

Aycan, Z. (2008). Cross-cultural approaches to work-family conflict. In K. Korabik, D. S. Lero, & D. L. Whitehead (Eds.), *Handbook of work-family integration research, theory, and the best practices* (pp. 353–370). London: Elsevier.

Bakker, A. B., & Demerouti, E. (2009). The crossover of work engagement between working couples: A closer look at the role of empathy. *Journal of Managerial Psychology, 24*, 220–236.

Bakker, A. B., & Demerouti, E. (2013). The Spillover-Crossover model. In J. Grzywacs & E. Demerouti (Eds.), *New frontiers in work and family research*. Hove, UK: Psychology Press.

Bakker, A. B., Demerouti, E., & Burke, R. (2009). Workaholism and relationship quality: A Spillover–Crossover perspective. *Journal of Occupational Health Psychology, 14*, 23–33.

Bakker, A. B., Demerouti, E., & Dollard, M. (2008). How job demands influence partners' experience of exhaustion: Integrating work-family conflict and crossover theory. *Journal of Applied Psychology, 93*, 901–911.

Bolger, N., DeLongis, A., Kessler, R., & Wethington, E. (1989). The contagion of stress across multiple roles. *Journal of Marriage and Family, 51*, 175–183.

Breevaart, K., & Bakker, A. B. (2012). The influence of job and parental strain on typically and atypically developing children: A vicious circle? *Community, Work and Family, 15*, 173–188.

Byron, K. (2005). A meta-analytic review of work-family conflict and its antecedents. *Journal of Vocational Behavior, 67,* 169–198.

Cabinet Office. (2006). *White Paper on the National Lifestyle.* Retrieved May 10, 2010, from http://www5.cao.go.jp/seikatsu/whitepaper/h18/01_honpen/index.html. Accessed November 13, 2013 (in Japanese).

Davies, P. T., & Cummings, E. M. (1998). Exploring children's emotional security as a mediator of the link between marital relations and child adjustment. *Child Development, 69,* 124–139.

Eby, L. T., Casper, W. J., Lockwood, A., Bordeaux, C., & Brinley, A. (2005). Work and family research in IO/OB: Content analysis and review of the literature (1980–2002). *Journal of Vocational Behavior, 66,* 124–197.

Edwards, J. R., & Rothbard, N. P. (2000). Mechanisms linking work and family: Clarifying the relationship between work and family constructs. *Academy of Management Review, 25,* 178–199.

Emery, R. E., & O'Leary, K. D. (1982). Children's perception of marital discord and behavior problems of boys and girls. *Journal of Abnormal Child Psychology, 10,* 11–24.

Ford, M. T., Heinen, B. A., & Langkamer, K. L. (2007). Work and family satisfaction and conflict: A meta-analysis of cross-domain relations. *Journal of Applied Psychology, 92,* 57–80.

Frone, M. R. (2000). Work-family conflict and employee psychiatric disorders: The National Comorbidity Survey. *Journal of Applied Psychology, 85,* 888–895.

Frone, M. R. (2003). Work-family balance. In J. C. Quick & L. E. Tetric (Eds.), *Handbook of occupational health psychology* (pp. 143–162). Washington, DC: American Psychological Association.

Fukumaru, Y. (2003). *Multiple roles of work and family among wives and husbands with pre-school children.* Tokyo, Japan: Kazama-shobo (in Japanese).

Greenhaus, J. H., & Beutell, N. J. (1985). Sources of conflict between work and family roles. *Academy of Management Review, 10,* 76–88.

Greenhaus, J. H., Parasuraman, S., Granrose, C. S., Rabinowitz, S., & Beutell, N. J. (1989). Sources of work-family conflict among two-career couples. *Journal of Vocational Behavior, 34,* 133–153.

Hammer, L. B., Allen, E., & Grigsby, T. D. (1997). Work-family conflict in dual-earner couples: Within-individual and crossover effects of work and family. *Journal of Vocational Behavior, 50,* 185–203.

Harvey, E. (1999). Short-term and long-term effects of early parental employment on children of the National Longitudinal Survey of Youth. *Developmental Psychology, 35,* 445–459.

Japan Institute for Labour Policy and Training. (2010). *Research findings on work characteristics, personal characteristics, and working time.* Retrieved January 18, 2011, from http://www.jil.go.jp/press/documents/20101207.pdf. Accessed November 13, 2013 (in Japanese).

Kanai, A. (2006). Economic and employment conditions, karoshi (work to death) and the trend of studies on workaholism in Japan. In R. J. Burke (Ed.), *Research companion to working time and work addiction* (pp. 158–172). Cheltenham, UK: Edward Elgar.

Kato, Y., & Kanai, A. (2006). The effect of coping behavior with work-family conflict in dual-career couples. *The Japanese Journal of Psychology, 76,* 511–518 (in Japanese).

Kato, Y., & Kanai, A. (2007). Work-family conflicts and in dual-career couples: Study of the crossover effect and the coping behavior as a mediator and a buffer. *Japanese Association of Industrial/Organizational Psychology Journal, 20,* 15–25 (in Japanese).

Koizumi, T., Sugawara, M., Maekawa, K., & Kitamura, T. (2003). Direct and indirect effects of negative spillover from work to family, on depressive symptoms of Japanese working mothers. *Japan Journal of Developmental Psychology, 14*, 272–283 (in Japanese).

Kovacs, M. (1997). Depressive disorders in childhood: An impressionistic landscape. *Journal of Child Psychology and Psychiatry and Allied Disciplines, 38*, 287–298.

Major, D. A., & Germano, L. M. (2006). The changing nature of work and its impact on the work-home interface. In F. Jones, R. J. Burke, & M. Westman (Eds.), *Work–life balance: A psychological perspective* (pp. 13–38). East Sussex, England: Psychology Press.

Ministry of Health, Labour and Welfare. (2010). *Current status of working women in 2009.* Retrieved January 18, 2011, from http://www.mhlw.go.jp/bunya/koyoukintou/josei-jitsujo/09.html. Accessed November 13, 2013 (in Japanese).

Neal, M. B., & Hammer, L. B. (2007). *Working couples caring for children and aging parents: Effects on work and well-being.* Mahwah, NJ: Lawrence Erlbaum Associates Publishers.

Ohashi, Y. (2000). Background of the tendency of single, late-marriage, and individualism. In K. Yoshizumi (Ed.), *Marriage and partnership: Revisiting the married couple* (pp. 27–55). Kyoto, Japan: Minerva Shobo (in Japanese).

Rebick, M., & Takenaka, A. (2006). The changing Japanese family. In M. Rebick & A. Takenaka (Eds.), *The changing Japanese family* (pp. 39–53). Oxon, MD: Routledge.

Seto, M., Morimoto, K., & Maruyama, S. (2004). Effects of work-related factors and work-family conflict on depression among Japanese working women living with young children. *Environmental Health and Preventive Medicine, 9*, 220–227.

Scholz, U., Gutierrez-Dona, B., Sud, S., & Schwarzer, R. (2002). Is general self-efficacy a universal construct? Psychometric findings from 25 countries. *European Journal of Psychological Assessment, 18*, 242–251.

Shimazu, A., Bakker, A. B., & Demerouti, E. (2009). How job demands affect the intimate partner: A test of the spillover–crossover model in Japan. *Journal of Occupational Health, 51*, 239–248.

Shimada, K., Shimazu, A., Bakker, A. B., Demerouti, E., & Kawakami, N. (2010). Work-family spillover among Japanese dual-earner couples: A large community-based study. *Journal of Occupational Health, 52*, 335–343.

Shimazu, A., Bakker, A. B., Demerouti, E., & Peeters, M. C. W. (2010). Work-family conflict in Japan: How job and home demands affect psychological distress. *Industrial Health, 48*, 766–774.

Shimazu, A., Demerouti, E., Bakker, A. B., Shimada, K., & Kawakami, N. (2011). Workaholism and well-being among Japanese dual-earner couples: A spillover-crossover perspective. *Social Science and Medicine, 73*, 399–409.

Shimazu, A., Kubota, K., Bakker, A. B., Demerouti, E., Shimada, K., & Kawakami, N. (2013). Dual experiences of work-to-family conflict and family-to-work conflict: A spillover-crossover perspective. *Journal of Occupational Health, 55*, 234–243.

Snir, R., & Harpaz, I. (2004). Attitudinal and demographic antecedents of workaholism. *Journal of Organizational Change Management, 17*, 520–536.

Sugawara, M., Yagishita, A., Takuma, N., Koizumi, C, Sechiyama, H., Sugawara, K., & Kitamura, T. (2002). Marital relations and depression in school-age children: Links with family functioning and parent attitudes toward child rearing. *Japanese Association of Educational Psychology, 50*, 129–140 (in Japanese).

United Nations Development Programme. (2009). *Human development report 2009.* Retrieved January 18, 2011, from http://hdr.undp.org/en/media/HDR_2009_EN_Complete.pdf. Accessed November 13, 2013.

Watai, I. (2011). Work-family conflict and mental health in dual-earner couples with elementary school children. Published thesis, The University of Tokyo, Bunkyo, Tokyo (in Japanese).

Watai, I., Nishikido, N., & Murashima, S. (2007). The impact of parents' employment on their parental attitude among Japanese dual earner couples with school children. *Research and Paper of the Meiji Yasuda Mental Health Foundation, 42*, 190–199 (in Japanese).

Watai, I., Nishikido, N., & Murashima, S. (2008). Gender difference in work-family conflict among Japanese information technology engineers with preschool children. *Journal of Occupational Health, 50*, 317–327.

Westman, M. (2001). Stress and strain crossover. *Human Relations, 54*, 557–591.

Westman, M. (2002). Crossover of stress and strain in the family and in the workplace. In P. L. Perrewé & D. C. Ganster (Eds.), *Research in occupational stress and well-being* (Vol. 2, pp. 143–181). Oxford, UK: JAI Press/Elsevier Science.

Westman, M. (2006). Crossover of stress and strain in the work–family context. In F. Jones, R. J. Burke, & M. Westman (Eds.), *Work–life balance: A psychological perspective* (pp. 163–184). East Sussex, England: Psychology Press.

Westman, M., & Etzion, D. L. (2005). The crossover of work-family conflict from one spouse to the other. *Journal of Applied Social Psychology, 35*, 1936–1957.

7

A Life Course Perspective on Immigrant Occupational Health and Well-Being

Frederick T.L. Leong
Michigan State University, USA

Donald E. Eggerth and Michael A. Flynn
National Institute for Occupational Safety and Health, USA

Introduction

With the exception of the subfield of developmental psychology, the field of psychology has tended to ignore the time dimension in its theory development and research paradigms (Zimbardo & Boyd, 1999). For example, much of the research on cross-cultural mental health in clinical and counseling psychology begins with the client presenting for treatment, yet their pre-clinical life course and life experiences may be highly critical to their current condition as well as the outcome of their treatment. Similarly, in occupational health psychology, much of the literature begins with a workplace crisis precipitating an intervention. This chasm also exists in the literature concerning the adjustment and adaptation of immigrant workers in the US. The application of the life course perspective (e.g., Baltes, 1987; Levinson, 1986) to studies of immigrant occupational health would provide a framework within which to remedy these conceptual shortcomings.

Early applications of the life course perspective in psychology can be found in the work of Jack Block (1971), Glen Elder (1985), and Erik Erikson (1950). In these applications, the life course paradigm replaced child-based and growth-oriented frameworks with models that emphasized timing, social context, and sequencing of events across the life-span. The life course paradigm actively seeks to identify connections between social change, developmental trajectories, and life-span development within the context of family and community, across historical time and place. The life course paradigm has increasingly been used to

Contemporary Occupational Health Psychology: Global Perspectives on Research and Practice, Volume 3,
First Edition. Edited by Stavroula Leka and Robert R. Sinclair.
© 2014 John Wiley & Sons, Ltd. Published 2014 by John Wiley & Sons, Ltd.

research life experience, health, and adaptation of diverse populations (e.g., Ben-Shlomo & Kuh, 2002; Moen, 1996).

Overview of the Life Course Perspective

Wethington (2005) provided an excellent summary of the life course perspective in health research. This paper will adopt her framework for application to immigrant occupational health. According to Wethington, the life course perspective has successfully been employed to look at health and health behavior throughout the human life-span in areas like medicine, public health, psychology, sociology, and education. This approach is unique in that it frames understanding the association between social context, historical events, and changes in population and group health over a time period instead of only at one point in time. The life course perspective allows for multiple, interconnected causal factors, such as life history, personality factors, and cultural differences, to account for group or individual differences in health.

Many researchers view the life course perspective not as a formal theory, but rather a model whose principles and concepts can bridge multiple disciplines (Wethington, 2005). This perspective has been widely used in sociology, but its application to other fields has been limited due to the difficulties in factoring of life history into study designs. In part, this arises because the approach was developed for basic research in the social sciences rather than as a template for translating research to practice. Recently, the perspective has been used in biological research on human development and aging along with research on social and historical change. Researchers have used this perspective to look at how group differences in health, behaviors, and mortality change or endure throughout time. For example, mortality and morbidity differ according to social status and class.

Wethington (2005) discussed seven key concepts related to using the life course perspective to measure individual change across time. The concepts were designed to be used to create testable hypotheses integrating the implications of an individual's adaptation to change over a period of time instead of looking at only one point in the individual's lifetime.

The first of these concepts is **trajectories**. Trajectories are patterns of health or behavior that remain stable over time such as chronic disease or tobacco use. Other examples of trajectories include social factors like the social network or social integration trajectory that an individual has that might influence their health maintenance. A common work-related trajectory is that of starting in positions that require few skills and no independence and over time advancing to more skilled positions and finally to one involving supervision of other workers. Typically, trajectories develop consistently and reinforce each other. Consequently, attempts to change a certain type of trajectory may not end up having a long-lasting change in behavior. This may be because other trajectories or aspects of life keep the trajectory in its current state (Wethington, 2005).

Another concept used in the life course perspective is **transitions**, which are significant changes in the social responsibilities or roles of an individual (Wethington, 2005). Transitions can be stressful and unanticipated, which can make it difficult for an individual to cope. However, transitions can also be positive, such as a job promotion, and can lead to increased commitment to the current trajectory. Often, transitions will affect more than just one life trajectory when impacting a social role.

Turning points are major life changes that alter the direction of a trajectory. Studies suggest that turning points are most likely to occur in the first third or half of life (Wethington, 2005). Turning points are less common than transitions and are less likely to support behavioral tendencies that already exist with the individual (Wethington, 2005). Some critics believe that turning points are too difficult to differentiate from transitions and consequently, the two terms have been used interchangeably in the literature. In this chapter, we differentiate between the two concepts in that we consider turning points to be more abrupt in onset, to occur over a discrete period, to be of shorter duration, and of greater peak intensity than transitions. A good metaphor might be found in geology. Earthquakes and erosion both have the power to radically reshape landscapes. However, the first does so quickly and violently, and the second so gradually that one is challenged to establish a meaningful timeline. In work-related terms, an example of a turning point would be an unexpected job loss requiring a change of career.

Culture and contextual influences focus on factors outside of the control of the individual. Examples include coming of age during historical events such as the Great Depression or the Civil Rights Movement and immutable characteristics such as race, ethnicity, or gender. Contextual influences in childhood and young adulthood have been shown to affect health throughout the lifetime. Given that trajectories are stable across time, advantages and disadvantages become more prominent as individuals age (Wethington, 2005). In the workplace, the influence of contextual factors may be seen in the generational differences regarding worker expectations of remaining with the same employer for most of one's working life.

Another important concept is the **timing of events** (Wethington, 2005). Long-lasting effects on a person may arise from events occurring during a vulnerable period (such as childhood) and can change both physical and psychological development. Being stressed during a vulnerable period can adversely impact an individual's ability to adapt to external demands for change for many decades.

The concept of **linked** or **interdependent lives** is concerned with how the development of an individual is affected by the influence or presence of others (Wethington, 2005). For example, younger construction workers report that they often feel pressured into adopting less safe work practices by older colleagues who have "always done it that way" (Flynn & Sampson, 2012).

The final concept discussed in Wethington's (2005) review of the life course perspective is **adaptive strategies**. These are approaches used by individuals to improve their lifestyle or well-being by better adapting to external changes. Ultimately, it is expected that individuals will make decisions to maximize personal gain while minimizing any personal loss.

A Life Course Perspective on Immigrant Occupational Health

It is estimated that 3% of the world population, nearly 191 million people, are international immigrants (United Nations, 2009. The majority (60%) of international immigrants move to economically developed countries. The US hosts the largest number of international immigrants, 38.4 million or approximately 13% of its total population. Approximately 9% of the population of Europe are international immigrants, with the largest numbers of immigrants being hosted by Russia (12.1 million), Germany (10.1 million), Ukraine (6.8 million), France (6.5 million), and the UK (5.4 million). Refugees account for only 7% of all international immigrants. Consequently, it would appear that the majority of international immigrants are motivated by a desire for economic betterment.

Many immigrants experience significant pressures to find and keep a job. For unauthorized immigrants, finding employment can pose such challenges that they are willing to accept jobs, wages, and working conditions that workers with more options would find unacceptable (Orrenius & Zavodny, 2009). Hudson (2007) found evidence that in the US, citizenship status accounts for more variance in predicting an individual's occupation than any other variable. Consequently, significant occupational health disparities can exist between immigrant workers and native-born workers. Researchers have found that Latin American immigrants working in the US have significantly higher rates of work-related injury and mortalities than native-born workers (Loh & Richardson, 2004; Richardson, Ruser & Suarez, 2003). Within the construction industry, Latin American immigrant workers were fatally injured at two to three times the rate of native-born workers doing the same jobs (Dong & Platner, 2004).

Employers in host countries will remain challenged for decades to come to optimally incorporate immigrants into the workforce. Application of the life course perspective to immigration holds the potential to both enrich such research efforts and provides a much needed theoretical paradigm to guide them. The concepts of trajectories, transitions, context, linkages, and adaption can easily be used to frame concerns that are central to the immigrant experience. The impact and scope of the stressors related to immigration is succinctly summarized in the term *culture shock*, coined by Furnham and Bochner (1986) to refer to the abruptness of change and the magnitude of emotional violence that can be associated with adapting to an unfamiliar environment.

Trajectory

The most frequently studied *trajectory* experienced by immigrants is *acculturation*, the overall process of adapting to life in a new country (Williams & Berry, 1991). Immigration can involve changes in ways of doing business, the use of technology, social interactions, and political activities. For the individual, acculturation can involve changes (*transitions*) in behavior, attitudes, beliefs, and self-image, giving rise to *adaptive strategies*. The term *acculturative stress* refers to the toll the individual pays in adapting to a new environment. For many immigrants, the workplace is the primary domain in which they must interact with the culture of the host country. This can easily add to the already signifi-cant stressors associated with acclimating to a new job.

Turning points

Within the life course perspective, the term *turning point* is used to describe transi-tions of such magnitude as to be immediately life changing. Perhaps the greatest turning point experienced by many undocumented immigrants is the experience of border crossing. Although many unauthorized international immigrants first enter their host countries using legal mechanisms such as a student or tourist visa (De Haas, 2008), many others go across international borders in ways that are life-threatening.

De Haas (2008) reports an unfortunate parallel between African migration to Europe and Latin American migration to the US. When attempting to cross the Mediterranean Sea from North Africa to Europe, boats carrying immigrants frequently sink in route due to poor maintenance or overloading. In North America, many Latin American immigrants cross its southern border in areas so remote that several days of hiking across a desert are required. They risk dying from exposure to the elements. Immigrants using the services of human smugglers may actually find the dangers of the border crossing increased. Immigrants are often abandoned in the desert by their guides at the least sign of trouble. Some are forced to assist with smuggling of drugs into the US. Female migrants face being coerced into exchanging sexual favors for preferential treat-ment or simply being raped (Eggerth, DeLaney, Flynn & Jacobson, 2012). The trauma of the border crossing experience is so extreme that after 5+ years later, it remained the number one stressor reported by a sample of Latin American immigrants to the US (Eggerth, 2007). Although acknowledged as important by immigrants, workplace hazards pale in comparison to the border crossing experience, thereby significantly increasing the challenges associated with implementing an effective occupational safety and health intervention with this group.

Cultural and contextual influences

As might well be expected, the life course perspective concepts of *cultural and contextual influences* are of great relevance to framing the immigrant experience. Of the cultural barriers immigrants face in adapting to their new home, language is perhaps the largest and, certainly, the most obvious. The inability to communicate in routine situations central to daily living, such as finding a place to live or speaking with a supervisor, can be a significant source of stress. In communities hosting large numbers of immigrants, it is not uncommon for social service agencies to offer language courses. Unfortunately, many immigrants are unable to take advantage of these offerings due to time constraints or poor academic preparation (Eggerth, DeLaney, Flynn & Jacobson, 2012). Attempting to learn another language with little or no academic knowledge of one's native tongue can increase the challenge of learning a second language to the point that many frustrated immigrants give up. Employers frequently use the most bilingual of their immigrant employees to serve as a communication conduit. This practice gives that individual significant power over their peers as they control the dialogue between workers and supervisors. Unscrupulous individuals can use this control to improve their own work conditions at the expense of their immigrant peers – all without the knowledge of the employer.

In addition to learning a new language, immigrants are forced to discover the common practices, shared meanings, and range of acceptable responses to daily situations in their host country. It is important to recognize that cultural differences impact workplaces as well as the broader society. For example, there may be signifi-cant differences between home and host countries regarding the proper relationship between worker and employer or how one should address workplace problems. When addressing culture, it is important to not only account for how immigrants deal with cultural differences between their home and host countries but also the receptiveness of the host country to immigrants.

Adapting to life in a new country is stressful under the best of circumstances. However, these efforts are often further frustrated by the legal, sociocultural, and political conditions of the host country. Many countries will often limit an immi-grant's ability to fully participate or integrate into society. These exclusions can range from ineligibility for benefits such as state-sponsored healthcare programs to barring immigrants or their children from becoming citizens. The most extreme example of restrictions on participation is the categorization of individuals as "illegal" which results in a class of immigrants living in a constant state of vulnerability and fear of deportation (De Genova, 2002). This vulnerability is heightened during times of increased immigration enforcement, usually during economic downturns, often coinciding with increased political rhetoric and legislation. Undocumented status can give rise to chronic stress among immigrants who live in constant fear of depor-tation (Berk & Schur, 2001). The routine targeting of undocumented immigrants in the host country not only presents an immediate physical and psychological threat to an individual's health but also results in an ongoing sense of alienation. Many undocumented immigrants believe they have fewer rights than they actually do and therefore do not take advantage of the resources legally available to them, thereby increasing their isolation, exploitability, and psychological distress (Flynn, 2010). Cavazos-Rehg, Zayas and Spitznagel (2007) reported that 39% of their sample of Latin American immigrants stated they did not visit social or government agencies due to deportation fears.

One particularly important example of a contextual feature is access to healthcare. Limited access to healthcare is a widespread if not global concern for immigrants (Casteneda, 2008, 2009; Eggerth, DeLaney, Flynn & Jacobson, 2012; Sinnerbrink et al., 1997). In countries with a fee-for-service healthcare delivery model, most individuals are covered by health insurance plans provided through employers. Many immigrants, particularly the unauthorized, work in low-paying, dangerous, or otherwise undesirable jobs that typically do not offer health insurance to employees, regardless of nativity. However, some employers, who otherwise might have offered health insurance to their workers, take advantage of unauthorized immigrants and do not do so with them. In addition, Heyman, Nunez and Talavera (2009) found that unauthorized status creates a web of direct (i.e., ineligibility for government social assistance programs) and indirect (i.e., limited mobility arising from fear of deportation) barriers to accessing healthcare. Eggerth, DeLaney, Flynn and Jacobson (2012) report instances of workers being denied time off to seek medical attention, even for work-related injuries. An immigrant worker who misses work for a medical condition, even one that is work related, is typically not paid for any time off work and risks being fired. Consequently, many immigrants work through injuries or illnesses, attempting to self-treat or hide medical problems from employers. Casteneda (2008, 2009, 2010) reported that in countries having national healthcare programs, unauthorized immigrants may experience even greater difficulties accessing healthcare because healthcare providers are mandated to report individuals not registered with the national system.

Adaptive strategies

Although *adaptation* is at the heart of the acculturation process, there is little in the literature directly addressing decision-making strategies. Rather, the studies have tended to concern correlates of acculturative stress. Clearly, the quality of these outcomes is predicated upon a host of decisions regarding how much of the host country's culture to embrace and how much of one's home country's to leave behind. Unfortunately, most studies have focused on outcomes and leave one needing to extrapolate backward to hypothesize exactly how this end was reached. It is clear that higher levels of acculturation are often associated with greater economic opportunities and less friction with the members of the host culture (Nwadiora & McAdoo, 1996; Shen & Takeuchi, 2001). However, higher levels of acculturation are also associated with higher levels of acculturative stress. Highly acculturated individuals can become alienated from family and friends and experience a loss of self-integration as new values and beliefs replace or come into conflict with the old. Hovey (2000) reported findings suggesting that family closeness, hopefulness for the future, and financial resources might buffer the impact of acculturative stressors among Mexican immigrants to the US.

In a study of immigrants from the former Soviet Union to the US, Aroian, Norris, Patsdaughter and Tran (1998) found that immigrants who were female, older, or more poorly educated or had poorer English language skills suffered higher levels of acculturative stress. Similarly, Ritsner, Ponizovsky, Nechamkin and Modai (2001) found female immigrants from the former Soviet Union to Israel tended to experience higher levels of acculturative stress than males. In a different study of immigrants from the former Soviet Union to Israel, Ritsner and Ponizovsky (1999) found distress experienced by the immigrants increased until 27 months following their arrival. At that point, stress levels began to diminish and continued to do so until at least the end of the fifth year following arrival.

One important implication for employers is to realize that immigrant employees will likely take far longer to settle into new jobs and communities than native-born workers. Consequently, employers may find it helpful to go to extra lengths to make such employees feel welcomed, understood, and supported.

Transitions

Research focusing on the component aspects or sequencing of the acculturation process frequently addresses topics that would be considered *transitions* within the life course perspective. Although it is easy to see how failures at understanding and adapting to a new culture can increase distress, success can also be stressful and challenge one's beliefs requiring changes or reinterpretations of deeply held expectations and patterns of behavior. Menjivar (1999) found that although Central American women perceived greater opportunities for work and experienced a higher self-esteem since migrating to the US, they also reported an uncomfortable disequilibrium regarding traditional gender roles. Specifically, their newfound economic independence challenged the traditional role of husband as provider, which sometimes gave rise to demeaning or violent behavior from their husbands' attempts to maintain or reestablish the traditional masculine role in the family.

Linked lives

Although many international immigrants move seeking greater economic opportunities, this betterment often comes with attendant costs. First among these is the cost of immigration itself. For many, this expense was paid with the pooled resources of the entire family. Those not having access to liquid assets often use property as collateral. Most families not only need to be repaid but also expect to share the economic benefits experienced by the immigrant in the form of *remittances*, money sent to family remaining in one's home country. For some countries, remittances are a major source of foreign exchange earnings and are a significant portion of the gross domestic product (United Nations, 2009). Unauthorized immigrants sometimes owe large amounts to the criminal organizations that smuggled them across international borders. Failing to repay these organizations can lead to loss of collateral property, as well as violence directed at both immigrants and their family members.

Family stressors

For many international immigrants, moving to a new country means separation from family and friends for an extended period of time (Grzywacz *et al.*, 2006). It may be years before they are prosperous enough to afford to visit their home countries. Unauthorized immigrants and refugees can face even greater obstacles. Unauthorized immigrants are unable to travel freely across international borders. Consequently, time between visits home is frequently greater and is complicated by the need to undergo another illegal border crossing on their return to their host country.

Many refugees despair of ever being reunited with their families (Sinnerbrink *et al.*, 1997; Steel *et al.*, 1999). For refugees, particularly those fleeing war zones or political persecution, communication with family members at home can be very difficult. The conditions that led them to seek asylum may make their return home unlikely or impossible. In addition, there is the constant concern that these same conditions are adversely impacting family members left behind.

For immigrants leaving spouses and children behind, there can be considerable pressure to reunite the families, either at home or in their host country (Eggerth, DeLaney, Flynn & Jacobson, 2012). Even when entire families are able to immigrate, there are significant stressors related to acculturation both as individuals and as a family group (Rogler, 1994). Sometimes, the individual viewed as being the prime force behind the family's immigration is held responsible by the remainder of the family for any negative consequences arising from the move. Further complicating the family dynamic are *mixed-status families*, in which at least one parent is unauthorized and at least one child is a citizen by virtue of being born within the country of residence or from having a parent who is either a citizen or a legal resident of that country (Castaneda, 2008). In the US, the majority (over 80%) of unauthorized families with children are mixed-status families (Passel, 2006). In a mixed-status family, the "citizen members" are eligible for state-sponsored social assistance programs and have far greater opportunities for education and employment. These differential advantages can undermine the basic sense of equality among siblings in the family and challenges the parental role as provider and protector. Children often acculturate faster than parents. This can lead to stress as family roles are reversed and parents come to depend on children to orient them in situations that would be considered routine in their home country, such as medical appointments or parent–teacher conferences. However, as Grzywacz, Quandt, Arcury and Marin (2005) report, stress related to family, while significant, is still likely to be lower than the stressors related to seeking employment and sending remittances home.

Mental health

Perhaps no area cuts across so many life course perspective concept areas as that of mental health. It is important that the differences of scope and/or kind of mental health concerns between economic immigrants and those who are refugees from conflict and/or oppression be recognized. Consequently, the following discussion refers to economic immigrants, and a separate section will discuss the unique concerns of refugees.

A paradoxical finding in the literature is the very different mental health trajectories experienced by immigrants to Europe and those to the US. Immigrants to Europe experience more mental health problems than the European population in general and, over time and across generations, tend to get better. Immigrants to the US tend to experience the opposite trajectory.

Vega, Sribney, Aguilar-Gaxiola and Kolody (2004) found that the prevalence of psychiatric disorders among Latin American immigrants to the US is less than half that of the general population in the US. Factors that increase the risk of a psychiatric disorder among Latin American immigrants have been identified. Some of these findings can be related to the life course perspective concept of timing in lives. For example, poor mental health outcomes are negatively associated with age at time of immigration and positively associated with length of time living in the US. It has been suggested by some that these findings reflect what has been dubbed the "healthy immigrant" effect (Vega, Sribney, Aguilar-Gaxiola & Kolody, 2004). This effect hypothesizes that typically it is the most physically and mentally healthy individuals who have the motivation and wherewithal to undertake the arduous challenges inherent to immigration. This represents a variation on the sampling bias plaguing most health outcome studies – the individuals most likely to participate in such a study are already the healthiest and the most health-minded individuals in the study population. In the occupational health literature, this is commonly referred to as the "healthy worker effect" (Li & Sung, 1999).

In any event, being a "healthy immigrant" is likely not genetic in origin as these differences begin to disappear within a generation following immigration, with the children and grandchildren of immigrants suffering psychiatric disorders at the same rate with the general population of the US (Alegria *et al.*, 2007). Vega, Sribney, Aguilar-Gaxiola and Kolody (2004) report that epidemiological studies conducted in Mexico indicate lower rates of mental illnesses as compared to the US, lending support for their argument that increasing rates of psychiatric disorders in the Mexican immigrant population can be attributed to acculturative stress. Hovey and King (1997) reached similar conclusions regarding the higher levels of suicide among Mexican immigrants to the US as compared to Mexicans remaining at home.

One argument against the "healthy immigrant" effect is that most international immigrants are among the "best and brightest" of their home countries (De Haas, 2008), and yet in Europe, researchers have found significantly higher rates of psychiatric problems among immigrant groups when compared to the host country's general population (Hutchinson & Haasen, 2004). A study comparing elderly Somali and Bengali immigrants with elderly white British living in the same London neighborhood found that the Bengalis were three times more likely to experience depression than Somalis or white British and both the Bengalis and Somalis reported significantly lower levels of life satisfaction than the white British (Silveira & Ebrahim, 1998). Hutchinson and Haasen (2004) reported that Caribbean immigrants to both the UK and the Netherlands experience significantly higher rates of schizophrenia than the general populations of these countries. They report that in the UK, these increased rates persist for several generations following immigration. In contrast, a study of black Caribbean immigrants to the US found lower lifetime rates of psychiatric disorders than in the general population (Williams *et al.*, 2007). However, as with Mexican immigrants, rates increased with each succeeding generation in the US. Zolkowska, Cantor-Graae and McNeil (2001) reported increased rates of psychosis among immigrants to Sweden with the highest rates occurring among immigrants from Asia and Africa. In a study of Southeast Asian, Pacific Island, and British immigrants to New Zealand, Pernice and Brook (1996) found elevated levels of depression and anxiety among the Asians and

Pacific Islanders. They related these findings to the discrimination experienced by these immigrants in nearly all life settings outside of the home. The British immigrants reported no discrimination. Indeed, they felt their social status has been enhanced since immigration. These findings suggest the important role cultural and contextual influences can have on outcomes.

If one considers the difficulties inherent to cross-cultural investigations of mental illness, it is not surprising that findings have been mixed. In addition to questions regarding the appropriateness of applying psychiatric criteria developed in the First World to individuals from vastly different cultural backgrounds, there are a host of practical difficulties, many related to simply overcoming barriers of language. In most host countries, there are not enough healthcare providers who speak the language(s) of the immigrants they serve. Consequently, many rely upon a family member or another member of the immigrant community to translate communications between healthcare providers and patients. In addition to cultural and contextual influences, this touches upon the concept of linked lives and of transitions. The latter concept is of particular importance as children are often required to serve as the communication link between parents and healthcare providers, thereby upsetting traditional family hierarchy.

The use of standardized questionnaires to assess aspects of the immigrant experience has the potential to eliminate some sources of bias, but new problem areas arise. It has long been accepted practice to develop alternate language forms of an existing instrument through the process of translation and back-translation by individuals who speak both languages. Most researchers assume that the psychometric properties of the original version will survive translation into another language. Unfortunately, the individuals doing the translation are typically more assimilated into Western culture and far better educated than the individuals who will be assessed. Consequently, one risks developing a questionnaire that contains unexamined cultural assumptions and is written at a level too high for most immigrants to fully comprehend. Flynn, Lawson, Eggerth and Jacobson (2008) reported that poorly educated Latin American immigrants to the US understood significant portions of a widely used questionnaire addressing physical and mental health needs in a manner very different than intended without either interviewer or interviewee realizing this was so. Follow-up cognitive testing of questionnaire items was needed to reveal this unhappy truth. Brunette (2005) suggested that the development of materials intended for use with immigrants should be an iterative and a collaborative process involving researchers, translators, and members of the immigrant community. The work of Fujishiro et al. (2010) found that following Brunette's suggestions did not eliminate the need for cognitive testing to ensure conceptual, as well as linguistic, equivalence of translations.

Refugees

As might be expected, studies conducted with immigrants fleeing situations involving extremes of deprivation, violence, and/or persecution have consistently found them to be at elevated risk for stress-related disorders such as posttraumatic stress disorder (PTSD). These research findings are particularly relevant to the life course perspective areas of turning points and timing in lives.

Research has been conducted with a range of different refugee groups in a number of different host countries. Mollica *et al.* (2001) reported that 45% of a sample of 528 Bosnian refugees then living in Croatia met the diagnostic criteria for depression alone, PTSD alone, or both together. In follow-up interviews conducted 3 years later, 28% of a sample of 222 still met the diagnostic criteria for one or both maladies. Marshall *et al.* (2005) conducted a study of 490 Cambodian refugees two decades after resettlement in the US. They found high rates of both PTSD (62%) and major depression (42%) among members of this sample. Neuner *et al.* (2004) reported that in a sample of 77 Sudanese refugees living in Uganda, 44 (56%) met the diagnostic criteria for PTSD. Indeed, PTSD was so prevalent in a sample of Vietnamese ex-political detainees, now in the US, that the researchers were able to identify a dose–response relationship between trauma and psychiatric symptoms (Mollica *et al.*, 1998). In a large study of Vietnamese refugees resettled in Australia, researchers found similar results (Steel, Silove, Phan & Bauman, 2002). It should be noted that trauma is not exclusive to refugees. In a sample of Latin American immigrants to the US who were not identified as refugees, Holman, Silver and Waitzkin (2000) found that well over half had experienced significant traumas. Among some Central American immigrants groups, they found as many as 76% had experienced traumas.

Sinnerbrink *et al.* (1997) argued that the increasingly stringent restrictions placed upon asylum seekers in Western countries have the potential to exacerbate the traumas of these immigrants. In a study of Mandaean refugees in Australia, Steel *et al.* (2006) found significant relationships between length of detention and the risk of ongoing PTSD and/or depression that persisted for several years after release. In a study of Tamil immigrants in Australia, Steel *et al.* (1999) found that 14% of the variance in PTSD symptoms could be attributed to postmigration stressors as compared to 20% of the variance attributable to premigration traumas.

This review of the immigrant mental health literature suggests that it is important for the employers of immigrants, particularly those who are refugees, to understand that these individuals may face ongoing challenges that will not necessarily be alleviated by mastering a new language or becoming familiar with local customs. Supervisory, human resources, and employee assistance program professionals may all require additional training to sensitize them to these special needs. In particular, it must be recognized that for some of these concerns, time does not always heal, but can actually worsen outcomes.

Summary

This chapter proposed the application of the life course perspective to the study of immigrant occupational health in order to correct psychology's tendency to ignore the time and contextual dimensions and use primarily static cross-sectional designs with decontextualized variables. Wethington's (2005) formulation of the life-span perspective across the concepts of trajectories, transitions, context, linkages, and adaption strategies was used to frame our study of the immigrant experience and illustrate how such a perspective can enrich a program of research as well as provide a much needed theoretical model to guide such research. The discussion of this paradigm provided specific examples of how application of the life course perspective can enhance understanding of the occupational health of immigrants and move us from a variable-centered approach to the person-centered approach.

What is needed next are research studies which incorporate the measurements of these dimensions of trajectories, transitions, context, and linkages to determine if they provide incremental validity above the traditional cross-sectional studies of immigrant occupational health. These studies should also help us identify important sub-group differences among immigrants due to differential life course dynamics which will ultimately help us design prevention and intervention programs with greater clinical utility and effectiveness.

In the pursuit of clarity of definition and rigor of measurement, research in psychology has increasingly sacrificed directly addressing the depth, interrelatedness, and richness of human experiences such as immigration. Although such an approach is more easily funded and published, it is not necessarily better or more relevant science. The life course perspective embraces the complexity, the interrelatedness, and, dare we say, the "messiness" of life that current psychology too often attempts to avoid, control, or contain. The challenges inherent to conceptualizing research within such a model represent the spirit, if not the essence, of developing a *nomological net* around one's research concepts, as advocated by Cronbach and Meehl (1955) in their classic work on construct validity. Consequently, the life course perspective does not ask psychology researchers to enter uncharted methodological waters, but rather to embrace more tightly a decades-old "best practice" of our discipline.

References

Alegria, M., Mulvaney-Day, N., Torres, M., Polo, A., Chao, Z., & Canino, G. (2007). Prevalence of psychiatric disorders across Latino subgroups in the United States. *American Journal of Public Health, 97*, 68–75.

Aroian, K. J., Norris, A. E., Patsdaughter, C. A., & Tran, T. V. (1998). Predicting psychological distress among former Soviet immigrants. *International Journal of Social Psychiatry, 44*, 284–294.

Baltes, P. B. (1987). Theoretical propositions of life-span developmental psychology on the dynamics between growth and decline. *Developmental Psychology, 23*(5), 611–626.

Ben-Shlomo, Y., & Kuh, D. (2002). A life course approach to chronic disease epidemiology: Conceptual models, empirical challenges and interdisciplinary perspectives. *International Journal of Epidemiology, 31*, 285–293.

Berk, M. L., & Schur, C. L. (2001). The effect of fear on access to care among undocumented Latino immigrants. *Journal of Immigrant Health, 3*, 151–156.

Block, J. (1971). *Lives through time.* Berkeley, CA: Bancroft.

Brunette, M. (2005). Development of educational and training materials on safety and health: Targeting Hispanic workers in the construction industry. *Family & Community Health*, *28*, 253–266.

Castaneda, H. (2008). Paternity for sale: Anxieties over "demographic theft" and undocumented migrant reproduction in Germany. *Medical Anthropology Quarterly*, *22*, 340–359.

Casteneda, H. (2009). Illegality as risk factor: A survey of unauthorized migrant patients in a Berlin clinic. *Social Science & Medicine*, *68*, 1552–1560.

Casteneda, H. (2010). Immigration ad health: Conceptual, methodological, and theoretical propositions for applied anthropology. *NAPA Bulletin*, *34*, 6–27.

Cavazos-Rehg, P. A., Zayas, L. H., & Spitznagel, E. L. (2007). Legal status, emotional well-being and subjective health status of Latino immigrants. *Journal of the National Medical Association*, *99*(10), 1126–1131.

Cronbach, L. J., & Meehl, P. E. (1955). Construct validity in psychological tests. *Psychological Bulletin*, *52*, 281–302.

De Genova, N. P. (2002). Migrant "illegality" and deportability in everyday life. *Annual Review of Anthropology*, *31*, 419–447.

De Haas, H. (2008). The myth of invasion: The inconvenient realities of African migration to Europe. *Third World Quarterly*, *29*, 1305–1322.

Dong, X., & Platner, J. W. (2004). Occupational fatalities of Hispanic construction workers from 1992 to 2000. *American Journal of Industrial Medicine*, *45*, 45–54.

Eggerth, D. E. (2007). *Occupational safety risk perceptions and acceptance among Hispanic immigrants in the United States*. Paper presented at the 12th International Metropolis Conference, Melbourne, Australia.

Eggerth, D. E., DeLaney, S. C., Flynn, M. A., & Jacobson, C. J. (2012). Work experiences of Latina immigrants: A qualitative study. *Journal of Career Development*, *39*(1), 13–30.

Elder, G. H., Jr. (1985). *Life course dynamics*. Ithaca, NY: Cornell University Press.

Erikson, E. H. (1950). *Childhood and society*. New York: Pelican Books.

Flynn, M. A. (2010). *Undocumented status and the occupational lifeworlds of Latino immigrants in a time of political backlash: The workers' perspective*. Master's thesis, University of Cincinnati, Cincinnati, OH. Retrieved June 9, 2011, from https://etd.ohiolink.edu/ap:0:0: APPLICATION_PROCESS=DOWNLOAD_ETD_SUB_DOC_ACCNUM:::F1501_ID: ucin1280776817,attachment.

Flynn, M. A., Lawson, R., Eggerth, D. E., & Jacobson, C. J. (2008, March 25–29). *Bloody noses, heart attacks, and other emotional problems: The importance of cognitive testing in survey adaptation and development*. Paper presented at the 68th Annual Meeting of the Society for Applied Anthropology, Memphis, TN.

Flynn, M. A., & Sampson, J. M. (2012). Trench safety – Using a qualitative approach to understand barriers and develop strategies to improve trench practices. *International Journal of Construction Education and Research*, *8*, 63–79.

Fujishiro, K., Gong, F., Baron, S., Jacobson, Jr., C. J., DeLaney, S., Flynn, M., *et al.* (2010). Translating questionnaire items for a multi-lingual worker population: The iterative process of translation and cognitive interviews with English-, Spanish-, and Chinese-speaking workers. *American Journal of Industrial Medicine*, *53*(2), 194–203.

Furnham, A., & Bochner, S. (1986). *Culture shock: Psychological reactions to unfamiliar environments*. London/New York: Methuen.

Grzywacz, J. C., Quandt, S. A., Arcury, T. A., & Marin, A. (2005). The work-family challenge and mental health: Experiences of Mexican immigrants. *Community, Work and Family*, *893*, 271–279.

Grzywacz, J. C., Quandt, S. A., Early, J., Tapia, J., Graham, C. N., & Arcury, T. A. (2006). Leaving family for work: Ambivalence and mental health among Mexican migrant farmworker men. *Journal of Immigrant and Minority Health, 8*(1), 85–97.

Healthcare Foundation of Greater Cincinnati, The (2006). *2005 Greater Cincinnati Hispanic/ Latino health survey*. Cincinnati, OH: Author. Retrieved November 18, 2013 from https://www.interactforhealth.org/docs/2005%20Hispanic%20Latino%20Health%20 Survey%20report.pdf

Heyman, J. M., Núñez, G. G., & Talavera, V. (2009). Healthcare access and barriers for unauthorized immigrants in El Paso County, Texas. *Family Community Health, 32*, 4–21.

Holman, E. A., Silver, R. C., & Waitzkin, H. (2000). Traumatic life events in primary care patients: A study in an ethnically diverse sample. *Archives of Family Medicine, 9*, 802–810.

Holmes, T. H., & Rahe, R. H. (1967). The social readjustment rating scale. *Journal of Psychosomatic Research, 11*(2), 213–218.

Hovery, J. D. (2000). Psychosocial predictors of acculturative stress in Mexican immigrants. *The Journal of Psychology, 134*, 490–502.

Hovey, J. D., & King, C. A. (1997). Suicidality among acculturating Mexican Americans: Current knowledge and directions for research. *Suicide and Life-Threatening Behavior, 27*, 92–103.

Hutchinson, G., & Haasen, C. (2004). Migration and schizophrenia: The challenges for European psychiatry and implications for the future. *Social Psychiatry and Psychiatric Epidemiology, 39*, 350–357.

Hudson, K. (2007). The new labor market segmentation: Labor market dualism in the new economy. *Social Science Research, 36*, 286–312.

Levinson, D. J. (1986). A conception of adult development. *American Psychologist, 41*(1), 3–13.

Li, C. Y., & Sung, F. C. (1999). A review of the healthy worker effect in occupational epidemiology. *Occupational Medicine, 49*, 225–229.

Loh, K., & Richardson, S. (2004). Foreign-born workers: Trends in fatal occupational injuries, 1996–2001. *Monthly Labor Review, 127*(6), 42–53.

Marshall, G. N., Schell, T. L., Elliot, M. N., Berthold, S. M., & Chun, C. (2005). Mental health of Cambodian refuges 2 decades after resettlement in the United States. *Journal of the American Medical Association, 294*, 571–579.

Menjívar, C. (1999). The intersection of work and gender: Central American immigrant women and employment in California. *American Behavioral Scientist, 42*, 601–627.

Moen, P. (1996). A life course perspective on retirement, gender and well-being. *Journal of Occupational Health Psychology, 1*, 131–144.

Mollica, R. F., McInnes, K., Pham, T., Smith-Fawzi, M. C., Murphy, E., & Lin, L. (1998). The dose-effect relationship between torture and psychiatric symptoms in Vietnamese ex-political detainees and a comparison group. *The Journal of Nervous and Mental Disease, 186*, 543–553.

Mollica, R. F., Sarajlic, N., Chernoff, M., Lavelle, J., Vukovic, I. S., & Massagli, M. P. (2001). Longitudinal study of psychiatric symptoms, disability, mortality, and emigration among Bosnian refugees. *Journal of the American Medical Association, 286*, 546–554.

Neuner, F., Schauer, M., Klaschik, C., Karunakara, U., & Elbert, T. (2004). A comparison of narrative exposure therapy, supportive counseling, and psychoeducation for treating posttraumatic stress disorder in an African refuges settlement. *Journal of Consulting and Clinical Psychology, 72*, 579–587.

Nwadiora, E., & McAdoo, H. (1996). Acculturative stress among Amerasian refugees: Gender and racial differences. *Adolescence, 31*, 477–487.

Orrenius, P. M., & Zavodny, M. (2009). Do immigrants work in riskier jobs? *Demography, 46*(3), 535–551.

Passel, J. (2006). *The size and characteristics of the unauthorized migrant population in the U.S. estimates based on the March 2005 current population survey.* Washington, DC: Pew Hispanic Center. Retrieved June 9, 2011, from http://pewhispanic.org/files/reports/61.pdf

Pernice, R., & Brook, J. (1996). Refugees' and immigrants' mental health: Association of demographic and post-immigration factors. *The Journal of Social Psychology, 136*, 511–519.

Richardson, S., Ruser, R., & Suarez, P. (2003). Hispanic workers in the United States: An analysis of employment distributions, fatal occupational injuries, and non-fatal occupational injuries and illnesses. In National Research Council (Eds.), *Safety is Seguridad* (pp. 43–82). Washington, DC: The National Academies.

Ritsner, M., & Ponizovsky, A. (1999). Psychological distress through immigration: The two-phase temporal pattern? *International Journal of Social Psychiatry, 42*, 125–139.

Ritsner, M., Ponizovsky, A., Nechamkin, Y., & Modai, I. (2001). Gender differences in psychological risk factors for psychological distress among immigrants. *Comprehensive Psychiatry, 42*, 151–160.

Rogler, L. H. (1994). International migrations: A framework for directing research. *American Psychologist, 49*, 701–708.

Seyle, H. (1956). *The stress of life.* New York: McGraw-Hill.

United Nations, Department of Economic and Social Affairs, Population Division (2009). *International Migration Report 2006: A Global Assessment.* New York, NY: Author.

Shen, B., & Takeuchi, D. T. (2001). A structural model of acculturation and mental health status among Chinese Americans. *American Journal of Community Psychology, 29*, 387–418.

Silveira, E. R., & Ebrahim, S. (1998). Social determinants of psychiatric morbidity and well-being in immigrant elders and whites in East London. *International Journal of Geriatric Psychiatry, 13*, 801–812.

Sinnerbrink, I., Silove, D., Field, A., Steel, Z., & Manicavasagar, V. (1997). Compounding of premigration trauma and postmigration stress in asylum seekers. *The Journal of Psychology, 131*, 463–470.

Steel, Z., Silove, D., Bird, K., McGorry, P., & Mohan, P. (1999). Pathways from war trauma to posttraumatic stress symptoms among Tamil asylum seekers, refugees, and immigrants. *Journal of Traumatic Stress, 12*, 421–435.

Steel, Z., Silove, D., Brooks, R., Momartin, S., Alzuhairi, B., & Susljik, I. (2006). Impact of immigration detention and temporary protection on mental health of refugees. *The British Journal of Psychiatry, 188*, 58–64.

Steel, Z., Silove, D., Phan, T., & Bauman, A. (2002, October 5). Long-term effect of psychological trauma on the mental health of Vietnamese refugees resettled in Australia: A population-based study. *The Lancet, 360*(9339), 1056–1062.

Vega, W. A., Sribney, W. M., Aguilar-Gaxiola, S., & Kolody, B. (2004). 12-month prevalence of DSM-III-R psychiatric disorders among Mexican Americans: Nativity, social assimilation, and age determinants. *The Journal of Nervous and Mental Disease, 192*, 532–541.

Wethington, E. (2005). An overview of the life course perspective: Implications for health and nutrition. *Journal of Nutrition Education and Behavior, 37*, 115–120.

Williams, C. C. (2003). Re-reading the IPSS research record. *Social Science and Medicine, 56(3)*, 501–515.

Williams, C. L., & Berry, J. W. (1991). Primary prevention of acculturative stress among refugees. *American Psychologist, 46*, 632–641.

Williams, D. R., Haile, R., Gonzalez, H. M., Neighbors, H., Baser, R., & Jackson, J. S. (2007). The mental health of black Caribbean immigrants: Results from the National Survey of American Life. *American Journal of Public Health, 97*, 52–59.

Zimbardo, P. G., & Boyd, J. N. (1999). Putting time in perspective: A valid, reliable individual-differences metric. *Journal of Personality and Social Psychology, 77*, 1271–1288.

Zolkowska, K., Cantor-Graae, E., & McNeil, T. F. (2001). Increased rates of psychosis among immigrants to Sweden: Is migration a risk factor for psychosis? *Psychological Medicine, 31*, 669–678.

8

Meaningfulness as a Resource to Mitigate Work Stress

Sharon Glazer[1]
University of Maryland, Center for Advanced Study of Language, USA

Malgorzata W. Kozusznik[2]
University of Valencia, Spain

Jacob H. Meyers
American Psychological Association, USA

Omar Ganai
University of Waterloo, Canada

For decades, psychologists have been searching to answer *why* some people develop strains, but others do not, when faced with the same stressors; philosophers and theologians have been chasing an answer for millennia. The answer that seemed to prevail 2000 years ago was faith (Rivera, n.d.). Faith, seeking enlightenment, and finding something to work for or look forward to seem to have been and continue to be a plausible explanation for why some people who face stressors interpret them as challenges to overcome or opportunities to seize, whereas others interpret stressors as threats. Anecdotally, it appears that meaningfulness in life has real and practical consequences for individuals and society.

The notion of meaningfulness in life is not new to the psychological literature. Viktor Frankl (1963), in *Man's Search for Meaning*, provides accounts of prisoners of war during the Holocaust who died very shortly after giving up on life. He wrote that those who kept living (as long as the Nazis did not take them first) for some real or imagined purpose did so despite their emaciated and tormented bodies. Frankl reminds us that "he who has a *why* to live for can bear almost any *how*" (p. 84).

[1] University of Baltimore, USA
[2] University of Exeter, UK.

Contemporary Occupational Health Psychology: Global Perspectives on Research and Practice, Volume 3,
First Edition. Edited by Stavroula Leka and Robert R. Sinclair.
© 2014 John Wiley & Sons, Ltd. Published 2014 by John Wiley & Sons, Ltd.

Moreover, he noted that everyone's purpose was unique to them and that this purpose could be found only if individuals exercised their personal responsibility in actualizing this meaning through concrete action(s) (Frankl, 1963). Popular literature, for example, *The Secret* (Byrne, 2006) and *The Last Lecture* (Pausch & Zaslow, 2008), also conveys the importance of finding purpose, fulfillment, and meaningfulness in life to make our lives feel more complete. Still, it is scientifically unclear if people who have a greater sense of meaningfulness are more resilient to stressors, and thus less susceptible to strains, than people whose lives are meaningless.

Over the past decade, scholars (e.g., Mascaro & Rosen, 2008; Pines, 2004a, b) have returned to existential philosophical roots to understand how meaningfulness in life might affect stressor–strain relationships. Pines (2004b) reminds us that the need to believe that our lives are meaningful and important (i.e., we serve a purpose greater than ourselves) helps to mitigate the effects of stressors on strains. In agreement with Pines (2004b), we propose that meaningfulness buffers against stressors' deleterious effects on strain and burnout. Furthermore, in concert with Schnell (2010), we assert that culture influences individuals' sense of meaningfulness.

Significance of Meaningfulness Research

Schnell (2010) reported that between 4% and 7% of a representative sample of Germans 16–85 years of age and a sample of German students, respectively, experienced low meaningfulness. This equates to roughly 2.8–4.8 million Germans.[1] Moreover, 35% and 37%, respectively (or about 24.8 million), were existentially indifferent; they "neither experience[d] their lives as meaningful nor suffer[ed] from this lack of meaning" (p. 363). To better contextualize the above figures, in general, 9% of adult Germans suffer from depression (Cynkar & English, 2011). These numbers are significantly lower than rates of Americans who suffer from depression (17%), probably even major depression, which afflicts approximately 14.8 million American adults (NIMH, n.d.).

As with depression, people who lack meaningfulness in life are more prone to substance abuse, think about committing suicide, feel less in control of their lives, and feel disengaged, depressed, disconnected, alienated, burned out, and lower general mental well-being (Debats, Drost & Hansen, 1995; Mascaro & Rosen, 2008; Newcomb & Harlow, 1986; Pines, 2004b). Existentially indifferent individuals, however, were no different in terms of anxiety and depression from those with high meaningfulness, but their mood and life satisfaction were significantly lower (Schnell, 2010).

In this chapter, we define stress and meaningfulness. This is followed by a literature review of theories and individual difference constructs that support our contention that meaningfulness plays an important role in mitigating stress. We further consider cultural implications of meaningfulness in life on the relationships between stressors and strains, as well as the role of the workplace in providing resources and opportunities for individuals to pursue goals in an effort to create meaningfulness.

Stress

Stress refers to a process by which people perceive and respond to environmental demands, opportunities, and constraints (i.e., stressors) that might lead to strains (Lazarus & Folkman, 1984). Individual differences, including how people appraise stressors, will determine when stressors yield strains. When a person appraises a stressor as a threat, she/he anticipates experiencing harm. A root of this perception is lack of self-efficacy to overcome the stressor and achieve desired goals. This sense of threat may deteriorate human performance and impede mental processes and provoke work dissatisfaction, turnover intentions, decreased well-being, and burnout (Peiró, Gonzalez-Romá, Tordera & Mañas, 2001). When a person appraises a stressor as a *challenge*, the person focuses on a potential gain or growth, which is typically associated with eagerness, excitement, and exhilaration. The person believes that he or she has potential and opportunities for overcoming barriers. Thus, the meaning given to a stressor may be partly related to what is meaningful to a person.

Meaningfulness

Meaningfulness refers to the amount of significance a life experience holds for the individual and varies from person to person (Pratt & Ashforth, 2003). Mascaro and Rosen (2008) define it as "the possession of a coherent framework for viewing life that provides a sense of purpose or direction, which, if lived with in accord, can bring about a sense of fulfillment" (p. 578). A purpose in life is a psychological state of creating or defining goals that carry meaning for a person. When people have purpose in life, they focus their energy on activities that help them maintain that state and fulfill their goals while also acting to overcome barriers that threaten goal fulfillment.

Psychological research suggests numerous benefits for people who feel their life is worth living. People who report meaning in life are better able to cope with stressors (Mascaro & Rosen, 2008). They feel more connected with others and are happier, more spiritual, more hopeful, and actively engaged in life (Auhagen & Holub, 2006; Debats, Drost & Hansen, 1995; Mascaro & Rosen, 2008). Finally, they are more likely to experience feelings of vitality and undergo self-actualization (Ryff & Singer, 1998). Personal well-being notwithstanding, Peterson, Park, Hall and Seligman (2009) reported that *zest*, a recurring approach to live life with enthusiasm, drive, and excitement, correlates with job satisfaction. This suggests that meaningfulness can also drive one to attain organizational goals. In sum, a life full of meaning and purpose relates to many positive life outcomes and is generally characterized by a healthy level of interest and engagement with the world.

Sense of purpose

Having a sense of purpose plays a pivotal role in the construction of the meaning and meaningfulness of work through its ability to connect present events to future anticipated events and states (Baumeister & Vohs, 2002). Work experiences can reinforce a sense that an individual's actions are purposeful and moving him or her closer to fulfilling desired future goals (Bunderson & Thompson, 2009). Sense of purpose is described as a sense of directedness and intentionality in life and an individual's identification of, and intention to pursue, particular highly valued, over-arching life goals (Damon, Menon & Bronk, 2003). Like goals, sense of purpose is a motivational construct that is defined by a desire to obtain a specific state, ability, or relationship (Elliot, 2006); however, goals tend to be relatively short in time, while purpose must last longer. Sense of purpose is a source of structure that unites an individual's actions over several discrete periods in the service of longer-term missions (Steger & Dik, 2010). It serves to bridge people from where they are now to the achievement of their future aspirations and accomplishments (Emmons, 2003). According to Frankl (1963), having a sense of purpose is so fundamental that people will not survive long without it. Sources that create a sense of purpose range from internally driven motivations or goals to externally or spiritually driven sense of purpose that one feels compelled or called to fulfill (Grant, 2008; Wrzesniewski, Dutton & Debebe, 2003).

Motivational Theories Supporting the Role of Meaningfulness

Self-determination theory

While having a purpose in life necessitates having goals to pursue, a person with goals does not necessarily lead a life with purpose (Ryan, Huta & Deci, 2008). In order to have purpose, the goals must align with personal sources of meaning (Schnell, 2010). Thus, goals that satisfy basic psychological needs help create meaning. These needs are:

1. *Autonomy*: need to exercise free will and feel volition in their behavior,
2. *Relatedness*: need for feeling close and connected to valued others, and
3. *Competence*: need for feeling effective and competent in one's behavior.

These basic psychological needs form the basis for self-determination theory (Deci & Ryan, 2000). When blocked from fulfilling these needs and pursuits are extrinsically motivated, people are likely to be unhappy and to want to leave their workplace (Vansteenkiste *et al.*, 2007). Likewise, Sagiv and Schwartz (2000) contend there are healthy values that promote well-being and unhealthy values that increase ill-being. A healthy value might be self-transcendence, that is, living life in pursuit of goals that are important for one's in-group or society (Schnell, 2010).

Values theory

Peterson, Park and Seligman (2005) concluded that living a happy life requires one to live in accordance with one's values. Living true to one's inner self ensures one has a meaningful life (Seligman, 2002). However, pursuing one's own hedonic pleasures does not necessarily promote well-being, because the person is focused on himself or herself instead of his or her relationship with others (Schnell, 2010).

In the following, we describe other values that might provide a stronger foundation for meaningfulness in life.

Human values are guiding principles in life ranked according to importance and internalized through cognitive development (Sagiv & Schwartz, 2000). Values serve as motivating factors that help people satisfy their biological and social welfare needs in a socially acceptable manner to promote effective coordination among individuals in social groups. Values might relate to meaningfulness in life because they (1) provide a *cognitive* framework that answers the question "What makes my life worth living?", (2) compel people to act toward satisfying them (i.e., they are *motivational*), and (3) can provide positive *affective* experiences once they are realized. However, certain values will more likely foster the psychological experience of purpose in life than will others.

Sagiv and Schwartz (2000) proposed that human values can be divided along a self-enhancement – a self-transcendence dimension and an openness to change – conservation dimension. Self-enhancement values include power, achievement, and hedonism because they emphasize the pursuit of self-interest. Individuals who value power want social status and prestige as well as control and dominance over resources and people. Pursuing power might involve taking advantage of or mistreating others, but more positively, it involves fulfillment of personal desires (Schwartz & Bardi, 2001). In contrast, the end goal of achievement is personal success through demonstrating competence according to social standards. Finally, hedonism is about the gratification of personal desires and sensuous pleasure.

Self-transcendence values include benevolence and universalism values and emphasize concern for the welfare and interest of others. An individual endorsing benevolence values (i.e., honesty, loyalty, helpfulness, forgiveness, responsibility) will generally enhance the welfare of someone they know and with whom they have a relationship. Individuals with universalism values (i.e., social justice, wisdom, broadminded, equality, a world at peace, protecting the environment) will focus and enhance the welfare of all others and nature, most significantly on those outside the person's own in-group (Schwartz & Bardi, 2001).

Openness to change values include self-direction, stimulation, and hedonism values (Schwartz & Bardi, 2001). These value types emphasize self-interests in pursuit of a varied, exciting, and independent life. Endorsement of self-direction values (e.g., creativity, choosing own goals, and self-respect), stimulation values (e.g., daring and exciting life), and hedonism values (e.g., pleasure and enjoying life) typically motivate personal pursuits that enhance an individual's quality of life without consideration of how those pursuits affect others. In contrast, conservation values reflect security, tradition, and conformity values (Schwartz & Bardi, 2001). Someone who endorses security values (e.g., national and family security, social order, cleanliness, sense of belonging), conformity values (e.g., obedience, politeness, and honor), and tradition values (e.g., respect for tradition) will generally display emotions, behave, and think in ways that conserve one's place in the group environment, without destabilizing the *status quo* and routine.

Both self-transcendence and conservation values should be more conducive for experiencing meaningfulness in life. Self-transcendence values reinforce healthy interest and engagement with the world, reaching beyond the self and connecting with others. One can achieve meaningfulness when individuals are able to view the world and their own purpose in relation to other human beings and believe that they can have an impact on the whole world, beyond their own geographical boundaries or culture. Self-transcendence means one is guided by principles of subordinating oneself to groups, experiences, or entities that transcend themselves. Conservation values reinforce the goal of stability and coherence that security, tradition, and conformity values offer. In contrast, self-enhancement and openness to change values should be less conducive for fostering the experience of meaningfulness in life because they are more about enhancing personal welfare at the expense of others, which requires a certain amount of detachment from the emotions and circumstances of others.

Conservation of resources theory

Conservation of resources (COR) theory (Hobfoll, 2001) provides a framework for understanding why it is important for individuals to develop meaningfulness as a psychological resource to maintain and enhance well-being. Moreover, it suggests that meaningfulness in life could be viewed as a precious resource that should be preserved.

According to Hobfoll (2001), it is important to invest in resources that help mitigate resource loss, improve recovery from losses, and stimulate obtainment of more resources. Resources may be objects (e.g., home, car), personal characteristics (e.g., positive outlook), conditions (e.g., good marriage, financial security) and energies (e.g., time, knowledge), or, as we propose, meaningfulness in life. Psychological resource gains contribute to improved well-being, health, and functioning (Gorgievski & Hobfoll, 2008).

Hobfoll's (2001) COR theory also stipulates that "resource loss is disproportionately more salient than resource gain" (p. 343), as people define who they are on the basis of what they do or do not have. When resources are drained or gaining resources becomes an intolerable struggle, strains develop. This is because people "strive to obtain, retain, foster and protect those things they centrally value" (Hobfoll, 2011, p. 117). Thus, individuals will strive to maintain meaningfulness in life when facing threats. Losses in meaningfulness in life will disproportionately reduce well-being compared to increases in well-being from gains in meaningfulness in life.

In short, threats to meaning could be stressful, making it important to seek ways of creating coherence in events to restore meaning. Imposing meaning onto events can protect people against subsequent work stressors. However, if people are unable to create meaning and sense meaningfulness in life, they become more susceptible to other kinds of resource loss, which may further degrade the ability to create meaning (Hobfoll, 2001). Thus, the preservation of meaningfulness in life as a psychological resource can serve as building blocks of stress resilience, but a loss in meaningfulness in life is likely more salient to individuals than a gain in meaningfulness in life.

Terror management theory

Terror management theory (TMT) provides a different perspective on meaning in life. It views the ability to find meaning as central to coping with frightening realities (Pyszczynski, Solomon & Greenberg, 2002). TMT suggests that human abilities to think causally, to anticipate events, and to take the self as an object of attention increase the awareness of the inevitability of death and the ever-present potential for pain and aversive experience (Greenberg *et al.*, 1992). We focus here on the similarities between TMT and meaning in life. According to TMT, two psychological mechanisms might be implemented to manage terror. First, individuals might try to understand and give meaning to the world by defending, affirming, and justifying their cultural worldview to keep their world meaningful and predictable. This approach can help a person gain a sense of value and the promise of symbolic immortality. Second, individuals might try to live up to the standards and values set by one's society and culture, thus increasing self-esteem. Living up to societal standards fulfills a fundamental need for psychological security, which is engendered by humans' awareness of their own vulnerability (Landau *et al.*, 2004). When facing an existential threat, people whose self-concept is, in part, reinforced by an enduring collective identity are likely to feel greater security and less psychological distress (e.g., anxiety; Routledge & Juhl, 2010). In other words, high meaningfulness buffers against the effects of demands (perceived as threats) on strains.

In the framework of TMT, having meaningfulness in life can help someone mitigate anxiety associated with thoughts of death (Simon *et al.*, 1998). This is because individuals become more connected to a cause, mission, and meaning that can persist and confer a sense of symbolic immortality. Similarly, we anticipate that meaningfulness can help mitigate work-related anxiety associated with thoughts of job insecurity. Like in COR theory, however, losing this sense of meaningfulness will likely exacerbate feelings of inevitable peril, as opposed to its presence facilitating pursuit of life. This type of negative affect has implications for the workplace, for example, Aquino, Lewis and Bradfield (1999) showed that negative affect accounts for 3–5% of variance in deviant organizational behaviors.

Sense of Coherence

Like negative affect, Antonovsky's (1987) theoretical conception of *sense of coherence* (SOC) is a pervasive, enduring, though dynamic, feeling of confidence that one's internal and external environments are predictable and that things will work out as well as can reasonably be expected. Individuals with a strong SOC are characterized by three coping resources, including comprehensibility, manageability, and meaningfulness.

Comprehensibility addresses individuals' perceptions of internal and external experiences as predictable, understandable, and ordered. Consistent and predictable experiences allow people to plan ahead and thus adapt in the best possible way. *Manageability* refers to individuals' perceptions that they have the personal and social resources to cope with internal and externals demands placed upon them. Finally, *meaningfulness* is characterized by individuals' feelings that the demands they face in life are challenges worthy of energy investment and engagement.

There is evidence that SOC has positive implications on well-being. Specifically, SOC negatively relates to individuals' perceptions of life events as stressful and positively relates to perceptions of a high quality of life (Delgado, 2007). Employees with a strong SOC report less burnout and more work engagement (Rothmann, Steyn & Mostert, 2005). Still, there is no evidence that its presence (like resource gain) would promote performance, but the absence of SOC could impair performance.

SOC also enhances individuals' ability to make cognitive sense of the workplace, perceive work experiences as challenges, and make emotional and motivational sense of work demands (Strümpfer, 1995). It positively relates with work engagement, work-related well-being, job satisfaction, positive perceptions, performance, efficiency, recognition, rewards, and promotion, all of which can become resources to further enhance the individual's SOC (Feldt, Kivimäki, Rantala & Tolvanen, 2004; Rothmann, Steyn & Mostert, 2005; Strümpfer, 1995). As a factor that might help to maintain health despite stress, as well as to improve work and career effectiveness, relationships, religious expression, and economic and political functioning, SOC might mitigate strain (Strümpfer, 2003). The workplace can contribute to a person's SOC by creating an environment in which incumbents' perceive high job control, social support, and opportunities for career development (Feldt, Kivimäki, Rantala & Tolvanen, 2004).

Based on the aforementioned theoretical approaches, considering meaningfulness as a motivational factor, we assert that work experiences can promote values that are meaningful to an individual, ensure resource gain, help preserve resources, support a SOC, and reduce perceptions of threats to one's well-being. Organizations that support employees in this way prevent deviant workplace behaviors that often occur when individuals feel inconsistency between organizational practices and individuals' work-related attitudes, beliefs, values, and identities (Shamir, 1991).

Is there a dispositional basis to meaningfulness?

This discussion on theories related to meaningfulness suggests that environmental factors might influence the extent to which people develop meaningfulness in life. However, there is also indication that there might be a dispositional basis to meaningfulness in life.

Resilience
Resilience can be understood as a set of attributes and resources. Resilience describes a person who has the capacity to get over adversities and recover, to get stronger, and to develop strengths and competencies despite exposure to stressors (Rutter, 1985).

It does not necessarily specify that the way to cope with adversities is through control; rather, it describes the character of a person who sees the silver lining in otherwise difficult situations. For example, compared to soldiers with low tolerance for stressors, resilient soldiers were less likely to develop disorders following the experience of life-threatening stressors (Maddi, 2005). Further, individuals who believe that they can learn from stressful experiences and achieve personal growth from coping with otherwise harmful stressors become more resilient (Bonanno, 2004). Thus, a patterned attitude of finding the good in bad experiences helps to transform perceptions of stressors into growth opportunities, which intensifies resilience against ongoing demands and pressures of everyday life. Kozusznik, Rodriguez and Tordera (2012) also showed that appraising stressors in a positive light increases resilience, which, in turn, increases engagement and psychological well-being and decreases burnout.

Self-efficacy
Self-efficacy refers to individuals' beliefs that they have the power and ability to produce an intended effect or make a difference (Bandura, 1977). At work, it enables individuals to feel capable and competent to change or control their environment, which contributes to meaningfulness (Baumeister & Vohs, 2002). Individuals with high self-efficacy set high personal goals, while individuals with low self-efficacy set relatively low goals (Lunenburg, 2011). Individuals who successfully overcome new challenges are likely to feel more personally competent and effective in their work (Spreitzer *et al.* 2005). Thus, having high self-efficacy can provide people with the motivation to overcome challenges, which in turn can provide a sense of meaning (Gecas, 1991).

Locus of control
Locus of control is a relatively stable personality trait that refers to a person's belief about what causes the successes and failures in their life (Ng, Sorensen & Eby, 2006). When someone believes that she/he is solely responsible for what happens to him/her in life, she/he is said to have an internal locus of control. In other words, internals believe that they are the masters of their fate and in control of their destiny. They often see a strong link between their actions and the resulting consequences. In contrast, when individuals believe that luck or other factors are responsible for what happens to them in life, they are said to have an external locus of control. Externals believe that they do not have direct control over their destiny; they believe that powerful others control their fate. Due to feelings of no control over their lives, externals often react to life events passively (Ng, Sorensen & Eby, 2006).

To derive meaning in life, individuals need to feel like they have the personal power to act on goals. Those with an internal locus of control might be more likely to take action to achieve their goals, given that they believe they are in control of their destiny. In contrast, those with an external locus of control may stall or avoid taking action to achieve their goals, given that they believe powerful others are in control of their successes and failures. Past psychological research indicates that internal locus of control positively relates to purposefulness in life (see Thompson, Coker, Krause & Henry, 2003) and external locus of control positively relates with meaninglessness (Newcomb & Harlow, 1986). This observation might partly explain results in Glazer, Stetz and Izso's (2004) cross-cultural study of locus of control and job stress. They concluded that people with an internal locus of control probably have lower "job stress" when their environment also encourages internal locus of control. For example, compared to Hungarian nurses with an internal locus of control, US nurses with an internal locus of control had significantly less job stress. Thus, when individuals feel they are in control of their destiny, they can create meaning in life (Frankl, 1963), but when societies limit individuals' freedoms to control their own lives, having an internal locus of control can be a detriment. It would be interesting to see if Hungarians are more existentially indifferent than Americans.

Role of Culture in the Stress Process

There is other developing evidence that perception of and reactions to workplace stressors might differ across cultures (Glazer & Beehr, 2005). Moreover, conditions conducive for engendering a sense of purpose in life may differ across cultures. We assert that in some national cultures, a sense of purpose beyond one's own needs is important for dealing with macro stressors (e.g., political conflict), and thus, these individuals will be better able to cope with micro daily life stressors (e.g., work role overload or conflict) than people in cultures where personal desires guide their purpose in life. This is because *culture* is a shared set of values, beliefs, assumptions, and normative behaviors that are transmitted from one generation to another; it is the key factor that *provides meaning* for the existence of a group of people (Glazer, 2008). That culture provides meaning suggests that it shapes perceived purpose in life. It follows that a culture's values might affect when meaningfulness will help mitigate strains. Few studies have considered the role of meaningfulness across cultures (e.g., Pines, 2004a, b). Studies that addressed cultural differences in meaningfulness suggest that its importance differs and therefore its role in moderating stressor–strain relationships also likely differs across cultures.

Pines (2004b) explains that Israelis experience less burnout despite similar levels of, or more, work stressors than Americans, because the Israeli culture emphasizes individuals working toward a greater good (i.e., survival of the nation) that has benefits beyond the immediate family. Therefore, with over a third of Schnell's (2010) research population reporting existential indifference, it would not be surprising if in Germany high meaningfulness would not statistically moderate the stressor–strain relationship, particularly because Germans tend to endorse openness to change and self-enhancement values. The congruence of personal values and the environment's values might protect against stressors effects on strains (e.g., Vandenberghe, 1999).

Further, there are numerous ways to foster meaningfulness in life, and these sources likely differ across cultures. People in cultures that value the welfare of the group might reinforce behaving in ways that take into consideration others' needs before their own, whereas people in cultures that value pursuing individually desired goals might create existential indifference (Schnell, 2010), which will not mitigate strains, but might reduce well-being. Given these cultural differences, the salience of meaningfulness in life as a resource that moderates the stressor–strain relationship is likely to differ across cultures, but only more research in different cultural contexts will elucidate this assertion.

Meaningfulness in life is also not something that others can do for someone; however, our environments (whether national and/or organizational cultures) could shape the way our sense of purpose is manifested. As Frankl (1963) noted, the environment of severe humiliation intensified some people's sense of meaningfulness in life and others' sense of defeat. Likewise, Pines (2004b) asserted that survival of a nation serves to provide meaningfulness in the lives of its constituents who develop existential reasons for living. Thus, occupational health scholars should be especially sensitive to differences in culture's values, as they too might shape the extent to which people develop a sense of meaningfulness, which then further influences the stress process.

As Glazer and Beehr (2005) highlighted, the entire stress process, including the perception of stressors, interpretation of stressors, availability of coping resource, application of coping resources, manifestation of strains, the type of strains that manifest, and the intensity of those strains, is immersed in a person's cultural context. Similarly, the extent to which people derive meaningfulness in life should be influenced by cultural factors. Therefore, in multinational companies, it is important that managers be conscientious about possible variations in values among employees and the ways they have developed a sense of meaning in life, in order to support employees' development of meaningfulness at work too.

Role of the Workplace in Creating Meaningfulness

In addition to identifying characteristics of the person in creating meaningfulness, it is important to identify how the workplace can foster an environment that helps one create meaningfulness in what one does. Meaning in life is derived from activities across the range of life roles, where work has a specific role for spurring more meaning and purpose (Ryff & Singer, 1998). Finding meaning in work is frequently a social endeavor and often takes place in the company of others, within the same work teams and departments (Weick, 1995). However, such efforts are not sufficient for creating meaningfulness, particularly because the working and unemployed populations appear to have similar levels of meaningfulness (Schnell, 2010).

For the workplace to play a role in individuals' sense of meaningfulness, it must provide access to resources and stimulating tasks. It then behooves the person to seek meaningfulness in the workplace by utilizing the organization's resources to set tasks that are intrinsically motivating and create a sense of purpose (Pratt & Ashforth, 2003). This implies that the person might need to alter his or her relationship with the organization and the people therein by associating with colleagues that promote the organization's goals, beliefs, and values. Moreover, by engaging in cognitively meaningful tasks, a person creates a sense of joy, which connects individuals to a larger good and to things viewed by them as important in life (Wrzesniewski, Dutton & Debebe, 2003). Thus, meaningfulness promotes work motivation and individual performance, job satisfaction, personal fulfillment, career development, and diminished stress (Dik & Duffy, 2009; Elangovan, Pinder & McLean, 2010; Hackman & Oldham, 1980; Kahn, 2007).

Interventions in the workplace to promote meaningfulness in work

As with many person-driven stress interventions (e.g., relaxation exercises and weight loss programs), organizations cannot force the application of the intervention, but they can offer opportunities for employees to seize. Similarly, organizations cannot command a person to have a sense of meaningfulness, but they can initiate work processes that stimulate employees' sense of meaningfulness. One way can be through job redesign. Hackman and Oldham's (1980) central tenet is that job meaningfulness is a product of the variety of skills used on the job, task significance, and task identity, plus autonomy in getting one's work done and knowledge of how one's performance is appraised. The concept of autonomy is related to Lawler, Mohrman and Benson's (2001) suggestion that empowerment will increase meaningfulness. When management believes in its people and gives them the resources they need to get their jobs done, they are more likely to approach the challenge with a sense of meaningfulness.

Path–goal leadership (Pratt & Ashforth, 2003) is also an effective way of creating meaningfulness in work. Here, the leader illuminates clear paths/goals for subordinates to fulfill their goals, thereby influencing their satisfaction and performance. This may also be accomplished by engaging in practices that focus on creating organizational culture, identities, and ideologies, applying, for example, visionary leadership (Kirkpatrick & Locke, 1996). At the very least, leaders should remove obstacles detrimental to performance, as obstacles can erode the meaningfulness of even the most inspiring of jobs (Fox & Spector, 1999). A transformational leader also inspires subordinates to pursue more complex goals, fosters trust, and creates pathways to obtaining opportunities to grow and develop both intellectually and in positions in the organization (Nielsen, Randall, Yarker & Brenner, 2008). However, the link between transformational leadership and meaningfulness is unclear, as it only indirectly relates to well-being through work characteristics (Nielsen, Randall, Yarker & Brenner, 2008).

Pratt and Ashforth (2003) further discuss the role of colleagues in the work environment. They assert that strengthening relationships with colleagues in the workplace can promote meaningfulness at work. When people believe that they are working for the greater good of their workgroup and individuals value such efforts, meaningfulness is strengthened. Fostering meaningfulness at work can occur through building an organizational community with intimate, family-like dynamics. This process should call attention to an organizational mission beyond the profit motive and attend to individuals' innate desires to form a kinship with others, specifically in the work context that is characterized by frequent collaborative interactions with fellow employees (Baumeister & Leary, 1995). Finally, calling attention to the organization's corporate social responsibility; making people feel they are providing an active, constructive service; and contributing toward general welfare in the context of society can help create meaningfulness at work (Pratt & Ashforth, 2003). Such tasks can have tremendous personal meaning if they are framed as connecting to something greater (Emmons, 2003).

Conclusion

Given the immense benefits associated with purpose in life and the potential costs associated with meaninglessness and existential indifference, it is alarming to note that our period in history has been characterized as the age of meaninglessness (Frankl, 1963), even as we have enjoyed relatively high levels of wealth, human rights, and (domestic) peace. Some scholars have noted our society has mastered *how* to live but not *why* to live (Mascaro & Rosen, 2008). Individuals born in the current time period have unprecedented levels of power, thanks to the furious and continuously accelerating pace of technological innovation (Friedman, 2003). However, many of these individuals have harnessed this power toward the pursuit of materialistic values, without regard to the psychological and environmental destruction it might have caused (Brown & Kasser, 2005). Such materialism might be the cause of a "shallow and superficial" life among a large proportion of existentially indifferent young adults (Schnell, 2010). Of particular concern is that these are also the same individuals who will become the next generation of leaders. Perhaps a renewed focus on leading a more complex, purposeful life, as opposed to a materialistic life, is needed.

To that end, psychologists and other social scientists can help in guiding individuals and society toward a more meaningful and sustainable future by actively studying the nature of meaningfulness in life. For that matter, what is the point of any endeavor that aims to improve the condition of human beings for the better if we cannot answer *why* it is important? Given the scope of the problem and the immense positive and negative consequences for individuals and society, there is an ethical imperative (Mascaro & Rosen, 2008) for psychologists to specify what enhances and what detracts from individuals experiencing their work lives as meaningful and to examine relationships between meaningfulness and other important psychological variables.

Future directions

This literature review elucidated a number of proximal research opportunities. First, a number of individual difference characteristics were identified as possibly enabling the development of meaningfulness. These variables, however, were not systematically evaluated in a convergent validation study. Future studies should validate measures of meaningfulness in life in relation to locus of control, self-efficacy, self-esteem, and resilience. Second, there might be a difference between purpose in life and zest as an approach to life. Third, future research should examine the relationship between purpose in life and values. Fourth, research on meaningfulness in life and non-stress-related organizational behaviors, for example, organizational commitment, organizational citizenship behavior, and performance across cultures, would also be fruitful. Finally, future studies should test how organizational practices foster or inhibit opportunities for individuals to develop meaningfulness. For example, goal setting, job enrichment programs, and leadership styles might influence employees' meaningfulness.

Note

1. These figures are based on July 2010 census data found in http://en.wikipedia.org/wiki/Demographics_of_Germany#Population.

References

Antonovsky, A. (1987). *Unraveling the mystery of health: How people manage stress and stay well*. San Francisco: Jossey-Bass.

Aquino, K., Lewis, M. U., & Bradfield, M. (1999). Justice constructs, negative affectivity, and employee deviance: A proposed model and empirical test. *Journal of Organizational Behavior, 20*, 1073–1091.

Auhagen, A. E., & Holub, F. (2006). Ultimate, provisional, and personal meaning of life: Differences and common ground. *Psychological Reports, 99*, 131–146.

Bandura, A. (1977). *Social learning theory*. Englewood Cliffs, NJ: Prentice-Hall.

Baumeister, R. F., & Leary, M. R. (1995). The need to belong: Desire for interpersonal attachments as a fundamental human motivation. *Psychological Bulletin, 117*, 497–529.

Baumeister, R. F., & Vohs, K. D. (2002). The pursuit of meaningfulness in life. In C. R. Snyder & S. J. Lopez (Eds.), *The handbook of positive psychology* (pp. 608–618). New York: Oxford University Press.

Bonanno, G. A. (2004). Loss, trauma and human resilience. Have we underestimated the human capacity to thrive after extremely aversive events? *American Psychologist, 59*, 20–28.

Brown, K. W., & Kasser, T. (2005) Are psychological and ecological well-being compatible? The role of values, mindfulness, and lifestyle. *Social Indicators Research, 74*, 349–368.

Bunderson, J. S., & Thompson, J. A. (2009). The call of the wild: Zookeepers, callings, and the double-edged sword of deeply meaningful work. *Administrative Science Quarterly, 54*, 32–57.

Byrne, R. (2006). *The secret*. New York: Atria Books.

Cynkar, P., & English, C. (2011, November 23). *Fewer report depression in Germany than in U.S., UK: Women more likely than men to report a depression diagnosis in all three countries*. Retrieved August 13, 2013, from http://www.gallup.com/poll/150944/-fewer-report-depression-germany.aspx

Damon, W., Menon, J., & Bronk, K. C. (2003). The development of purpose during adolescence. *Applied Developmental Science, 7*, 119–128.

Debats, D. L., Drost, J., & Hansen, P. (1995). Experiences of meaning in life: A combined qualitative and quantitative approach. *British Journal of Psychology, 86*, 359–375.

Deci, E. L., & Ryan, R. M. (2000). The "what" and "why" of goal pursuits: Human needs and the self-determination of human behavior. *Psychological Inquiry*, *11*, 227–268.

Delgado, C. (2007). Sense of coherence, spirituality, stress, and quality of life in chronic illness. *Journal of Nursing Scholarship 39*, 229–234.

Dik, B. J., & Duffy, R. D. (2009). Calling and vocation at work. *The Counseling Psychologist*, *37*, 424–450.

Elangovan, A. R., Pinder, C. C., & McLean, M. (2010). Callings and organizational behavior. *Journal of Vocational Behavior*, *76*, 428–440.

Elliot, A. (2006). The hierarchical model of approach-avoidance motivation. *Motivation and Emotion*, *30*, 111–116.

Emmons, R. A. (2003). Personal goals, life meaning, and virtue: Wellsprings of a positive life. In C. L. M. Keyes & J. Haidt (Eds.), *Flourishing: Positive psychology and the life well-lived* (pp. 105–128). Washington, DC: American Psychological Association.

Feldt, T., Kivimäki, M., Rantala, A., & Tolvanen, A. (2004). Sense of coherence and work characteristics: A cross-lagged structural equation model among managers. *Journal of Occupational and Organizational Psychology*, *77*, 323–342.

Frankl, V. E. (1963). *Man's search for meaning: An introduction to logotherapy*. Oxford, England: Washington Square Press.

Fox, S., & Spector, P. E. (1999). A model of work frustration-aggression. *Journal of Organizational Behavior*, *20*, 915–931.

Friedman, T. L. (2003), *Longitudes and attitudes: The world in the age of terrorism*. New York: Anchor.

Gecas, V. (1991). The self-concept as a basis for a theory of motivation. In J. A. Howard & P. L. Callero (Eds.), *The self-society dynamic: Cognition, emotion, and action* (pp. 171–187). New York: Cambridge University Press.

Glazer, S. (2008). Cross-cultural issues in stress and burnout. In J. R. B. Halbesleben (Ed.), *Handbook of stress and burnout in health care* (pp. 79–93). Hauppauge, NY: Nova Science.

Glazer, S., & Beehr, T.A. (2005). Consistency of the implications of three role stressors across four countries. *Journal of Organizational Behavior*, *26*, 467–487.

Glazer, S., Stetz, T. A., & Izso, L. (2004). Individual difference variables and subjective job stress across five countries. *Personality and Individual Differences*, *37*, 645–658.

Gorgievski, M., & Hobfoll, S. (2008). Work can burn us out or fire us up: Conservation of resources in burnout and engagement. In J. R. B. Halbesleben (Ed.), *Handbook of stress and burnout in health care* (pp. 7–22). New York: Nova Science.

Grant, A. M. (2008). The significance of task significance: Job performance effects, relational mechanisms, and boundary conditions. *Journal of Applied Psychology*, *93*, 108–124.

Greenberg, J., Solomon, S., Pyszczynski, T., Rosenblatt, A., Burling, J., Lyon, D., *et al*. (1992). Assessing the terror management analysis of self-esteem: Converging evidence of an anxiety-buffering function. *Journal of Personality and Social Psychology*, *63*, 913–922.

Hackman, J. R., & Oldham, G. R. (1980). *Work redesign*. Reading, MA: Addison-Wesley.

Hobfoll, S. E. (2001). The Influence of culture, community, and the nested-self in the stress process: Advancing Conservation of Resources Theory. *Applied Psychology*, *50*, 337–370.

Hobfoll, S. E. (2011). Conservation of resource caravans and engaged settings. *Journal of Occupational and Organizational Psychology*, *84*, 116–122.

Kahn, W. A. (2007). Meaningful connections: Positive relationships and attachments at work. In J. E. Dutton & B. R. Ragins (Eds.) *Exploring positive relationships at work: Building a theoretical and research foundation* (pp. 189–206). Mahwah, NJ: Erlbaum.

Kirkpatrick, S. A., & Locke, E. (1996). Direct and indirect effects of three core charismatic leadership components on performance and attitudes. *Journal of Applied Psychology, 81,* 36–51.

Kozusznik, M. W, Rodriguez, I., & Tordera, N. (2012). The appraisal of eustress as a predictor of burnout, work engagement and well-being: The mediating role of resilience. In C. Carvalho, P. R. Lourenco, y C. F. Peralta (Eds.), *A Emocao nas Organizacoes* [The emotion in organizations] (pp. 93–110). Viseu, Portugal: PsicoSoma.

Landau, M. J., Solomon, S., Greenberg, J., Cohen, F., Pyszczynski, T., Arndt, J., *et al.* (2004). Deliver us from evil: The effects of mortality salience and reminders of 9/11 on support for President George W. Bush. *Personality and Social Psychology Bulletin, 30,* 1136–1150.

Lawler, E. E., Mohrman, S., & Benson, G. (2001). *Organizing for high performance: The CEO report on employee involvement, TQM, reengineering, and knowledge management in Fortune 1000 companies.* San Francisco: Jossey-Bass.

Lazarus, R. S., & Folkman, S. (1984). *Stress appraisal and coping.* New York: Springer.

Lunenburg, F. C. (2011). Self-efficacy in the workplace: Implications for motivation and performance. *International Journal of Management, Business, and Administration, 14,* 1–6.

Maddi, S. (2005). On hardiness and other pathways to resilience. *American Psychologist, 60,* 261–262.

Mascaro, N., & Rosen, D. H. (2008). Assessment of existential meaning and its longitudinal relations with depressive symptoms. *Journal of Social & Clinical Psychology, 27,* 576–599.

Ng, T. W. H., Sorensen, K. L., & Eby, L. T. (2006). Locus of control at work: A meta-analysis. *Journal of Occupational Behavior, 27,* 1057–1087.

Newcomb, M. D., & Harlow, L. L. (1986). Life events and substance use among adolescents: Mediating effects of perceived loss of control and meaninglessness in life. *Journal of Personality and Social Psychology, 51,* 564–577.

Nielsen, K., Randall, R., Yarker, J., & Brenner, S. (2008). The effects of transformational leadership on followers' perceived work characteristics and psychological well-being: A longitudinal study. *Work & Stress, 22,* 16–32.

NIMH. (n.d.). *The numbers count: Mental disorders in America.* Retrieved August 6, 2009, from http://www.nimh.nih.gov/health/publications/the-numbers-count-mental-disorders-in-america/index.shtml

Pausch, R., & Zaslow, J. (2008). *The last lecture.* New York: Hyperion.

Peiró, J. M., González-Romá, V., Tordera, N., & Mañas, M. A. (2001). Does role stress predict burnout over time among health care professionals? *Psychology & Health, 16,* 511–525.

Peterson, C., Park, N., Hall, N., & Seligman, M. E. P. (2009). Zest and work. *Journal of Organizational Behavior, 30,* 161–172.

Peterson, C., Park, N., & Seligman, M. E. P. (2005). Orientations to happiness and life satisfaction: The full life versus the empty life. *Journal of Happiness Studies, 6,* 25–41.

Pines, A. M. (2004a). Adult attachment styles and their relationship to burnout: A preliminary, cross-cultural investigation. *Work and Stress, 18,* 66–80.

Pines, A. M. (2004b). Why are Israelis less burned out? *European Psychologist, 9,* 69–77.

Pratt, M. G., & Ashforth, B. E. (2003). Fostering meaningfulness in working and at work. In K. S. Cameron, J. E. Dutton, & R. E. Quinn (Eds.), *Positive organizational scholarship* (pp. 309–327). San Francisco: Berrett-Koehler.

Pyszczynski, T., Solomon, S., & Greenberg, J. (2002). *In the wake of 9/11: The psychology of terror.* Washington, DC. American Psychological Association.

Rivera, R. (n.d.). *Faith and anxiety*. Retrieved January 16, 2012, from http://www.chabad.org/theJewishWoman/article_cdo/aid/1742915/jewish/Faith-and-Anxiety.htm

Rothmann, S., Steyn, L. J., & Mostert, K. (2005). Job stress, sense of coherence and work wellness in an electricity supply organisation. *South African Journal of Business Management, 36*, 55–63.

Routledge, C., & Juhl, J. (2010). When death thoughts lead to death fears: Mortality salience increases death anxiety for individuals who lack meaning in life. *Cognition and Emotion, 24*, 848–854.

Rutter, M. (1985). Resilience in face of adversity: Protective factors and resistance to psychiatric disorder. *British Journal of Psychiatry, 1*, 598–611.

Ryan, R. M., Huta, V., & Deci, E. L. (2008). Living well: A self-determination theory perspective on eudaimonia. *Journal of Happiness Studies, 9*, 139–170.

Ryff, C. D., & Singer, B. H. (1998). The contours of positive human health. *Psychological Inquiry, 9*, 1–28.

Sagiv, L., & Schwartz, S. H. (2000). Value priorities and subjective well-being: Direct relations and congruity effects. *European Journal of Social Psychology, 30*, 177–198.

Schnell, T. (2010). Existential indifference: Another quality of meaning in life. *Journal of Humanistic Psychology, 50*, 351–373.

Schwartz, S. H., & Bardi, A. (2001). Value hierarchies across cultures: Taking a similarities perspective. *Journal of Cross-Cultural Psychology, 32*, 268–290.

Seligman, M. E. P. (2002). *Authentic happiness: Using the new positive psychology to realize your potential for lasting fulfillment*. New York: Free Press.

Shamir, B. (1991). Meaning, self and motivation in organizations. *Organization Studies, 12*, 405–424.

Simon, L., Arndt, J., Greenberg, J., Pyszczynski, T., & Solomon, S. (1998). Terror management and meaning: Evidence that the opportunity to defend the worldview in response. *Journal of Personality, 66*, 3359–3382.

Spreitzer, G. M., Sutcliffe, K. M., Dutton, J. E., Sonenshein, S., & Grant, A. M. (2005). A socially embedded model of thriving at work. *Organization Science, 16*, 537–549.

Steger, M. F., & Dik, B. J. (2010). Work as meaning: Individual and organizational benefits of engaging in meaningful work. In P. A. Linley, S. Harrington, & N. Garcea (Eds.), *Oxford handbook of positive psychology and work* (pp.131-142). Oxford, England: Oxford University Press.

Strümpfer, D. J. W. (1995). The origin of health and strength: From "salutogenesis" to "fortigenesis". *South African Journal of Psychology, 25*, 81–89.

Strümpfer, D. J. W. (2003). Resilience and burnout: A stitch that could save nine. *South African Journal of Psychology, 33*, 69–79.

Thompson, N. J., Coker, J., Krause, J. S., & Henry, E. (2003). Purpose in life as a mediator of adjustment after spinal cord injury. *Rehabilitation Psychology, 48*, 100.

Vandenberghe, C. (1999). Organizational culture, person-culture fit, and turnover: A replication in the health care industry. *Journal of Organizational Behavior, 20*, 175–184.

Vansteenkiste, M., Neyrinck, B., Niemiec, C., Soenens, B., De Witte, H., & Van den Broeck, A. (2007). On the relations among work value orientations, psychological need satisfaction and job outcomes: A self-determination theory approach. *Journal of Occupational and Organizational Psychology, 80*, 251–277.

Weick, K. E. (1995). *Sensemaking in organizations*. Thousand Oaks, CA: Sage.

Wrzesniewski, A., Dutton, J. E., & Debebe, G. (2003). Interpersonal sensemaking and the meaning of work. *Research in Organizational Behavior, 25*, 93–135.

9

Progress and Challenges in Occupational Health and Safety Research

Peter Y. Chen, Yiqiong Li, and Michelle Tuckey
University of South Australia, Australia

Konstantin P. Cigularov
Old Dominion University, USA

Estimates by the International Labour Organization (ILO, 2012) reveal that each year two million workers die at work, 160 million workers suffer from work-related diseases, and approximately 270 million workers experience non-fatal work-related accidents. The ILO further estimated that 4% of the world's GDP is lost every year as a result of occupational diseases and accidents. These grim statistics are not new, and efforts to address occupational health and safety (OHS) in research and practice can be traced back to the turn of the last century (Münsterberg, 1913; Viteles, 1932). In part because of the many contributions of OHS research, injury rates have declined over time in many countries (Occupational Safety and Health Administration [OSHA], 2013; Stout & Linn, 2002); however, important challenges remain in efforts to improve workplace health and safety.

To reflect the major progress of OHS research, as well as highlight challenges ahead, we focus on four themes in this chapter. First, we review the advancement of safety climate research, which is arguably the most vibrant OHS research over the past two decades. Then, we review a construct related to safety climate, psychosocial safety climate (PSC) (Dollard & Bakker, 2010), which focuses on organizational climate for psychosocial safety. Third, we bring the attention to (im)migrant workers (within and/or between borders) who have experienced disproportional OHS disparity over years. Finally, we will focus on to what extent survey respondents from different groups or populations differ in how they interpret and respond to measures assessing various aspects of safety constructs. At the end of the chapter, we

Contemporary Occupational Health Psychology: Global Perspectives on Research and Practice, Volume 3,
First Edition. Edited by Stavroula Leka and Robert R. Sinclair.
© 2014 John Wiley & Sons, Ltd. Published 2014 by John Wiley & Sons, Ltd.

offer our observations pertaining to challenges and research directions related to the correspondent themes mentioned earlier.

Safety Climate

In recent years, safety climate has earned the reputation of being a significant leading indicator of safe work practices across industries and occupations and as a result has received a great deal of attention from OHS researchers. Safety climate reflects perceptions shared by workers about how safety policies, safety procedures, and safety practices are actually implemented and managed in organizations, as well as the relative priority of safety over schedules and production (Snyder *et al.*, 2008; Zohar, 2011). One can also view safety climate as a snapshot of the safety culture at a particular time and place, and it informs managers about the "temperature" of the safety system with their units, departments, or organizations (Huang, Chen & Grosch, 2010).

Over the past 30 years, the number of published studies on safety climate has drastically increased. Huang, Chen and Grosch (2010) searched for "safety climate" in abstracts of published peer-reviewed journal articles to find one article published in 1980 (Zohar, 1980), two articles published during 1981–1990, 28 articles published during 1991–2000, and 89 articles published during 2001–2008. We extended their search to reveal 134 new articles published between 2009 and 2013. The *NIOSH WorkLife Initiative* (2008) stated that effective safety and health programs and policies cannot be achieved and sustained without having a healthy organizational culture and leadership commitment to workers' health and safety. Similarly, the NORA Construction Sector Council (2008) also highlighted safety climate as a key contributor to safety and health performance. In fact, recent meta-analyses have demonstrated the usefulness of safety climate for both research and practice as evidenced by its consistent positive effects on safety behaviors and outcomes, including accidents and injuries (e.g., Christian, Bradley, Wallace & Burke, 2009; Clarke, 2010).

There are at least four plausible reasons why safety climate exhibits the aforementioned relationships. First, safety climate serves a sensemaking function, which guides employees in discerning the relative priority of safety versus production and other goals (e.g., quality) in their organization based on observed patterns of management-enacted safety policies and procedures (Zohar, 2011). In other words, safety climate reflects the degree to which organizations are perceived to be serious about and committed to their safety policies, procedures, and practices (Zohar & Luria, 2005). For example, when safety issues and procedures are clearly and consistently ignored or made contingent upon production demands, employees will likely develop a highly shared understanding (i.e., strong safety climate) of the low priority of safety in their organization (i.e., negative safety climate). Second, because safety climate perceptions focus on enacted (rather than espoused) safety policies and procedures, employees learn through their work experiences the probable consequences of (un) safe behaviors. More specifically, safety climate perceptions help employees form expectations of what behaviors are rewarded and what behaviors are discouraged at work, thus directing employee work efforts (Zohar, 2011).

Third, the employee shared perceptions and behaviors related to safety create group and organizational norms, which inform employees about others' values, beliefs, attitudes, and actions pertaining to safety (Hayes, Peranda, Smecko & Trask, 1998). As a result, employees experiencing positive or negative safety climate would presumably follow the group/organizational norms and would be more likely to behave safely or unsafely, respectively. Finally, organizations with positive safety climates value employees' contributions and feedback regarding safety risks and/or concerns (Cigularov, Chen & Rosecrance, 2010). Viewing employees as subject matter experts and involving them in upward communications and decision-making and goal-setting processes can not only improve organizational policies and practices regarding safety but can also provide employees with a sense of authority and responsibility for their decisions and actions, which can further motivate their safety efforts at work (Vinodkumara & Bhasi, 2010).

Psychosocial Safety Climate

Dollar and Bakker (2010, p. 580) defined PSC as shared perceptions about "policies, practices, and procedures for the protection of worker psychological health and safety". In contrast to safety climate that has traditionally focused on physical aspects of health and safety, the emphasis of PSC is on psychological health and safety at work and reflects freedom from psychological harm. The core features of PSC, similar to safety climate, are management priority toward psychological health and safety, organizational communication regarding psychological health and safety, organizational participation from all levels in identifying any issues that impact on psychological safety, and the level of commitment by senior management to resolve such issues and protect worker health (Idris, Dollard, Coward & Dormann, 2012).

The confirmatory factor analysis in Australian and Malaysian samples has shown that the construct of PSC is distinct from other climate constructs including safety climate and team PSC (Idris, Dollard, Coward & Dormann, 2012). Additional evidence has shown that levels of PSC vary across organizations (e.g., Law, Dollard, Tuckey & Dormann, 2011) and across teams, work units, and work locations within organizations (e.g., Bond, Tuckey & Dollard, 2010; Idris, Dollard, Coward & Dormann, 2012).

PSC plays an important role in process of preventing stressful job conditions. Specifically, PSC is theorized as an antecedent to psychosocial features of the job and work context described in job stress models such as Karasek's (1979) Demand–Control Model and Job Demands–Resources Model (Demerouti, Bakker, Nachreiner & Schaufeli, 2001). In a longitudinal study, Dollard and Bakker (2010) found that PSC predicted levels of psychological distress and emotional exhaustion reported through its relationship with work pressure and emotional demands. Likewise, Idris, Dollard, Coward & Dormann (2012) found that PSC was negatively related to job demands (emotional demands and role conflict), which mediated the relationship with burn-out. Evidence that PSC plays a role in employee motivation has also emerged, show-ing that PSC boosts work engagement through the perception of increased job resources (Idris, Dollard, Coward & Dormann, 2012; Law, Dollard, Tuckey & Dormann, 2011). Thus, PSC can be viewed as a leading indicator of psychological health and safety in workplaces and is envisaged as playing a key role in the primary prevention of occupational stress (Dollard & Karasek, 2010).

The other main function of PSC is in weakening the association between job demands and poor psychological health. For example, it has been demonstrated that PSC moderates the impact over time of workplace bullying on outcomes such as posttraumatic stress symptoms (Bond, Tuckey & Dollard, 2010), psychological dis-tress and emotional exhaustion (Law, Dollard, Tuckey & Dormann, 2011), and the relationship over time between emotional demands and emotional exhaustion (Dollard & Bakker, 2010). Further, a recent longitudinal study showed that the potential protective effect of emotional job resources on the relationship between emotional job demands and emotional exhaustion was seen only in the context of high levels of PSC (Dollard et al., 2012). That is, PSC may provide the right context for workers to utilize available resources to offset the demands they face. Hence, PSC plays a dual role in protecting worker health and safety; fostering PSC has indirect effects through its impact on job design and also moderating effects that minimize psychological harm.

OHS Threats to Migrant Workers

Over the past three decades, there have been steadily increasing cross-border (e.g., migrant workers from other countries who moved to the US, Singapore, Northern Europe to seek out jobs) and cross-province (e.g., migrant workers from rural areas in China and Australia who moved to cities to seek out jobs) migration. These changes in workforce composition are, however, accompanied by health and safety disparities between migrant and non-migrant workers (Ahonen, Benavides, & Benach, 2007; ILO, 2004; National Research Council, 2003). The European Agency for Safety and Health at Work (2008) has shown disproportionally high acci-dent rates among migrant workers in Europe including France, Germany, and Spain. The European Foundation for the Improvement of Living and Working Conditions (2007) further revealed that migrant workers with a non-Western background tended to experience poor health conditions and be exposed to hazards at work, in addition to high work accident rates. A high work-related injury rate was also found among male migrants in Canada compared with natives (Smith & Mustard, 2009).

Migrant workers also have much higher exposures to dangerous substances at work compared with native workers. For example, Lee, McGuinness and Kawakami (2011) quoted the finding from a study conducted by the Korea Occupational Safety and Health Agency that exposure to lead at work resulted in a significantly higher blood-lead level of migrant workers in Korea at 4.9% (38 per 788) compared to native workers at 0.4% (7 per 1581). In addition, exposure to urinary methylhippuric acid, a cancer-causing agent, has led 0.5% of migrant workers (6 per 1109) to have unsafe urinary methylhippuric suspension levels, while no native Korean workers have reported above the safe level.

Similar to the aforementioned inequalities, Loh and Richardson (2004) found that the occupational fatality rate in the US during 1996 and 2001 was 15% higher among wage and salary foreign-born workers (4.5 per 100,000) than that of native-born workers (3.9 per 100,000). Moreover, foreign-born workers have experienced the increase of fatalities at work, even though the overall number of work-related fatalities in the US has declined over the same period. As the largest group of migrants in the US, Latino migrants suffered from significantly higher rates of workplace mortalities (5.9 per 100,000) compared with all workers (4.0 per 100,100) in the year 2006 (Centers for Disease Control and Prevention, 2008). Australia shows an even worse situation wherein the workplace mortality rate in 2007 among temporary migrant workers holding 457 visas was 5.8 deaths per 100,000 workers, which is almost twice the rate (3 deaths per 100,000 workers) of native Australian workers (Sutton, 2008).

Migrant workers are far more prevalent in 3D (dirty, dangerous, and degrading) jobs, with inherently greater health and safety risks (Lee, McGuinness & Kawakami, 2011; Leong et al., 2012; Smith & Mustard, 2009) because of their limited employment choices. The vast majority of migrants work in sectors such as the construction, manufacturing, transportation, agriculture, and fishing sectors, where occupational accidents and injuries are concentrated. For instance, Hispanic construction workers in the US are more likely to suffer fatal and non-fatal injuries at work than any other ethnic group across all ages (Dong, Fujimoto, Ringen & Men, 2009; Dong & Platner, 2004).

However, job type alone does not seem to be the only reason for the aforementioned disparities on safety and health at work. Migrant workers tend to lack sufficient education and knowledge to identify work hazards and understand safety requirements of new countries (Brunette, 2005). They also do not receive essential safety training and have little skills and prior work experience (Brunette, 2005; ILO, 2004; O'Connor et al., 2005).

In addition to the aforementioned contributing factors of disparity, poor proficiency in the host country language appears to be an important risk factor associated with occupational risk (Acosta-Leon, Grote, Salem & Daraiseh, 2006). Evidence in the US and Australia shows that migrants with poor proficiency in English have higher fatality and injury rates than their English-proficient counterparts (Corvalan, Driscoll & Harrison, 1994; Davila, Mora & Gonzalez, 2011). Indeed, language difficulties may constrain these workers from communicating risks and understanding safety training materials and safety regulations. In a study of non-English-speaking construction workers in Australia, Trajkovski and Loosemore (2006) found that nearly half of the workers misunderstood instructions and procedures, and many of them attempted to skip safety training delivered in an English format. The latter scenario has also been observed in the largest private construction project in the US (Gittleman *et al.*, 2010), when safety training was delivered in English to all non-English-speaking crews.

In addition to the earlier problems, language difficulty may limit knowledge and awareness of available health services for injured workers, which increases the risk for prolonged disability. For example, workers from non-English-speaking countries (34%) were less likely to apply for workers' compensation compared with those born in Australia (44%) and those born in other English-speaking countries (45%) (SafeWork Australia, 2011). This result could also be that migrant workers are fearful of the impact on future work options if they submit a compensation claim, especially given the limited job choices. Perhaps they believe that having made a claim will mean that they are passed over for new opportunities.

Cultural barriers could be another important risk factor that influences how migrants perceive and cope with health and safety hazards (Faucett *et al.*, 2001; Leong *et al.*, 2012). Some studies indicate that migrant workers may be less risk averse than natives for a number of reasons, which explains why migrant workers are willing to accept risky jobs. For instance, Hispanic migrant workers tend to be exposed to hazardous working conditions in their own countries and, as a result, become accustomed to them. They may also have low expectation about management's commitment to safety (Brunette, 2005). Furthermore, the meaning of safety may be interpreted through a different frame of reference by migrant workers. Migrant workers may consider pain, injuries, and illness as an inevitable part of their jobs. Faucett *et al.* (2001) found that Hispanic migrant workers tend to describe their musculoskeletal symptoms as "bothersome discomforts" but not "pain". Thus, they believe that they can continue to work because there is no pain.

Finally, cultural beliefs of fatalism about their lives and cultural values of maintaining social harmony may also affect how migrant workers interpret and react to hazardous conditions. According to Leong *et al.* (2012), Hispanic migrant workers tend to believe fate is not controlled by them. In turn, this belief may lead such workers to accept the conditions they face without taking measures to report or reduce risks. Likewise, influenced by their collectivistic values, Asian migrants in the US are less likely to utilize social support to cope with job stress in order to maintain social harmony in the social groups.

Measurement Equivalence in Safety Surveys

Various survey instruments have been used to assess safety issues such as safety risks, safety attitudes, safety motivation, safety leadership, and safety climate (Guldenmund, 2007; Zohar, 2011). Yet it is unclear whether these measures are interpreted in the same frame of reference among respondents from different backgrounds. In this section, we use the safety climate literature to provide a useful illustration of the need to demonstrate measurement equivalence of safety measures.

As shown earlier, safety climate has been shown to predict behavior and outcomes. Because of its utility as a leading indicator of accidents and injuries, there has been an increased interest in examining the mean levels of safety climate measures across different populations of interest, for example, based on job position and organizational level (Findley, Smith, Gorski & O'Neil, 2011; Gittleman et al., 2010), industry (Glendon & Litherland, 2001), type of organization (Cheyne, Oliver, Tomas & Cox, 2002), and gender (Wu, Liu & Lu, 2007). And yet, little is known about the extent to which respondents representing the aforementioned different groups differ in how they interpret and respond to safety climate measures.

If migrant workers and workers born in host countries hold qualitatively different views of safety climate due to their cultural values and work experiences, then confirmation of mean difference among groups on a safety climate measure could be misleading because these responses are not comparable. To ensure we compare apples to apples rather than "sandwiches to sand wedges" (Vandenberg & Lance, 2000, p. 40), measurement equivalence has become a prerequisite for comparing means between groups of interest, particularly when respondents are from diverse backgrounds.

This issue is exemplified well by a study from Parker et al. (2007), who found that employees who did not speak English perceived higher workplace safety compared to English-speaking employees. The findings were contrary to their expectations, and the researchers struggled to explain the observed mean differences. As suggested from the earlier discussion, migrant workers may have different expectations about working conditions and workplace safety. Thus, interpretation of mean differences on safety climate measures should be made cautiously because the observed mean difference may be attributed to different frames of reference shaped by different cultural backgrounds. This example highlights the importance of establishing the measurement equivalence of safety measures prior to conducting mean comparisons. It should be emphasized that statistically controlling for group membership is not a magic wand that can "equalize" the frame of reference because researchers are at risk of masking substantive differences (Spector, Zapf, Chen & Frese, 2000).

Assessing measurement equivalence is most often conducted with a multi-group confirmatory factor analysis (MGCFA) in a stepwise process. This process is illustrated by using studies of Cigularov et al. (2013a, b) as examples. Both studies assessed the measurement equivalence of a safety climate measure across different construction trades and ethnic groups in four steps following recommendations in the literature (Cheung & Rensvold, 2002; Vandenberg & Lance, 2000): (1) configural equivalence, (2) metric equivalence, (3) scalar equivalence, and (4) invariant uniqueness. Prior to the measurement equivalence tests involving all groups simultaneously, separate within-group CFAs were conducted to establish a well-fitting baseline measurement model for each group. After demonstrating adequate fit for the measurement model in each group, Cigularov et al. proceeded to test the measurement models simultaneously across the groups of interest in a sequence of four increasingly stringent tests as follows.

In the first step, Cigularov *et al.* (2013a, b) examined the configural equivalence or the equality of factor structure (i.e., same number of factors and pattern of factor loadings) of the baseline measurement models across the groups. In both studies, they found support for the configural equivalence of the safety climate measure across the studied groups. Establishing configural equivalence suggested that the safety climate items were answered with the same frame of reference by respondents from different groups. Lack of configural equivalence would suggest the inappropriateness of conducting mean comparisons of these groups or mixing these groups while conducting other statistics.

At the second step, the researchers assessed metric equivalence by constraining the factor loadings of the safety climate items to be equal across the groups and comparing the fit of the more restrictive (metric) model to the less restrictive (configural) model. The results from both studies revealed that there was no substantial reduction in model fit, lending support for the metric equivalence of the safety climate measure across both trade and ethnic groups of construction workers. This result suggested that respondents used the same metric to respond to the safety climate items. Non-equivalence of factor loadings would suggest that the differences on item scores are the result of different units employed by different groups of respondents.

Scalar equivalence is tested at the third step. Scalar equivalence suggests that the item intercepts are equal across the groups, which infers no systematic group differences in response bias. Finding support for scalar equivalence (along with configural and metric equivalence) is considered as strong evidence for measurement equivalence, and it is a prerequisite before conducting *latent* mean comparisons in safety climate (Meredith, 1993). Cigularov *et al.* (2013a) examined change in model fit between the scalar and the metric models and found a negligible reduction in fit, indicating that there was no systematic difference in response bias across the 10 construction trade groups. However, Cigularov *et al.* (2013b) found a reduction in model fit after imposing an equality constraint on the safety climate item intercepts across the three ethnic groups. This result suggested that the assumption of full scalar equivalence was not tenable. Then, they proceeded to explore partial scalar equivalence by releasing the equality constraints on the unequal intercepts one at a time after carefully considering modification indices, parameter estimates, and item content until no substantial reduction in model fit was observed. This process identified group differences in seven item intercepts (37% of the items), suggesting possible response bias. They also conducted latent mean comparisons and found no significant true differences in safety climate under conditions of partial scalar equivalence, after accounting for the seven unequal item intercepts.

Invariant uniqueness is the fourth and most stringent step to test measurement equivalence, which is established by demonstrating that item error variances are equal across the groups. This is accomplished by setting an additional constraint to the previous (most often scalar) equivalence model in the form of equal error variances and comparing model fit. Despite concerns that this might be an overly strict test of measurement equivalence, Cigularov *et al.* (2013a, b) examined invariant uniqueness of the safety climate measure, because it was a prerequisite for testing *observed* mean differences in safety climate, which represented a more common practice in organizational safety assessments compared to latent mean comparisons. Findings from both studies indicated only a mild deterioration in model fit, which provided some support for the invariant uniqueness of the safety climate measure under investigation.

As demonstrated previously, evaluating the measurement equivalence of safety measures is a research step that is complex and yet necessary. This step ensures that the safety assessments, which are often used by organizations for developing occupational safety interventions and programs, produce valid results that are generalizable across different groups of employees. For example, establishing measurement equivalence is essential when an organization plans to use group mean differences in safety perceptions to develop safety interventions targeting specific underperforming groups of employees or employees at a higher risk for injuries. Measurement equivalence is particularly important for organizations using safety climate measures, which are inherently perception based; establishing measurement equivalence should be an important consideration for multinational organizations, as the climate measures may or may not be directly transportable across borders, cultures, and languages.

Challenges and Future Research Directions

Over the past century, OHS researchers and practitioners have witnessed some improvements in workers' safety through enacted legislation, improved job designs, engineered safer tools, and the establishment of safety regulations and policies. Yet challenges in OHS remain. In the final section, we offer our observations about challenges and research directions regarding the themes we have reviewed.

Process and synergy of psychosocial safety climate and safety climate

As a relatively new concept, research on PSC is gaining momentum outside of traditional OHS research focusing on physical and environmental aspects of safety and health. Yet, knowledge is limited regarding the mechanisms through which PSC shapes the job and work context and moderates the impact of job demands. Likewise, the processes through which PSC is formed in an organization, and by which it varies within different parts of an organization, are unknown. While Dollard and Bakker (2010) suggested that key mechanism of transfer of PSC to the frontline is through leadership, no data are available on this issue.

Traditionally, safety climate is thought to be the leading cause of safety and health outcomes. Yet, it is possible that both safety climates and PSC can be affected by adverse outcomes. In other words, it is likely that both the job and work context, and psychological health and safety outcomes, have reciprocal effects on climate. Injury incidents and mental health problems occurring at work, as well as costs associated with lost productivity and increased absence, may send urgent signals to management teams about these risks, which motivate them to change their safety policies and practices which in turn may influence climate.

Although this issue has not been investigated in either safety climate or PSC literature, there is evidence suggesting that reciprocal causal relationships are indeed plausible. Beus *et al.* (2010) found that the injury → safety climate relationship ($\rho = -.29$) is stronger than safety climate → injury ($\rho = -.24$). Other studies also support both burnout → depression and depression → burnout relationships (Ahola & Hakanen, 2007), mental health → burnout and burnout → mental health relationships (Zapf, Dormann & Frese, 1996), and stressor → strain and strain → stressor relationships (Spector, Zapf, Chen & Frese, 2000). In their review of the occupational stress literature, Cigularov, Brusso and Callan (in press) point out that researchers rarely test reverse or reciprocal causal relationships. Clearly, there is a need for more attention to the possibility of reciprocal relationships between safety climate constructs and safety outcomes, such as accidents and injuries.

Finally, there is a need to explore potential synergy between safety climate and PSC and their interactions with other competing priorities. As Zohar (2010) voiced in his reflection of 30 years of safety climate research, the improvement of safety climate needs to go beyond the focus on safety in isolation and also pay attention to the forces of other competing elements in organizations such as production. Thus, it seems logical to strategically align both climates with production, which is driven by economic pressure. The notion of alignment implies that positive climates for health and safety (i.e., OHS climates) do not need to be subordinate to, or competing against, other priorities. Given that occupational injuries and illnesses cost organizations billions of dollars every year (e.g., US companies incurred 51.1 billion dollars in direct worker compensation costs in 2010; Liberty Mutual Research Institute for Safety, 2012), OHS climates should be viewed as leading indicators[1] integral to the larger management system, and consequently, as is the case with any typical management process, they should be implemented in a structured, systematic way in order to encourage successful performance. At the strategic level, OHS goals and objectives can be aligned with the business goals and objectives of the organization and play a role in mapping the ultimate direction of the organization. At the practical level, OHS climates along with other leading safety indicators can be aligned with how employee job performance is measured and rewarded in the company, thus linking them to key performance indicators implemented in the whole organization.

Migrant workers and OHS disparities

The increase of migrant workers has inevitably created OHS challenges concerning possible safety and health disparities. These disparities, in part attributed to their limited awareness of their legal rights, inadequate PPEs, and poor working conditions, may create social conflicts and threaten social stability (Zhu, Chen & Zhao, 2013). A recent report by ILO (2011) highlights the widespread discrimination, deterioration in working conditions, and increased xenophobia, violence, and often harsh political and social realities facing migrant workers in both developed and developing countries, especially in times of economic downturn. In fact, numerous news and government reports from around the world have linked unfair and discriminatory employment practices directed at migrant workers to increased crime rates and social unrest, including organized labor strikes and protests, which in turn have prompted local and international government bodies to take measures to address the social and political implications of (mis)managing increased migrant labor flows (China Labour Bulletin, 2012; French, 2006; Liow, 2003; Lum, 2006). The following recent events and trends across the globe validate the aforementioned concerns:

- In 2008, more than 60 migrants were killed and 10,000 were left homeless in South Africa by locals demanding their departure ("Fighting discrimination at work," 2011).
- Between 1993 and 2009, organized protests in China rose from 10,000 to 90,000, 75% of which involved workers and peasants (Leung & Ngai, 2009). Mass protests have seen the most dramatic increase in areas with high migrant worker populations (Becker, 2012).
- In January 2010, the shooting of two African workers in Rosarno, Italy, prompted a two-day riot of migrant workers, which resulted in 53 injured individuals (18 police, 14 locals, and 21 immigrants) and the evacuation of all migrant workers and their families from the town (Hooper, 2010).
- In March 2012, 70 Latino tomato pickers staged a six-day hunger strike in front of the headquarters of a major grocery store chain in Lakeland, Florida. The strike was part of an ongoing protest and labor conflict between tomato pickers (and community supporters) and their employer, raising concerns about the underpayment for migrant agricultural workers in the US (Weisenmiller, 2012).

To address potential influences of language and culture on OHS disparities, Leong *et al.* (2012) suggested that culturally tailored, language-concordant interventions should be developed and implemented for workers from different backgrounds. Moreover, ethnic group-specific and host country-specific research is called for to improve data on migrants from different ethnic/cultural backgrounds and in different host countries. These approaches would help identify unique OHS hazards and exposure and develop appropriate surveillance tools (Leong *et al.*). For instance, a peer-training approach has been suggested by several researchers to overcome cultural and language barriers in training (Williams *et al.*, 2010). This approach involves training a worker to act as an onsite trainer for OHS issues among migrant peers from the same ethnic group. Furthermore, the local community organizations and religious groups may play key roles in promoting workers' safety practices and awareness, encouraging them to participate in safety training, and assisting them to recognize their safety rights (Forst *et al.*, 2004; Lee, McGuinness & Kawakami, 2009).

Finally, OHS regulations and policies, as well as management commitment to safety, should be equally applied to migrant workers and their counterparts.

Measurement Equivalence Implications

In practice, needs assessment surveys are used to evaluate organizational needs related to physical and psychosocial health and safety. Based on the strengths and weaknesses identified, companies would implement safety prevention programs to remediate problems or prevent injuries and illnesses (Gittleman et al., 2010). Thus, the verification of measurement equivalence of surveys administered to workers from different populations (e.g., migrant and non-migrant workers) has important implications in organizational diagnosis, decision making, and change related to safety policies and practices. Imagine the situation where an organizational intervention is not endorsed for migrant workers because there is no mean difference on management commitment to safety (a key component in safety climate), even though the survey fails to show adequate measurement invariance across groups. The potential costs (both direct and indirect) could be detrimental to organizations and individuals when decisions are made based on erroneous results.

Another important implication about measurement equivalence, beyond the measurement issue, is to obtain a better understanding of cultural values and beliefs, as well as other contributing factors that may influence workers' frames of references about safety and risks, safety practices, safety leadership, safety behaviors, and so on, which in turn affect their interpretations and responses to survey questions. Future research may explore qualitatively how items of safety measures are comprehended and interpreted by workers from different backgrounds and the reasons underlying these interpretations. For instance, potential respondents could provide their thought processes in a more in-depth way to explain how and why they respond to each item. In addition, inclusion of these potential contributing factors in quantitative as well as qualitative safety research would offer invaluable information to improve safety research and practices (e.g., how to communicate risks and hazards at the tool box meetings).

Building strong climate for OHS

The UK Committee on Safety and Health at Work (1972) has attributed the OHS problem to a sense of apathy because injuries or illnesses are often infrequent and because managers often face competing short-term priorities such as productivity. Furthermore, the health consequences of many occupational diseases (e.g., black lung or hearing loss) may not be apparent until workers have extended periods of exposure to hazards. The combination of infrequent and longer-term consequences and competing short-term priorities makes it understandably challenging for managers to focus on safety concerns.

In the process of aligning OHS with productivity, the alignment between enacted and espoused priorities (Zohar, 2011) is one of the key driving forces to build a strong safety climate. Stated differently, it is the companies' commitment to safety and willingness to be responsible to address OHS *in action*, or talk the talk and walk the walk (Gittleman *et al.*, 2010), that promotes a strong and positive OHS climate. Our own field experience suggests that companies often react to OHS *problems* or lagging indicators (e.g., workers' compensation insurance premiums, lost time injury, or recordable injuries/illness) quickly and forcefully yet are less responsive to leading indicators (e.g., monitoring management commitment to safety), even though these indicators underpin a major portion of OHS problems.

In conclusion, there is a need to understand factors that contribute to changes in safety and examine the process of transformation at both micro and macro levels. What factors lead organizations to embrace societal values to build enduring institutions, people, and society? How can organizations be encouraged to adopt a preventative focus on building healthy workplaces rather than simply reacting to accidents and injuries? How can top management be consistent in both espoused and enacted priorities (what it says it does and what it does) and be strategic in aligning priorities for safety versus production?

Note

1. Leading indicators measure and track factors that are precursors to worker accidents, injuries, or illnesses and can be used to prevent injuries and fatalities (NORA Construction Sector Council, 2008).

References

Acosta-Leon, A. L., Grote, B. P., Salem, S., & Daraiseh, N. (2006). Risk factors associated with adverse health and safety outcomes in the US Hispanic workforce. *Theoretical Issues in Ergonomics Science, 7*, 299–310.

Ahola, K., & Hakanen, J. (2007). Job strain, burnout, and depressive symptoms: A prospective study among dentists. *Journal of Affective Disorders, 104*, 103–110.

Ahonen, E. Q., Benavides, F. G., & Benach, J. (2007). Immigrant populations, work and health – A systematic literature review. *Scandinavian Journal of Work, Environment & Health, 33*(2), 96–104.

Becker, J. (2012). The knowledge to act: Chinese migrant labor protests in comparative perspective. *Comparative Political Studies, 44*(11), 1379–1404.

Beus, J. M., Payne, S. C., Bergman, M. E., & Arthur Jr., W. (2010). Safety climate and injuries: An examination of theoretical and empirical relationships. *Journal of Applied Psychology, 95*, 713–727.

Bond, S. A., Tuckey, M. R., & Dollard, M. F. (2010). Psychosocial safety climate, workplace bullying, and symptoms of posttraumatic stress. *Organization Development Journal, 28*, 37–56.

Brunette, M. J. (2005). Development of educational and training materials on safety and health: Targeting Hispanic workers in the construction industry. *Family & Community Health, 28*, 253–266.

Centers for Disease Control and Prevention. (2008). Work-related injury deaths among Hispanics – United States, 1992–2006. *Morbidity and Mortality Weekly Report, 57*, 596–600.

Cheung, G. W., & Rensvold, R. B. (2002). Evaluating goodness-of-fit indexes for testing measurement invariance. *Structural Equation Modeling, 9*, 233–255.

Cheyne, A., Oliver, A., Tomas, J., & Cox, S. (2002). The architecture of employee attitudes to safety in the manufacturing sector. *Personnel Review, 31*, 649–670.

China Labour Bulletin. (2012, March). *A decade of change: The workers' movement in China 2000–2010.* Retrieved November 12, 2013, from http://www.clb.org.hk/en/sites/default/files/File/research_reports/Decade%20of%20the%20Workers%20Movement%20final.pdf

Christian, M. S., Bradley, J. C., Wallace, J. C., & Burke, M. J. (2009). Workplace safety: A meta-analysis of the roles of person and situation factors. *Journal of Applied Psychology, 94*, 1103–1127.

Cigularov, K. P., Adams, S., Gittleman, J. L., Haile, E., & Chen, P. Y. (2013a). Measurement equivalence and mean comparisons of a safety climate measure across construction trades. *Accident Analysis & Prevention, 51*, 68–77.

Cigularov, K. P., Brusso, R. C., & Callan, R. C. (in press). Longitudinal research in occupational stress: A review of methodological issues. In C. Cooper & P. Y. Chen (Eds.), *Wellbeing in the workplace: From stress to happiness.* Oxford/New York: Wiley-Blackwell.

Cigularov, K. P., Chen, P. Y., & Rosecrance, J. C. (2010). The effects of error management climate and safety communication on safety: A multi-level study. *Accident Analysis and Prevention, 42*, 1488–1497.

Cigularov, K. P., Lancaster, P. G., Chen, P. Y., Gittleman, J. L., & Haile, E. (2013b). Measurement equivalence of a safety climate measure among Hispanic and White non-Hispanic construction workers. *Safety Science, 54*, 58–68.

Clarke, S. (2010). An integrative model of safety climate: Linking psychological climate and work attitudes to individual safety outcomes using meta-analysis. *Journal of Occupational & Organizational Psychology, 83*, 553–578.

Corvalan, C. F., Driscoll, T. R., & Harrison, J. E. (1994). Role of migrant factors in work-related fatalities in Australia. *Scandinavian Journal of Work, Environment & Health, 20*, 364–370.

Davila, A., Mora, M. T., & Gonzalez, R. (2011). English-language proficiency and occupational risk among Hispanic immigrant men in the United States. *Industrial Relations, 50*, 263–296.

Demerouti, E., Bakker A. B., Nachreiner, F., & Schaufeli, W. B. (2001). The Job Demands–Resources model of burnout. *Journal of Applied Psychology, 86*, 499–512.

Dollard, M. F., & Bakker, A. B. (2010). Psychosocial safety climate as a precursor to conducive work environments, psychological health problems, and employee engagement. *Journal of Occupational and Organizational Psychology, 83*, 579–599.

Dollard, M. F., & Karasek, R. (2010). Building psychosocial safety climate: Evaluation of a socially coordinated PAR risk management stress prevention study. In J. Houdmont & S. Leka (Eds.), *Contemporary occupational health psychology: Global perspectives on research and practice* (pp. 208–234). Chichester, UK: Wiley Blackwell.

Dollard, M. F., Opie, T., Lenthall, S., Wakerman, J., Knight, S., Dunn, S., *et al.* (2012). Psychosocial safety climate as an antecedent of work characteristics and psychological strain: A multilevel model. *Work & Stress, 26*(4), 385–404.

Dong, X. S., Fujimoto, A., Ringen, K., & Men, Y. (2009). Fatal falls among Hispanic construction workers. *Accident Analysis and Prevention, 41,* 1047–1052.

Dong, X., & Platner, J. W. (2004). Occupational fatalities of Hispanic construction workers from 1992 to 2000. *American Journal of Industrial Medicine, 45,* 45–54.

European Agency for Safety and Health at Work. (2008). *Literature study on migrant workers.* Retrieved November 12, 2013, from https://osha.europa.eu/en/publications/literature_reviews/migrant_workers

European Foundation for the Improvement of Living and Working Conditions. (2007). *Fourth European working conditions survey.* Luxembourg City, Luxembourg: Office for Official Publications of the European Communities. Retrieved November 12, 2013, from http://www.eurofound.europa.eu/pubdocs/2006/98/en/2/ef0698en.pdf

Faucett, J., Meyers, J., Tejeda, D., Janowitz, I., Miles, J., & Kabashima, J. (2001). An instrument to measure musculoskeletal symptoms among immigrant Hispanic farmworkers: Validation in the nursery industry. *Journal of Agricultural Safety and Health, 7,* 185–198.

Fighting discrimination at work: Progress at risk (2011, August 5). *World of Work, 72,* 6–19.

Findley, M., Smith, S., Gorski, J., & O'Neil, M. (2011). Safety climate differences among job positions in a nuclear decommissioning and demolition industry: Employees' self-reported safety attitudes and perceptions. *Safety Science, 45,* 875–889.

Forst, L., Lacey, S., Chen, H. Y., Jimenez, R., Bauer, S., Skinner, S., *et al.* (2004). Effectiveness of community health workers for promoting use of safety eyewear by Latino farm workers. *American Journal of Industrial Medicine, 46,* 607–613.

French, H. W. (2006). China success story chokes on its own growth. *The New York Times.* Retrieved November 12, 2013, from http://www.nytimes.com/2006/12/19/world/asia/19shenzhen.html

Gittleman, J., Gardner, P., Haile, E., Sampson, J., Cigularov, K. P., Ermann, E. D., *et al.* (2010). City Center and Cosmopolitan Construction Projects, Las Vegas, Nevada: Lessons learned from the use of multiple sources and mixed methods in a safety needs assessment. *Journal of Safety Research, 41,* 263–291.

Glendon, A., & Litherland, D. (2001). Safety climate factors, group differences and safety behavior in road construction. *Safety Science, 39,* 157–188.

Guldenmund, F. W. (2007). The use of questionnaires in safety culture research – An evaluation. *Safety Science, 45,* 723–743.

Hayes, B. E., Peranda, J., Smecko, T., & Trask, J. (1998). Measuring perceptions of workplace safety: Development and validation of the workplace safety scale. *Journal of Safety Research, 29,* 145–161.

Hooper, J. (2010, January). Southern Italian town world's 'only white town' after ethnic cleansing. *The Guardian.* Retrieved November 12, 2013, from http://www.theguardian.com/world/2010/jan/11/italy-rosarno-violence-immigrants

Huang, Y. H., Chen, P. Y., & Grosch, J. W. (2010). Safety climate: New developments in conceptualization, theory, and research. *Accident Analysis and Prevention, 42,* 1421–1422.

Idris, M. A., Dollard, M. F., Coward, J., & Dormann, C. (2012). Psychosocial safety climate: Conceptual distinctiveness and effect on job demands and worker psychological well-being. *Safety Science, 50,* 19–28.

International Labour Organization [ILO]. (2004). *Towards a fair deal for migrant workers in the global economy.* Retrieved November 12, 2013, from http://www.ilo.org/global/publications/ilo-bookstore/order-online/books/WCMS_PUBL_9221130436_EN/lang–en/index.htm

ILO (2011). *Equality at work: The continuing challenge*. Retrieved November 12, 2013, from http://www.ilo.org/asia/whatwedo/publications/WCMS_164949/lang--en/index.htm

ILO (2012). Occupational safety and health. Retrieved November 12, 2013, from http://www.ilo.org/global/standards/subjects-covered-by-international-labour-standards/occupational-safety-and-health/lang-en/index.htm

Karasek, R. A. (1979). Job demands, job decision latitude, and mental strain: Implications for job design. *Administrative Science Quarterly*, 24, 285–308.

Law, R., Dollard, M. F., Tuckey, M. R., & Dormann, C. (2011). Psychosocial safety climate as a lead indicator of workplace psychosocial hazards, psychological health and employee engagement. *Accident Analysis & Prevention*, 43, 1782–1793.

Lee, K., McGuinness, C., & Kawakami, T. (2011). *Research on occupational safety and health for migrant workers in five Asia and the Pacific countries: Australia, Republic of Korea, Malaysia, Singapore and Thailand*. ILO Asian and the Pacific Working Paper Series. Retrieved November 12, 2013, from http://www.ilo.org/wcmsp5/groups/public/–asia/–ro-bangkok/–sro-bangkok/documents/publication/wcms_170518.pdfLee, P. T. (2009). Occupational and environmental health. In C. Trinh-Shevrin, N. S. Islam, & M. J. Rey (Eds.), *Asian American communities and health: Context, research, policy and action*. San Francisco: Jossey-Bass.

Leong, F. T. L., Eggerth, D., Flynn, M., Roberts, R., & Mak, S. (2012). Occupational health disparities among racial and ethnic minorities. In P. L. Perrewé, J. R. B. Halbesleben, & C. C. Rosen (Eds.), *The Role of the economic crisis on occupational stress and well being*. Emerald Group Publishing Limited, UK.

Leung, P. N., & Ngai, P. (2009). Radicalization of the new Chinese working class: A case study of collective action in the gemstone industry. *Third World Quarterly*, 30, 551–565.

Liberty Mutual Research Institute for Safety. (2012). *2012 Liberty mutual workplace safety index*. Hopkinton, MA: Author.

Liow, J. (2003). Malaysia's illegal Indonesian migrant labour problem: In search of solutions. *Contemporary Southeast Asia*, 25(1), 44–64.

Loh, K., & Richardson, S. (2004). Foreign-born workers: Trends in fatal occupational injuries, 1996–2001. *Monthly Labor Review*, 127, 42–53.

Lum, T. (2006, May). *Social unrest in China* (CRS Report No. RL33416). Retrieved November 12, 2013, from Congressional Research Service website: http://www.fas.org/sgp/crs/row/RL33416.pdf

Meredith, W. (1993). Measurement equivalence, factor analysis and factorial equivalence. *Psychometrika*, 58, 525–543.

Münsterberg, H. (1913). *Psychology and industrial efficiency*. Boston, MA: Houghton Mifflin Company.

National Institute of Occupational Safety and Health. (2008). *NIOSH worklife initiative: Essential elements*. Retrieved November 12, 2013, from http://www.cdc.gov/niosh/docket/archive/docket132.html

National Research Council. (2003). *Safety is seguridad*. Washington, DC: National Academy of Sciences.

NORA Construction Sector Council. (2008). *National construction agenda for occupational safety and health research and practice in the U.S. construction sector*. Retrieved November 12, 2013, from http://www.cdc.gov/niosh/nora/comment/agendas/construction/pdfs/ConstOct2008.pdf

Occupational Safety and Health Administration, U.S. Department of Labor. (2013). *Commonly used statistics*. Retrieved November 12, 2013, from https://www.osha.gov/oshstats/commonstats.html

O'Connor, T. M., Loomis, D., Runyan, C., dal Santo, J. A., & Schulman, M. (2005). Adequacy of health and safety training among young Latino construction workers. *Journal of Occupational and Environmental Medicine, 47*, 272–277.

Parker, D., Brosseau, L., Samant, Y., Pan, W., Xi, M., Haugan, D., *et al.* (2007). A comparison of the perceptions and beliefs of workers and owners with regard to workplace safety in small metal fabrication businesses. *American Journal of Industrial Medicine, 50*, 999–1009.

SafeWork Australia. (2011). *Work-related injuries in Australia: Who did and didn't receive workers' compensation in 2009–10.* Retrieved November 12, 2013, from http://www.safeworkaustralia.gov.au/sites/SWA/about/Publications/Documents/644/Who%20did%20and%20did%20not%20receive%20workers%20compensation%202009-10.pdf

Smith, P. M., & Mustard, C. A. (2009). Comparing the risk of work-related injuries between immigrants to Canada and Canadian-born labour market participants. *Occupational and Environmental Medicine, 66*, 361–367.

Snyder, L. A., Krauss, A. D., Chen, P. Y., Finlinson, S., & Huang, Y. H. (2008). Occupational safety: Application of the job demand-control-support model. *Accident Analysis & Prevention, 40*, 1713–1723.

Spector, P. E., Zapf, D., Chen, P. Y., & Frese, M. (2000). Why negative affectivity should not be controlled in job stress research: Don't throw out the baby with the bath water. *Journal of Organizational Behavior, 21*, 79–95.

Stout, N. A., & Linn, H. I. (2002). Occupational injury prevention: Progress and priorities. *Injury Prevention, 8*(Suppl. IV), iv9–iv14.

Sutton, J. (2008). Asia-Pacific labour mobility and the two track labour market. *People and Place, 16*, 85–91.

Trajkovski, S., & Loosemore, M. (2006). Safety implications of low-English proficiency among migrant construction site operatives. *International Journal of Project Management, 24*, 446–452.

UK Committee on Safety and Health at Work. (1972). *Safety and health at work: Report of the committee, 1970–72.* London: H. M. Stationery Office.

Vandenberg, R., & Lance, C. (2000). A review and synthesis of the measurement invariance literature: Suggestions, practices, and recommendations for organizational research. *Organizational Research Methods, 3*, 4–70.

Vinodkumara, M. N., & Bhasi, M. (2010). Safety management practices and safety behaviour: Assessing the mediating role of safety knowledge and motivation. *Accident Analysis & Prevention, 42*(6), 2082–2093.

Viteles, M. S. (1932). *Industrial psychology.* New York: W. W. Norton.

Weisenmiller, M. (2012). *Protest highlights underpayment of U.S. migrant farm workers.* Retrieved November 12, 2013, from http://news.xinhuanet.com/english/world/2012-03/27/c_122884690.htm

Williams, Q., Ochsner, M., Marshall, E., Kimmel, L., & Martino, C. (2010). The impact of a peer-led participatory health and safety training program for Latino day laborers in construction. *Journal of Safety Research, 41*, 253–261.

Wu, T., Liu, C., & Lu, M. (2007). Safety climate in university and college laboratories: Impact of organizational and individual factors. *Journal of Safety Research, 38*, 91–102.

Zapf, D., Dormann, C., & Frese, M. (1996). Longitudinal studies in organizational stress research: A review of the literature with reference to methodological issues. *Journal of Occupational Health Psychology, 1*, 145–169.

Zhu, Y., Chen, P. Y., & Zhao, W. (2013). Injured workers in China: Injustice, conflict and social instability. Submitted for publication.

Zohar, D. (1980). Safety climate in industrial organizations: Theoretical and applied implications. *Journal of Applied Psychology*, *65*, 96–102.

Zohar, D. (2010). Thirty years of safety climate research: Reflections and future directions. *Accident Analysis & Prevention*, *42*, 1517–1522.

Zohar, D. (2011). Safety climate: Conceptual and measurement issues. In J. C. Quick & L. E. Tetrick (Eds.), *Handbook of occupational health psychology* (2 ed., pp. 141–164). Washington, DC: American Psychological Association.

Zohar, D., & Luria, G. (2005). A multilevel model of safety climate: Cross-level relationships between organization and group-level climates. *Journal of Applied Psychology*, *90*, 616–628.

10

The WHO Healthy Workplace Model: Challenges and Opportunities

Evelyn Kortum

World Health Organization, Switzerland

While the importance of the workplace in protecting and promoting health, and in ensuring healthy behaviors, for workers and their families has been recognized for quite some time (WHO Global Strategy for Occupational Health for All, 1996), there is still ample room for action in this regard. In addition, recent changes in the global world of work, partly linked to global economic and social transitions, have affected actions related to workers' health. For example, job insecurity, having risen in the past decade, has been shown to negatively affect physical and mental health (Ferrie *et al.*, 1998; Metcalfe *et al.*, 2003; Ostry & Spiegel, 2004; Pollard, 2001; Virtanen *et al.*, 2005). Globalization has certainly contributed to an exacerbation of job insecurity, and, in addition, has resulted in an increase of the size of the informal sector, with informal workers mostly being unprotected by any national labor law. Evidence-based findings link social determinants, such as social status, stress, early life, social exclusion, work, unemployment, social support, addiction, food, and transport, to health in its broad sense (Wilkinson & Marmot, 2003). Many of these determinants are linked to working conditions and, hence, demonstrate that ill-health outcomes, particularly non-communicable and mental health problems, can be related to adverse employment and working conditions, in addition to limited possibilities to pursue healthy lifestyles.

But why should one address workers' health? Apart from the ethical obligation to protect and promote health for the whole population, including the working population, there are obvious benefits to society as a whole. Ensuring better health for the working population will undoubtedly result in improved productivity and, consequently, economic performance. This, in turn, will ensure the stability of society and will reflect in an improved health status of the population as a whole.

Contemporary Occupational Health Psychology: Global Perspectives on Research and Practice, Volume 3,
First Edition. Edited by Stavroula Leka and Robert R. Sinclair.
© 2014 World Health Organization.

In many parts of the world, however, and particularly after the recent financial crisis, sustainable economic recovery will not be achieved unless key employment and social challenges are addressed including skills development (Kortum, 2012).

The increasing evidence about the high burden of disease related to sub-standard working and employment conditions, together with the enhanced understanding of the socio-economic benefits of preventive actions to improve these conditions, is starting to show effect through two major transitions in approaches to protecting and promoting workers' health. The first is the fact that, more and more, workers' health is seen as a part of overall public health. The working population is a major part of the population as a whole, and improving their health will directly result in improved health of the population as a whole. In addition, good health of the working population will positively affect the health of their families and communities. The second transition is a move towards considering all factors affecting health at work in a holistic manner, rather than addressing individual types of risk. Addressing these separately, without accounting for other potential or synergistic effects, may not result in improving workers' health.

The Role of WHO

As the global directing and coordinating authority for health within the United Nations system, the World Health Organization (WHO) has the responsibility to provide leadership on global health matters, to shape the health research agenda, to set health-related norms and standards, to articulate evidence-based policy options, to provide technical support to countries, and to monitor and assess health trends (WHO Constitution, 1946). The WHO Constitution recognizes that "the enjoyment of the highest attainable standard of health is one of the fundamental rights of every human being without distinction of race, religion, political belief, economic or social condition" (WHO, 1946). This certainly applies to the working population, constituting almost half of the world's population. And while work is essential to providing income to support human needs and, hence, positively impacts on the health and well-being of individuals and on the social and economic status of societies, it is clear that sub-standard working conditions are linked to certain risks in the work environment, with social factors, behaviors, and access to health services being other determinants of workers' health (Ivanov & Kortum, 2008).

Health at the workplace has, therefore, been part of WHO's work since its inception. The World Health Assembly (WHA), the supreme governing body of WHO, has adopted, over the years, a number of resolutions supporting the work of the organization in the field of occupational health, stressing its importance as part of public health, and promoting action by member states to increase their capacities for management of occupational health services and diseases (resolutions WHA 25.63, 28.73, and 29.57). In resolution WHA 33.31, adopted by the 33rd WHA in 1980, a global program of action on workers' health was established with the aim of supporting developing countries and facilitating experience and knowledge, as well as promoting the coordination of work at national level. In 1996, the 49th WHA endorsed the Global Strategy on Occupational Health for All as a comprehensive policy framework for WHO's work on workers' health (resolution WHA 49.12).

Global processes have also supported a major role for WHO in the field of health at the workplace. The World Summit on Sustainable Development held in Johannesburg in 2002 recommended that WHO's program to "reduce occupational deaths, injuries and illness, and link occupational health with public health promotion as a means of promoting public health education" be strengthened and promoted (United Nations, 2002).

In its resolution WHA 60.26, the 60th WHA in 2007 endorsed the Global Plan of Action (GPA) on Workers' Health 2008–2017. The resolution called on governments to work jointly with workers, employers, and their organizations in devising national policies and implementation plans for the GPA and to strive towards full coverage of all workers, including those in the informal economy, small- and medium-sized enterprises, as well as agricultural and migrant workers, with regard to essential interventions and basic occupational health services for primary prevention of work-related diseases and injuries. The GPA includes workers' health as an important component of general public health but also recognizes its importance for policies addressing sustainable development, poverty reduction, employment, trade, environmental protection, and education.

The GPA provides a new policy framework for concerted action to protect, promote, and improve the health of all workers. WHO's global action on workers' health has five major elements: (1) devising and implementing policy instruments on workers' health; (2) protecting and promoting health at the workplace, (3) improving the performance of, and access to, occupational health services; (4) providing and communicating evidence for action and practice; and (5) incorporating workers' health into other policies. Since healthy and safe workplaces are, *inter alia*, an essential prerequisite for preventing accidents and for preventing the spread of infectious public health threats (e.g., SARS or H5N1), it is evident that action on protecting workers' health and safety can contribute in a major way to global public health security. Thus, WHO views actions on workers' health as part and parcel of ensuring global health security.

Then, in May 2013, at the 66th WHA, WHO member states recognized the importance of and endorsed the action plans for non-communicable diseases and mental health for the period 2013–2020. The major actions relevant to workers' health in the non-communicable action plan include developing programs for healthy workplaces, connecting occupational health services to primary health care, and addressing occupational non-communicable diseases. Objective three of the mental health action plan specifically focuses on the promotion of participation in work and return-to-work programs for those affected by mental and psychosocial disorders, as well as the promotion of safe and supportive working conditions, with attention to work organizational improvements, training on mental health for managers, and the provision of stress management courses and workplace wellness programs. It, furthermore, focuses on tackling stigmatization and discrimination, as well as on workplace initiatives for suicide prevention.

Burden of Disease due to Workplace Hazards

Earlier studies on ill-health effects of unhealthy and unsafe working conditions revealed that these result in about two million deaths per year around the world (Driscoll *et al.*, 2005). With regard to non-communicable diseases, occupational risk factors accounted for 37% of back pain, 16% of hearing loss, 13% of chronic obstructive pulmonary disease, 11% of asthma, 8% of injuries, 9% of lung cancer, and 2% of leukemia (Concha-Barrientos *et al.*, 2004). In the case of depression, 8% was attributed to occupational risks (Prüss-Üstün & Corvalán, 2006). The WHO action plan on non-communicable diseases makes reference to the fact that 48% of overall cardiovascular diseases, 12% of chronic obstructive pulmonary diseases, and 21% of cancers are preventable. Out of these, 26% of cardiovascular diseases and chronic obstructive pulmonary diseases and 11% of cancers are preventable through interventions at the workplace. This is close to half of preventive potential in the workplace, hence underlining the importance of workplace interventions.

More recently, a meta-analysis of data from 13 European cohorts with 197,473 men and women demonstrated that job strain is associated with an elevated risk of chronic heart disease, suggesting that prevention of work-related stress may lead to a reduction in chronic heart disease incidence (Kivimäki *et al.*, 2012).

Ill-health in the working population leads to an increased level of absence from the workplace. In addition, the number of people who leave the labor market permanently with a health problem or condition is increasing around the globe. This comes at a time when economic considerations require that society aims at benefiting from a maximum number of productive years from as many people as possible, so that the ratio of earners (working population) to dependants (children, pensioners, unemployed) is kept high. With life expectancy increasing, this becomes an even more urgent need. Good health is a prerequisite for an extended healthy working life. In the UK, recent statistics show that out of a working population of 27.6 million, 2.5% are off sick on average and 26% have a permanent health condition or disability. This relates to 8.8 million "inactive" and 2.5 million unemployed, among whom 49% and 31%, respectively, live with a health condition or disability (DWP, 2012).

Workers' health is determined by a variety of different factors, the first being hazards in the work environment. These may be of mechanical, physical, chemical, biological, ergonomic, or psychosocial nature and are often encountered in combinations. Secondly, work-related health practices may have a substantive effect on workers' health. Among those, unhealthy habits such as smoking and drinking and lack of physical exercise and the prevalence of sedentary work, unhealthy diet, and behaviors related to an increased risk taking and neglecting personal protection are common. Thirdly, social factors may contribute to health outcomes of workers. Such factors include occupational status, employment conditions, income level, and perceived or real inequities due to gender, race, age, religion, or others. Finally, access to health services is a key determinant of workers' health. This relates to both preventive occupational health services and curative care and rehabilitation services. Also, the availability of health and accident insurance schemes is a major component of accessibility of health services, which is largely a privilege of formal sector workers.

The most common reasons for absence from work in industrialized countries are musculoskeletal problems and common mental health problems (e.g., DWP, 2012). In fact, psychosocial risk factors have often been neglected, though their importance cannot be stressed enough. The high prevalence across the population, paired with the fact that often little or no objective disease or impairment is seen and that most episodes settle rapidly, even though symptoms often persist or recur, points to the fact that in those instances, simple, early interventions can really make a difference. These may include improved work organization, coupled with sound managerial behavior and leadership (Nielsen, Randall & Brenner, 2008). This by no means signifies that psychosocial risk factors have no serious effects, since the relationship between these and serious chronic disease outcomes has been clearly demonstrated as outlined earlier in this chapter.

It is important to reinforce the approach that occupational health should not be addressed separately from general public health given the intricate relationship between risk factors at work and outside of it and the close interaction between the various factors, mechanical, social, behavioral, and access related, in determining potential health impacts. It is, therefore, important to note that work *per se* is a determinant of health.

The Need for an Integrated Approach

A well-functioning society, which performs well in economic and social terms, requires a high-performing, resilient workforce to ensure enhanced productivity. This, in turn, necessitates that the workforce is healthy and engaged and that the organizations they work in are safe and well managed. Ensuring good health of workers requires concerted action involving a variety of actors and addressing workers' health in a holistic manner. Key prerequisites include a capable and an informed leadership, innovative and forward-looking management structures and approaches, consideration of the need to ensure a working environment that prevents ill-health outcomes and ensures resilience and engagement of the workforce, the integration of traditional occupational health and safety with health promotion and well-being, accommodation of chronic conditions at the workplace through return-to-work programs, and application of public health measures and approaches in the workplace (e.g., DWP, 2012; WHO, 2007, 2010, 2012).

The WHO Healthy Workplace Model

Against the background of the need to take a holistic view towards workers' health and with the understanding that occupational health is part of general public health, the WHO healthy workplace model was developed (WHO, 2010). The model considers the various dimensions of workers' health and its determinants, as well as the fact that various key players contribute to ensuring it. The model covers both content and process, without being prescriptive to avoid the wrong impression of a "one-size-fits-all" approach. On the contrary, the model is presented as a flexible framework, and individual enterprises/businesses are encouraged to adapt it to their needs, considering their own workplace, their own culture, and their own country's legislative framework.

The model refers to a number of core values that apply to business ethics, including personal and social codes of behavior, the business case relating costs of prevention to those resulting from accidents and illnesses and the legal case showing that business liability will enhance adherence to relevant legislation and policies. Key criteria of the model include management commitment, the involvement of workers, a continuous learning approach, as well as the need to work towards achieving sustainability. In this context, sustainability strategies are those means applied by businesses in order to engage in improving health protection and health promotion and to ensure social well-being for workers and their families, with the goal of integrating these approaches into the business culture (Kortum, 2013, chapter in press).

The healthy workplace initiative thus aims at facilitating the application and implementation of comprehensive approaches to workplace health promotion and protection. Such approaches are in line with the broad definition of health as an integrated value in the 1948 Constitution of the WHO, which states that health is "a state of complete physical, mental and social well-being, and not merely the absence of disease". Later on, in May 1984, the 37th WHA took the historic decision to adopt resolution WHA 37.13, which made the "spiritual dimension" part and parcel of WHO member states' strategies for health. Fourteen years later, the special group of the WHO Executive Board for the review of the Constitution proposed that the preamble be modified to read as follows: "Health is a state of complete physical, mental, spiritual and social well-being and not merely the absence of disease". Hence, the WHO definition of a healthy workplace is based on this broad view of health in general and considers, in addition, evidence from best practice in research and applied policies (WHO, 2010). As such, it is also adaptable to a variety of cultures that want to further develop the health component of their national policies and programs.

The WHO healthy workplace model encompasses four avenues of influence, covering, in terms of content, actions that can best be taken and, in terms of process, the most effective ways that can be followed by employers and workers to implement such actions.

Therefore, a healthy workplace is one in which workers and managers jointly develop, apply, and continuously improve a comprehensive process to protect and promote the health, safety, and well-being of all workers and the sustainability of the workplace. In applying such an approach, the following issues need to be considered in a flexible manner, taking into account specific identified needs and priorities:

- Health and safety concerns in the physical work environment;
- Health, safety, and well-being concerns in the psychosocial work environment including organization of work and workplace culture;

- Personal health resources (available choices) in the workplace provided by the employer; and
- Ways of participating in the community to improve the health of workers, their families, and other members of the community.

The four avenues of influence of the model in Figure 10.1 refer to content and not process. Each of the four avenues is explained in Figure 10.1, including some examples of interventions to make the workplace healthier and safer. It is important to note that the four avenues are not to be considered as separate, since they do interact, overlap, and have common denominators (WHO, 2010).

The physical work environment is the part of the workplace that can be detected by human or electronic senses, including the structure, air, machines, furniture, products, chemicals, materials, and processes that are present or that occur in the workplace, which can affect the physical or mental safety, health, and well-being of workers. If the worker performs his or her tasks outdoors or in a vehicle, then that location is the physical work environment. Examples of interventions include:

- Eliminating a toxic chemical or substituting with one less hazardous,
- Installing machine guards or local exhaust ventilation,
- Training workers on safe operating procedures,
- Providing personal protective equipment such as respirators or hard hats.

Personal health resources in the workplace encompass the supportive environment and the choices provided to include health services, information, resources, opportunities, and flexibility an enterprise provides to workers to support or motivate their efforts to improve or maintain healthy personal lifestyle practices. They also enable them to monitor and support their ongoing physical and mental health. Examples include:

- Providing fitness facilities, classes, or equipment for workers;
- Providing healthy food choices in the cafeteria and vending machines;
- Putting no smoking policies in place and providing smoking cessation assistance;
- Providing information about alcohol and drugs and employee assistance counseling;
- Providing confidential medical services such as health assessments, medical examinations, medical surveillance, and medical treatment if not accessible in the community (e.g., antiretroviral treatment for HIV).

The psychosocial work environment includes the organization of work and organizational culture and the attitudes, values, beliefs, and practices that are demonstrated on a daily basis in the enterprise/organization, which affect the mental and physical well-being of employees. These are sometimes generally referred to as workplace stressors, which may cause emotional or mental stress to workers. Examples of interventions include:

- Reallocating work to reduce workload;
- Enforcing zero tolerance for harassment, bullying, or discrimination;

- Allowing flexibility in how and when work is done to respect work–family balance;
- Recognizing and rewarding good performance appropriately;
- Allowing meaningful worker input into decisions that affect them.

Enterprise–community involvement or business responsibility comprises the activities, expertise, and other resources an enterprise engages in or provides to the social and physical community or communities in which it operates and which affect the physical and mental health, safety, and well-being of workers and their families. It includes activities, expertise, and resources provided to the immediate local environment but also the broader global environment. Examples include:

- Providing free or affordable primary health care to workers and including access for family members, employees from small and medium enterprises, and informal workers;
- Providing free supplemental literacy education to workers and their families;
- Providing leadership and expertise related to workplace health and safety to small and medium enterprises in the community;
- Implementing voluntary controls over pollutants released into the air or water;
- Providing financial support to worthwhile community causes without an expectation of concomitant enterprise advertising.

Clearly, not every enterprise may have the immediate need or capacity to address each of these four avenues at the same time. The way an enterprise addresses the four avenues must be based on the needs and priorities identified through an

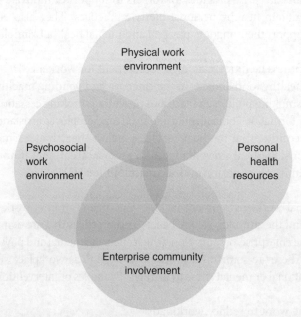

Figure 10.1   The Four Avenues of Influence.

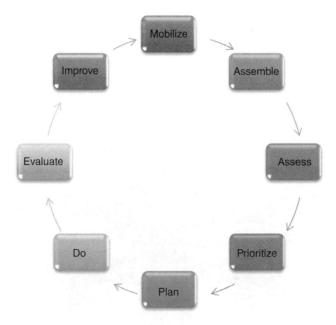

Figure 10.2   Risk Assessment and Management Cycle.

assessment process that involves extensive consultation with workers and their representatives through health and safety committees. Lack of capacity (or need) to address all components should not be a reason not to start acting on what can be achieved. However, actions in all four avenues need to be planned and addressed in time as these are synergistic and have shown to be more efficient than actions in isolation on one of the avenues of influence only.

Implementing a healthy workplace program that is sustainable and effective in meeting the needs of workers and employers requires more than knowing what kinds of issues to consider. To successfully create such a healthy workplace, an enterprise must follow a process that involves continuous improvement (a management systems approach). This is graphically represented by the continual improvement loop of mobilize, assemble, assess, prioritize, plan, do, evaluate, and improve, graphically demonstrated in Figure 10.2.

Two core principles are basic requirements that underlie this model: management commitment and workers' involvement. They are featured in the center of Figure 10.3, which is the healthy workplace model including all its components. These principles are not merely steps in the process, but are fundamental requirements for the successful implementation of a healthy workplace. They describe circumstances or conditions that must be tapped into at every stage of the process.

The Five Keys: A Simple Roadmap to Implementing the WHO Healthy Workplace Model

To provide assistance to enterprises in establishing and maintaining healthy workplaces, an overview of the five main elements of the healthy workplace model

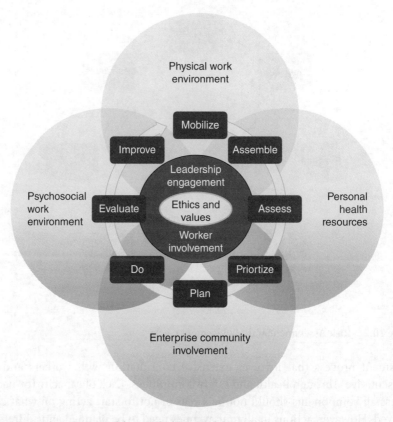

Figure 10.3 The WHO Healthy Workplace Model.

and its implementation requirements was developed by WHO and launched in 2013 in a variety of languages. The document entitled *Five keys to healthy workplaces: no business wealth without workers' health* is published on the WHO website. The guidance is comprised of five action areas, denominated "keys", which describe what needs to be done to achieve a healthy workplace (Table 10.1). Again, if action is possible only on some of the keys, depending on identified needs or limited capacity, then it should be taken, rather than delaying action until all five keys can be addressed. The process can be incremental until all keys are addressed.

The five keys are the following: (1) leadership commitment and engagement, requiring the mobilization and gaining of commitment from major stakeholders, such as senior management and union leadership, to integrate healthy workplaces into the business goals and values, including the obtainment of necessary permissions, resources, and support; (2) involvement of workers and their representatives to ensure that due to their active participation as partners in all steps of the risk assessment and management process, from planning to evaluation, they see themselves as co-owners of the process; (3) ensuring adherence to business ethics and legality through securing employees' health and safety, adhering to workers' social and ethical codes within their broader community, enforcing occupational

Table 10.1 Five Keys for Healthy Workplaces: No Business Wealth without Workers' Health

Key 1: Leadership commitment and engagement	• Mobilize and gain commitment from major stakeholders (e.g., senior leadership, union leadership) to integrate healthy workplaces into the enterprise's business goals and values • Get necessary permissions, resources, and support • Provide key evidence of this commitment by developing and adopting a comprehensive policy that is signed by the enterprise's highest authority which clearly indicates that healthy workplace initiatives are part of the organization's business strategy
Key 2: Involve workers and their representatives	• Workers and their representatives must not simply be "consulted" or "informed" but must be actively involved in every step of the risk assessment and management process from planning to evaluation, considering their opinions and ideas • It is critical that workers have some collective means of expression
Key 3: Business ethics and legality	• One of the most basic of universally accepted ethical principles is to "do no harm" to others and to ensure employees' health and safety • Adhere to workers' social and ethical codes as part of their role in the broader community • Enforce occupational health codes and laws • Take responsibility for workers, their families, and the public and avoid undue risks and human suffering
Key 4: Use a systematic, comprehensive process to ensure effectiveness and continual improvement	• Mobilize strategic commitment to a healthy workplace • Assemble the resources required • Assess the current situation and the desired future • Develop priorities • Develop a comprehensive overall plan and specific project action plans by learning from others, for example, consult experts from a local university or ask experienced union leaders to act as mentors, visit other enterprises, consult the virtual world • Implement the plan • Evaluate the acceptance and effectiveness of the plan • Improve when circumstances indicate it is needed

(Continued)

Table 10.1 *(Continued)*

Key 5: Sustainability and integration	• Gain senior management commitment to use a health, safety, and well-being "filter" for all decisions
	• Integrate the healthy workplace initiatives into the enterprise's overall strategic business plan
	• Use cross-functional teams or matrices to reduce isolation of work groups and establish a health and safety committee and a workplace wellness committee
	• Evaluate and continuously improve
	• Measure not only financial performance but also customer knowledge, internal business processes, and employees' learning and growth to develop long-term business success
	• Maintain a comprehensive view to workplace health and safety and examine all aspects to identify a wider range of effective solutions
	• Consider external influences such as lack of primary health care and resources in the community
	• Reinforce and recognize desired behavior through performance management systems that set behavioral standards and output targets

health codes and laws, and taking responsibility for workers, their families, and the public; (4) use of a systemic, comprehensive process to ensure effectiveness and continual improvement, recognizing that lessons learned from developing, apply- ing, and monitoring the process should be applied to make necessary changes and improvements whenever needed; and (5) ascertaining sustainability and integration through, *inter alia*, gaining senior management commitment to use a health, safety, and well-being "filter" for all decisions, integrating the healthy workplace initiative into their overall business plan – also described as the DNA of the business – and reinforcing and recognizing desired behavior through performance management systems that set behavioral standards and output targets.

Challenges and Opportunities: An Outlook

Evidence shows that holistic, integrated approaches to workers' health show many advantages over traditional approaches. Evidence also shows that a public health approach to workers' health is a more rational one, given that almost half of the world's population are economically active and that ensuring good health in the work environment, and linking with health services of the community in which workers live, will ultimately result in securing a healthier life of the population in general. This is evident from the fact that while traditional occupational health practices (1) provide actions at the workplace only, (2) address only work-related health issues, (3) consider only those permanently employed, (4) cover only the workers themselves, and (5) display a limited responsibility of the employer, the public health approach provides actions beyond the workplace. It (1) addresses workers' families and the community in which they work and live; (2) addresses all health determi- nants and not only those that are work-related; (3) considers all workers, including contracted ones which are part of the informal economy; (4) provides an overall policy and legal framework for action rather than being limited to the responsibility of the employers; and (5) involves all relevant stakeholders within and around a given enterprise.

   Such integrated approaches, exemplified by the WHO healthy workplace initiative, face a number of challenges besides offering important opportunities. Challenges include the following:

- Approaches to managing workers' health to date have been fragmented, both from a professional and from an institutional point of view. Addressing safety aspects are often covered by special occupational hygiene inspection institutions and address, in general, mainly physical hazards. Health surveillance is in the hands of occupational health services, and psychosocial risks are hardly recognized, let alone addressed. Integrating these services and ensuring that they understand each other and communicate and act in a concerted manner is a learning process requiring leadership but also openness and willingness to change.

- While protection measures, particularly against physical hazards, are common and while curative actions are taken once an ill-health outcome appears, a preventive culture in a broad sense is fairly uncommon. The benefits of addressing determinants of workers' health, including those related to psychosocial risk factors, and tackling the root causes are not fully recognized.
- Disciplines relevant to managing health aspects of the work environment are hardly interlinked in most parts of the world. Interactions among them are scarce, and the understanding of the importance of other disciplines and of the limitations and remits of one's own is limited.
- In particular, psychosocial risks are often underestimated and partly ignored, despite the growing body of evidence about their relation to a large number of ill-health outcomes including mental and chronic, non-communicable diseases, as well as injuries and musculoskeletal disorders. Seen in the context of their potential health impact, it would be prudent to tackle the root causes here rather than waiting for the negative health outcomes to become evident.
- There is a clear underestimation of the economic effects of occupational illnesses, despite the high degree of absenteeism seen in many enterprises and services worldwide, which relate to physical, ergonomic, and social risks. The cost of such outcomes is high if addressed only at the far end of the cycle, rather than managing the initial risk factors.
- There is a tendency to have a "tunnel vision" towards addressing health in the work environment separately and ignoring the larger public health impacts. This has structural reasons in terms of division of responsibility but is socially and economically unjustified.
- The lack of understanding of the need to apply a public health approach to workers' health also hampers the establishment of sound enterprise–community interactions to ensure that the worker is not seen independently from his/her family or the community he/she lives in, but that improving health at the workplace and eliminating or reducing health risks within and around an enterprise will have beneficial effects on the health of the community and, consequently, ensure a healthy and more productive workforce.

Among the many opportunities offered by integrated approaches to workers' health are the following:

- Addressing workers' health in a holistic, public health-oriented manner and taking a broader view towards addressing relevant key determinants of health in a concerted, preventive manner are bound to ensure good health of the working population in the broader sense of health beyond the absence of illness and infirmity.
- Economic benefits are evident from various aspects: a healthy and engaged workforce will ultimately be more productive, particularly if it takes ownership of the work produced for an enterprise that cares about its health. An enterprise which takes a broader responsibility towards its workers, their families, and the communities they live in will ultimately gain from its good reputation and will be able to attract engaged, qualified staff.

- Linking workers' health to public health in general is of benefit to society as a whole. The funding of public health services will be shared, reducing the overall cost to society, and addressing many root causes of disease by tackling risk factors within and around the workplace will prevent ill-health outcomes and result in societal benefits from a health and an economic point of view.
- Adopting a culture of prevention will also motivate individuals to adopt healthy lifestyles and to take responsibility for their own health and that of those living and working with and around them.
- A healthy workforce in a work environment in which a healthy workplace culture prevails will no doubt be characterized by increased job satisfaction, a sense of ownership, and a feeling of trust that will all lead to increased productivity and a decrease in illness and absenteeism.
- A healthy workplace culture promotes the approach towards achieving a modern society of shared ownership and responsibility of employers and employees, towards which we all aim, while keeping in mind that there is no business wealth without workers' health.

We are at the beginning of a long journey towards achieving a holistic approach to workers' health and the establishment of the healthy workplace as the golden standard for work life management. But the first steps in awareness raising and implementation have been made, and they are promising.

References

Concha-Barrientos, M., Nelson, D. I., Driscoll, T., Steenland, N. K., Punnett, L., Fingerhut, M. A., et al. (2004). Selected occupational risk factors. In M. Ezzati, A. D. Lopez, A. Rodgers, & C. J. L. Murray (Eds.), *Comparative quantification of health risks: Global and regional burden of diseases attributable to selected major risk factors* (pp. 1651–1801). Geneva, Switzerland: WHO.

Department for Work and Pensions (DWP). (2012). *Annual population survey/labour force survey*. London: UK Office for National Statistics of the UK Government.

Driscoll, T., Takala, J., Steenland, K., Corvalan, C., & Fingerhut, M. (2005). Review of estimates of the global burden of injury and illness due to occupational exposures. *American Journal of Industrial Medicine, 48*, 491–502.

Ferrie, J. E., Shipley, M. J., Marmot, M. G., Stansfeld, S. A., & Smith, G. D. (1998). An uncertain future: The health effect threats of employment security in white-collar men and women. *American Journal of Public Health, 88*(7), 1030–1036.

Ivanov, I., & Kortum, E. (2008). WHO strategies and action to protect and promote the health of workers. *Medicina y Seguridad el Trabajo, 209*, 1–4.

Kivimäki, M., Nyberg, S. T., Batty, G. D., Fransson, E. I., Heikkilä, K., Alfredsson, L., *et al.* (2012). Job strain as a risk factor for coronary heart disease: A collaborative meta-analysis of individual participant data. *Lancet, 380*(9852), 1491–1497. Retrieved November 15, 2013, from the Lancet website http://www.thelancet.com/journals/lancet/article/PIIS0140-6736(12)60994-5/fulltext.

Kortum, E. (2012). Editorial: A need to broaden our perspective to address workers' health effectively in the 21st century. *Industrial Health, 50*, 71–72.

Kortum, E. (2014, in press). The WHO global approach to protecting and promoting health at work. In C. Biron, R. J. Burke, & C. L. Cooper (Eds.), *Creating healthy workplaces: Reducing stress, improving well-being and organizational effectiveness* 23–35. Farham, UK: Gower Publishing.

Metcalfe, C., Smith, G. D., Sterne, J. A., Heslop, P., Macleod, J., & Hart, C. (2003). Frequent job change and associated health. *Social Science and Medicine, 41*, 210–216.

Nielsen, K., Randall, R., & Brenner, S. O. (2008). The effects of transformational leadership on followers' perceived work characteristics and psychological well-being: A longitudinal study. *Work and Stress, 22*(1), 16–32.

Ostry, A. S., & Spiegel, J. M. (2004). Labor markets and employment security: Impacts of globalization on service and healthcare-sector workforces. *International Journal of Occupational and Environmental Health, 10*, 368–374.

Pollard, T. M. (2001). Changes in mental well-being, blood pressure and total cholesterol levels during workplace reorganization: The impact of uncertainty. *Work and Stress, 15*(1), 14–28.

Prüss-Üstün, A., & Corvalán, C. (2006). *Preventing disease through healthy environments.* Geneva, Switzerland: WHO.

United Nations. (2002). *Report of the world summit on sustainable development* (A/CONF.199/20). Johannesburg, South Africa, August 26–September 4. Retrieved November 15, 2013, from the World Summit website http://www.un.org/jsummit/html/documents/summit_docs/131302_wssd_report_reissued.pdf.

Virtanen, M., Kivimäki, M., Joensuu, M., Virtanen, P., Elovainio, M., & Vahtera, J. (2005). Temporary employment and health: A review. *International Journal of Epidemiology, 34*, 610–622.

Wilkinson, R., & Marmot, M. (2003). *Social determinants of health: The solid facts* (2nd ed.). Copenhagen, Denmark: The Regional Office for Europe of the WHO.

World Health Organization (WHO) Global Strategy for Occupational Health for All. (1996). *Recommendation of the second meeting of the WHO Collaborating Centres in Occupational Health,* October 11–14, 1994, Beijing, China.

WHO. (1946). *Constitution of the World Health Organization.* Geneva, Switzerland: WHO. Retrieved November 15, 2013, from the WHO website http://apps.who.int/gb/bd/PDF/bd47/EN/constitution-en.pdf.

WHO Global Strategy for Occupational Health for All (1996). *Recommendation of the second meeting of the WHO Collaborating Centres in Occupational Health,* Beijing, China, October 11–14, 1994.

WHO. (2007). *Workers' health: Global plan of action. 60th World Health Assembly.* Geneva, Switzerland: WHO.

WHO. (2010). *Healthy workplaces: A model for action. For employers, workers, policy-makers and practitioners.* Geneva, Switzerland: WHO.

WHO. (2012). *Five keys to healthy workplaces: No business wealth without workers' health.* Retrieved July 31, 2013, from the WHO website on http://www.who.int/occupational_health/5keys_healthy_workplaces.pdf.

11

A Sound Change: Ways to Support Employees' Well-Being during Organizational Restructuring

Krista Pahkin and Pauliina Mattila-Holappa
Finnish Institute of Occupational Health, Finland

Karina Nielsen
Norwich Business School, University of East Anglia, UK

Maria Widerszal-Bazyl
Central Institute of Labour Protection – National Research Institute, Poland

Noortje Wiezer
Netherlands Organization for Applied Scientific Research TNO, The Netherlands

According to the European Restructuring Monitor (ERM) database, which contains information on large-scale restructuring events reported in the principal national media in each EU member state, approximately 17,000 restructuring events have occurred in Europe from 2002 to present. This number includes only cases in which at least 100 jobs have been lost or created or employment effects affecting at least 10% of a workforce of more than 250 people. The number of smaller restructuring cases is probably even higher. The number of restructuring cases is increasing day by day.

It is evident that different kinds of restructuring activities are part of modern work life, and most employees will face restructuring at some point during their working life. In this chapter, we give a short overview of the effect of restructuring on the well-being of employees and present the main principles of a sound organizational change process that would ensure employee's health and well-being during restructuring. We also try to shed light on what in practice could be done during the change process in organizations. We base our views on the findings of our research project called Psychological health and well-being in restructuring: key effects and mechanisms (PSYRES)[1] (Wiezer et al., 2011), in which both quantitative and qualitative data from Denmark, Finland, the Netherlands, and Poland were utilized, and on other research studies carried out in the field of restructuring. We know that there is no single or simple answer on how restructuring influences the health and well-being of individual employees or what the best way to manage the restructuring process is. However, we hope that this chapter will motivate researchers and practitioners to consider the restructuring process so that its final outcome is sound from the viewpoint of both the employer and employee.

Defining Restructuring

The term "restructuring" has become associated with the enactment of structural change at the sector, company, and establishment level. In this chapter, the focus will be on restructuring at the company and establishment level, one could say at the workplace level. We focus on the consequences of the "necessary response of the organization to the long term forces of economic development" (Storrie, 2006) on employees and their well-being. Restructuring of organizations is seen to be driven by the need to maintain or enhance profitability and to, therefore, ensure the survival of the company (and thus jobs) in the long term. It is defined to be an organizational change that is more significant than commonplace changes (Kieselbach *et al.*, 2009). Restructuring is a word which often evokes negative reactions from employees. It is often linked with downsizing activities, such as risk of losing jobs. However, certain types of restructuring can be growth oriented (Storrie, 2006) and include expansion of business, like mergers.

The PSYRES project showed that restructuring (no matter what type) is a process that influences the health and well-being of employees across national borders. Employees' reactions to restructuring were similar across countries and occupations: uncertainty about the future, the question about what will happen to me and to my workmates. For employees, restructuring may mean changes in the way work is done, with whom it is done, where it is done, who the employer is, and so on. Different types of change happening at the workplace at the same time may also present a challenge. For example, there may be outsourcing of some of the activities of the organization, and at the same time, a new production line may be started; or the next restructuring process may start before the previous one is finalized.

Consequences of Restructuring on Employees' Well-Being

As mentioned earlier, restructuring is often associated with "crisis"-like events, such as closure, layoffs, and downsizing. A lot of attention has been paid to employees who lose their jobs (are being made redundant) as a consequence of restructuring. The impact of job loss has been described extensively in the unemployment literature, and numerous studies show the negative consequences of job loss on well-being (Paul & Moser, 2009). However, research evidence shows that the health and well-being of employees who keep their jobs after restructuring may also suffer. Paying attention to this group of employees is also crucial, since they are the ones ultimately responsible for meeting the production-oriented goals of restructuring.

Longitudinal studies among employees who experienced downsizing but kept their jobs show, for example, that going through the downsizing process in their workplace caused health effects like faster declining self-rated health (Kivimäki *et al.*, 2000b), higher diagnosed long-term sickness absence rates (Vahtera, Kivimäki & Pentti, 1997), and increased risk of cardiovascular mortality (Vahtera *et al.*, 2004). Downsizing has also been associated with increased psychological distress, anxiety, and burnout (see review of Ferrie *et al.*, 2008).

Studies show that expansion of business may also influence employees' well-being. Like in the case of downsizing, merger experience has been found to elevate the prevalence of subjective stress, anxiety, and impatience (Haruyama *et al.*, 2008) and increase the risk of generalized anxiety disorders (GAD) (Wang *et al.*, 2012). Employees generally view merger-related experiences as stressful (Scheck & Kinicki, 2000), and a mere announcement of a merger may increase stress levels (Haruyama *et al.*, 2008). So the effect of increasing versus decreasing production restructuring, in many cases, can be very similar from the viewpoint of the employees' health and well-being.

In addition to these direct effects mentioned earlier, there are different mechanisms which influence the effects of restructuring. For example, downsizing can lead to increased job insecurity, which plays a significant role in the incidence of ill-health (De Witte, 2005; Kivimäki *et al.*, 2001; Kivimäki, Vahtera, Pentti & Ferrie, 2000a; Sverke, Hellgren & Naswall, 2002). However, the findings of PSYRES (Wiezer *et al.*, 2011) showed that restructuring affects a wide range of psychosocial working conditions, not only in terms of job insecurity or workload. Also, emotional demands, the amount of conflicts with colleagues or supervisors, the adaptive culture (e.g., the co-operation in the organization to create the changes), participation in decision making, effort–reward imbalance, work–family conflict, are affected, and they, in turn, mediate (i.e., explain) the influence of restructuring on employees' well-being. The findings, for example, showed that prolonged restructuring increases emotional demands and this, in turn, decreases job satisfaction and increases sickness absenteeism. In the same way, prolonged restructuring may increase conflicts with supervisors, and this, in turn, decreases job satisfaction and causes more sickness absenteeism (see Figure 11.1).

The effect of restructuring on employees' own work tasks and the way the restructuring process is experienced (appraisal of the changes) seem to be of particular importance. Change experiences are subjective appraisals of an individual's perceptions of the advantages and disadvantages caused by a change in the work situation (tasks, colleagues, a supervisor) and also include an appraisal of how the change is managed by the organization (management and supervisors). The decrease or increase in employees' well-being due to restructuring partly depends on the appraisal of the impact of the restructuring. The results of the PSYRES project (Wiezer *et al.*, 2011) suggest that restructuring influences employees' health and well-being through the way employees appraise the change. If the appraisal of the restructuring is positive and/or if the job position of the employee is improved as a result of restructuring, employee's health and well-being remain stable or improve. If the appraisal is negative, the consequences are more likely to be poor

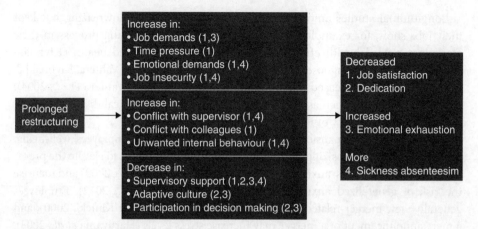

Figure 11.1   Work-Related Factors Which Mediate the Influence of Prolonged Restructuring on Employees' Well-Being. The number after the variable refers to outcome which the variable affects.
Source: Reproduced with permission of Wiezer *et al.* (2011).

health and well-being. The larger the number of work areas changed, the stronger appears to be the effect of restructuring on employees' well-being. Change experiences were also found to influence future reactions to change: if an employee experiences changes negatively, it is more likely that their reaction to the next change will also be negative. Change experience does not always increase employees' flexibility or readiness for change.

Other research has shown that negative change experiences can also threaten the mental health of employees in the long term. A negative change experience increases the risk of mental health problems, like the use of prescribed psychotropic drugs, hospitalizations for psychiatric disorders, or attempts/committed suicide after organizational mergers (Väänänen *et al.*, 2011). However, personal resources can protect employees from negative change experiences. One of these is the sense of coherence (see Antonovsky, 1987), which characterizes a general orientation to life. A person with a strong sense of coherence feels that life makes sense emotionally, perceives stimuli in a clearly structured way, and is confident that adequate coping resources are available. Employees with strong sense of coherence prior to the restructuring have been found to be at a considerably lower risk of reacting negatively to the change. But those employees with a weak pre-merger sense of coherence who reacted to the restructuring negatively were at risk of having mental health problems later in life (Pahkin *et al.*, 2011b). Also, the results of the PSYRES project showed that employees who had a strong sense of coherence and who had the necessary work-related skills and the ability to handle stressful situations, especially by using task-oriented coping, experienced the restructuring more positively. In addition to personal resources, social support, for example, has been found to affect the way organizational change is experienced (Väänänen, Pahkin, Kalimo & Buunk, 2004).

What Are the Principles of a Sound Change Process?

It has been suggested that the lack of success of restructuring and the later threat to occupational health may be related to an underestimation of the significance of the quality of the change process (e.g., Dahl-Jørgensen & Saksvik, 2005; Nytrø et al., 2000). Therefore, paying attention to how the change process is managed and how employees' feel is important. An important question is how organizational change may be managed to ensure a good quality change, a sound change that is good for both organizational outcomes and employees.

In addition to the effects of restructuring on employees' health and well-being, one of the goals of the PSYRES project was to shed light on how the restructuring process should be handled and identify good practices in organizational change. Both quantitative and qualitative findings indicate that the way the change process is handled, the level of support employees get, and the way employee feels that they are treated by the organization (e.g., if they feel they are respected and their points of view are considered) influence employees' health and well-being. In other words, employees that had better work-related well-being (i.e., higher job satisfaction, work ability, engagement, innovative behavior, performance, and lower stress and exhaustion) (Wiezer et al., 2011):

- Could count on *good communication and support from top management*: which means that management informed them clearly about the goals and the state of change, considered the point of view of the personnel, and made sure that there were sufficient change support services for the whole staff
- Could count on *good communication and support from their direct supervisor*: which means that the direct supervisor informed his or her employees clearly about the goals and the state of change, clarified the new roles of subordinates, and solved problems that emerged during the change process
- Were *involved in the process of restructuring*: which means that employees had the opportunity to give their views on the changes before they were implemented
- Had *trust*: meaning that employees believed that the leader of the change knew what he or she was doing, was well informed, and had good reason for change

Other studies have highlighted similar key elements of a sound (healthy) change. In a review, Westgaard and Winkel (2011) found that factors like employee participation, information and communication, management style, organizational and social support, and perceived justice are important factors which can be influenced by the organization. Also, the findings of Tvedt, Saksvik and Nytrø (2009) support the notion that a responsive process (awareness of diversity, manager availability, role clarification, constructive conflicts) is important. It was found that even though the responsive process may not reduce the additional demands produced by organizational change, it may still be able to reduce the experience of stress and facilitate coping with stress.

Sørensen and Hasle (2009) highlighted the importance of trust for successful organizational change. The employees' trust in the management is essential because the management, as the most powerful party and often the initiator or endorser of internal organizational change, have many opportunities to "betray" the trust of the employees. Social relations with management and leadership style are potential sources of stress at work for employees also in general (Sutherland & Cooper, 1988). Restructuring processes may change and violate the psychological contract (Rousseau, 1995) which represents the mutual beliefs, perceptions, and informal obligations between the employer and employee. For example, employees may have thought that the employer will take care of them until they retire, and any threat for the work contract might be perceived as a violation of that trust.

What in Practice Should Be Done during the Change Process?

But what do good communication, support, trust, and participation mean in practice? First of all, what is important to take into account is that restructuring is a process, and it is a process where some phases are repeated (Wiezer *et al.*, 2011) and to which the reactions of employees differ (modified from Arikoski & Sallinen, 2007; Blau, 2007; Saarelma-Thiel, 1994) (Figure 11.2). Different types of activities are needed during the change process.

Researchers (e.g., Cox & Cox, 1993; Leather *et al.*, 1999) have taken the view that all psychosocial hazards at work can be most effectively managed within the framework of risk management that has proven successful in managing the more tangible hazards found in the workplace. Traditionally, the distinction regarding psychosocial risk management approaches has been made between organizational,

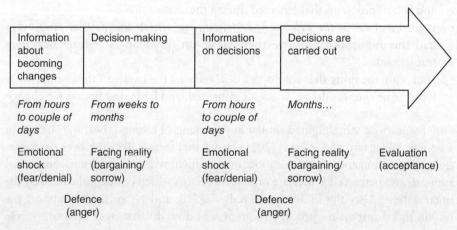

Figure 11.2   The Phases of Change Process, Their Duration, and Employees' Reactions to Them.
Source: Adapted and reproduced with permission of Wiezer *et al.* (2011).

task/job level, and individual orientations. Intervention programs are seen to be most effective and mutually reinforcing when they include both person-directed and organizational-/environment-directed strategies (e.g., LaMontagne *et al.*, 2004).

In the PSYRES project, examples of good practices were collected through interviews and workshops (with managers, employee representatives, and human resources and occupational health representatives) arranged in participating countries (Pahkin *et al.*, 2011a). The initiatives and activities were divided into four levels: activities aimed at the individual, activities aimed at the group, activities aimed at the manager or supervisor, and finally, activities aimed at changing organizational procedures and practices (see Anderson, 2012). This separation of employees into individual/employee (no-supervisor position), and into manager/supervisor, addresses the challenges of the change process to individuals in different positions but also the meaning of work group and the organization and how the activities targeted to bigger groups can act as a resource for the individual employee too. As mentioned earlier, restructuring is a process in which different actions are needed in different phases. Furthermore, the employees' reactions to different phases vary. Therefore, a wide range of supportive activities should be organized during the process (Table 11.1).

The activities in all of the aforementioned levels and phases of change concern *communication*, opportunities to *participate* in the change process, and *support* available for individuals from the management, supervisor (and employee representatives), and colleagues and, when necessary, from external experts, like occupational safety and health (OSH) experts. It is important to remember that appropriate activities depend on the type and the magnitude of the changes. There are no "one size fits all" solutions on how to manage the organizational change process, and in each restructuring situation, the best possible way of acting has to be discussed together with different actors in the organization. Something may work well in one organization, but this does not mean it will work exactly in same way in another. For example, when the organization is forced to lay off employees, one organization may prefer sending a notice letter to their home address giving employees the opportunity to adapt to the situation and then have a face-to-face meeting when employees have had time to adapt to the news and be more ready to discuss future possibilities and support available, while another organization may prefer having a face-to-face meeting, presenting a more personal approach for giving the notice. In both cases, it is important to have written information about the options for those being laid off, in terms of support, training, job search, etc. (Wiezer *et al.*, 2011).

The PSYRES results (Wiezer *et al.*, 2011) indicated that the principles, "the golden rules", of a sound change were the same across countries and different occupations and sectors. What is essential during the change process is that a clear plan is made on how information is given, the use of different communication channels, and making sure that the "voice" of different target groups is heard and that the communication is truly a "two-way communication", not only information provision.

Table 11.1 Activities during a Sound Change According to Their Target Group and the Phase of the Change Process

Phase of the process (duration)	Information about the becoming changes (up to couple of days)	Decision making (weeks)	Information on decisions (up to couple of days)	Decision are carried out (months)
Individual employee	**Support for understanding the news:** confidential discussions with supervisor, employee representative, or OSH expert	**Preparation for the future:** coaching, analysis of competencies, participating in decision making of future work tasks (sometimes through employee representatives)	**Support for understanding the news:** confidential discussions with supervisor, employee representative, or OSH expert	**Support for addressing challenges:** getting the needed competencies (training), taking care of work ability (with the help of OSH expert if needed) and own employability
Supervisor/ manager	**Support for communication:** instructions on what, when, and whom to inform; who will inform; why restructuring is taking place now; what is the future goal of the changes; what are the future steps; who to contact (for information, for support) **Support for understanding the news:** discussion with management	**Support for change management** (to supervisors and employee representatives): own inner meetings to discuss the changes, training for communication (how to talk about the changes, what kind of reactions to expect), participation to decision making (being involved to change groups), training on how to analyze competencies, temporary division of supervisor's day-to-day work	**Support for communication:** instructions on what the decisions are, their effect, what the future steps are, who to contact (for information, for support)	**Support for addressing challenges:** participation in planning the future tasks of the work unit, support/training for transformation (how to implement changes, how to develop functionality of the work group, whom to take care of, employability of employees and their well-being), support for communication (future oriented), improving resilience of the organization (own inner meetings to discuss about the change process, how it was handled, what were lessons learned)

Work group	**Support for understanding the news:** "venting meetings" where employees have the opportunity to ask critical questions and vent their frustrations	**Preparation for the future:** developing ground rules for communication, mapping competencies at the group level, taking care of well-being (risk assessment, use of inner well-being coordinators), participation in decision making on the tasks of the group	**Support for understanding the news:** "venting meetings" where employees have the opportunity to ask critical questions and vent their frustrations	**Support for addressing challenges:** support for transformation (transition rituals, development activities), taking care of well-being (risk assessment, use of inner well-being coordinators), taking care of expertise (e.g., training, mobile learning units), participation in planning of the future tasks of the work group
Organization	**Support for understanding the news:** general communication on the becoming change – joint meetings, press briefings, newsletters	**Preparation for the future:** general communication on how the process is going, what the next steps are, when the decisions are expected, and etc., to make sure that rumors and the feeling of insecurity do not take over; using different communication channels (e.g., questions and answers column); taking care of well-being (risk assessment)	**Support for understanding the news:** general communication on what has been decided – joint meetings, press briefings, newsletters	**Support for addressing challenges:** general communication on how the process is going, what the next steps are, etc.; improving employability (training) and resilience of the organization (risk assessment, evaluation of the change process and learning from it)

Source: From Wiezer *et al.* (2011).

With good communication, it could also be possible to support employees' personal resources, like sense of coherence, by addressing:

- What is going on? Why are we restructuring? (*meaning*)
- Why it is going on? Where are we going? (*comprehensibility*)
- What can be done? What opportunities do employees have to influence the process? (*manageability*)

Realistic communication, in the form of a realistic view on how the change will affect employees, has been found to stabilize the amount of uncertainty and its associated outcomes during the process and, over time, to return fate to the organization's trustworthiness, honesty, and caring as well as self-reported performance (Schweiger & Denisi, 1991).

It is also important to consider how individual employees and work groups can participate in the planning of changes and implementing changes as this may create a feeling of ownership of the changes and employees can commit themselves to the changes. Employee participation has been found to be one of the key factors in the success of interventions (Nielsen & Randall, 2012). It is equally important to consider different kinds of support actions to meet the needs of employees. Special attention should be paid to the supervisor, because they have an essential role of carrying out the change process and making sure that everyday work tasks are completed, a double role which is not easy to carry out. An active role of supervisors during change, for example, in the case of implementing team organization, has been found to affect restructuring outcomes (Nielsen & Randall, 2009).

Future Needs

A lot is known about the consequences of structuring on employees' health and well-being, and there is some information on how the change process should be managed and the kind of supportive activities that are used to carry out the change process. However, there are still several questions which need to be answered and new approaches which need to be studied. Next, we give some ideas for the future needs of restructuring research.

The aforementioned activities (Table 11.1) can be viewed from the different levels of intervention (primary, secondary, tertiary). Generally, in primary-level interventions, the aim is to prevent the harmful effects or phenomena to emerge, whereas in secondary-level interventions, the aim is to increase individual resources, and in tertiary-level interventions, the focus is on the treatment of manifested ill-health (Cooper & Cartwright, 1997).

Most of the previously mentioned activities can be categorized as secondary-level interventions. The aim of many of the activities mentioned is to reverse, reduce, or slow the negative consequences of restructuring on employees' health and well-being. This can be done, for example, by supporting the employees' ability to manage the situation by increasing their knowledge, skills, and/or coping resources. Only some of the mentioned activities are tertiary-level interventions, rehabilitative interventions by nature, like the confidential discussions with OSH experts to overcome the shocking news. What is mostly lacking are the primary-level interventions which are proactive by nature.

Some activities presented in Table 11.1, for example, increasing employability by training, can be viewed as primary-level interventions. However, these interventions mentioned in the last phase of the change process are presented as tools to prepare the organization for the *next* change which might happen in the future. The research findings show that employees with good personal resources in a healthy workplace *before* the change are the ones which can view the coming changes more positively and whose well-being is supported, and not weakened, by the changes (Pahkin *et al.*, 2011b; Väänänen, Pahkin, Kalimo & Buunk, 2004; Wiezer *et al.*, 2011). Therefore, carrying out primary-level interventions is important already before restructuring is even expected to happen.

More attention should be paid to psychosocial working conditions prior to initiating the change process. For example, social support is often defined as one of the job-related resources in the process of promoting well-being (Demerouti, Bakker, Nachreiner & Schaufeli, 2001), and it has been found to be a significant factor also during restructuring. If the support of supervisors and colleagues decreases during the change process, this can lead to poor employee's health and well-being. Conversely, if employees feel that they have strong support from their colleagues, they experience less job insecurity (Wiezer *et al.*, 2011). The situation can thus be challenging (workload, the amount support available) for employees even before any changes are introduced, and this may diminish their resources to manage restructuring. Paying attention to the social climate already before any changes take place is important, since restructuring, and the job insecurity related to it, can lead to different kinds of problems in social interactions, sometimes even bullying or inappropriate behavior (De Cuyper, Baillien & De Witte, 2009; Hoel & Cooper, 2000) and workplace violence (Baron & Neuman, 1996), which in turn decrease well-being (Vartia, 2001).

A closely related concept to social climate is resilience of the organization. In the business environment, resilience has been used to describe how organizations respond to rapid changes of economics (Hamel & Välikangas, 2003). Resilient organizations are seen to be organizations that have the necessary culture and capacity to deal effectively with the side effects of the crisis and accordingly equip employees with effective coping skills for job security threats. Hamel and Välikangas (2003), however, point out that *successful* organizations should be able to renew themselves even when there is no financial crisis going on (strategic resilience). Organizational resilience is nowadays a part of a "healthy organizations" (Cooper & Cartwright 1994), organizations that will have (1) healthy practices for structuring and managing the work processes that influence the development of (2) healthy employees and (3) healthy organizational outcomes (Salanova, Llorens, Cifre & Martínez, 2012). According to Salanova and colleagues, a healthy and resilient organization (HERO) is an organization that develops systematic, planned, and proactive efforts in improving the employee and the financial health of the organization. This kind of organization carries out healthy organizational practices, and resources are aimed at improving the work environment at the task, social, and organizational levels, especially during turbulence and changing times.

Since resilience is seen to begin with management setting priorities, allocating resources, and making the commitment to build organizational resilience throughout the enterprise, attention should be paid to management skills and in particular management/leadership that supports the development of employee resilience. Another component of organizational resilience is enterprise culture. A resilient culture is built on the principles of organizational empowerment, purpose, trust, and accountability. If the organizational goal is to be resilient, what needs to be considered is how this goal can be achieved in practice, the kind of interventions that would help organization to become resilient, and, finally, whether resilient organizations actually cope better during restructuring. One task is to develop ways (interventions) that help organizations and their employees' to cope, to become more resilient, in the unstable world of work.

A closer look of employability may also be needed in the future, since it offers a promising approach to tackling insecure working environments. At the individual level, self-perceived employability helps employees self-regulate and experience positive emotions and self-control over their career, effectively manage job loss or cope with job insecurity, and secure their position in the labor market (e.g., De Cuyper et al., 2008; Fugate, Kinicki & Ashford, 2004). Also, employees with higher perceived employability tend to experience better self-reported health and well-being in the long run (Berntson & Marklund, 2007). At the organizational level, strong employability culture can also lead to greater job satisfaction and less turnover intention among employees (Nauta et al., 2009). Employability opens up thus new opportunities for the promotion of coping with constant changes both from the individual and organizational perspectives.

In addition to considering the different types of interventions, a closer look at the tools used nowadays and the way interventions are evaluated is also needed. For example, many organizations conduct annual attitude surveys and monitor well-being through traditional health and safety surveys using standardized measures of working conditions and health and well-being; however, these rarely capture change conditions and concerns of staff during restructuring. In the PSYRES project, a questionnaire was developed that captures key elements of the restructuring process (Wiezer et al., 2011). There is, however, a wider need to incorporate relevant measures related to restructuring into existing tools. An example of a method to develop tailored initiatives that target adverse working conditions during restructuring is the participatory intervention from an organizational perspective (PIOP) approach (Nielsen, Stage, Abildgaard & Brauer, 2013) in which the working conditions that may be influenced by restructuring are tackled head on.

In evaluating the usefulness of interventions, the nature of the restructuring process should also be taken into account. During an actual restructuring process, it might be too demanding to evaluate interventions by using traditional demands of intervention studies: randomized measurement before and after the intervention and including a control group in the study design. Especially the use of a control group is challenging since all employees should have the opportunity to be involved in support activities arranged by the organization during the restructuring process. Perhaps, one of the future challenges is to measure success of interventions by paying more attention to the quality of the process and things happening during the intervention.

Conclusions

Restructuring, in its different forms, is part of working life and almost unavoidable. Much is already known about the consequences of restructuring on the health and well-being of employees. Even though the consequences are often reported to be negative, it is promising that recent research suggests that it is possible to manage the restructuring process in such a way that it leads to enhanced well-being of employees. Unfortunately, less is known about how in practice the different types of change processes should be handled in organizations to guarantee that employees stay well while and after going through the process. However, good examples do exist, and the future goal would be to make sure that the lessons learned are utilized and awareness of how to carry out organizational changes in sound way is increased.

Note

1. PSYRES project. More information: www.psyres.pl.

References

Anderson, D. L. (2012). *Organization development: The process of leading organizational change*. Thousand Oaks, CA: Sage Publications.

Antonovsky, A. (1987). *Unrevealing the mystery of health*. San Francisco: Jossey-Bass.

Arikoski, J., & Sallinen, M. (2007). *Muustosvastarinnasta vastarannalle [From change resistance to the other side]*. Helsinki, Finland: Finnish Institute of Occupational Health.

Baron, R. A., & Neuman, J. H. (1996). Workplace violence and workplace aggression: Evidence on their relative frequency and potential causes. *Aggressive Behaviour, 22*(3), 161–173.

Berntson, E., & Marklund, S. (2007). The relationship between perceived employability and subsequent health. *Work & Stress, 21*, 279–292.

Blau, G. (2007). Partially testing a process model for understanding victim responses to an anticipated worksite closure. *Journal of Vocational Behavior, 71*, 401–428.

Campbell-Jamison, F., Worral, L., & Cooper, C. (2001). Downsizing in Britain and its effects on survivors and their organisations. *Anxiety, Stress and Coping, 14*, 35–58.

Cox, T., & Cox, S. (1993). *Psychosocial and organizational hazards at work: Control and monitoring. European Occupational Health Series (No. 5)*. Copenhagen, Denmark: WHO Regional Office for Europe.

Cooper, C. L., & Cartwright, S. (1994). Healthy mind: Healthy organization – A proactive approach to occupational stress. *Human Relations, 47*, 455–471.

Cooper, C. L., & Cartwright, S. (1997). An intervention strategy for workplace stress. *Journal of Psychosomatic Research, 43*(1), 7–16.

Dahl-Jørgensen, C., & Saksvik, P. O. (2005). The impact of two organizational interventions on the health of service workers. *International Journal of Health Service, 35*(3), 529–549.

De Cuyper, N., Baillien, E., & De Witte, H. (2009). Job insecurity, perceived employability and targets' and perpetrators' experiences of workplace bullying. *Work & Stress, 23*(3), 206–224.

De Cuyper, N., Bernhard-Oettel, C., Berntson, E., De Witte, H., & Alarco, B. (2008). Employability and employees' well-being: Mediation by job insecurity. *Applied Psychology: An International Review, 57*, 488–509.

De Cuyper, N., Raeder, S., Van Der Heijden, B., & Wittekind, A. (2012). The association between workers' employability and burnout in a reorganization context: Longitudinal evidence building upon the conservation of resources theory. *Journal of Occupational Health Psychology, 17*(2), 162–174.

Demerouti, E., Bakker, A. B., Nachreiner, F., & Schaufeli, W. B. (2001). The job demands-resources model of burnout. *Journal of Applied Psychology, 86*, 499–512.

De Witte, H. (2005). Job insecurity: Review of the international literature on definitions, prevalence, antecedents and consequences. *Journal of Industrial Psychology, 31*(4), 1–6.

European Restructuring Monitor (ERM). http://www.eurofound.europa.eu/emcc/erm/index.htm.

Ferrie, J. E., Westerlund, H., Virtanen, M., Vahtera, J., & Kivimäki, M. (2008). Flexible labor markets and employee health. *Scandinavian Journal of Work Environment and Health, 6*, 98–110.

Fugate, M., Kinicki, A. J., & Ashford, B. E. (2004). Employability: A psycho-social construct, its dimensions and applications. *Journal of Vocational Behavior, 65*, 14–38.

Haruyama, Y., Muto, T., Ichimura, K., Yan, Y., & Fukuda, H. (2008). Changes of subjective stress and stress-related symptoms after a merger announcement: A longitudinal study in a merger-planning company in Japan. *Industrial Health, 46*, 183–187.

Hamel, G., & Välikangas, L. (2003). The quest for resilience. *Harvard Business Review, 81*(9), 52–63.

Hoel, H., & Cooper, C. L. (2000). *Destructive conflict and bullying at work*. Manchester, UK: Manchester School of Management, University of Manchester Institute of Science and Technology (UMIST).

Kieselbach, T., Armgarth, E., Bagnara, S., Elo, E.-L., Jefferys, S., Joling, C., et al. (2009). *Health in restructuring: Innovative approaches and policy recommendations*. München-Mering, Germany: Hampp.

Kivimäki, M., Vahtera, J., Ferrie, J. E., Hemingway, H., & Pentti, J. (2001). Organizational downsizing and musculoskeletal problems in employees: A prospective study. *Occupational and Environmental Medicine, 58*, 811–817.

Kivimäki, M., Vahtera, J., Pentti, J., & Ferrie, J. E. (2000a). Factors underlying the effect of organizational downsizing on health of the employees: A longitudinal cohort study of changes in work, social relationships and health behaviours. *British Medical Journal, 320*, 971–975.

Kivimäki, M., Vahtera, J., Pentti, J., Thomson, L., Griffiths, A., & Cox, T. (2000b). Downsizing, changes in work, and self-rated health of employees: 3-wave panel study. *Anxiety Stress and Coping, 14,* 59–73.

LaMontagne, A. D., Barbeau, E., Youngstom, R. A., Lewiton, M., Stoddard, A. M. McLelland, D., et al. (2004). Assessing and intervening on OSH programmes: Effectiveness evaluations of the Well-works-2 interventions in 15 manufacturing worksites. *Occupational and Environmental Medicine, 61,* 651–660.

Leather, P., Beale, D., Lawrence, C., Brady, C., & Cox, T. (1999). Violence and work: Introduction and overview. In P. Leather, C. Bardy, C. Lawrence, D. Beale, & T. Cox (Eds.), *Work-related violence. Assessment and Intervention* (pp. 3–18). London: Routledge.

Nauta, A., van Vianen, A., van der Heijden, B., van Dam, K., & Willemsen, M. (2009). Understanding the factors that promote employability orientation: The impact of employability culture, career satisfaction, and role breadth self-efficacy. *Journal of Occupational and Organizational Psychology, 82,* 233–251.

Nielsen, K., & Randall, R. (2009). Managers' active support when implementing teams: The impact on employees' well-being. *Applied Psychology: Health and Well-Being, 1,* 374–390.

Nielsen, K., & Randall, R. (2012). The importance of employee participation and perceptions of changes in procedures in a teamworking intervention. *Work & Stress, 26,* 91–111.

Nielsen, K., Stage, M., Abildgaard, J. S., & Brauer, C. V. (2013). Participatory intervention from an organizational perspective: Employees as active agents in creating a healthy work environment. In G. Bauer & G. Jenny (Eds.), *Concepts of salutogenic organizations and change: The logics behind organizational health intervention research.* New York: Springer Publications.

Nytrø, K., Saksvik, P. Ø., Mikkelsen, A., Bohle, P., & Quinland, M. (2000). An appraisal of key factors in the implementation of occupational stress interventions. *Work & Stress, 13,* 213–225.

Paul, I. K., & Moser, K. (2009). Unemployment impairs mental health: Meta-analyses. *Journal of Vocational behavior, 74*(3), 264–282.

Pahkin, K., Mattila-Holappa, P., Nielsen, K., Wiezer, N., Widerszal-Bazyl, M., de Jong, T., et al. (2011a). *Steps towards sound change – Initiatives for ensuring employee well-being during restructuring.* Warsaw, Poland: Central Institute for Labour Protection – National Research Institute.

Pahkin, K., Väänänen, A., Koskinen, A., Bergbom, B., & Kouvonen, A. (2011b). Organizational change and employees' mental health: The protective role of sense of coherence in organizational merger: prospective study on psychiatric disorders. *Journal of Occupational and Environmental Medicine, 53,* 118–123.

Rousseau, D. M. (1995). *Psychological contracts in organizations: Understanding written and unwritten agreements.* Thousand Oaks, CA: Sage.

Saarelma-Thiel, T. (1994). *Eteenpäin kriisistä [For forth from a crises].* Helsinki, Finland: Finnish Institute of Occupational Health.

Salanova, M., Llorens, S., Cifre, E., & Martínez, I. M. (2012). We need a Hero! Towards validation of the Healthy and Resilient Organization (HERO) model. *Group and Organization Management, 37*(6), 785–822.

Scheck, C. L., & Kinicki, A. J. (2000). Identifying antecedents of coping with an organizational acquisition: A structural assessment. *Journal of Organizational Behavior, 21,* 627–648.

Schweiger, D., & Denisi A. (1991). Communication with employees following a merger: A longitudinal field experiment. *Academy of Management Journal, 34*(1), 110–135.

Sørensen, O., & Hasle, P. (2009). The importance of trust in organizational change. In P. Saksvik (Eds.), *Prerequisites for Healthy Organizational Change* (pp. 10–29). The Netherlands: Bentham Science Publisher Ltd.

Storrie, D. (2006). *Restructuring and employment in the EU: Concepts, measurement and evidence*. Dublin, Ireland: European Foundation for the Improvement of Living and Working Conditions.

Sutherland, V., & Cooper, C. (1988). Sources of work stress. In J. J. Hurrell, L. R. Murphy, S. L. Sauter, & G. L. Cooper (Eds.), *Occupational stress: Issues and developments in research*. London: Taylor & Francis.

Sverke, M., Hellgren, J., & Naswall, K. (2002). No security: A meta-analysis and review of job insecurity and its consequences. *Journal of Occupational Health Psychology, 7*, 242–264.

Tvedt, S., Saksvik, P., & Nytrø, K. (2009). Does change process healthiness reduce the negative effects of organizational change on the psychosocial work environment? *Work & Stress, 23*(1), 80–98.

Vahtera, J., Kivimäki, M., & Pentti, J. (1997). Effect of organisational downsizing on health of employees. *Lancet, 350*, 1124–1128.

Vahtera, J., Kivimäki, M., Pentti, J., Linna, A., Virtanen, M., Virtanen, P., et al. (2004). Organisational downsizing, sickness absence, and mortality: 10-town prospective cohort study. *British Medical Journal, 328*, 555–560.

Vartia, M. (2001). Consequences of workplace bullying with respect to the well-being of its targets and the observers of bullying. *Scandinavian Journal of Work Environment Health, 27*(1), 63–69.

Väänänen, A., Ahola, K., Koskinen, A., Pahkin, K., & Kouvonen, A. (2011). Organizational merger and psychiatric morbidity: A prospective study in a changing work organization. *Journal of Epidemiological Community Health, 65*, 682–687.

Väänänen, A., Pahkin, K., Kalimo, R., & Buunk, B.P. (2004). Maintenance of subjective health during a merger: The role of experienced change and pre-merger social support at work in white- and blue-collar workers. *Social Science and Medicine, 58*, 1903–1915.

Wang, J. L., Patten, S., Currie, S., Sareen, J., & Schmitz, N. (2012). Business mergers and acquisitions and the risk of mental disorders: A population based study. *Occupational and Environmental Medicine, 69*, 569–573.

Westgaard, R. H., & Winkel, J. (2011). Occupational musculoskeletal and mental health: Significance of rationalization and opportunities to create sustainable production systems. A systematic review. *Applied Ergonomics, 42*, 261–296.

Wiezer, N., Nielsen, K., Pahkin, K., Widerszal-Bazyl, M., de Jong, T., Mattila-Holappa, P., et al. (2011). *Exploring the link between restructuring and employee well-being*. Warsaw, Poland: Central Institute for Labour Protection – National Research Institute.

12

Making Safety Training Stick

Autumn Krauss and Tristan Casey
Sentis, USA

Peter Y. Chen
University of South Australia, Australia

Introduction

Despite improvements in safety performance over the past 30 years, workplace injuries continue to occur (Geldart, Shannon & Lohfeld, 2005). Every 15 seconds, 160 workers globally experience a work-related injury or fatality (ILO, 2008), highlighting the need for continued investment in improving employees' safety at work. Financially, safety incidents cost Australia, the US, and the UK more than $330 billion annually (HSE, 2011; Leigh, 2011; Safe Work Australia, 2012). Moreover, as multinational companies expand operations into new territories and developing countries such as China and India experience unprecedented economic growth, there is an increased need for safety awareness and injury prevention efforts. Put simply, continued empirical research and practical interventions targeting workplace safety are necessary to protect human life and foster organizational effectiveness.

One intervention that organizations use to improve employees' safety at work is safety training (Smith-Crowe, Burke & Landis, 2003). Safety training increases workers' knowledge, skills, and motivation with the goal of employees performing safety behaviors more frequently and effectively and, hence, experiencing less safety incidents at work (Burke *et al.*, 2006). The prevalence of safety training is high, with virtually any job for which safety is a concern requiring some type of safety training. Unfortunately, employees may receive a lot of safety training but that does not guarantee that it is effective in improving their safety outcomes; in fact, most injured workers have previously participated in safety training (ABS, 2010). This finding points to a potential problem with either adequate learning in

Contemporary Occupational Health Psychology: Global Perspectives on Research and Practice, Volume 3,
First Edition. Edited by Stavroula Leka and Robert R. Sinclair.
© 2014 John Wiley & Sons, Ltd. Published 2014 by John Wiley & Sons, Ltd.

the training program or sufficient application of learning upon return to the workplace. Given that substantial empirical findings and several integrative reviews have established that employees learn new skills and knowledge during training (e.g., Arthur, Bennett, Edens & Bell, 2003; Blume, Ford, Baldwin & Huang, 2010), this problem seems to be less about learning and more about post-training application (Krauss, 2005).

This "training transfer problem" (Baldwin & Ford, 1988) is well acknowledged within the psychology, learning, and professional training and education literatures and represents a significant challenge for organizations seeking to maximize the return on their training investment. Importantly for safety, training that fails to transfer can lead to much more serious consequences than reduced ROI – it can determine the difference between an employee who successfully avoids a safety incident and one who experiences a debilitating injury. Thus, there is a raft of reasons – financial, operational, and ethical – for researchers and practitioners to address the training transfer problem, particularly within the context of safety training.

Accordingly, this chapter leverages current research in the areas of occupational safety and employee training to build a model of safety-specific training transfer. The objectives of this chapter are to (1) highlight the training transfer problem within the context of workplace safety, (2) outline research to support an evidence-based model of safety training transfer, (3) identify the key predictors of safety training transfer, and (4) provide suggested interventions for practitioners and organizations to increase safety training transfer. The remainder of this chapter is structured around these objectives, beginning with an overview of the safety training transfer problem.

Safety Training and the Transfer Problem

To achieve safe operations, organizations seek to control hazards and reduce risk. Besides engineering-based strategies (e.g., redesigning equipment to remove hazards), methods such as developing safe work practices and procedures, creating warning signs and alert systems, and providing personal protective equipment (PPE) are routinely used (Khanzode, Maiti & Ray, 2012). Importantly, as the risk-reduction intervention increasingly requires an action on the part of the worker (e.g., requiring a particular piece of PPE to be worn when completing a certain task), reliance on workers' safety knowledge and skills grows (Colligan & Cohen, 2004). Workers must also be motivated to engage in these actions, which may be challenging when the hazard is deemed low risk, the appropriate action takes considerable effort, or existing social norms discourage the behavior from being performed (DeJoy, 1996). Hence, training is often used to improve safety as it improves employee knowledge, skills, and motivation.

Indeed, safety training serves an integral role within most safety management systems and creates a foundation for strong individual, team, and organizational safety performance as well as symbolizes the importance of safety across a company (Khanzode, Maiti & Ray, 2012; Vredenburgh, 2002). Tangibly, safety training goes by many different guises according to the type of skill or knowledge being trained, the availability of training resources, and the job context, among other factors. Safety training ranges from passive lecture-based formats such as site safety inductions and technical training in safety legislation to active and engaging programs targeting workers' self-regulatory abilities, safety-related cognitions, and performance of particular safety behaviors (Burke *et al.*, 2006).

Given the ubiquitous nature of safety performance issues across industries, it is not surprising that a significant percentage of companies' training expenditure is allocated to safety-specific initiatives. For instance, during 2012, the Australian mining industry invested $1.1 billion or an average 5.5% of payroll in employee safety training; within the US, approximately a quarter of employees' total training time across all industries is allocated to safety-related topics (Waehrer & Miller, 2009). Overall, safety training represents a significant investment of money, time, and effort by both employers and employees.

Despite this considerable investment, workplace injuries and fatalities continue to happen. Notably, a recent survey of the Australian workforce questioned the effectiveness of safety training, with 82% of injured workers reporting participation in safety training before their injuries (ABS, 2010). Further, incident investigations, empirical research, and industry reports consistently identify training-related deficits as key contributors to catastrophic safety events across a wide range of industries (Skogdalen, Utne & Vinnem, 2011; Zontek, Isernhagen & Ogle, 2009). Given evidence that workplace training generally (Arthur, Bennett, Edens & Bell, 2003) and safety training specifically (Burke *et al.*, 2006) can be effective in increasing employees' knowledge, skills, and motivation, one could argue that challenges exist in the application of these learnings upon return to the workplace (Krauss, 2005).

Training transfer refers to the generalization of learned skills and knowledge to an employee's job following training as well as the maintenance of new skill and knowledge use over time (Baldwin & Ford, 1988). For the purposes of this chapter, safety training transfer is defined as employees' application of learned *safety-specific* knowledge, skills, and motivation when back at work and employees' ongoing use of these learnings over time. In situations where safety training fails to be used in the workplace, we define this as the safety training transfer problem.

Estimates of the training transfer problem vary markedly, with anywhere between 60% (Fitzpatrick, 2001; Saks, 2002) and 90% (Cromwell & Kolb, 2004; Lim & Morris, 2006) of training failing to transfer immediately after the training event. Moreover, survey research conducted by Saks (2002) indicated that the transfer problem increases over time, with an estimated 40% of workers failing to apply learning after one year. Reviews such as the one carried out by Arthur, Bennett, Stanush and McNelly (1998) suggest a much greater long-term transfer problem, with as much as 90% of learned skills and knowledge decaying after one year. Overall, despite much empirical work to explore this issue, the transfer problem still persists (Salas, Tannenbaum, Kraiger & Smith-Jentsch, 2012), resulting in substantial lost opportunity to improve job performance. In the absence of safety training-specific estimates of the transfer problem, we can only draw on studies that show most injured workers previously received safety training and, hence, may have failed to apply learned knowledge and skills on return to work (e.g., ABS, 2010).

Following earlier calls (Baldwin & Ford, 1988) to explore the training transfer problem in more detail, research efforts focused on investigating antecedents and moderators of training transfer (e.g., Salas, Tannenbaum, Kraiger & Smith-Jentsch, 2012), with the result being the creation of myriad transfer models and identification of a slew of transfer predictors (e.g., Burke & Hutchins, 2008; Holton, Bates & Ruona, 2000). To simplify this large body of research, scholars then began to pinpoint the common factors shown to have the strongest relations with training transfer. By adopting Baldwin and Ford's (1988) three component conceptual model as a guiding framework, researchers have now established key training transfer predictors at the levels of the individual trainee, the training design, and the work environment (e.g., Grossman & Salas, 2011; Salas, Tannenbaum, Kraiger & Smith-Jentsch, 2012).

Understanding Safety Training Transfer

Similar to other topics within organizational psychology being ported over to study the phenomenon in a safety-specific context (e.g., motivation, leadership, climate), researchers and practitioners have applied the existing body of work focused on employee training to the study of safety training specifically. As a result, the science and practice of safety training has benefited greatly from the general training literature, with the findings informing safety training design and implementation as well as transfer of safety training research studies. To date, the work conducted within safety training-specific contexts supports many of the assertions and conclusions of the general training transfer literature. Yet, we contend that some of the established training transfer predictors may have different conceptualizations and/or strengths of relationships with transfer in the safety training context due to the unique characteristics of safety training. Furthermore, there are likely individual and work environment characteristics that are only relevant for predicting safety training transfer, not the transfer of other types of training. Accordingly, in this section, we consider how the general training transfer literature is relevant to particularly safety training transfer by drawing on workplace safety research. To do so, we rely on the model of training transfer originally put forward by Baldwin and Ford (1988), which is a relevant framework to discuss the predictors and process of safety training transfer.

Defining features of safety training

Safety training, although similar to other types of employee training in some respects, has several unique characteristics that warrant a contextualized model of training transfer. At the trainee level, employees are more likely to possess long-held and deeply ingrained attitudes, beliefs, and values toward safety, as compared to other types of training topics (e.g., a new computer program), in part because individuals develop ideas about and have experiences with safety from their childhood continuing through their life outside of work. For instance, culture has been shown to impact the effectiveness of safety training (Burke *et al.*, 2008), with communities developing shared ways of thinking and acting in relation to safety. These ecological effects, combined with previous personal and professional safety experiences, are likely to shape malleable cognitions (e.g., readiness to change, locus of control). Additionally, it is likely that these characteristics contextualized to safety (e.g., readiness to change safety behavior, safety locus of control) will be more effective predictors of safety training transfer than the general constructs. Finally, it is also likely that employees will have previous experience engaging in the behaviors targeted by safety training, which are most often safety compliance behaviors. In this case, employees' safety behaviors may already be highly routinized and hence difficult to change through interventions such as training.

Regarding the design and implementation of safety training, several unique features must be considered. The vast majority of safety training is mandated by organizations. Within the general training transfer literature, the effects of mandatory versus voluntary training on transfer are mixed; however, mandatory training seems to result in slightly better transfer outcomes, likely due to the fact that transfer would also be enforced or closely monitored by the organization (Salas, Tannenbaum, Kraiger & Smith-Jentsch, 2012). In the case of safety training, mandated training attendance may interact with trainees' safety characteristics in ways that influence training outcomes and consequently training transfer. This effect may be most pronounced when trainees' existing safety attitudes are negative, with these safety cognitions reducing transfer *via* low motivation to learn during training. Also, dependent upon the organization's safety climate, mandatory safety training may be perceived as either a tangible sign of management's commitment to safety and therefore facilitate training transfer (Burke *et al.*, 2008; Krauss, 2005) or as merely paying "lip service" to safety and therefore reducing training transfer. Overall, this suggests a need for thoughtful consideration as to how to prepare trainees for attendance at safety training events, since trainees will be bringing existing safety attitudes and behaviors along with perceptions of management's commitment to safety with them to training.

Regulated safety training also has implications for safety training transfer. As some safety training is prescribed by national and/or state regulations, it is highly likely that employees will experience similar incarnations of safety training over the course of their profession. If delivered using passive training techniques (e.g., lectures), employees may fail to leave with even a renewed motivation to use the safety knowledge they already possessed. In this case, training design factors become even more important to increase safety training transfer. Finally, some of the knowledge and skills taught during safety training may only be needed during emergencies and other abnormal events. Indeed, workplace safety has been described as the management of a "dynamic non-event" (Weick, 1991). Consequently, there may be little opportunity for workers to apply what they have learned immediately following safety training. This means the retention of their learning could be prone to faster decay compared to other learned knowledge and skills that can be frequently used after safety training.

Turning now to the broader organizational context in which safety training takes place, well-established factors such as safety training transfer climate, co-worker and supervisor support for safety, and employee reward and recognition for certain safety behaviors are likely to impact transfer. Whereas general training transfer climate has been studied extensively, the safety-specific manifestation of this construct has received less attention. That being said, it is likely that safety training transfer climate is an important predictor of the transfer of safety training and likely interacts with other organizational factors like the company's safety climate and management's safety leadership to predict safety training transfer. For instance, frontline leaders may vary in the importance they place on safety in general and safety training in particular. Hence, the organization may expect employees to apply their learning from safety training, but local team conditions such as production pressure, supervisor behaviors that are interpreted as being against safety training, or unfavorable behavioral norms shared by co-workers may interfere with transfer. Finally, safety training is commonly tied to employee performance evaluation, meaning employees are expected to use their safety training and consequences are possible if this does not occur. While this practice may increase the *frequency* of transfer of safety training, it may inhibit transfer *effectiveness*, particularly if the reward system targets only certain trained behaviors, focuses on outcomes rather than the quality of the behavior, uses extrinsic motivators as the reward scheme, or incorporates a large punitive aspect.

Together, these features of safety training distinguish it from other forms of employee learning and development. The primary implication is the need to consider the predictors and process of training transfer specifically in the safety context. By drawing on the themes presented in this section, the general training transfer literature, and the occupational safety literature, we discuss in the succeeding text the trainee, training design, and work environment characteristics specifically relevant for safety training transfer.

Trainee characteristics

Within the general training transfer literature, numerous studies have shown that trainee characteristics (e.g., locus of control, conscientiousness, pre-training motivation, self-efficacy) predict learning during training, which in turn predicts post-training motivation and self-efficacy to apply the learned knowledge and skills (Colquitt, LePine & Noe, 2000). In the workplace safety literature, individual safety characteristics (e.g., safety beliefs, attitudes, values) are consistently found to predict safety knowledge and motivation. Accordingly, we suggest that these safety characteristics influence safety training transfer indirectly through proximal training antecedents such as motivation to learn and self-efficacy during training. In the succeeding text, we discuss in more detail one of these distal safety antecedents to safety training transfer, namely, safety locus of control.

Safety locus of control

Locus of control refers to the extent to which consequences are seen to be determined by personal actions and behavior (internal locus) or by the environment and other people (external locus) (Rotter, 1966). In general, an internal locus of control is associated with positive workplace outcomes, including job engagement and motivation (Ng, Sorensen & Eby, 2006), and safety performance (Christian, Bradley, Wallace & Burke, 2009). Applied to training, internally locussed individuals are more likely to use their training back at work because they believe that using their new knowledge and skills will enable them to achieve successful outcomes (Noe, 1986), with Colquitt, LePine and Noe (2000) finding that internal locus of control is positively associated with training transfer, supporting this notion. Importantly, research has demonstrated that locus of control beliefs are context-specific, meaning that individuals may have certain cognitions about behavior-outcome contingencies for work compared to home or safety at work compared to other work topics like promotions (Jones & Wuebker, 1993; Spector, 1988).

Only one study has explicitly examined the role played by locus of control in safety training transfer; however, the results were inconclusive and the author examined work locus of control rather than safety locus of control (Krauss, 2005). Krauss (2005) hypothesized that while individuals with an internal locus of control would engage in effective safety training transfer irrespective of external factors, individuals with an external locus of control would be more sensitive to organizational factors (e.g., safety training transfer climate) to determine whether they would transfer their safety training. Another related study did find that following a safety training intervention, participants' locus of control beliefs became more internal, resulting in more safety behaviors targeted by the intervention (Huang & Ford, 2012).

Although these studies did not specifically examine safety locus of control, as mentioned earlier, we contend that safety locus of control will be the most relevant operationalization of locus of control to predict safety training transfer. In particular, there are two mechanisms by which safety locus of control may influence safety training transfer. First, training activities that facilitate a shift in beliefs toward a more internally locussed safety orientation are likely to increase the transfer of learned safety knowledge and skills. Second, individuals with externally locussed safety beliefs could potentially be more influenced by environmental cues such as the safety training transfer climate to determine their safety training transfer. Consequently, the causal paths through which safety locus of control influences safety training transfer may differ depending on the individual's orientation (internal or external), which has implications for the relative importance of training design and work environment factors that we turn to next.

Training design characteristics

Psychological research findings have long since pointed to the importance of training design factors in predicting training outcomes (Gegenfurtner, 2013). As a result, the criticality of instructional design is widely recognized by workplace training practitioners, with 46% of members of the American Society for Training and Development indicating that they use specific training design strategies to improve learning transfer (Burke & Hutchins, 2008).

In the particular case of safety training, the findings from a concerted research program carried out by Burke and colleagues (2006, 2008, 2011) emphasized the importance of instructional design in predicting safety training transfer, primarily through processes that increase learner engagement in the training program (leading to more learning and transfer). To explore the effects of these safety training design characteristics and others on transfer, we modeled the training process using the following three components: pre-implementation, implementation, and embedding. *Pre-implementation* involves training design elements used to increase employees' readiness to change and their motivation and confidence to learn. *Implementation* focuses on maximizing the amount of knowledge and skills employees learn during the program, and the aim of *embedding* is to facilitate transfer and encourage the maintenance of transferred skills over time.

Pre-implementation

There are parallels between unsafe behavior at work and other types of negative health behaviors that people engage in (e.g., smoking, poor diet). In these situations, the negative health behaviors are associated with negative events (e.g., safety incident, cancer, cardiovascular disease) that could possibly occur at some distant point in the future. Considering neuroscience principles, we know that this type of rationale for engaging in safe and healthy behavior is plagued by cognitive biases (e.g., temporal discounting; Fellows, 2004), making effective decisions and sustained changes in behavior difficult. Nevertheless, interventions have been successful in changing peoples' decisions and associated behaviors, when their current thought processes and readiness for change are taken into consideration.

The transtheoretical model proposes that people progress through a series of steps during the behavior change process and their success at doing so is predictive of whether their behavioral change is sustained over time (Prochaska, Redding & Evers, 2008). The model consists of the following six stages: *Precontemplation* (no intention to make a change), *Contemplation* (intention to make a change), *Preparation* (intention to make a change and actions to prepare for the change), *Action* (initial change of behavior), *Maintenance* (sustained change of behavior), and *Termination* (no temptation to relapse and 100% confident of change being maintained) (Prochaska, Redding & Evers, 2008).

Although the transtheoretical model has been utilized extensively in clinical settings, ranging from smoking cessation (Prochaska & DiClemente, 1983) to problematic drinking (Carbonari & DiClemente, 2000), the model has not often been applied to organizational training design, much less to a safety-specific training context. The handful of studies that have been conducted in an organizational training setting support the notion that individuals' psychological preparedness to change their behavior influences important training antecedents and outcomes. Specifically, Steele-Johnson, Narayan, Delgado and Cole (2010) found that individuals' change readiness was positively related to their motivation to learn in training. Harned, Dimeff, Woodcock and Skutch (2011) found that after a training intervention, participants in *Action* were more likely to use their learned skills during the week following the training than those in a control condition. These results suggest that acknowledging participants' readiness for change and designing training to correspond to the psychological change process would have beneficial effects on training factors that predict transfer.

Applied to safety training, we propose that the transtheoretical model holds particular merit, as a way to understand how employees may be "placed" at different stages within the change process when it comes to their current safety attitudes and behavior as well as their intention to change these. Specifically, employees in *Precontemplation* would lack motivation to learn during safety training, as they would likely perceive a low level of risk in their environment and believe that their current safety choices are sufficient to keep them safe at work. Employees in *Contemplation*, *Preparation*, and *Action* may be more motivated to learn during safety training, because they have a greater awareness of the potential risk and hazards at work and recognize the opportunity to make better safety choices. Finally, individuals in *Maintenance* may be seeking reinforcement of current safety attitudes and opportunities to practice existing safety behaviors as a way to sustain the changes that they have already made. Overall, using this time prior to training implementation to take stock of participants' readiness to change their safety behavior and possibly move them further through the stages of change has the potential to increase participants' motivation to learn and self-efficacy during training and hence result in greater learning and increased safety training transfer.

Implementation

Safety training is delivered using methods ranging from passive (e.g., lectures, instructional videos) to interactive (e.g., role-plays, demonstrations). These methods are used to achieve diverse safety training objectives, such as gaining factual knowledge about safe work protocols, procedural knowledge about how to correctly complete a job safety analysis, cognitive skills for stress management, or motivation to demonstrate safety citizenship. It is widely recognized that certain training methods foster trainee engagement more than others, with a meta-analysis of 95 safety training studies finding that trainee engagement, which was influenced by training delivery method, significantly predicted training transfer (Burke *et al.*, 2006). A follow-up study confirmed this finding and extended it by showing that the effects of training method and associated trainee engagement may differ depending on the focus of the safety training (Burke *et al.*, 2011). More specifically, when training content is focused on lower risk hazards (e.g., slips), trainee engagement does not seem to matter as transfer occurs similarly across passive and engaging instructional methods. Alternatively, when higher-risk topics are the focus of training (e.g., electrocution), engaging instructional methods significantly improve training transfer.

Engaged trainees are more likely to learn new safety knowledge and skills and apply their learning in the workplace, because the methods used to create engagement (e.g., role-plays, case study) facilitate deeper learning through developing "open" skills rather than "closed" skills (Burke *et al.*, 2006). In sum, given evidence that engaging safety training is roughly three times more effective in fostering training transfer than non-engaging training (Burke *et al.*, 2006), organizations should invest resources in incorporating interactive and experiential learning opportunities into safety training. Further, this investment may be particularly worthwhile when high-risk hazards are the focus of safety training.

Embedding

Assuming that employees learn something useful in their safety training and feel motivated and confident to use it, having adequate opportunities to apply this learning upon return to the workplace is crucial for training transfer (Burke & Hutchins, 2007; Lim & Johnson, 2002). These opportunities are determined by whether employees recognize instances when the training can be applied and whether characteristics of the job and workplace (e.g., workload, job autonomy, availability of resources) facilitate the use of the training.

Unfortunately, there are circumstances that may limit trainees' opportunities to apply their learning, reducing the likelihood of transfer in the short term and easy recall of learned knowledge and skills when they are needed in the long term. Safety training sometimes targets knowledge and skills that are rarely required during normal operations (e.g., emergency response), so there is (hopefully) limited opportunity to apply these at work. Even though drills are possible, some types of safety scenarios are simply too dangerous or costly for organizations to simulate (Salas *et al.*, 2009). Also, safety training often teaches concepts in isolation from their contexts, so when back at work, employees may struggle with identifying relevant cues that prompt the use of trained safety behaviors. Finally, some organizations adopt a strict approach to safety management, which can discourage employees from practicing learned safety skills at times when they are not required (e.g., performing a new type of risk assessment on job tasks that have already been assessed by someone else). Taken together, these circumstances suggest that safety training should always touch on when and how the training should be used at work, and it should be followed by post-training interventions to create and promote clear opportunities for transfer.

Work environment characteristics

Along with investigating predictors of training transfer that occur before and during training, researchers have looked beyond the training event to identify post-training factors predictive of training transfer (Salas, Tannenbaum, Kraiger & Smith-Jentsch, 2012). At the individual level, situational factors such as the experience of punishments/rewards and support from other people help or hinder employees as they look to apply their learning (e.g., Chiaburu & Marinova, 2005; Facteau *et al.*, 1995). At the work group and organizational levels, shared perceptions of these barriers and enablers are collectively conceptualized as "training transfer climate", which has been shown to significantly predict the transfer of training (Rouiller & Goldstein, 1993; Tracey, Tannenbaum & Kavanagh, 1995). Safety training transfer is particularly sensitive to these situational workplace factors, in part due to signals from co-workers and leaders that convey the extent to which safety overall, including the transfer of safety training, is valued and rewarded in the workplace. These predictors, including safety training transfer climate, safety climate, and safety support, are described in more detail in the succeeding text.

Safety training transfer climate
As mentioned earlier, training transfer climate has been shown to explain significant incremental variance in individual training transfer (Rouiller & Goldstein, 1993). By integrating the safety climate and training transfer climate literatures, researchers proposed a construct of safety training transfer climate. Specifically, Smith-Crowe, Burke and Landis (2003) operationalized safety training transfer climate as a multidimensional construct consisting of 10 factors that collectively create an organizational context conducive to the use of safety training. In a comparison of two worksites, they found that the relationship between safety knowledge and safety performance was stronger in the presence of a positive safety training transfer climate. Using the framework put forward by Smith-Crowe et al., Krauss (2005) showed *via* a multi-level study that safety training transfer climate at the group level was positively related to workers' transfer of safety training. Taken together, these preliminary studies examining safety training transfer climate suggest that consideration of this safety-specific transfer climate construct may be beneficial for improving the transfer of safety training.

Safety climate
Safety climate refers to employees' perceptions of whether safety is valued and prioritized by the organization (Zohar, 1980), with consistent and favorable perceptions leading to more frequent and effective safety behaviors being demonstrated by employees. In organizations where a strong and positive safety climate exists, safety training transfer is likely to be high because (1) the value of safety is clearly conveyed, which encourages employees to reciprocate with effective safety performance, including the transfer of safety training; (2) safety training is based on an accurate needs assessment and therefore relevant and appropriate to transfer back to the workplace; and (3) the training environment is supportive of safety-related ideas and behaviors – increasing motivation to learn during training and encouraging transfer of training when back at work (Burke *et al.*, 2008). Indeed, a meta-analytic study investigating the relationship between safety climate and safety training transfer found that for organizations with more positive safety climates, the effect of safety training on safety outcomes (e.g., injuries) was greater (Burke *et al.*, 2008).

There may be situations where an organization's safety climate is positive, yet the safety training transfer climate is less positive. This phenomenon may occur in situations where training is generally deprioritized by management (e.g., small businesses) or there are reduced resources available for training-based programs such as following a cost-cutting initiative. In this case, organizations should seek to enhance the broader safety climate in which safety training is delivered to still leverage the social context of safety as a means to foster safety training transfer.

Social support

While a well-established predictor of the transfer of training (Burke & Hutchins, 2008; Salas, Tannenbaum, Kraiger & Smith-Jentsch, 2012), social support from co-workers and supervisors may be particularly influential on the transfer of safety training. This is due to the fact that social support for safety is already an important predictor of safety behavior through its positive influence on safety norms (Fugas, Meliá & Silvia, 2011; Fugas, Silva & Meliá, 2012) and positive links with workers' safety knowledge and motivation (Christian, Bradley, Wallace & Burke, 2009). Following employee safety training, frontline leaders serve a crucial role in encouraging workers to use what they have learned, by removing barriers to transfer, identifying opportunities for workers to apply learning, providing corrective feedback, and integrating training concepts within existing processes (e.g., pre-start briefings and safety meetings). Co-workers encourage safety training transfer through sharing experiences (e.g., success stories of applying learning), refreshing and reinforcing knowledge of training concepts, and establishing helpful social norms (e.g., showing co-workers that it is acceptable to practice learned skills on the job). In these ways, social support at an individual worker level may be important to safety training transfer, independent of the group-level influences of safety training transfer climate and safety climate.

Interventions to Increase Safety Training Transfer

In the previous sections, we identified specific factors across three categories of transfer predictors (trainee, training design, and environmental characteristics) that have particular relevance for the transfer of safety training. With the ultimate aim of improving the transfer of safety training, possible interventions targeting these factors must now be considered. By integrating what we know from the practice of and research in safety training, we have proposed several intervention strategies in the succeeding text, organized by the timeline for a safety training event.

Before safety training

- Clearly communicate the objectives of the training as well as observable and realistic changes that the training is meant to create back in the workplace.
- Ensure that all levels of leadership (executive to frontline) participate in the safety training program, even a reduced form, so that the concepts and skills can be driven meaningfully from the top down.
- Implement the training using a phased approach, starting with a representative and influential group of team members in each department to increase training awareness and build energy and interest in the program.

- Collect diagnostic data (e.g., safety training transfer climate, safety climate, individual readiness to change safety behavior) and adjust the training approach to reflect strengths and opportunities across these areas.
- Integrate the safety training program into a broader initiative to improve the organization's safety climate.
- Facilitate coaching/mentoring of frontline leaders by middle or senior managers in techniques to encourage workers' transfer of safety training (e.g., providing feedback more effectively, dealing with resistance among more experienced workers).

During safety training

- Open the program with an introduction by a senior leader or other employee who has significantly benefited from it, as a way to demonstrate organizational commitment to and tangible benefits arising from the program.
- Identify and discuss tangible examples of when the training concepts could be applied at work.
- Encourage participants to experiment with safety skills taught during the training and provide constructive feedback on any errors made.
- Identify and discuss the potential barriers to using the training upon return to work (at least ask this on the training evaluation form).
- Ensure the program provides ample opportunities for participants to interact socially and involves them actively in the learning process (e.g., group discussions, role-plays).
- Explore novel ways to simulate workplace conditions and scenarios during the training session (e.g., delivering parts of the training in the workplace, hiring simulators, developing realistic case studies or scenarios using workers' experiences onsite).

After safety training

- Use pre-start meetings to refresh training concepts and terminology (e.g., rotating trained concepts and skills).
- Align safety tools and documentation with training concepts and terminology (e.g., modifying the language of a risk assessment to reinforce learned knowledge).
- Through discussions with team members, "simulate" or anticipate situations where safety training could be applied and prompt them to consider how they would respond using their learned knowledge and skills.
- Incorporate trained behaviors into performance evaluation criteria, which are supported by both organizational (e.g., safety observations) and team (e.g., safe peer of the month) recognition programs.
- Identify "coaches" responsible for ongoing championing of training concepts within the workplace.

- Provide dedicated spaces (virtual such as online forums and physical such as the team lunch area) where employees can share their experiences using safety training and pose questions to leaders and colleagues.
- Support safety knowledge retention by providing employees with follow-up exercises and activities (e.g., web-based modules, situational judgment questions) that are also discussed during team meetings.

Conclusion

Although the science of training transfer has advanced greatly over the past 30 years, relatively little work has been done to define and understand how the unique characteristics of safety training may impact transfer. With this in mind, we identified features of safety training that have implications for the trainee, training design, and contextual factors predictive of safety training transfer. This was an attempt to call attention to certain concepts that we think have particular relevance for the transfer of safety training; admittedly, those that we chose to focus on do not reflect an exhaustive list of characteristics that should be considered. It is likely that through further research specifically focused on safety training transfer, the list of pertinent characteristics will be both expanded and refined.

Finally, we offered some practical strategies that may be implemented before, during, and after safety training, with the goal of fostering safety training transfer. Put simply, safety training is a practice that is commonplace in organizations operating in a high-risk environment, and these organizations want to improve their training return on investment. Interventions targeting safety training transfer represent an excellent opportunity for occupational health psychologists to better an existing organizational safety practice and ultimately improve employees' workplace safety outcomes.

References

Arthur, W., Jr., Bennett, W., Jr., Edens, P. S., & Bell, S. T. (2003). Effectiveness of training in organizations: A meta-analysis of design and evaluation features. *The Journal of Applied Psychology*, 88(2), 234–245.

Arthur, W., Jr., Bennett, W., Jr., Stanush, P. L., & McNelly, T. L. (1998). Factors that influence skill decay and retention: A quantitative review and analysis. *Human Performance*, 11(1), 57–101.

Australian Bureau of Statistics [ABS]. (2010). *Work-related injuries, Australia, 2009–10, 6324.0*. Retrieved from http://www.abs.gov.au/ausstats/abs@.nsf/mf/6324.0/.Accessed on November 12, 2013.

Baldwin, T. T., & Ford, J. K. (1988). Transfer of training: A review and directions for future research. *Personnel Psychology*, 41(1), 63–105.

Blume, B. D., Ford, J. K., Baldwin, T. T., & Huang, J. L. (2010). Transfer of training: A meta-analytic review. *Journal of Management*, 36(4), 1065–1105.

Burke, L. A., & Hutchins, H. M. (2007). Training transfer: An integrative literature review. *Human Resource Development Review*, 6(3), 263–296.

Burke, L. A., & Hutchins, H. M. (2008). A study of best practices in training transfer and proposed model of transfer. *Human Resource Development Quarterly, 19*(2), 107–128.

Burke, M., Smith-Crowe, K., Salvador, R., Chan-Serafin, S., Smith, A., & Sonesh, S. (2011). The dread factor: How hazards and safety training influence learning and performance. *The Journal of Applied Psychology, 96*(1), 46–70.

Burke, M. J., Chan-Serafin, S., Salvador, R., Smith, A., & Sarpy, S. A. (2008). The role of national culture and organizational climate in safety training effectiveness. *European Journal of Work and Organizational Psychology, 17*(1), 133–152.

Burke, M. J., Sarpy, S. A., Smith-Crowe, K., Chan-Serafin, S., Salvador, R. O., & Islam, G. (2006). Relative effectiveness of worker safety and health training methods. *American Journal of Public Health, 96*(2), 315–324.

Carbonari, J. P., & DiClemente, C. C. (2000). Using transtheoretical model profiles to differentiate levels of alcohol abstinence success. *Journal of Consulting and Clinical Psychology, 68*(5), 810–817.

Chiaburu, D. S., & Marinova, S. V. (2005). What predicts skill transfer? An exploratory study of goal orientation, training self-efficacy and organizational supports. *International Journal of Training and Development, 9*(2), 110–123.

Christian, M. S., Bradley, J. C., Wallace, J. C., & Burke, M. J. (2009). Workplace safety: A meta-analysis of the roles of person and situation factors. *The Journal of Applied Psychology, 94*(5), 1103–1127.

Colligan, M. J., & Cohen, A. (2004). The role of training in promoting workplace safety and health. In J. Barling & M. Frone (Eds.), *The psychology of workplace safety*. Washington, DC: APA.

Colquitt, J. A., LePine, J. A., & Noe, R. A. (2000). Toward an integrative theory of training motivation: A meta-analytic path analysis of 20 years of research. *The Journal of Applied Psychology, 85*(5), 678–707.

Cromwell, S. E., & Kolb, J. A. (2004). An examination of work-environment support factors affecting transfer of supervisory skills training to the workplace. *Human Resource Development Quarterly, 15*(4), 449–471.

DeJoy, D. M. (1996). Theoretical models of health behavior and workplace self-protective behavior. *Journal of Safety Research, 27*(2), 61–72.

Facteau, J. D., Dobbins, G. H., Russell, J. E., Ladd, R. T., & Kudisch, J. D. (1995). The influence of general perceptions of the training environment on pretraining motivation and perceived training transfer. *Journal of Management, 21*(1), 1–25.

Fellows, L. K. (2004). The cognitive neuroscience of human decision making: A review and conceptual framework. *Behavioral and Cognitive Neuroscience Reviews, 3*(3), 159–172.

Fitzpatrick, R. (2001). The strange case of the transfer of training estimate. *Industrial-Organizational Psychology, 39*(2), 18–19.

Fugas, C., Meliá, J., & Silvia, S. (2011). The 'is' and the 'ought': How do perceived social norms influence safety. *Journal of Occupational Health Psychology, 16*(1), 67–79.

Fugas, C. S., Silva, S. A., & Meliá, J. L. (2012). Another look at safety climate and safety behavior: Deepening the cognitive and social mediator mechanisms. *Accident Analysis & Prevention, 45*, 468–477.

Gegenfurtner, A. (2013). Dimensions of motivation to transfer: A longitudinal analysis of their influence on retention, transfer, and attitude change. *Vocations and Learning, 6*(2), 1–19.

Geldart, S., Shannon, H. S., & Lohfeld, L. (2005). Have companies improved their health and safety approaches over the last decade? A longitudinal study. *American Journal of Industrial Medicine, 47*(3), 227–236.

Grossman, R., & Salas, E. (2011). The transfer of training: What really matters. *International Journal of Training and Development, 15*(2), 103–120.

Harned, M. S., Dimeff, L. A., Woodcock, E. A., & Skutch, J. M. (2011). Overcoming barriers to disseminating exposure therapies for anxiety disorders: A pilot randomized controlled trial of training methods. *Journal of Anxiety Disorders, 25*(2), 155–163.

Holton III, E. F., Bates, R. A., & Ruona, W. E. (2000). Development of a generalized learning transfer system inventory. *Human Resource Development Quarterly, 11*(4), 333–360.

HSE. (2011). *Costs to Britain of workplace injuries and work-related ill health: 2010/11 update.* Retrieved from http://www.hse.gov.uk/statistics/pdf/cost-to-britain.pdf. Accessed on November 12, 2013.

Huang, J. L., & Ford, J. K. (2012). Driving locus of control and driving behaviors: Inducing change through driver training. *Transportation Research Part F: Traffic Psychology and Behaviour, 15*(3), 358–368.

ILO. (2008). *Safety and health at work.* Retrieved from http://www.ilo.org/global/topics/safety-and-health-at-work/lang--en/index.htm. Accessed on November 12, 2013.

Jones, J. W., & Wuebker, L. J. (1993). Safety locus of control and employees' accidents. *Journal of Business and Psychology, 7*(4), 449–457.

Khanzode, V. V., Maiti, J., & Ray, P. K. (2012). Occupational injury and accident research: A comprehensive review. *Safety Science, 50*(5), 1355–1367.

Krauss, A. D. (2005). *The transfer problem: Examining the direct and interactive effects of safety training transfer climate and work locus of control on the transfer of safety training.* Unpublished doctoral dissertation, Colorado State University, Fort Collins, CO.

Leigh, J. (2011). Economic burden of occupational injury and illness in the United States. *Milbank Quarterly, 89*(4), 728–772.

Lim, D. H., & Johnson, S. (2002). Trainee perceptions of factors that influence learning transfer. *International Journal of Training and Development, 6*(1), 36–48.

Lim, D. H., & Morris, M. L. (2006). Influence of trainee characteristics, instructional satisfaction, and organizational climate on perceived learning and training transfer. *Human Resource Development Quarterly, 17*(1), 85–115.

Ng, T. W., Sorensen, K. L., & Eby, L. T. (2006). Locus of control at work: A meta-analysis. *Journal of Organizational Behavior, 27*(8), 1057–1087.

Noe, R. A. (1986). Trainees' attributes and attitudes: Neglected influences on training effectiveness. *Academy of Management Review, 11*(4), 736–749.

Prochaska, J. O., & DiClemente, C. C. (1983). Stages and processes of self-change of smoking: Toward an integrative model of change. *Journal of Consulting and Clinical Psychology, 51*(3), 390–395.

Prochaska, J. O., Redding, C. A., & Evers, K. (2008). The transtheoretical model and stages of change. In K. Glanz, B. Rimer, & K. Viswanath (Eds.), *Health behavior and health education: Theory, research and practice* (pp. 170–222). San Francisco: Jossey-Bass.

Rotter, J. B. (1966). Generalized expectancies for internal versus external control of reinforcement. *Psychological Monographs, 80*, 1–28.

Rouiller, J. Z., & Goldstein, I. L. (1993). The relationship between organizational transfer climate and positive transfer of training. *Human Resource Development Quarterly, 4*(4), 377–390.

Safe Work Australia. (2012). *Key work health and safety statistics booklet Australia*. Retrieved from http://www.safeworkaustralia.gov.au/sites/swa/statistics/pages/statistics. Accessed on November 12, 2013.

Saks, A. M. (2002). So what is a good transfer of training estimate? A reply to Fitzpatrick. *The Industrial-Organizational Psychologist, 39*(3), 29–30.

Salas, E., Rose, M. A., Weaver, S. J., Held, J. D., & Weissmuller, J. J. (2009). Guidelines for performance measurement in simulation-based training. *Ergonomics in Design: The Quarterly of Human Factors Applications, 17*(4), 12–18.

Salas, E., Tannenbaum, S. I., Kraiger, K., & Smith-Jentsch, K. A. (2012). The science of training and development in organizations: What matters in practice. *Psychological Science in the Public Interest, 13*(2), 74–101.

Skogdalen, J. E., Utne, I. B., & Vinnem, J. E. (2011). Developing safety indicators for preventing offshore oil and gas deepwater drilling blowouts. *Safety Science, 49*(8), 1187–1199.

Smith-Crowe, K., Burke, M. J., & Landis, R. S. (2003). Organizational climate as a moderator of safety knowledge–safety performance relationships. *Journal of Organizational Behavior, 24*(7), 861–876.

Spector, P. E. (1988). Development of the work locus of control scale. *Journal of Occupational Psychology, 61*(4), 335–340.

Steele-Johnson, D., Narayan, A., Delgado, K. M., & Cole, P. (2010). Pretraining influences and readiness to change dimensions: A focus on static versus dynamic issues. *The Journal of Applied Behavioral Science, 46*(2), 245–274.

Tracey, J. B., Tannenbaum, S. I., & Kavanagh, M. J. (1995). Applying trained skills on the job: The importance of the work environment. *The Journal of Applied Psychology, 80*(2), 239–252.

Vredenburgh, A. G. (2002). Organizational safety: Which management practices are most effective in reducing employee injury rates? *Journal of Safety Research, 33*(2), 259–276.

Waehrer, G., & Miller, T. (2009). Does safety training reduce work injury in the United States? *The Ergonomics Open Journal, 2*, 26–39.

Weick, K. E. (1991). Organizational culture as a source of high reliability. *California Management Review, 29*(1), 112–127.

Zohar, D. (1980). Safety climate in industrial organizations: Theoretical and applied implications. *The Journal of Applied Psychology, 65*(1), 96–102.

Zontek, T. L., Isernhagen, J. C., & Ogle, B. R. (2009). Psychosocial factors contributing to occupational injuries among direct care workers. *Journal of the American Association of Occupational Health Nurses, 57*(8), 338–347.

13

Sustainable Business Practice in a Norwegian Oil and Gas Company: Integrating Psychosocial Risk Management into the Company Management System

Linn Iren Vestly Bergh

University of Nottingham, UK, Statoil ASA, Norway

Siri Hinna

Statoil ASA, Norway

Stavroula Leka

University of Nottingham, UK

Introduction

Norway's oil and gas resources belong to the Norwegian society and are managed for the maximum benefit of present and future generations. Today, about 50 Norwegian and foreign companies are active on the Norwegian Continental Shelf (NCS). The current oil production and its importance for the Norwegian economy are immense. The petroleum sector is Norway's largest industry with 76 fields in production, 16 fields under development, and 84 fields undergoing evaluation (Hansen & Rasen, 2012).

Like all Scandinavian countries, Norway has a sound custom for employee–management cooperation and participation in the working environment. The "working life democratization" in Norway, which started in the 1960s, had great influence on the Norwegian working environment. This included the establishment of the Norwegian Working Environment Act (1977). The law specifically states that the working environment shall give employees full protection against physical and psychological hazards. The employees are also entitled to a meaningful job where they are encouraged to participate and take control over their working situation. This has also influenced Norwegian oil and gas companies' health and safety efforts.

Contemporary Occupational Health Psychology: Global Perspectives on Research and Practice, Volume 3,
First Edition. Edited by Stavroula Leka and Robert R. Sinclair.
© 2014 John Wiley & Sons, Ltd. Published 2014 by John Wiley & Sons, Ltd.

Furthermore, initiatives to improve safety and control hazards related to its overall risk picture have been evoked by large-scale accidents and serious incidents. In the 1970s and early 1980s, technological and safety challenges were the main focus. During this period, several serious accidents occurred, the most serious ones being the Alexander Kielland breakdown (1980) where 123 people were killed and the Bravo Blowout (Ryggvik & Smith-Solbakken, 1997), which led to a high focus from both companies and authorities on health, safety, and the environment (HSE). This includes the prevention of ill-health due to the working environment as well as the prevention of major accidents. The focus for this chapter will be on one particular company whereas the above mentioned characteristics were important building blocks when strengthening, refining, and professionalizing the management of the psychosocial working environment.

Psychosocial risks in the oil and gas industry

Aspects related to the organization, design, and management of work, also known as psychosocial factors, have over the past decade been introduced as an emerging risk area also in the oil and gas industry. The concept was introduced by the International Labour Organization (ILO) in 1986. Psychosocial hazards are defined as those aspects of work design and the organization and management of work, and their social and environmental context, that have the potential for causing psychological, social, or physical harm (Cox & Griffiths, 1995). Psychosocial hazards can be categorized into ten broad categories as shown in Table 13.1 (Leka & Jain, 2010).

There are a number of examples in the oil and gas industry where accidents are linked to underlying factors related to the organization, design, and management of work. One example is the loss of the Piper Alpha oil platform with 167 deaths caused by poor communication at shift handover compounded by leadership failures in 13 emergency responses (Cullen, 1990). The understanding of accidents in light of human error and poor working environment conditions has gained maturity. This has improved the understanding of accident causation (Petroleum Safety Authority Norway, 2012).

A poor psychosocial work environment can also be related to the development of ill-health due to long-term exposure to poor working conditions. An extensive number of articles have been published on stress and burnout and how they correlate with psychological and physiological outcomes (Cox, Griffiths & Rial-González, 2000; Leka & Jain, 2010; Maslach, Schaufeli & Leiter, 2001; Schaufeli & Enzmann, 1998). Workers' experience of work-related stress is linked to their exposure to psychosocial hazards. This may be associated with symptoms such as poor sleep quality, excessive drinking, feeling depressed, feeling anxious and jittery, and inattention which, in turn, may result in people becoming momentarily distracted, making dangerous errors in judgement, and/or failing in normal activities (Hoffmann & Stetzer, 1996; Leka & Jain, 2010; Mearns, 2001; Payne et al., 2009; Proctor et al., 1996). Stress has been shown, for example, to be associated with lower levels of work situation awareness for drilling personnel on oil and gas installations (Sneddon, Mearns & Flin, 2013).

Table 13.1 Psychosocial Hazards

Category	Examples
Job content	Lack of variety or short work cycles, fragmented or meaningless work, under-use of skills, high uncertainty, continuous exposure to people through work
Workload and work pace	Work overload or underload, machine pacing, high levels of time pressure, continually subjected to deadlines
Work schedule	Shift working, night shifts, inflexible work schedules, unpredictable hours, long or unsociable hours
Control	Low participation in decision-making, lack of control over workload, pacing, shift working, etc.
Environment and equipment	Inadequate equipment availability, suitability or maintenance; poor environmental conditions such as lack of space, poor lighting, excessive noise
Organizational culture and function	Poor communication, low levels of support for problem solving and personal development, lack of definition of, or agreement on, organizational objectives
Interpersonal relationships at work	Social or physical isolation, poor relationships with superiors, interpersonal conflict, lack of social support, violence, harassment, bullying
Role in organization	Role ambiguity, role conflict, and responsibility for people
Career development	Career stagnation and uncertainty, under-promotion or over-promotion, poor pay, job insecurity, low social value to work
Home–work interface	Conflicting demands of work and home, low support at home, dual career problems

Source: Leka & Jain (2010), with permission from WHO.

The industry has learned that it cannot sit and wait for the next incident to occur or work-related illness to develop. It has, therefore, introduced a whole string of risk management measures in order to promote health and safety. Actions to prevent accidents go hand in hand with making operations more reliable, which also have an impact on workers' health and well-being.

International frameworks on psychosocial risk management

In recent years, there have been a number of initiatives and guidance that focus on managing the psychosocial work environment. An example is the Psychosocial Risk Management Excellence Framework (PRIMA-EF), funded by the European Commission's 6th Framework Programme. A standard on psychosocial risk management (PRIMA) in the form of a Publicly Available Specification (PAS1010) has also been developed on the basis of PRIMA-EF by the British Standards Institution (BSI, 2011). The BSI standard is meant to help companies address this area of workplace health by setting a benchmark for good practice for the process of psychosocial risk assessment and management.

PRIMA-EF has further been incorporated into the World Health Organization's (WHO) Global Framework for Healthy Workplaces (WHO, 2010). This framework combines evidence-based approaches and principles of health protection and health promotion and is meant to be used by companies, countries, and international stakeholders. For the oil and gas industry with its high focus on HSE, it is beneficial to implement internationally acknowledged frameworks and best practices and also to manage the psychosocial work environment. However, in order for companies to successfully use theory and the frameworks launched by international projects and bodies such as WHO and BSI, it is essential to re-interpret and adjust them to fit the language and systems of particular business contexts.

Management systems in the oil and gas industry

Oil and gas companies operating on the Norwegian continental shelf are responsible for complex processes which demand that well-developed management systems are in place. Management systems contain a set of principles, policies, processes, and requirements which support the organization in fulfilling the tasks required to achieve its objectives. Furthermore, they consist of several elements such as company values, performance management system, monitoring system, and governing documents. Business performance, high-quality decision-making, fast and precise execution, and continuous learning are supported by the management system contributing to safe, reliable, and efficient operations.

When introducing a system for managing psychosocial risk, it is imperative that methods and tools are implemented into the existing management system. It needs to be integrated and followed up into daily operations (Leka, Cox & Zwetsloot, 2008). By establishing a fully integrated solution, companies will be able to manage the risk in a sustainable manner. International frameworks relevant for psychosocial work environment are general descriptions of best practice and meant to be applicable in different contexts. In order to be able to use these frameworks, the content must be adjusted to fit different occupational sectors, such as the oil and gas industry. As such, the frameworks and best practice principles for PRIMA need to be re-interpreted and translated into the existing management systems and thus protect and promote the health, safety, and welfare of employees.

This chapter will describe the implementation and integration of PRIMA into a Norwegian oil and gas company's management system (Figure 13.1). This included:

1. Establishment of the business case
2. Integration into relevant governing documents, including established methods
3. Training programs for managers and employees
4. Development of HSE indicators and follow-up actions as part of the performance management system
5. Development of a psychosocial verification tool as part of the monitoring system

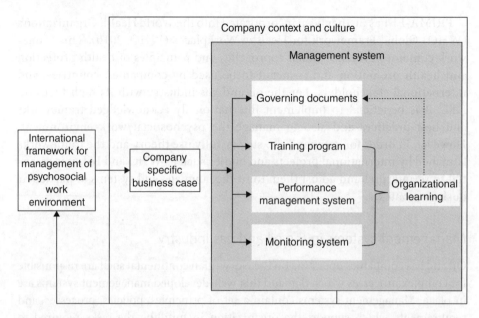

Figure 13.1   Integration of International Framework for PRIMA into Practice and Internal Business Processes.

Establishing a Business Case

One of the biggest challenges is to ensure that research related to the management of the psychosocial work environment is continually translated into workplace interventions. As with health and safety in general, the successful promotion of a sound psychosocial work environment requires that it is integrated in daily work processes and not treated as a separate project. The first step when implementing PRIMA into existing business practices is to get top management attention and buy-in (Cox, 1993; EU-OSHA, 2012; Leka, Cox & Zwetsloot, 2008). In order to see their role in the prevention strategy, leaders need knowledge of how management of the psychosocial work environment is highly relevant to business results.

As such, to ensure management commitment, it is critical to establish a business case. The purpose of a business case is to describe the business rationale for starting a project (Schmidt, 2002). As such, the business case for strengthening the integration of the management of the psychosocial work environment needs to answer the question: what are the business reasons for encouraging line management to put effort into managing the psychosocial work environment? Furthermore, the business outcome must be described. This can be financial reasons, non-financial reasons, and a combination of the two, for example, how promotion of a good psychosocial work environment characterized by low sickness absence, acceptable turnover, safe behavior, and high work engagement is linked to achieving a cost-efficient and value-based operation. Business cases are created to help decision-makers ensure that the proposed initiative will add value and have priority.

The business case should be tailored to the size and risk of the organization. For example, in the oil and gas industry, with its high risk potential, it is critical to create a business case where the initiatives are linked to both the prevention of ill-health and the promotion of safe and reliable operations. In order to show the link between the psychosocial work environment, stress, ill-health, and safe and reliable operations, experiences from internal and external investigations and reports from the industry were utilized. These investigations and reports often highlight human and organizational factors as critical causes for preventing work-related illness as well as accidents. The business case should reflect a balance between knowledge from research, the internal experiences and context of the company, and its internal requirements. These sources should shape both the content and construction of the business case and workplace interventions, ensuring commitment from the mangers in the organization. By doing this, the business case will be recognizable as well as the key elements in the case proposed will be justified. As such, a business case for a multinational oil and gas company, with pressure from governmental regulations as well as high HSE and reputational risk, will differ from a business case developed for a small company in, for example, the media industry.

The language in the business case should not be underestimated; the proposal must be understandable. For example, if an organization has a tradition of using risk management as a cornerstone in their decision-making process related to HSE issues, it is important to use the same concepts when preparing the business case for managing the psychosocial work environment. For example, the risk management of chemicals is a familiar concept within the oil and gas industry, so when describing the business case related to the psychosocial work environment, the same terminology should be applied: identification of psychosocial hazards, likelihood of developing ill-health and other outcomes, severity of exposure, mitigation actions, residual risk, etc. Furthermore, there should be a clear description of how the business managers need to proceed in order to initiate relevant effort with regard to the management of the psychosocial work environment. In this particular company, the business case was built on pre-existing HSE policy with a goal of zero harm to people and assets.

Governing Documentation

Health and safety regulations are meant to protect and promote the health, safety, and welfare of employees in different industries. However, again, they are general in nature and designed to fit different types of companies. As such, companies need to translate policies, laws, requirements, and standards into a company-specific context, that is, the internal management system. A company's internal governing documents consist of policies, requirements, work processes, and guidelines. The purpose of the governing documentation is to ensure the standardization and the deployment of best practice across the business. The internal governing documents must be sensitive with regard to the business context, for example, size, risk level, type of operation, and complexity. Governing documents are established for areas that are important in supporting the company's ambition and strategies.

As previously addressed, the international frameworks and standards on PRIMA developed over the past years are not industry specific and need further translation into company internal management systems. Therefore, when implementing internal requirements for the psychosocial work environment, it is important to first assess the pre-existing requirements and management system in the company. Decisions on how to integrate requirements for the psychosocial work environment should be based on this assessment.

In the Norwegian oil and gas industry, HSE is a very important aspect of business operations and is linked to the license to operate. Due to the impact of the psychosocial work environment on health and safety aspects, it is important to include it in the governing documents related to HSE. The industry has established a substantial amount of requirements related to HSE, and the implementation of psychosocial requirements and guidelines should be integrated into this system. It should be noted that companies should strive towards developing a solution that is fully integrated and not establish a separate system for such activities. The following section describes how this company has integrated requirements and methods into its internal governing documents.

Establishing corporate requirements for the psychosocial work environment

In the process of establishing psychosocial requirements into the company's corporate requirements, it was clear that individual treatment and follow-up was already addressed through existing company systems and occupational health services. However, there was a need for strengthening the requirements related to reducing risk at source. A focus on the design, management, and organization of work needed to be incorporated into the existing requirements. It was seen as particularly important to describe the requirements for psychosocial risk in a similar way as for other HSE risk factors, such as chemicals or noise. Furthermore, this entailed following the same hierarchy of control measures in order to prevent harm to people. These corporate requirements are furthermore linked to the internal HSE risk management process.

The psychosocial requirements that were added into the existing requirements stated that: "workplaces and work processes should be organized in a way that prevents employees from being exposed to psychosocial hazards with risks of developing ill-health. Effort should be made to avoid work-related stress and ill-health due to the psychosocial working environment. Coarse psychosocial hazard identification should be performed regularly on an annual basis. Attention should be paid to determinants such as job content, workload and work schedule, job control, interpersonal relationships at work, role in organization, bullying, home–work interface, and organizational change. Health and working environment risks, including psychosocial risk, should be managed in a systematic, ongoing manner within the organizational context. Results from the coarse psychosocial hazard identification should indicate where to implement further in-depth assessments in line with best practice principles for PRIMA described in the guideline for the PRIMA approach. The requirements in relation to the psychosocial work environment also include hazards such as violence, bullying, and harassment at work. Complaints of bullying should be handled in accordance with the internal work process for handling bullying cases".

In order to fully integrate requirements for the psychosocial work environment into the management system, it was necessary to keep within the frames of the pre-existing HSE requirements. This meant that the requirements ended up being general in description, referencing best practice guidelines and work processes.

Guideline for psychosocial risk management (PRIMA)

The guideline for PRIMA is part of the company's internal requirements; it ensures the use of best practice principles when following up psychosocial risk. The guideline is based on the method originally developed at the University of Nottingham (Cox, Griffiths & Rial-González, 2000). This method was later adapted through the PRIMA-EF (Leka & Cox, 2008). Some adjustments were made in order to fit the company's management system. One of the more important adjustments was to introduce "upside risk" into the guideline for managing psychosocial risk. This was in line with how the company defines risk in two dimensions: upside and downside risk. In this company, risk is defined as the deviation from a specified reference value and the associated uncertainty, that is, positive deviation = upside risk and negative deviation = downside risk.

A guideline is, in this company, listed as advisory documentation and is a description of recommended practices, techniques, methods, and user manuals. It is based on the principles of prevention in line with the control cycle (Cox, Griffiths & Rial-González, 2000).

Steps in the PRIMA process include:

1. In-depth psychosocial risk assessment is triggered by HSE indicators.
2. Start-up and familiarization: Plan ahead and prepare the organization.
3. Risk identification and assessment: Identify psychosocial factors that may affect employees' health (both upside and downside risks should be included).
4. Identify interventions: Involve employees in the discussions when identifying interventions. Make action plan.
5. Risk intervention: Implement action plan in order to deal with the identified factors.
6. Evaluation: Recommendations and further work must include an evaluation of the short-term and long-term effect of the measures.

Findings and interventions should be evaluated and included in a systematic and continuous evaluation and improvement of the psychosocial work environment. It is important to include the entire control cycle and through this process achieve organizational development and training.

PRIMA is based on the process of triangulation: using multiple data collection methods and cross-checking the reliability and validity of the data collected (Leka, Cox & Zwetsloot, 2008). The method is based on a review of organizational documentation and systems, qualitative methods (such as interviews and focus groups), and quantitative methods (surveys). PRIMA is facilitated by experts with appropriate training and experience.

Work process for the prevention and handling of bullying cases

Bullying at work (sometimes referred to as mobbing, harassment, psychological violence, or mistreatment) involves repeated negative, unfriendly, or offensive behavior, actions, and practices (e.g., tormenting, undermining, socially excluding) that are directed at one or more employees (Einarsen, Hoel, Zapf & Cooper, 2011). The behavior is unwelcome to the target and carried out in circumstances where the targets have difficulty in defending themselves. To become bullied is a psychosocial risk situation that may cause serious mental and physical harm. Moreover, bullying at work can be a consequence of a poor psychosocial work environment (Leka, Cox & Zwetsloot, 2008).

The prevention and handling of bullying cases is an important part of the management of the psychosocial work environment, and complaints of bullying should be handled according to best practice principles. Due to the similarities between the best practices for handling bullying and HSE investigations in the company, it was decided to establish a work process for handling bullying cases building on the principles of HSE investigations.

The objective of the work process was to describe how complaints of bullying will be handled in order to ensure that bullying incidents are identified and brought to an end, with all parties in a bullying case being treated fairly and impartially, adhering to the principles of natural justice, that is, the rule against bias and the right to a fair hearing. Describing the handling of bullying as a work process in the management system meant that roles and responsibilities were particularly highlighted. Both preventive advice and clear guidelines for solving specific cases were included in the work process. The work process applies to all employees, with particular roles identified for line managers, HR managers, HSE managers, and HSE professionals, including occupational health and other personnel responsible for the HSE system and quality at all levels.

Psychosocial Risk and Performance Management Practices: Ambition to Action

Today, many companies, particularly larger companies within the oil and gas industry, have chosen to implement structured performance management systems. This is to meet changes in the nature of work, competition, and external demands. The performance management system translates company strategies into more specific strategic objectives. The purpose of having a performance management system is to achieve the best possible performance in a company by creating conditions and providing tools necessary for managers and teams to utilize their full potential in a dynamic and unpredictable business environment. The balanced scorecard is likely to be the best-known method for translating strategy into action, offering a robust framework, capable of helping organizations to successfully navigate the uncertainties of competition and changing dynamics (Kaplan & Norton, 2006; Neely, 1998; Niven, 2006). Thus, if health and safety are a critical area for success, as is the case for the oil and gas industry, these should be included in the system.

In this specific company, the performance management process is called Ambition to Action and is based on the balanced scorecard. Ambition to Action is a process that balances alignment, going from strategic objectives to individual goals. In this process, the company (1) defines its most important strategic change areas; (2) chooses indicative measures for the strategic deliverables; (3) sets concrete actions and expected deliverables, including clear deadlines and accountabilities targeting the strategic objectives; (4) as well as translates the deliverables into individual performance goals.

The Ambition to Action system covers five perspectives. These perspectives are people and organization, HSE, operation, market, and finance. There are key performance indicators (KPIs) for the five different perspectives in the Ambition to Action system. Within the HSE perspective, the KPIs can be either proactive or reactive in nature. Over the last years, evidence from experience and research related to stress, work-related ill-health, and human reliability has highlighted the need to increase focus on proactive actions and implement indicators that can reveal underlying factors in the way work is organized, designed, and managed. As such, a balanced scorecard should also make use of indicator measures related to psychosocial risks, including human and organizational aspects.

In order to integrate PRIMA into the organization's internal performance management system, an HSE performance indicator for psychosocial risk was developed. The Ambition to Action system was utilized in order to follow up initiated actions. In the following, the process of establishing an HSE indicator for psychosocial risk will be outlined.

Developing and implementing an HSE risk indicator for psychosocial risk (PRI)

To strengthen the internal risk management process and close the PRIMA loop, the company has established an exposure indicator for psychosocial risk. The indicator, called psychosocial risk indicator (PRI), is instrumental in guiding management in prioritizing risk areas with appropriate follow-up measures (Bergh, Hinna, Leka & Jain, 2014). The indicator is part of a more comprehensive system generating risk data from PRIMA follow-up. Through the performance indicator for psychosocial risk, the company can more easily document and follow up psychosocial risks across the organization.

PRI was developed on the basis of existing validated instruments on psychosocial risk assessment as well as internal company data. It has been formulated in a way that fits the annual employee survey. PRI is published automatically in the internal performance management system alongside other HSE indicators. Furthermore, the PRI is used in combination with other sources of information in the risk management process. This is to provide line management with a comprehensive risk picture. Even though the different indicators within HSE are important on their own, it is the combination of indicators that provides managers with a navigation path to corrective actions, by highlighting the business areas that need the most attention. By ensuring the implementation of proactive indicators focused on psychosocial risks in addition to other more traditional indicators, the company enforces a more holistic approach to the HSE risk picture. This strengthens the likelihood of business decisions being based on a balanced view of risk and enables prioritization of follow-up activities.

The indicator is communicated through control banding (red, yellow, and green light), and special attention has been dedicated to make PRI both simple to communicate and user-friendly in best practice principles for development of indicators (Øien, Utne & Herrera, 2011; Øien, Utne, Tinmannsvik & Massaiu 2011). The indicator score is available for benchmarking across business units, showing all units in a business area. This is an easy and accessible way of presenting results and supporting line management in prioritizing where to initiate appropriate follow-up based on the identified risk level. Line management is provided with guidance on how to follow up the indicator scores in accordance with best practice principles. These best practice principles are described in the company's internal guideline for PRIMA.

The process of establishing PRI incorporated the elements of evidence-based practice (Briner, 2012). In the evidence-based practice model, decision-making is based on four aspects: the company context, key stakeholders' preference, practitioners' experiences, as well as research evidence. As such, these sources shaped both the content and construction of the indicator. The development of the indicator consisted of several interrelated steps (Figure 13.2): (1) theoretical framework establishment, (2) establishment of baseline data to the indicator, (3) development of the PRI, (4) evaluation of the usability of the indicator as input to the risk picture, and (5) implementation of the indicator as part of the company internal performance management system (Bergh, Hinna, Leka & Jain, 2014).

Documentation and follow-up of interventions related to the psychosocial work environment

Implementation of actions related to the psychosocial work environment is a crucial phase and needs to be carefully managed (BSI, 2011; Leka, Cox & Zwetsloot, 2008). The actions are designed to attain the potential related to upside risk as well as mitigate and/or reduce downside risk. Ownership and participation of managers and workers are essential for successful implementation of actions. The process of identifying interventions and actions should include all relevant personnel.

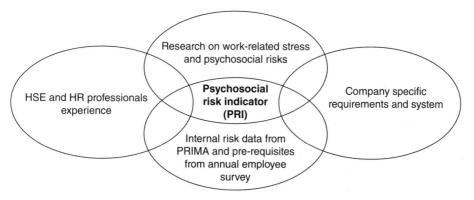

Figure 13.2   Evidence-Based Practice Model for PRI Development.
Source: Adapted from Bergh, Hinna, Leka & Jain (2014), with permission from Elsevier.

This can be done by conducting workshops where employees are included in the dialogue. The management should provide mandates to narrow the scope for interventions and by this ensure that the proposed initiatives are easy to implement.

When identifying the appropriate actions, it is important that they are flexible, are easy to follow up, give status and always support the strategic objectives, and, in addition, improve the probability of reaching the various indicator targets. For example, the interventions can be linked to initiatives/issues identified through PRIMA or the PRI. In order to ensure commitment and ownership from line management, actions and interventions are documented and followed up as an integrated part of the Ambition to Action process. By linking the interventions into the Ambition to Action process, it is more likely that they are implemented into the day-to-day work.

It is important to evaluate whether the actions are implemented as discussed. Regular management meetings as well as unit meetings are an arena where progress is traced. If progress comes to a halt, it is important to re-establish discussions to detect why progress is lacking. Examples of why progress is lacking may be the following: the intervention is not directed at the underlying factor; the intervention is too complicated to implement; the solution lies at a different organizational level; and the underlying factor has already changed due to other change initiatives. When the underlying factor is revealed, appropriate actions should be re-established and progress evaluated. These potential problems with the intervention process need to be anchored and handled by management. As such, the Ambition to Action system provides a tool for actions to be more systematically monitored and recorded.

Training Program on the Psychosocial Work Environment

Large oil and gas companies operate in a complex and diverse context, ranging from offshore to onshore projects and plants. This gives rise to a number of health and safety risks that need to be managed. In order to do so, there are requirements related to training of managers and employees. Such training involves the acquisition of knowledge, skills, and competencies related to health and safety. The goal of the training program is to improve managers' and employees' capabilities, capacities, and performance.

Many companies are faced with increasing globalization, changing nature of work, and significant demographic changes (EU-OSHA, 2012). In order to be in the forefront of a competitive market, it is imperative to ensure high-quality competencies for staff to meet new challenges. Some of these challenges are closely linked to psychosocial risks and the experience of work-related stress. For example, many employees in the modern workplace experience high work pace and heavy workload. International growth leads to more business travel and work across time zones. However, managers and employees often do not have enough training or even awareness of how to prevent negative effects caused by a poor psychosocial work environment (EU-OSHA, 2012). As such, to promote a good psychosocial work environment and prevent ill-health, it is essential to establish training and awareness programs. The training and awareness programs should be targeted at employees, managers, occupational health specialists, and other practitioners. They should include information to raise awareness as well as tools for the prevention and management of psychosocial risks, in addition to already existing programs. Following is a practical example of how to integrate the training and awareness programs related to the psychosocial work environment into the existing management system.

Awareness raising program focused on the prevention of work-related stress

To create awareness related to the prevention of work-related stress, it was decided to establish various awareness raising initiatives. These consist of presentations, workshops, but also written materials such as folders or posters that are handed out in the business areas. Internal webpages have also been established in order for employees and managers to have easy access to information about internal requirements, tools, and methods. The internal webpages are also used in order to showcase good examples for managing psychosocial risk in the business as well as publishing newsletters about various campaigns related to work-related stress, bullying, etc.

The presentations and workshops are targeted at both organizational units and management teams where the focus is on proactive and reactive strategies for coping with work-related stress. These awareness programs are off-the-shelf deliverables that can easily be used in various business settings. These more basic awareness raising initiatives are an important tool in order to create a common language for issues that pertain to the psychosocial work environment.

It is, however, important to note that these general awareness raising initiatives are not sufficient as training in themselves. In order to further ensure competence on this issue, training programs are targeted at specific groups that are important for the management of the psychosocial work environment.

Training programs for management teams and professionals

Experience has shown that management competence with regard to the psychosocial work environment is the key with regard to the promotion of health and safety. Newer research on psychosocial safety climate shows that top management commitment is linked to the health of employees in the organization (Dollard *et al.*, 2012). In order to increase managers' competence in relation to the psychosocial work environment, a training program has been established. This covers different topics such as leadership teams working systematically to manage their own as well as their employees' workload. Through the provision of training, managers become more aware of psychosocial risks and work-related stress and, hence, better able to address these topics. The training program has been developed and is facilitated by occupational health and working environment professionals.

The aim is to work in a process over a 12-month period involving approximately six training sessions. It was important to integrate this training program into the already established management meetings. The time spent varies according to the topic and the needs of the management team. Training covers theory, practical exercises, reflection, and sharing of experiences. The topics covered through the training program are conflict, work engagement, psychosocial factors, burnout, etc. Between the sessions, participants are expected to work systematically on controlling psychosocial risks. The experience gained through the training has been shown not only to increase managers' knowledge but also to enable peer support in the management team.

Health and safety professionals play a key role in facilitating the organization when improving the work environment. Health and safety professionals also need to be trained on how to identify psychosocial risks within the work environment. To promote standardized good practice across the company, a manual has been developed.

Two different yet interrelated training modules have been developed for professionals. The first module is designed for personnel with interest or responsibility in relation to the psychosocial work environment. The second module is tailored for professionals that will conduct and facilitate the organization while implementing PRIMA. This training program covers both theory and practical group work and includes a dedicated mentor assigned to help each professional follow the implementation of PRIMA for the first time.

Both the training programs for management teams and for professionals have been integrated into the company's internal learning portal alongside other HSE training initiatives. This portal is web-based and can be easily accessed by all employees.

Integration into the Internal Monitoring System (Auditing/ Verifications)

As mentioned before, one of the key success criteria when conducting risk assessment and follow-up of the psychosocial work environment is to ensure high management commitment and buy-in. In order to initiate corrective actions, it is crucial that management have the necessary mandate and resources in place and that they are able to address problems or challenges at the right level in the organization. This demands high-level commitment and willingness to change (Armenakis & Bedeian, 1999; BSI, 2011; Griffths, 1999; Kotter & Schlesinger, 1979).

Monitoring is conducted in order to manage risk and drive performance and learning. It ensures quality and effectiveness in how we run our business, as well as quality of the products and services provided. The purpose of the monitoring system is to assure compliance with the management system and to provide a basis for improvement. The monitoring plan is decided at high level in the organization, and the outcomes (reports) are documented in a common IT tool, an audit management system, which again is linked to the scorecard for calculation of KPIs and status reporting. Incorporating psychosocial risk into this system ensures attention and awareness of such risk. Furthermore, it promotes awareness and commitment from high-level management to the follow-up of psychosocial risk assessment and management.

The scope and frequency of internal monitoring depends on an assessment of risks performed by line managers, process owners, and corporate staff functions. In this company, monitoring activities are sectioned into different activities, whereas verification is one of them. Verification is the confirmation, through the provision of objective evidence, that the requirements for a specific intended use or application have been fulfilled. For our purpose, verification was a suitable tool to be developed in order to increase the company's control of psychosocial risk; as such, a project was initiated to develop and test such a verification tool.

The piloted verification tool for the psychosocial work environment is called Psychosocial Risk Verification (PRV). PRV is the verification of the psychosocial factors, for example, how work is designed, organized, and managed, in relation to business requirements. To ensure compliance with requirements to PRIMA and to drive organizational learning, PRV was aligned with existing verification activities. It is intended to be a structured and detailed process that is objective in nature, which applies checklists, and where findings are classified into predefined categories and reported into the internal audit management system. If PRV is decided to be implemented, it should be linked to the overall management of the psychosocial work environment.

The PRV pilot checks whether business is compliant with minimum requirements for the work environment stating that workplaces and work processes shall be organized in a way that prevents employees from being exposed to psychosocial hazards with risks of developing ill-health. Key aspects of the verification tool are the following:

- Structured and detailed process.
- Objective in nature and evidence-based results through triangulation.
- Performed by neutral third-party professionals.
- Check whether business is compliant with minimum requirements.
- Identification of psychosocial risk factors/conditions that have a higher probability for causing ill-health.

The internal requirements state that the following conditions should be paid particular attention to: job demands, job control, role in organization, and interpersonal relationships and support. The requirements are broadly defined so that they fit different contexts across the organization such as projects, offshore operations, plants, and field developments. To facilitate this process, it was important to establish a checklist that describes standards applicable to the psychosocial work environment, linked to internal requirements, in order to check that the conditions are satisfactory.

Main Learning Points and Way Forward

Integrating management of the psychosocial work environment into the existing management system of a large business is a stepwise process that needs careful consideration. As such, there are some important aspects that need to be addressed early on in the process.

Even though research, various frameworks, and standards highlight the importance of integration, few organizations fully succeed in achieving this. A recent report from the European survey of enterprises on new and emerging risks (ESENER) addresses the need for existing legislation and frameworks to be complemented by practical examples at both national and organizational levels (EU-OSHA, 2012). International bodies and networks within occupational health and occupational health psychology have in the recent years highlighted a pressing need to understand how research and best practices can be translated into sustainable business practice.

When introducing concepts and systems for managing psychosocial risk, it is important to evaluate the current knowledge base on psychosocial risk. Traditionally, top management has often lacked sufficient understanding on how to manage the psychosocial work environment in a practical and effective manner which translates into poor management of the psychosocial work environment (EU-OSHA, 2012). In this regard, it is also interesting to note that even though the knowledge related to psychosocial risk factors, or human and organizational factors, has progressively increased over the last 20 years, newer reports still point out a lack of focus on these issues in the industry (Atoosa, Thunem, Kaarstad & Thunem, 2009). This represents a serious threat to the organizations' ability to prevent ill-health and accidents due to psychosocial risk. In order to ensure good business practice, it is important to provide the organization with easy access to practical tools and methods that are applicable into daily operations. As such, the process of translating international frameworks into the company-specific context has contributed to the establishment of practical tools and methods that are accessible to line management.

Furthermore, it is important to assess whether the organization has access to professional support with in-depth knowledge about PRIMA. Professionals are important with regard to the integration of the management of the psychosocial work environment into the management system. It is equally important to ensure professional support to line management in the follow-up of the psychosocial work environment. In this company, in-house professionals have the necessary competence to advise and facilitate management on how to implement an integrated system as well as conducting risk assessment processes (as emphasized by Nielsen, Randall, Holten & Rial-Gonzalez, 2010).

When introducing the management of the psychosocial work environment, it is important to apply familiar terminology and processes as those used in the company management system. In order to highlight the logic behind a holistic HSE risk management and to fully integrate the psychosocial work environment into the risk management loop, it was decided to include the keywords "psychosocial" and "risk" into the new tools and methods. The term psychosocial was as such introduced into the already existing internal risk management framework.

When starting up a process for integrating a system for PRIMA, it is important to have realistic expectations with regard to other ongoing or planned initiatives. As such, it is important to carefully consider the various stakeholders' needs and/or perspectives. Furthermore, it is essential to explore if there are any shared interests and/or interfacing initiatives. If this is not managed properly, it can become very time consuming and, in the worst case scenario, a "showstopper". Within the oil and gas industry, human factor and organizational safety initiatives often have interfacing interest in promoting good management of issues related to the design, organization, and management of work.

The following success criteria have been identified in the overall process:

- An organization with high awareness of the importance of health and safety issues
- Utilization of available research, experience, and best practice principles as main input to the integration into the existing management system
- Linking the management of the psychosocial work environment to business requirements and law
- Top management buy-in and support
- Describing and showing a clear link between the management of psychosocial risk and business outcomes
- Adjusting the language and terminology to fit the existing management system in the organization
- Learning from and cooperating with other relevant disciplines, such as quality management and safety technology
- Establishing practical tools and methods for line management
- Access to internal professional resources, with knowledge of the psychosocial work environment and the management of health and safety
- An organization that is able and willing to apply an iterative process and learn as the process "goes along"

Conclusion

In this chapter, we have described the implementation and integration of PRIMA into a company's existing management system. The relevant context in this particular case is the oil and gas industry with its high risk potential and its high focus on HSE.

Through the implementation process, the various components of the internal management system have been thoroughly assessed in order to ensure sufficient integration. PRIMA has been integrated into the governing documentation, training programs, performance management system, and monitoring system. In this particular example, the business was guided in how to benefit from the abundance of frameworks and research in order to manage the psychosocial work environment. The international frameworks have been adapted into the organizational context and re-interpreted to fit the existing business case. This is in line with recommendations from existing frameworks and standards such as PRIMA-EF, PAS1010, and the WHO's Global Framework for Healthy Workplaces, highlighting the importance of fully integrating psychosocial work environment into companies' operations.

References

Armenakis, A. A., & Bedeian, A. G. (1999). Organizational change: A review of theory and research in the 1990s. *Journal of Management, 25*, 293–315.

Atoosa, P.-J., Thunem, A. P.-J., Kaarstad, M., & Thunem, H.P.-J. (2009). *Vurdering av organisatoriske faktorer og tiltak i ulykkesgranskning* [Evaluation of organizational factors and initiatives in accident investigations] (Rapportnummer IFE/HR/F-2009/1406). Norwegian, Norway: Petroleum Safety Authority Norway.

Bergh, L. I. V., Hinna, S., Leka, S., & Jain, A. (2014). Developing a performance indicator for psychosocial risk in the oil and gas industry. *Safety Science, 62*, 98–106.

Briner, R. B. (2012). Developing evidence-based occupational health psychology. In J. Houdmont, S. Leka, & R. Sinclair (Eds.), *Contemporary occupational health psychology: Global perspectives on research and practice* (Vol. 2, pp. 36–57). Chichester, England: Wiley-Blackwell.

British Standards Institution [BSI]. (2011). *Guidance on the management of psychosocial risks in the workplace: PAS1010*. London: British Standards Institution.

Cox, T. (1993). *Stress research and stress management: Putting Theory to work (HSE Contract research Report, No. 61/1993)*. Sudbury, ON: Health and Safety Executive.

Cox, T., & Griffiths, A. (1995). The nature and measurement of work stress: Theory and practice. In N. Corlett & J. Wilson (Eds.), *Evaluation of human work: A practical ergonomics methodology* (pp. 783–803). London: Taylor & Francis.

Cox, T., Griffiths, A., Barlowe, C., Randall, R., Thomson, L., & Rial-Gonzalez, E. (2000). *Organisational interventions for work stress: A risk management approach (Contract Research Report 286/2000)*. Sudbury, ON: Health and Safety Executive.

Cox, T., Griffiths, A., & Rial-Gonzalez, E. (2000). *Research on work-related stress*. Luxembourg City, Luxembourg: Office for Official Publications of the European Communities.

Cullen, L. (1990). *The public inquiry into the piper alpha disaster* (Vols. 1 and 2). Report to Parliament by the Secretary of State for Energy by Command of Her Majesty. London: HMSO.

Dollard, M. F., Opie, T., Lenthall, S., Wakerman, J., Knight, S., Dunn, S., *et al.* (2012). Psychosocial safety climate as an antecedent of work characteristics and psychological strain: A multilevel model. *Work and Stress, 26*(4), 385–404.

Einarsen, S., Hoel, H., Zapf, D., & Cooper, C. (2011). *Bullying and harassment in the workplace: Developments in theory, research, and practice* (2nd ed.). London: CRC Press.

EU-OSHA. (2012). *Drivers and barriers for psychosocial risk management: An analysis of the findings of the European Survey of Enterprises on New and Emerging Risks (ESENER).* Luxembourg City, Luxembourg: Publications Office of the European Union.

Griffiths, A. (1999). Organizational interventions: Facing the limitations of the natural science paradigm. *Scandinavian Journal of Work Environment and Health, 25*(6), 589–596.

Hansen, J. Ø., & Rasen B. (Eds.). (2012). *Facts 2012: The Norwegian petroleum sector.* Oslo, Norway: Norwegian Ministry of Petroleum and Energy.

Hoffmann, D. A., & Stetzer, A. (1996). A cross-level investigation of factors influencing unsafe behaviours and accidents. *Personnel Psychology, 49*, 307–339.

Kaplan, R. S., & Norton, D. P. (2006). *Alignment: Using the balanced scorecard to create corporate synergies.* Boston: Harvard Business School Publishing.

Kotter, J. P., & Schlesinger, L. A. (1979). Choosing strategies for change. *Harvard Business Review, 57*, 106–115.

Leka, S., & Cox, T. (2008). *The European framework for psychosocial risk management: PRIMA-EF* (pp. 1–16). Nottingham, UK: I-WHO Publications.

Leka, S., Cox, T., & Zwetsloot, G. (2008). The European framework for psychosocial risk management (PRIMA-EF). In S. Leka & T. Cox (Eds.), *The European framework for psychosocial risk management: PRIMA-EF* (pp. 1–16). Nottingham, UK: I-WHO Publications.

Leka, S., & Jain, A. (2010). *Health impact of psychosocial hazards at work: An overview.* Geneva, Switzerland: WHO.

Leka, S., Vartia, M., Hassard, J., Pahkin, K., Sutela, S., Cox, T., *et al.*(2008b). Best practice in interventions for the prevention and management of work-related stress and workplace violence and bullying. In S. Leka & T. Cox (Eds.), *The European framework for psychosocial risk management: PRIMA-EF.* Nottingham, UK: I-WHO Publications.

Maslach, C., Schaufali, W. B., & Leiter, M. P. (2001). Job burnout. *Annual Review of Psychology, 52*, 397–422.

Mearns, K. (2001). Human and organizational factors in the offshore safety. *Work and Stress, 15*(2), 144–160.

Neely, A. D. (1998). *Measuring business performance: Why, what and how.* London: The Economist Books.

Nielsen, K., Randall, R., Holten, A. L., & Rial-Gonzalez, E. (2010). Conducting organizational-level occupational health interventions: What works? *Work and Stress, 24*(3), 234–259.

Niven, P. R. (2006). *Balanced scorecard: Step by step.* Hoboken, NJ: Wiley-Blackwell.

Øien, K., Utne, I. B., & Herrera, I. A. (2011a). Building safety indicators. Part 1 – Theoretical foundation. *Safety Science, 49*(2), 148–161.

Øien, K., Utne, I. B., Tinmannsvik, R. K., & Massaiu, S. (2011). Building safety indicators. Part 2 – Application, practices and results. *Safety Science, 49*(2), 162–171.

Payne, S. C., Bergman, M. E., Beus, J. M., Rodriguez, J. M., & Henning, J. B. (2009). Safety climate: Leading or lagging indicators of safety outcomes? *Journal of Loss Prevention in the Process Industries, 22,* 735–739.

Petroleum Safety Authority Norway (PSA) (2008). *Hydrocarbon leaks and fires.* Available at: http://www.ptil.no/process-integrity/hydrocarbon-leaks-and-fires-article4162-902.html. Accessed April 2013.

Proctor, S. P., White, R. F., Robins, T. G., Echeverria, D., & Rocskay, A. Z. (1996). Effect of overtime work on cognitive function in automotive workers. *Scandinavian Journal of Environmental Health, 22,* 124–132.

Ryggvik, H., & Smith-Solbakken, M. (1997). *Norsk oljehistorie – Blod, svette og olje [Norwegian oil history – Blod, sweat and oil]* (Norsk petroleumsforening, Vol. 3). Oslo, Norway: Ad Notam Gyldendal.

Schaufeli, W. B., & Enzmann, D. (1998). *The burnout companion to study and practice: A critical analysis.* London: Taylor & Francis.

Schmidt, M. J. (2002). *The business case guide* (2nd ed.). Boston: Solution Matrix.

Sneddon, A., Mearns, K., & Flin, R. (2013). Stress, fatigue, situation awareness and safety in offshore drilling crews. *Safety Science, 56,* 80–88.

WHO. (2010). *Health workplaces: A model for action. For employers, workers, policy-makers and practitioners.* Geneva, Switzerland: WHO.

14

An Analysis of the Coverage of Psychosocial Factors at Work in Corporate Social Responsibility Instruments and Standards

Aditya Jain
Nottingham University Business School, UK

Daniel Ripa and Juan Herrero
University of Oviedo, Spain

Introduction

The International Labour Organization (ILO) defines psychosocial factors in terms of the interactions among job content, work organization and management, and other environmental and organizational conditions, on the one hand, and the employees' competencies and needs, on the other, that may have a hazardous influence over employees' health through their perceptions and experience (ILO, 1986). There is a reasonable consensus on the nature of psychosocial factors, which have been categorized under 10 broad areas: job content, workload and work pace, work schedule, control, environment and equipment, organizational culture and function, interpersonal relationships at work, role in organization, career development, and home–work interface (Cox, 1993; WHO, 2003, 2008). When exposure to psychosocial factors is perceived to be negative, then they are referred to as psychosocial hazards which are recognized as one of the major contemporary challenges for workers' health and well-being and are linked to such workplace problems as work-related stress, harassment or bullying and workplace violence (Leka, Jain, Zwetsloot & Cox, 2010).

A large body of evidence shows an association between exposure to psychosocial hazards, or to an interaction between physical and psychosocial hazards, and a multitude of individual and organizational level outcomes. A recent review by the WHO (2010) highlights the detrimental impact of psychosocial hazards on workers'

Contemporary Occupational Health Psychology: Global Perspectives on Research and Practice, Volume 3,
First Edition. Edited by Stavroula Leka and Robert R. Sinclair.
© 2014 John Wiley & Sons, Ltd. Published 2014 by John Wiley & Sons, Ltd.

physical, mental, and social health. Other studies have shown the direct and indirect effect of a poor psychosocial work environment on absenteeism, productivity, job satisfaction, and intention to quit (e.g., Michie & Williams, 2003; van den Berg, Elders, de Zwart & Burdorf, 2009). In addition, a reduction in physical and psychological health through the experience of stress can cause suboptimal performance that may lead to accidents and to other quality problems and reduced productivity, thereby augmenting operational risks (Nahrgang, Morgenson & Hofmann, 2011).

Despite the available evidence, the prevention and management of psychosocial hazards and associated risks has not been high on the policy-making agenda, and only in recent years has there been a growing movement at the intra-national, national, and organizational level to develop policies, measures, and programs, both regulatory and voluntary, to this aim (Leka, Jain, Zwetsloot & Cox, 2010). Policy-level interventions in the area of psychosocial risk management and the promotion of workers' health can take various forms. These may include the development of legislation, the specification of best practice standards at national or stakeholder levels, the signing of stakeholder agreements toward a common strategy, the signing of declarations, and the promotion of social dialogue and corporate social responsibility (CSR) in relation to the issues of concern (Leka et al., 2011).

Regulatory policies outline the minimum requirements for working conditions and employee protection at the workplace that must be adopted by enterprises. However, such an approach is only effective where an adequate enforcement framework is available to effectively translate policy into practice. Furthermore, there are very few specific regulations to address psychosocial hazards at work, and, where they exist, they are often limited in scope (Leka et al., 2011). Therefore, the need for implementing supplementary strategies to prevent the potential negative effect of psychosocial hazards and manage associated risks in the workplace using a "CSR-inspired" approach is being increasingly debated and propagated. A CSR-inspired approach to the management of psychosocial issues at work can be characterized by five key components (Jain, Leka & Zwetsloot, 2011):

1. Making sure that the strategic importance of the management of psychosocial issues is recognized
2. Integrating psychosocial issues in strategies, plans, and processes for organizational development
3. Organizing a good balance between implementation of systems, internalization of values, and organizational learning processes
4. Being aware of the societal impacts of psychosocial risks in the workplace but also of the business impact of psychosocial issues in society
5. Engaging with stakeholders, including non-traditional stakeholders

Acknowledgment:
Daniel Ripa gratefully acknowledges the support provided by a pre-doctoral fellowship from the Foundation for the Promotion of Applied Scientific Research and Technology (FICYT) and the Government of Asturias, Spain

To enable and further the promotion of a "CSR-inspired" approach to prevent and manage psychosocial hazards at work, this chapter analyzes the extent to which psychosocial factors are included in CSR tools and instruments. While a number of tools and instruments have been developed to promote CSR initiatives, the high number of existing standards has also led to considerable overlap resulting in dilution of practice (Tate, Ellram & Kirchoff, 2010). The chapter therefore begins with a review of key tools and instruments and then thematically analyzes these instruments to identify specific indicators in relation to psychosocial hazards.

CSR as a Mean of Improving Working Conditions and the Management of Psychosocial Issues

Over the years, numerous definitions of CSR have been proposed. The various definitions do have a commonality of themes in the context of stakeholder involvement, environment, ethics, governance, and sustainability (Dahlsrud, 2008). In 2011, the European Commission proposed a new, broader and simpler definition: "Corporate Social Responsibility is the responsibility of enterprises for their impact on society. Respect for applicable legislation and for collective agreements between the social partners, is a prerequisite for meeting that responsibility" (EC, 2011). CSR is applicable from the multi-nationals to the small- and medium-sized enterprises (SMEs) and should generally be viewed as responsible business practices aimed at both internal and external stakeholders of the enterprise, relevant to enterprises of all sizes and operating sectors (EC, 2001).

The internal dimension of CSR includes human resources management, health and safety at work, adaptation to change, and management of environmental impacts and natural resources, while the external applies to local communities, business partners, suppliers and consumers, human rights, and global environmental concerns (EC, 2001). Recent theoretical developments and research on CSR reveal an emerging global consensus on basic standards of corporate behavior, which include several aspects of working conditions, including psychosocial hazards at work (Goel & Cragg, 2005; GRI, 2011; Paine, Deshpande, Margolis & Bettcher, 2005). For example, an OECD review (2009), based on the analysis of OECD Guidelines, ILO Multinational Enterprises (MNE) Declaration, and the Global Compact, identified 12 labor issues in major CSR instruments: freedom of association and collective bargaining; elimination of all forms of forced and compulsory labor; abolition of child labor; non-discrimination in respect of employment and occupation; general development; employment promotion; training; wages and benefits; hours of work; safety and health; social protection; and industrial relations.

CSR Standards and Instruments

Since the late 1990s, there has been a massive surge in CSR interest, as a consequence of pressures from social movements, corporate scandals, and a growing international awareness of global sustainability problems (Carroll & Shabana, 2010; Lee, 2008).

Table 14.1   Types of CSR Tools and Instruments

	What are they?	Main instruments
Codes of behavior and ethics principles	A group of broadly agreed principles which business can sign. They define standards for company responsible behavior, but do not provide external assurance. They usually include mechanisms to inform stakeholders about the company's follow-up of implementation. Some of them are written specifically for a company or a sector	Global Compact, OECD Guidelines, ILO Guidelines for MNE, Sullivan Principles
Auditing and management systems	CSR management systems or frameworks aiming to integrate values into daily practices, processes, and activities. They can be certified against a standard after external assurance. These certifications include CSR labels to be placed on the packaging of products in order to influence purchasing decisions by consumers (e.g., Fairtrade Label, Fairtrade Labelling Organization (FLO); Ecolabel)	SA8000, Good Corporation Standard, FLO
Sustainability and social reporting	Guides to standardize social and environmental reporting, according to stakeholders' expectations (GRI). By promoting transparency, social accountability improves. Initially, based on triple bottom line, today, these are more focused on stakeholders and in the development process (AA1000). These can include external verification or an assurance process by stakeholders or external partners	GRI, CSR-SC Project, AA1000
Social and environmental investment indexes	Used by investment agencies or socially responsible investors to recognize responsible business. These measure companies' performance. Companies must be previously part of financial indexes to appear in social ones. There are inclusion and exclusion criteria, according to company activities. Focus is given to risk management. Sometimes supported by shareholder activism or institutional pension funds	FTSE4Good Index Series, Dow Jones Sustainability Index, KLD Ratings
CSR reputation and social rankings	A rating of companies according to several economic, social, or environmental practices, creating a ranking showing the leaders by areas, which increases corporate reputation	Fortune, Social Index
Multi-method self-improvement instruments	A set of tools to promote self-improvement. They can also be management systems or guidelines, although they are not audited. They work as a benchmarking tool and are implemented using guidance from governing organizations	Ethos Institute Indicators, ISO 26000, HRCA Checklist

Source: Adapted from Ripa and Herrero (2012), with permission of Daniel Ripa and Juan Herrero.

CSR standards, tools, and instruments have been central to this surge in interest and were developed for helping companies "to integrate CSR values into their strategy and operations, either by setting out principles for responsible behaviour, providing a set of procedures and implementation steps, or offering indicators and measurement methodologies to evaluate and report on performance" (EC, 2004, p. 7). Table 14.1 describes the main types of CSR tools, standards, and instruments.

Over the last 15 years, hundreds of new standards appeared as businesses sought a "golden rule" to implement CSR initiatives. As a consequence, there is an expansive infrastructure in the CSR field, which includes instruments, standards, regulations, and institutions (Waddock, 2008). However, there is also a considerable overlap among them (Tate, Ellram & Kirchoff, 2010). For this reason, over the past few years, scholars and CSR institutions have made strong efforts to rationalize these initiatives and help practitioners and managers understand which instruments they should use. Old initiatives have been updated, standardized, made more comprehensive, and linked to other standards.

For some authors, this process is not more than a "flight forward" (Van Oosterhout & Heugens, 2008), because the rapid expansion of the CSR infrastructure usually has not followed specific theories and dimensions, and theories have often not been the basis for creating instruments. However, despite these concerns, standards and instruments are crucial for CSR. They influence behavior in a "recognizable and reproducible" way (Goel & Cragg, 2005, p. 4), and they fill "the numerous governance gaps for which hard law is either non-existent or is weakly enforced" (Rasche, 2010, p. 283). As a consequence, CSR instruments can contribute to improving working conditions and the management of psychosocial hazards at work. They could potentially help companies go further than meeting requirements of existing legislation in new areas of interest such as employees' well-being. Therefore, an analysis of the issues that are included in CSR standards becomes fundamental.

The Current Research

Despite the comprehensive coverage of labor issues in CSR instruments, employees' well-being in relation to CSR initiatives has not always received adequate interest from research. This research, therefore, examines two research questions:

1. Are psychosocial factors adequately covered in CSR instruments and standards?
2. Which factors related to psychosocial issues (such as work-related stress, violence, bullying, and harassment) are included in CSR instruments and standards?

Methodology

Sample

A literature review of CSR tools and instruments, using CSR monographs, international and institutional CSR reports, and articles in academic journals, was conducted.

It should be noted that not all tools are directly comparable, arising from the fact that CSR instruments are developed with different objectives in mind. To accommodate these differences, the thematic areas of the instruments were considered.

More than 200 instruments were identified, many of them cited in McKague and Cragg's (2007) compendium of ethics codes and instruments of CSR. Instruments were selected and further analyzed from this population if they met the following inclusion criteria: recent (developed or updated post-2000), publicly available, applicable across regions and sectors, and included a labor dimension. Table 14.2 presents the list of selected instruments.

Table 14.2   CSR Tools and Instruments Included in the Analysis

Amnesty International Human Rights Principles for Companies (1998)	1.
BLIHR (2009)	2.
Caux Round Table Principles for Responsible Business (including the Stakeholder Management Guidelines and the People, Performance, Well-Being Guidelines) (2008, 2010)	3.
CSR-SC Project (2006)	4.
Dow Jones Sustainability Indexes (SAM Research, 2009, 2011)	5.
Ethos Institute Indicators (2009)	6.
Ethical Trading Initiative Base Code (2010)	7.
European Union Questionnaire to raise SME awareness of CSR (2007)	8.
Fair Labor Association: Workplace Code of Conduct (1997, 2011)	9.
Fairtrade Mark – Fairtrade Standards: FLO-CERT Public Criteria List, Hired Labour (2011)	10.
FTSE4 Good Index Inclusion Criteria (2006, 2011)	11.
GRI – 3.0, 3.1, and 4.0 (2006, 2011, 2013)	12.
Global Sullivan Principles (1999)	13.
Good Corporation Standard (2010)	14.
HRCA (2006)	15.
IFC Performance Standard (World Bank Group) (2010, 2012)	16.
ILO Tripartite declaration of principles concerning multinational enterprises and social policy (2006)	17.
IndicaRSE (Indicators for Central America) (2008)	18.
ISO 26000 (2010)	19.
Environmental, Social and Governance Ratings Criteria SOCRATES: KLD Ratings (2007)	20.
OECD Guidelines for Multinational Enterprises (2008, 2011)	21.
SA8000 (2008) and Guidance Document (2004)	22.
SGE 21: Ethical and CSR Management System, Forética (2008)	23.
Sigma: Sigma guide to sustainability issues (2006)	24.
United Nations Global Compact (2000)	25.
United Nations Guiding Principles on Business and Human Rights (2011)	26.
WBCSD Measuring Impact Framework (2008)	27.
XERTATU (2007)	28.

Analysis

Framework analysis was used following the key stages reported by Ritchie and Spencer (1994). A list of psychosocial hazards outlined by the WHO (2003) was used as the analytical framework. CSR instruments and standards were then thematically analyzed, using a top-down approach based on this framework (Braun & Clarke, 2006). Any relevant information was coded under these themes.

Findings

The final results were categorized under the 10 broad areas: job content, workload and work pace, work schedule, control, environment and equipment, organizational culture and function, interpersonal relationships at work, role in organization, career development, and home–work interface. These 10 first-order themes included 26 second-order themes and 97 third-order themes. The following sections present the themes and identify the instruments which include them (identified by the number assigned to each instrument in Table 14.2).

Job content

Psychosocial hazards related to job content have been characterized as lack of variety or short work cycles, fragmented or meaningless work, under-use of skills, high uncertainty, and continuous exposure to people through work (WHO, 2003). The analysis indicated that the coverage of such issues in CSR instruments was mainly limited to continuous exposure to people through work, as presented in Table 14.3.

Only three instruments included indicators which required companies to monitor the exposure of employees to people through their work, which could lead to stress, violence, or harassment from customers. For instance, indicator A.6.1.7 of the Human Rights Compliance Assessment (HRCA) Checklist seeks information of whether companies take "special measures to protect workers from the harassing, violent and threatening conduct of outsiders, such as customers, vendors and clients." In addition to exposure to people at work, job enrichment appears in only one instrument (IndicaRSE) in terms of job rotation.

Table 14.3 Sub-themes: Job Content

Job content	Continuous exposure to people through work	Measures to protect workers against harassment, violence, and threats from external persons	15
		Prevention of stress in specific sectors, with high exposure to clients or in dangerous activities and processes	6, 12, 15
	Job rotation	Rotation among different job positions at the same hierarchical level	18

Table 14.4   Sub-themes: Workload and Work Pace

Workload and work pace	Workload planning	Review of workload and need for extra workforce	4, 6, 10, 15, 19, 22, 28
		Analysis of accidents and worker turnover related to work overload	6, 15,19, 22

Workload and work pace

The workload and work pace group of psychosocial hazards includes work overload or underload, high levels of time pressure, and being continually subjected to deadlines (WHO, 2003). As presented in Table 14.4, the analysis indicated that CSR instruments included two themes: workload planning and breaks and days off.

Some CSR instruments inquire whether organizations review workload and take necessary measures to prevent peaks of work during the year rather than making workers work overtime. These include the analysis of level of accidents that are related to work overload and fatigue in comparison to company industry/sector or activity (e.g., Social Accountability 8000 (SA8000), HRCA, A.6.5.11). For example, Fairtrade Mark, indicator 1.5.1.13.2, requests the company "to prepare an annual overview of the company's need for workforce indicating the periods when non-permanent workers will be needed." CSR instruments also include indicators on working hours within the context of workload, for example, Ethos Institute, indicators I.16.13–16.17, compare the average of extra hours per year worked by employee with the average of workers' accident per year to ascertain the impact of workload on accidents.

Work schedule

Psychosocial hazards related to work schedule include shift working, night shifts, inflexible work schedules, unpredictable hours, and long or unsociable hours (WHO, 2003). Two themes emerged from the analysis which included issues relating to information and clarity about work schedules and long working hours including overtime (Table 14.5).

Three themes relevant to provision of information and clarity about work schedules emerged.These included providing employees access to written contracts, collective agreements and information about their rights, and working conditions in a fair and transparent manner. Several CSR instruments emphasize that enterprises adhere to fair, favorable, and legally recognized (either in national laws or in international standards) working conditions. This includes decent conditions of work with regard to hours of work (e.g., Fairtrade Mark, indicator 1.5.1.7.1.), weekly rest, and holidays (e.g., ISO 26000, section 6.4.4, Labour practices, issue 2), including access to written contracts or collective agreements (e.g., Business Leaders Initiative on Human Rights (BLIHR), 15.a.; SA8000, standard 7). Recommendations on the analysis and reporting of non-standard schedules are also included in some CSR instruments (e.g., Sigma

Table 14.5   Sub-themes: Work Schedule

Work schedule	Information and clarity about work schedules	Fair and legally compliant work schedules clearly communicated to workers (e.g., through written contracts, collective agreements)	2, 10, 16, 19, 22, 24, 28
		Paid holidays	2, 10, 15, 19, 22, 24
		Non-standard schedules (shift working, night shifts, etc.)	4, 22, 24
	Working hours	Maximum weekly hours – schedules, requirements, days off	2, 4, 7, 9, 10, 11, 15, 19, 21, 22, 24, 28
		Provision of breaks during work hours	10, 15
		Recording incidence of overtime	4, 6, 7, 9, 10, 15, 19, 22, 24, 28

guide to sustainability issues: Flexible working). Setting limits on extra hours, linked to long schedules, appears in several CSR instruments; for example, HRCA Checklist indicator A.6.5.1 states, "company work hours are limited to 48 per week by both company policy and in practice (or fewer hours if provided by national law or industry standards." Some instruments also recommend that overtime should be compensated for, and not required on, a regular basis; for instance, the Ethical Trading Initiative Base Code notes, "…workers shall be provided with at least one day off for every 7 day period on average. Overtime shall be voluntary, shall not exceed 12 hours per week, and shall not be demanded on a regular basis."

Control

Psychosocial hazards related to control include low participation in decision making and lack of control over workload, pacing, and shift working (WHO, 2003). The analysis indicated that there was broad coverage of these hazards in CSR instruments (Table 14.6), with detailed coverage of issues relating to industrial relations systems and involuntary or forced work.

CSR instruments emphasize the importance of employee involvement and communication and the existence of effective grievance systems. These include mechanisms which stimulate upward communication, follow up employees' suggestions or complaints, and allow remediation for any human right impacts. While some instruments promote a broader approach in decision-making processes and structures, establishing two-way communication processes with company stakeholders (ISO 26000, section 6.2.3), others are more directive on requirements.

Table 14.6   Sub-themes: Control

Control	Communication and involvement	Communication and suggestions: upward communication from employees	3, 6, 10, 14, 18, 19, 22, 23, 27, 28
		Workers' participation in decision-making part of corporate governance	4, 6, 8, 17, 18, 20, 21, 28
		Involvement of workers (or representatives) in health and safety committees, joint labor management programs, and professional development (internal mobility)	2, 6, 7, 10, 12, 15–17, 19, 21, 22, 24
		Communication, dialogue, or negotiation with trade unions and employees prior to organizational changes	3, 5, 6, 12, 15, 17–19, 21, 23
	Employee grievances	Grievance system: provision of information and accessibility to employees	2, 3, 5, 10, 11, 12, 14–17, 19–23, 25–27
		Grievance system which ensures transparency of the process and includes feedback from management and workers' representatives	10, 15–17, 19, 21, 26
	Industrial relations system	Freedom for workers' organization and collective bargaining including non-interference from the company	1, 2, 4, 7, 9–25, 27
		Employee representation and collective bargaining: well-functioning system and recognition by the company	2, 6, 7, 11, 14, 15, 17–22, 25
		Penetration of representation system within the company	4–6, 10, 11, 12, 18, 22, 28
		Actions and guarantees when no existence of trade unions in the area or company	1, 4, 7, 10, 11, 15–17, 19, 21, 22, 24
		Negotiation and adherence to collective bargaining agreements – at company and at sector level	5, 6, 10, 12, 15–17, 21, 22, 25
		Support to trade union functioning to improve representation and collaboration with the company	6, 10, 15, 17–19, 21, 22
	Control over involuntary/ forced work	Fair and transparent conditions regarding termination of employment	2, 7, 10, 15, 22, 25
		Elimination of compulsory or involuntary overtime	7, 10, 15, 19, 22

Control at work is also included in several CSR instruments as a feature of an industrial relations system which includes freedom of workers to organize and engage in collective bargaining and their rights to strike, assemble, elect representatives, bargain, and express their view directly or through their representative. For example, the OECD Guidelines for Multinational Enterprises state that "Enterprises should (…) 1. a) b) Respect the right of workers employed by the multinational enterprise to have trade unions and representative organizations of their own choosing recognized for the purpose of collective bargaining, and engage in constructive negotiations, either individually or through employers' associations, with such representatives with a view to reaching agreements on terms and conditions of employment."

Finally, also linked to control at work, some CSR instruments require companies to prohibit involuntary or forced work. This includes employee's lack of control about the decision of leaving the work, involuntary overtime, and lack of control over an employee's own work schedules. For example, the HRCA Quick Check (indicator A.1.1.9) assesses whether a "company takes all necessary measures to ensure that it (…) does not coerce or compel employees to work involuntary (overtime) hours (or work itself) by the use of threat or force."

Environment and equipment

Physical work environment and equipment relate to inadequate equipment availability, suitability, or maintenance and poor environmental conditions such as lack of space, poor lighting, and excessive noise (WHO, 2003). The analysis indicated that these hazards are broadly addressed in CSR instruments, as presented in Table 14.7.

Table 14.7 Sub-themes: Environment and Equipment

Environment and equipment	Equipment: availability, suitability, and maintenance	Safe protective equipment and machinery	2, 10, 12, 15, 16, 18, 19, 21, 22
		Employees' access to instructions about equipment and protective measures	2, 5, 6, 10, 11, 15, 17, 18, 22, 23, 25, 28
	Physical work environment	Optimal environment: noise, light, heat, ventilation, air	2, 10, 15, 16, 19, 22
		Safe facilities and services	2, 7, 10, 15–17, 19, 22, 27
		Safe processes and protection against dangerous substances and techniques	2, 10, 15, 16, 19, 21, 22
		Emergency action plans	2, 5, 10, 12, 15, 16, 19, 21, 22

CSR instruments were found to include indicators which require companies to ensure the provision of safe equipment and machinery, such as provision of free protective equipment; regular inspection, maintenance, and repair of machinery; and provision of tools to deal with risks and emergencies. Some indicators require companies to provide employees access to health and safety instructions about equipment and protective measures (e.g., through on-site training, training in a language known by the worker, training for new workers, new training in the case of accidents or reassignment). CSR instruments also require companies to provide optimal environmental conditions, safe facilities, and services to enable workers to safely and effectively perform their role. These include adherence to safe processes which include ensuring adequate protection (physical and psychological) against dangerous substances and processes through regular tests, records, cautionary measures, and presence of emergency action plans which include worker's rights to refuse or leave work when posed with imminent and serious danger.

Organizational culture and function

Psychosocial hazards related to organizational culture and function include poor communication, low levels of support for problem solving and personal development, and lack of definition of, or agreement on, organizational objectives (WHO, 2003). The analysis indicated that while these hazards were covered in some instruments, the focus was on non-discrimination. Table 14.8 presents the key themes that emerged in this area.

CSR instruments include several indicators aimed at improving organizational climate. These include ensuring regular downward communication about the company's initiatives and policies, mechanisms to assess the work climate within the company which can be used to detect structural problems and the presence of other psychosocial hazards and in turn promote employees' job satisfaction and well-being. Another theme that appears in several CSR instruments is the sharing of profits and organizational justice. Instruments take into account the percentage and kind of compensation of these mechanisms. For example, the Sigma Guidelines on Sustainability Issues state: "The payment to directors and other senior employees of salary, bonuses, compensation and other payments out of keeping with organizational performance or misaligned to remuneration of the full range of employees (…) can have a destabilizing effect on the workforce and other stakeholders, such as investors." Assessing the level of conflicts within the company, monitoring information regarding disciplinary measures, legal actions by workers, impact of strikes, and prevention of such industrial disputes through provision conciliation mechanisms, was also found to be included in CSR instruments as a means of promoting organizational culture.

CSR instruments also recommend that companies monitor health and safety performance (including workers' perceptions of their health and safety climate) by having effective monitoring and evaluation mechanisms in place. For example, item LA6 of the Global Reporting Initiative (GRI) 4.0 assesses whether companies record "type of injury and rates of injury, occupational diseases, lost days, and absenteeism,

Table 14.8 Sub-themes: Organizational Culture and Function

Organizational culture and function	Organizational climate	Regular downward communication	3, 4, 14, 18, 19, 27
		Measuring work climate and job satisfaction and promoting a positive work environment	4–6, 18, 23, 27, 28
		Organizational justice and addressing salary inequalities	3, 6, 12, 20, 24, 28
		Sharing of profits and corporate performance-based compensation	5, 6, 20, 28
	Conflict resolution	Level of conflicts within the company and disciplinary dismissals	4, 10, 18, 22, 27, 28
		Avoidance of disciplinary deductions from wages	2, 4, 7, 10, 15, 19, 22, 24
		Provision of conciliation machinery	3, 10, 17, 19, 22
	Continual improvement in health and safety performance	Health and safety compliance in all countries, certifications, excellence, and budget	1, 3–7, 9–23, 25, 28
		Implementation of health and safety policies	1–3, 5, 6, 8–11, 13–23, 25
		Implementation of health and safety management systems	2, 4–6, 10, 11, 15–17, 19–23
		Minimization of hazards and impact assessment of health and safety risks	2, 4, 5, 7, 10, 16, 17, 19, 21, 22, 24, 25
		Investigation, documentation, and evaluation of work-related injuries, diseases, and accidents	2, 4–6, 10–12, 15, 16, 19, 22, 25, 27, 28
		Training in health and safety	2, 6, 7, 10–12, 14–19, 21, 22, 27, 28
		Awareness raising and educational campaigns in health promotion	2, 6, 12, 18, 19, 21
		Monitoring worker satisfaction on health and safety	6, 15, 22, 24, 27
	Equal opportunities and non-discrimination	Non-discrimination against any group or person	All instruments
		Policies and mechanisms to avoid discrimination against vulnerable groups and to monitor diversity in the workforce	All instruments

Table 14.8   *(Continued)*

	Affirmative policies to promote development of vulnerable groups	2, 4, 6, 10, 16–21
	Promotion of diversity and culturally sensitive environments	2, 6, 15, 19, 20, 22, 24, 28
	Policies to avoid discrimination due to marriage, pregnancy, or parenthood	2, 6, 10, 12, 15, 19, 21, 22
Ethics and human rights	Promoting an ethical and human rights culture including respect for workers' civil and human rights and ILO fundamental principles and rights at work	All instruments
	Fair and legally compliant working conditions clearly communicated to workers	1–3, 7, 9, 10, 14–16, 18, 19, 22, 24
	Monitoring working conditions and human rights for staff and agency workers	1, 2, 5, 10–12, 14, 16, 19, 21–23, 25, 26
	Elimination of forced or compulsory labor	1–7, 9–27
	Elimination of child labor	1, 2, 4–7, 9–27
	No limitations of movements after work and freedom of accommodation	10, 15, 16, 22

and total number of work-related fatalities, by region and by gender." Provision of training in health and safety was also a recurring theme. This relates to companies providing managers, employees, and their representatives access to occupational health and safety training and instructions and educational campaigns and awareness raising in health and safety. Ensuring compliance with set legislation/standards, and having in place relevant policies and actions plans (including preventative ones), is also recommended by most CSR instruments, which should be consistent for all workers regardless of the company location, age, gender, and ethnicity, to ensure workers' health and safety, where adequate provisions are made for vulnerable workers.

The existence of equal opportunity and non-discrimination policies were one of the key areas included in most CSR instruments in relation to organizational culture and function. For example, the Sigma Guidelines highlight that companies should "Ensure equal opportunities for all in an organization without unfair restrictions or barriers. Good practice in this area (…) helps an organization 'fit' into its surroundings, matching its workforce and supplier mix to that of the locale." These instruments require companies to avoid any kind of discrimination to any group or person, even when national laws in the operating country are silent or even promote discrimination. CSR instruments also mention several areas where there may be a need to implement affirmative policies and also ensure non-discrimination.

CSR instruments often encourage the promotion of an ethical organizational culture and also emphasize respect for workers' and community civil and human rights, often requiring the monitoring of working conditions (e.g., due diligence to identify, prevent, and mitigate direct or indirect impacts on individuals) and a remediation of human right impacts (e.g., GRI 4.0 indicators HR 9 and12; UN Guiding Principles). Another topic that appears in CSR instruments is forced labor. This includes aspects such as elimination of forced and child labor, limitation of movements after work (e.g., freedom to leave company facilities after work), and freedom of accommodation to workers (e.g., possibility to choose own accommodation, freedom to leave the company's accommodation after work), which is a key issue if workers are migrants (or irregular migrants) or isolated from their families and social networks.

Interpersonal relationships at work

Interpersonal relationships at work include social or physical isolation, poor relationships with superiors, lack of social support, interpersonal conflict, harassment, bullying, and violence (WHO, 2003). The findings indicated that most indicators from CSR instruments were limited to harassment, bullying, and violence at work and to some extent social or physical isolation (Table 14.9).

Employees can be subject to bullying, harassment, and violence from their superiors (managers, supervisors), work colleagues, and even company security personnel. Some CSR instruments require company and managers to avoid the use – or acceptance – of corporal disciplinary punishment and mental, verbal, sexual, or physical coercion or harassment. These include provision of training to management and prohibit the use any corporal, mental, or moral abuse; clear codes of conduct and written policies about treating employees with dignity; and the existence of clear and proportional disciplinary procedures, which should be communicated, monitored, and publicly reported and in which remedial action should be taken. For example, the Fair Labour Association Workplace of Conduct includes a requirement which states: "Harassment or Abuse: Every employee shall be treated with respect and dignity. No employee shall be subject to any physical, sexual, psychological or verbal harassment or abuse."

Role in organization

Psychosocial hazards related to role in the organization have been characterized as role ambiguity, role conflict, and responsibility for people (WHO, 2003). The analysis indicated that the coverage of these hazards in CSR instruments was mainly limited to reduction of role ambiguity, as presented in Table 14.10.

Three themes relate to the reduction of role ambiguity. While three CSR instruments cover the initial training to recently hired workers (e.g., IndicaRSE, section Dialogue and

Table 14.9   Sub-themes: Interpersonal Relationships at Work

Interpersonal relationships at work	Poor relationships with superiors: harassment and violence from superiors	Written policies, training and procedures to avoid physical, psychological, or verbal abuse, violence, or harassment from superiors	1–3, 6, 7, 9–16, 18, 19, 22, 24–26
		Monitoring of abuses, violence, and harassment	10, 12, 15, 22, 23, 26
		Complaint and appeal system about disciplinary procedures or bad treatment to workers	1, 6, 10, 15, 18, 25
		Investigation of incidents and remedial action taken	1, 12, 15, 26
	Bullying, harassment, and violence from colleagues	Written policies to avoid physical, psychological, or verbal abuse, violence, bullying, and harassment (among staff)	1–3, 6, 7, 9, 10, 12, 14–16, 18, 19, 22, 24, 25
		Monitoring of abuses, violence, bullying, and harassment from colleagues	10, 12, 22, 23
		Complaint and appeal system about bullying and harassment from colleagues	6, 10, 15, 18, 25
		Prevention of interpersonal conflicts and tensions leading to violence	12, 15
		Investigation of incidents and remedial action taken	1, 12, 15

participation, indicator 6; Fairtrade Mark, indicator 1.1.2.5.2; BLIHR 15.c), job analysis and review of job roles (often as part of performance reviews) appear in several instruments. For instance, SGE 21 (section 6.4.6) states: "Organizations are to keep-up-to-date records, available to all personnel, on the job descriptions. Said descriptions will include

Table 14.10   Sub-themes: Role in Organization

Role in organization	Reduction of role ambiguity	Job analysis and role reviews	3, 5, 8, 10, 12, 14, 18, 23
		Induction training	2, 10, 18
		Description of responsibilities within the company	2, 10, 23, 27

requirements for the post, responsibilities, hierarchical and functional relationships, as well as the systems and parameters for performance evaluation." Some CSR instruments also inquire of the availability of a statement or written document which describes the responsibilities of managers and employees within the company.

Career development

The career development group of psychosocial hazards includes career stagnation and uncertainty, under-promotion or over-promotion, poor pay, job insecurity, and low social value to work (WHO, 2003). The analysis indicated that the coverage of these hazards in CSR instruments included six themes related to career development: training and development, employee retention and promotions, reducing job insecurity, support to retiring employees, pay and benefits, and promoting diversity and non-discrimination in career development, as presented in Table 14.11.

CSR instruments include several indicators which recommend or require companies to provide training and development to employees as well as assess its quality and impact. For instance, the Good Corporation Standard notes: "the organization encourages employees to develop skills and progress in their careers." Employee retention and promotion includes ensuring the implementation of a fair and transparent performance management system and the analysis of internal promotion and the retention of employees, including interns, apprentices, and people with learning contracts.

CSR instruments also include indicators which encourage companies to take measures to reduce job insecurity. This includes analyzing the impact of company actions of employee layoffs and mitigating the adverse effects of restructuring while taking into consideration the needs of vulnerable groups, including temporary workers and workers close to retirement. The International Finance Corporation (IFC) states in their Performance Standard Labour and Working Conditions: "where the client proposes to implement collective dismissals, an analysis for alternatives to retrenchment will be conducted. If the analysis does not identify alternatives to retrenchment, a retrenchment plan will be developed and implemented to mitigate the adverse impacts of retrenchment on workers." Provisions of adequate pay and benefits are also included in several CSR instruments. These relate to assessing whether organizations provide living wages, assessing employee satisfaction about salary, limiting variable remuneration, and providing fair pay and benefits, ensuring non-discrimination among all staff specifically in relation to pay and benefits and ensure non-discrimination in career development more broadly.

Table 14.11 Sub-themes: Career Development

Career development	Training and development	Promoting employability and professional development of employees	3–6, 8, 10–15, 17–19, 21, 23, 24, 27, 28
		Measurement of training provision and assessment of outcomes	4–6, 10–12, 14, 18, 27, 28
		Support for continuing and finishing formal education	5, 6, 18, 24, 27
		Provision of training and guidance in apprenticeship, internship programs	4, 6, 8, 15, 19, 20, 22, 28
		Avoidance of discrimination in the provision of training and development opportunities for all staff	3, 4, 6, 10, 7, 12, 15, 17, 19, 21, 23, 27
		Skill mapping and assessment of development needs	4–6, 10, 12, 14, 18, 23
	Employee retention and promotions	Internal promotion and recognition	4, 6, 18, 27, 28
		Advancement from an internship, apprenticeship, or learning contract	4, 6, 7, 19, 28
		Objective and fair job performance reviews	3, 5, 8, 12, 14, 18
	Reducing job insecurity	Impact assessment of company actions in relation to employee retrenchment and turnover	3–6, 10, 12, 16–20, 22, 27, 28
		Mitigation of adverse effects of mergers, takeovers, and transfers, causing major effects on employees	3, 5, 6, 12, 15–19, 21, 23
		Promotion of stable employment and job security for workers	1, 3, 7, 10, 12, 17, 19, 22, 28
	Support to retiring employees	Support and guidance for retiring employees	3, 6, 12, 14, 18
		Provision of financial support, company pension in addition to social security benefits	6, 10, 12, 14, 17–20, 28

(continued)

Table 14.11   (*Continued*)

Pay and benefits	Payment of adequate living wages	1–4, 6, 7, 9, 10, 12–15, 17, 19, 21, 22, 24, 27, 28
	Payment of extra hours and premium rate	2, 6, 7, 9, 10, 15, 18, 19, 22, 28
	Health insurance, sick leave, and social security benefits which cover compensation for accidents, maternity	2, 6, 7, 10, 12, 15–19, 22, 28
	Assessment of economic benefits: impact, value, kind of benefits, link of company's services to their actual costs	3–6, 10, 12, 14, 18, 27, 28
	Remuneration based on production, quotas, or piecework	5, 6, 10, 15, 18, 22
	Satisfaction about salary	6, 22
Non-discrimination in career development	Non-discrimination of temporary/subcontracted staff	1, 4, 6, 10, 12, 14, 16, 18, 19, 22, 28
	Non-discrimination on pay and benefits	1, 2, 4–7, 9, 10, 12, 15–17, 21, 23, 28
	Monitoring of non-discrimination in career advancement and promotion	3–6, 10–12, 18–20, 27, 28

Home–work interface

Psychosocial hazards related to home–work interface have been characterized as conflicting demands of work and home, low support at home, and problems arising out of dual careers (WHO, 2003). The analysis indicated that the coverage of these hazards in CSR instruments was focused on provisions of support made by the employers to deal with issues related to the home–work interface, as presented in Table 14.12.

Several instruments, such as the FTSE4Good Index and ISO 26000, included indicators which required companies to provide support to employees for managing conflicting demands of work and home. These included providing benefits which help employees to manage their work–life balance, such as accommodation, flexible arrangements in working patterns, transportation, and educational and leisure opportunities. CSR instruments also cover provision of support for parenthood and family demands which includes parental leave and breastfeeding breaks, childcare facilities, parenting guidance programs, as well as supporting child development and education. Some instruments recommend organizations to monitor the number of employees with children responsibilities to ensure adequate support is provided.

Table 14.12   Sub-themes: Home–Work Interface

Home–work interface	Provision of support	Benefits for work–life balance	2, 4, 6, 10, 11, 12, 15, 18–20, 23, 24, 27, 28
		Flexible arrangements in working patterns and transportation	4, 6, 8, 10, 11, 18–20, 23, 24, 28
		Support to workers' parenthood	2, 4, 6, 10–12, 15, 18–20, 24, 27, 28

Discussion

This research set out to examine which psychosocial factors and related issues such as work-related stress, violence, bullying, and harassment are covered in CSR instruments and standards. The findings clearly indicate that CSR instruments and standards provide a broad coverage of several psychosocial factors. Since most CSR standards and instruments cover labor dimensions and working conditions which include basic labor themes originating from international labor standards and regulations (e.g., ILO Fundamental Conventions, Universal Declaration of Human Rights, OECD Guidelines), a number of psychosocial factors are directly or indirectly addressed by these instruments. For example, ISO 26000 – section 6.4.6, Labour practices, issue 4, health and safety at work – includes direct reference to psychosocial hazards, stating that organizations should "strive to eliminate psychosocial hazards in the workplace, which contribute or lead to stress and illness."

Increasingly, human resource policies (e.g., recruiting, promoting, training, payment, dismissals) are also covered in various CSR instruments. This is particularly important as regulations, particularly in developing countries, do not cover many of these issues, and voluntary approaches, such as codes of conduct and governance documents, can help promote best practices, as these practices are linked to workers' well-being, job satisfaction, and organizational commitment (Standing, 2007). As such, CSR is increasingly becoming part of the daily work of human resource managers. Moreover, CSR instruments increasingly take into account the needs of vulnerable groups, and specific actions are suggested (e.g., drawing a profile of diversity, risk analysis, policies and statements, non-discrimination in human resources, affirmative policies, and protection and grievance mechanisms and awareness raising). Non-gender discrimination in wages and creation of culturally -neutral environments are one of the key aspects to ensure equal rights for minority groups included in the instruments. Besides, specific instruments for vulnerable groups have been launched (McKague & Cragg, 2007).

However, despite the broad coverage of these issues in CSR instruments, their inclusion in individual instruments varies considerably among different instruments. Furthermore, since several psychosocial factors are not considered within basic labor themes, their coverage in CSR instruments was found to be lacking or generic. While psychosocial factors relating to work schedules, control at work, physical work environment and equipment, career development, and home–work interface were covered by at least some instruments, there was hardly any coverage of psychosocial factors related to job content (such as lack of variety, fragmented or meaningless work, under-use of skills) and role in the organization (such as role ambiguity, role conflict, and responsibility for people). Also, in the case of factors such as organizational culture and function, the focus was on non-discrimination, while the coverage of hazards relating to interpersonal relationships at work was limited to harassment, bullying, and violence at work and, to some extent, to social or physical isolation. Hazards such as work pace, low levels of support for problem solving and personal development, poor relationships with superiors, and lack of social support were not found to be included in CSR instruments. Thus, there is a need for further development and revision of existing CSR instruments so that they adequately cover all issues relating to the psychosocial work environment. This is essential because "like any tool, a CSR instrument can be used well or poorly – or left on the shelf to be admired or to rust, but the better it is made, the greater the chance it will fill its intended purpose" (Paine, Deshpande, Margolis & Bettcher, 2005, p. 2).

Improving working conditions and promoting the health, safety, and well-being of workers are clearly relevant to the CSR activities of the firm(Montero et al., 2009), as can also be seen in the increased reporting of these issues in annual company CSR reports (Vuontisjärvi, 2006). Looking after the workforce and developing its capacity (mentally, socially, etc.) has strategic importance for organizations and society alike, especially if one considers current challenges such as workforce ageing and organizational restructuring (Jain, Leka & Zwetsloot, 2011). As enterprises are increasingly expected to "think and act inclusive," that is, by taking into account the consequences of their business activities for society and for stakeholders external to and within the organization, engagement in CSR, or responsible business practices, becomes increasingly important. It is clear that CSR involves social concerns, which include aspects of the psychosocial work environment and workers' health, safety, and well-being. Also, as challenges in enforcing legislative requirements increase, due to issues of resources, creative compliance (Gold & Duncan, 1993), lobbying for changes (Bain, 1997), blatant disregard for legislation, and less success in developing countries (Joubert, 2002), CSR is expected to continue to play a more important role for achieving higher standards of practice. Engaging in responsible business practices which incorpo-rate the psychosocial work environment has been reported to potentially lead to increased long-term stability for the business, a better public image, and improved employer reputation (Jain, Leka & Zwetsloot, 2011). It is, therefore, important that CSR instruments and standards cover these aspects, so that they can be used by companies to self-improve in these areas.

Practitioners and researchers in Occupational Health Psychology (OHP) must play a key role in this endeavor, and it is hoped that this study will provide them with guidance to support companies in this area. This would allow OHP research and practice to further develop and promote employee health, safety, and well-being through a sustainability approach.

References

Bain, P. (1997). Human resource malpractice: The deregulation of health and safety at work in the USA and Britain. *Industrial Relations Journal, 28*(3), 176–191.

Braun, V., & Clarke, V. (2006). Using thematic analysis in psychology. *Qualitative Research in Psychology, 3*(2), 77–101.

Carroll, A. B., & Shabana, K. M. (2010). The business case for corporate social responsibility: A review of concepts, research and practice. *International Journal of Management Reviews, 12*(1), 85–105.

Cox, T. (1993). *Stress research & stress management: Putting theory to work*. Sudbury: HSE Books.

Dahlsrud, A. (2008). How corporate social responsibility is defined: An analysis of 37 definitions. *Corporate Social Responsibility and Environmental Management, 15*, 1–13.

European Commission (EC). (2001). Green Paper: Promoting a European framework for corporate social responsibility. *Official Journal of the European Communities, 32*(L183), 1–8.

EC. (2004). *ABC of the main instruments of Corporate Social Responsibility*. Luxembourg City, Luxembourg: Office for Official Publications of the European Communities.

EC. (2011). *Communication from the Commission to the European Parliament, the Council, the European Economic and Social Committee and the Committee of the Regions. A Renewed EU Strategy 2011–2014 for Corporate Social Responsibility (COM(2011) 681 final)*. Luxembourg City, Luxembourg: Office for Official Publications of the European Communities.

Global Reporting Initiative (GRI). (2011). *Sustainability reporting guidelines: Version 3.1*. Amsterdam, the Netherlands: Author. Retrieved August 31, 2013 from https://www.globalreporting.org/resourcelibrary/G3.1-Sustainability-Reporting-Guidelines.pdf

Goel, R., & Cragg, W. (2005). *Guide to instruments of Corporate Responsibility: An overview of 16 tools*. Victoriaville, Canada: Schulich School of Business.

Gold, M., & Duncan, M. (1993). EC Health and Safety Policy – Better safe than sorry. *European Business Journal, 5*(4), 51–56.

International Labour Office (ILO). (1986). *Psychosocial factors at work: Recognition and control*. Report of the Joint International Labour Office and World Health Organization on Occupational Health, Ninth Session, Geneva, September 18–24, 1984. Occupational Safety and Health Series No. 56. Geneva, Switzerland: Author.

Jain, A., Leka, S., & Zwetsloot, G. (2011). Corporate social responsibility and psychosocial risk management. *Journal of Business Ethics, 101*(4), 619–633.

Joubert, D. M. (2002). Occupational health challenges and success in developing countries: A South African perspective. *International Journal of Occupational and Environmental Health, 8*(2), 119–124.

Lee, P. (2008). A review of the theories of corporate social responsibility: Its evolutionary path and the road ahead. *International Journal of Management Reviews, 10*(1), 53–73.

Leka, S., Jain, A., Widerszal-Bazyl, M., Żołnierczyk-Zreda, D., & Zwetsloot, G. (2011). Developing a standard for psychosocial risk management: PAS1010. *Safety Science, 49*(7), 1047–1057.

Leka, S., Jain, A., Zwetsloot, G., & Cox, T. (2010). Policy-level interventions and work-related psychosocial risk management in the European Union. *Work and Stress, 24*(3), 298–307.

McKague, K., & Cragg, W. (2007). *Compendium of ethics codes and instruments of corporate responsibility*. Toronto, Canada: York University. Retrieved August 31, 2013 from http://www.yorku.ca/csr/_files/file.php?fileid=fileCDOICwJieiandfilename=file_ Codes_Compendium_Jan_2007.pdf

Michie, S., & Williams, S. (2003). Reducing work related psychological ill health and sickness absence: A systematic literature review. *Occupational and Environmental Medicine, 60*(1), 3–9.

Montero, M. J., Araque, R. A., & Rey, J. M. (2009). Occupational health and safety in the framework of corporate social responsibility. *Safety Science, 47*(10), 1440–1445.

Nahrgang, J. D., Morgeson, F. P., & Hofmann, D. A. (2011). Safety at work: A meta-analytic investigation of the link between job demands, job resources, burnout, engagement, and safety outcome. *Journal of Applied Psychology, 96*, 71–94.

Organization for Economic Co-operation and Development (OECD) (Ed.). (2009). Overview of selected initiatives and instruments relevant to corporate social responsibility. In *Annual report on the OECD Guidelines for Multinational Enterprises 2008 employment and industrial relations* (pp. 235–260). Paris: OECD Publishing.

Paine, L., Deshpande, R., Margolis, J. D., & Bettcher, K. E. (2005). Up to code: Does your company's conduct meet world-class standards? *Harvard Business Review, 83*(12), 122–133.

Rasche, A. (2010). The limits of corporate responsibility standards. *Business Ethics: A European Review, 19*(3), 280–291.

Ripa, D., & Herrero, J. (2012). Corporate social responsibility: Standards and instruments. In A. K. Jain, B. B. Puplampu, K. Amponsah-Tawiah, & N. J. A. Andreou (Eds.), *Occupational safety and health and Corporate Social Responsibility in Africa: Repositioning Corporate Social Responsibility towards national development* (pp. 75–91). Cranfield, UK: Cranfield Press.

Ritchie, J., & Spencer, J. (1994). Qualitative data analysis for applied policy research. In A. Bryman, & R. G. Burgess (Eds.), *Analysing qualitative data* (pp. 173–194). London: Routledge.

Standing, G. (2007). *Decent workplaces, self-regulation and CSR: From puff to stuff? (UN DESA Working Paper No. 62)*. New York: United Nations Department of Economic and Social Affairs.

Tate, W. L., Ellram, L. M., & Kirchoff, J. F. (2010). Corporate social responsibility reports: A thematic analysis related to supply chain management. *Journal of Supply Chain Management, 46*(1), 19–44.

van den Berg, T. I. J., Elders, L. A. M., de Zwart, B. C. H., & Burdorf, A. (2009). The effects of work-related and individual factors on the Work Ability Index: A systematic review. *Occupational and Environmental Medicine, 66*, 211–220.

Van Oosterhout, J. V., & Heugens, P. P. (2008). Much ado about nothing. A conceptual critique of CSR. In A. Crane, A. McMilliams, D. Matten, J. Moon, & D. S. Siegel (Eds.), *The Oxford handbook of corporate social responsibility* (pp. 197–223). New York: Oxford University Press.

Vuontisjärvi, T. (2006). Corporate social reporting in the European context and human resource disclosures: An analysis of Finnish companies. *Journal of Business Ethics, 69*(4), 331–354.

Waddock, S. (2008). Building a new institutional infrastructure for corporate responsibility. *Academy of Management Perspectives, 22*(3), 87–108.

World Health Organization [WHO]. (2003). *Work organization and stress*. Geneva, Switzerland: World Health Organization.

World Health Organization (WHO). (2008). *PRIMA-EF: Guidance on the European Framework for Psychosocial Risk Management: A Resource for Employers and Worker Representatives. Protecting workers' health 9th Series*. Geneva: World Health Organization.

WHO. (2010). *Health impact of psychosocial hazards at work: An overview*. Geneva, Switzerland: World Health Organization.

Index

Contemporary Occupational Health Psychology: Global Perspectives on Research and Practice

CONTENTS OF PREVIOUS VOLUMES

Volume 1

Contemporary Occupational Health Psychology: Global Perspectives on Research and Practice, Volume 3,
First Edition. Edited by Stavroula Leka and Robert R. Sinclair.
© 2014 John Wiley & Sons, Ltd. Published 2014 by John Wiley & Sons, Ltd.